Advance Praise for

The Evolutionary Testament of Co-Creation

Barbara Marx Hubbard has given us a deeply personal, prophetic inter-pretation of the New Testament. This book radiates the cosmic spirit of evolution. In it we find both comfort and challenge for our own journey.

David Richo,
Author of The Power of Grace

The Evolutionary Testament of Co-creation is a guide to the self-fulfilling prophecy of the Universal Humanity we are to become. In this ground-breaking book, Barbara Marx Hubbard brings a fresh and updated mes-sage of what Jesus taught 2000 years ago. People have referred to Jesus as a revolutionary; however, through Barbara's eyes we discover he was in fact an evolutionary, describing for us how to achieve the Christ state both as individuals and as the entire human race. Barbara calls this col-lective transformation the Planetary Pentecost, a life-affirming alterna-tive to Armageddon.

The promise will be kept is a call to action for humanity to awaken as a Planetary Social Body. It inspires each individual to awaken to his or her divine nature and fulfill the promise of performing even great-er miracles than those once performed by Jesus. It carries a message for Unity amongst religions, as well as an invitation for us not to abandon the Church, but to evolve it.

Juan Carlos Kaiten
Social Alchemist
The Hague Center for Global
Governance, Innovation and Emergence

In Barbara's new book, *The Evolutionary Testament of Co-Creation*, some-thing profound is being offered for those with ears to hear. I have no doubt this book will become a mainstay for all ministers, preachers, and serious students of the New Testament. Her inspired reflections offer a fresh presentation of the words of Jesus that provide h⋯
clear vision to see us through the currer

ʟ

D1382905

In The Evolutionary Testament of Co-Creation, visionary futurist Barbara Marx Hubbard elaborates an evolutionary perspective on Christ consciousness, seeing in Christ an archetype for humanity's current journey from egocentric, to ego freedom. This book will resonate with followers of her ideas—and may also build a bridge between the New Age spirituality movement and Christian fundamentalists with its inspired interpretations of scriptural passages.

Daniel Pinchbeck
Author of Breaking Open The Head: A Psychedelic
Journey Into the Heart of Contemporary Shamanism,
and co-founder of the Evolver Network

The Evolutionary Testament of Co-Creation provides a modern commentary on selected passages from the New Testament that can be delighted in by all who are open to new wisdom. Although Barbara Marx Hubbard relies on the scriptures of Christianity and the symbol of Christ in her work, her writing transcends a given faith by offering us a wonderful vision for the future of all humankind.

Hubbard views Jesus as "the future human" and speaks of the Jesus everyone can recognize and be inspired by, whether they're a deeply committed religious person or equally committed agnostic. Hers are not merely lofty philosophical and theological ideas. Rather, Hubbard points to current life situations and explains how ancient wisdom from the Bible can impact us in useful ways today. As a futurist, Hubbard is elegantly familiar with the history of scientific and cultural breakthroughs, as well as cutting edge envisioning. She brings this future vision to bear on many ancient passages from the New Testament, rendering them as fresh as if we were reading today's newspaper—or even next decade's newspaper (if they're still around by then).

Although she claims to be neither a scholar nor a theologian, Hubbard, writes in the style of Origen, the vastly influential second century Christian theologian and teacher. Origin believed there were three levels of understanding within the Bible: the literal, the moral, and the spiritual. A literal interpretation of the words is but the first stage of any scriptural exploration. Those further along conduct a moral investigation into the text, while the most mature readers seek a spiritual interpretation, which involves a metaphorical and mystical reading of the scriptures. Hubbard writes from the highest level of the metaphorical and mystical, in that she plumbs the depths of these passages and finds in them new, highly relevant messages for today's world.

This is a book to be read slowly and fully digested. Study groups make an ideal setting for this, because they invite us to think in new and fresh ways and enable us to move beyond the deadening debate of literalism and doctrinaire trivia. What a world ours would be if even just the Christians would read and hear the New Testament in this refreshing way.

My own vision, as a New Testament scholar and mystic, expanded while I was reading Hubbard's words. The word "Spirit" (in both Hebrew and Greek) is the same word for breath, and this book provides a breath of the fresh air of Spirit for today. Hubbard says, "My personal mystical experience of the living Christ in 1980 catalyzed this book's creation." Like all the mystics throughout the ages (including Jesus) her words have been inspired by her own mystical experience. She practices what she preaches about the reality of receiving direct communications from Christ, and at times writes words that come to us straight from Spirit, using italics to distinguish these sections from her own voice.

This book is aflame with countless wisdom sparks, like: "Bureaucracy offers us less than the sum of its parts," and, "Within each of us exists a wellspring of inner scriptures." This notion of 'inner scriptures' echoes the Old Testament thought of God's word being written on our hearts, as well as the New Testament primacy of speaking the prophetic word direct from Spirit.

This is, in one sense, a new "translation" of parts of the New Testament for those interested in what Spirit is saying to us now—through the lens of what Spirit has said to us in the sacred scriptures of the New Testament.

A modern day mystic, Hubbard's spirit is clearly in touch with the Spirit of Christ. Even so, her feet are firmly planted on Earth while her heart points toward a more beautiful human future.

Rev Paul R. Smith, retired Baptist minister
Author of *Integral Christianity: The Spirit's Call to Evolve*

The

EVOLUTIONARY
TESTAMENT
of
CO-CREATION

THE PROMISE WILL BE KEPT

BARBARA MARX HUBBARD

LOS ANGELES   SANTA BARBARA

Muse Harbor Publishing
Los Angeles Santa Barbara

The Evolutionary Testament of
Co-Creation: The Promise Will Be Kept

A Muse Harbor Publishing Book

PUBLISHING HISTORY

Muse Harbor Publishing paperback edition
published November, 2015

Published by Muse Harbor Publishing, LLC
Los Angeles, California
Santa Barbara, California

Interior design: Typeflow

Scripture taken from The Holy Bible,
Updated King James Version: "I love Jesus (UKJV),"
http://www.oocities.org/updatedkjv/.
Used by permission.

ISBN 978-1-61264-172-0

Visit Muse Harbor Publishing at
http://www.museharbor.com

With great gratitude I dedicate *Evolutionary Testament: The Promise Will be Kept* to Lawrence Rockefeller, who recognized its purpose to help "bring forth the Christ of the 21st Century" and supported me in forming The Foundation for Conscious Evolution to bring it forward into the world.

Contents

Acknowledgments

Sidney Lanier, an Episcopal priest and my beloved partner for 25 years until his passing, co-founded The Foundation for Conscious Evolution, and affirmed the vision of the evolutionary meaning of the life of Jesus for our generation. In his book *The Sovereign Person: The Soul's Call to Conscious Evolution*, which I edited from his journal writings, he eloquently enlarges upon this meaning for us all.

Noel McInnis, former editor of *The Brain Mind Bulletin*, who served as editor and guide in the development of the teachings of Co-Creation as expressed in the 1600 pages of original writings from which *Evolutionary Testament: The Promise Will be Kept* is extracted.

John Zwerver who founded the first New Order of the Future, called for in the text, for "self-selected souls who are here to carry the miracle of the resurrection into action as the transformation of humanity from *Homo sapiens sapiens* to *Homo universalis.*"

Rev. Peggy Basset who with Rev. Roger Teel of Mile High Church in Denver first introduced these writings to the New Thought Movement.

Dr. Thomas Paine, Administrator of NASA during the Apollo program who recognized in the writings the inspiration of Teilhard de Chardin and offered his guidance in the use of technology when infused with Christ love.

Juan Carlos Kaitan, Mona Rhabie, and Anne Marie Vooheuve, who are guiding the Wheel of Co-Creation to be manifested as a process of global cooperation starting in Mexico and Cairo, and to Nina Patrick of Chicago, who are introducing the Wheel as an expression of Christ's message to Love One Another, and to do the work that he did and even greater work.

To Prof. David Smith who made the first movie inspired by the New Testament writings.

Lt. Col. John J. Whiteside, a Southern Baptist, who co-founded The Committee for the Future to bring forth positive options for the Future in Washington D.C and who affirmed the meaning of the evolutionary guidance given through the life of Jesus.

My son Lloyd Frost Hubbard, my fifth child, and now a Christian Scientist, as a young man in the Air Force who gave 10 copies of *The Revelation*, the first part of the writings published, to send to his Air Force friends.

Foreword

By Neale Donald Walsch

From the beginning of time humans have been trying to figure out Life. We've been doing everything we know how to do to understand what is going on here, what its purpose is, who we are in relation to all of it, and how we can apply in our lives what we imagine ourselves to know with a certainty on this subject.

In this ongoing effort we've sought help from as many sources as we could rally. Not the least of these have been the words and teachings of those whom millions of us, past and present, have acknowledged to be spiritual masters, and whose words have been recorded in our Holy Scriptures. And not the least of those scriptures has been the New Testament of the Bible, which centers around the life and teachings of Jesus Christ.

An enormous number of people have used this Testament as their touchstone, their main point of reference, their guidepost on life's journey. Yet what if some of what we've come to understand about Jesus and the teachings in the New Testament is mistaken—or at the very least, incomplete? What if much of it is? Would it make a difference? Would it matter?

Of course it would. Which is why it's important to never,

ever, discontinue the search, end the quest, or stop asking Life's most daring questions. And here is one with which we might start: Is it possible that there is something we do not fully understand about God and about Life, *the understanding of which could change everything?*

To me it is clear that the answer is yes.

And might some of what we don't fully understand have to do with this man called Jesus, and with the Testament that grew up around him?

Again, to me it is clear that the answer is yes. Surely there is at least room for further exploration. And even (dare I say it?) further revelation. Or must exploration and revelation have stopped two thousand years ago, and now—no matter how pure the encounter, no matter how wondrous the experience—be called blasphemy, heresy, or apostasy?

Even asking this question, to say nothing of answering it, requires a willingness to step outside the boundaries laid down by virtually every religion. Yet now along comes someone who has done both.

Now along comes Barbara Marx Hubbard, an ordinary human being who has had an extraordinary experience—an experience of direct revelation—of such magnitude that it offers all the world a chance to view Jesus and the New Testament in a brand new way; a way that could dramatically alter humanity's fundamental understanding and expression of what it means to be human; a way that could change forever and for the better how life is experienced upon the Earth.

What is extraordinary about this experience is not that it has happened. God is talking to all of us, all the time. The question is not, "To whom does God talk?" The question is: "Who listens?" What is extraordinary here is the depth, the breadth, and the scope of what this ordinary human being has placed before us.

It is equally extraordinary that she has had the determination to do so in the face of the fact that very few people believe that human beings receive direct revelation today. (In days gone by, yes, but in this day and age, no.)

There seems to be little disagreement among our species that those human beings upon whose messages the world's great religions are based experienced a direct revelation from The Divine. Indeed, among those who believe in God at all, the idea that God has been revealed to humanity *through* humanity goes virtually unchallenged.

Yet most people firmly believe that God *stopped talking to humanity* a very, very long time ago, or that Divinity has been revealed to and through only one person in all of human history, and no one else before or since. Thus, anyone who claims a direct revelation from The Divine in this moment is to be viewed with extreme skepticism at best, or put in prison or put to death at worst. (We see in this that things have not changed very much in these "modern times".)

So yes, it took great determination on the part of Barbara Marx Hubbard to bring forward what has been revealed to her—just as it will take determination on the part of everyone and anyone who would dare to read this material. For to even consider exploring ideas, concepts, and understandings of The Divine other than those with which we have all have been raised can be unsettling ... and, for some, actually frightening.

Still, our awareness that God is declaring God's presence in and through every one of us is increasing as our species evolves, and I believe that this heart-opening, mind-expanding, soul-revealing gift from Barbara Marx Hubbard will be remembered by all of humanity as a once-in-a-thousand-year treasure.

I hope you will give yourself the gift of this breathtaking exploration of larger possibilities regarding who Jesus was and what he was modeling for all of us. Was he modeling what it means to be a one-of-a-kind expression of Divinity? Or was he modeling who and what we *all* are—and what we all can express and experience were we merely to accept his demonstration as evidence of our potential?

That is the question of the millennium. And Barbara Marx Hubbard has dared to ask it. Should you explore it with her, you will have joined the great explorers within our human family. And we need explorers such as you. How else are we to proceed beyond the limited boundaries of our current understandings?

—Neale Donald Walsch
February 2015

Introduction

The Evolutionary Testament of Co-Creation: The Promise Will Be Kept comes to you as an inspirational writing awakened by the wisdom of the New Testament. My personal, mystical experience in 1980 of the living Christ catalyzed its creation. I had been writing a book on the future of humanity, in which I asked a question of the universe: "What kind of person can handle all this new power?" By that, I meant the new capacities I saw emerging from science and technology—breakthroughs that provided us with the awesome capacities we used to attribute to gods. Where was a new image of a human being who would be able to use these new powers for the good? I could not find any description of such a person.

Hampered by writer's block, I took a walk in the beautiful hills of Santa Barbara. The day shimmered with beauty. Before long I came upon a beautiful monastery high upon a hill—Mount Calvary Monastery—and entered the grounds. In the garden I noticed a large wooden cross reaching upward toward the mountains. Suddenly, a flock of hang gliders jumped in tandem off one of the higher mountains. They floated high above the cross, spreading their butterfly-colored wings.

In that instant an image of mass metamorphosis flashed

through my mind. The resurrection. The risen Christ. The ascension. The promise that we shall all be changed. I could hear the words of St. Paul sounding inside my head: "*Behold, I show you a mystery: We shall not all sleep; but we shall all be changed in a moment, in the twinkling of an eye, at the last trumpet. For the trumpet shall sound ...*"

An epiphany flashed through me. It was all coming true. This is the last trump of this phase of evolution. The trumpet is sounding right now for humanity. We cannot continue to fight, pollute, overpopulate and destroy our environment because we remain trapped in the illusion of separation. We're already all being changed by our new capacities, as well as our new crises. We will either evolve toward a higher order of love and creativity, or we will self-destruct.

A ray of hope illuminated my consciousness. As a futurist, I realized that if we could combine our new innovations in science and technology—to heal, to produce in abundance, to leave the earth in chariots of flaming fire, to communicate around the world with the speed of light—with ongoing advances in biotechnology, nanotechnology, robotics, artificial intelligence, quantum computing, accessing zero point energy and space travel, and if we could also infuse these new capacities with Christ love, we will indeed all be changed. I remembered Jesus's words: "You will do the work that I do, and even greater work shall you do in the fullness of time. ..." Jesus was calling out us to live up to our full potential as human beings.

The mass metamorphosis vision I witnessed by the cross became, for me, the image of the evolved humans we were already becoming. The resurrection offered a vision for the next phase of human evolution beyond our current condition. In that instant of inspiration, I realized that the person who could indeed handle all our awesome powers for the good would be a natural Christ: one who embodied the qualities Jesus demonstrated so beautifully throughout his own life.

With a feeling of awe and mystery, I knocked on the door of the monastery and entered the sanctuary with its polished wood floors, portraits of saints and rich aroma of incense. A nearby sign announced that there was to be a silent retreat held at the monastery that next weekend, "To meet the Lord in silence." I signed up right there.

While browsing through the library on the first morning of that retreat, I selected a Bible from the shelves and opened the New Testament to St. Paul's famous saying, "Behold I show you a mystery...." I then began to write. The floodgates of my mind opened. It appeared to me that the life of Jesus forecasted immense potential for the future human, by revealing a new humanity now struggling to be born. As I read various passages of scripture, I simply asked: *What does this mean for us now?* I then allowed the inspired insights to guide my thoughts, while holding in my awareness a dawning realization that the Bible is coded evolution, just now coming true.

The promise is being kept.

In six months I wrote a 1,600-page manuscript covering the Gospels, Acts, Epistles and the Book of Revelation. I named the entire work *The Book of Co-Creation*. Although I was a Jewish, agnostic futurist, the experience elevated me into a new awareness of Jesus as the embodiment of our highest potential self—a future human. It revealed the long-term goal of humanity to be the fullest actualization of ourselves as universal humans. In that, we become willing co-creators with the divine: natural Christs.

Mine is not a scholarly interpretation of the Bible, but a mystical expression based on my inspired insights. It therefore cannot be compared with the New Testament writings of the many distinguished scholars and theologians who have analyzed these same passages over the centuries. I have read with great interest and appreciation many in-depth scholarly and theological works about the Bible; however, I am neither a theologian nor a Biblical scholar. Bringing my futurist's perspective to the Bible, it seemed to me that the hidden evolutionary thrust of the work could not be revealed until after the birth of a generation that possessed the technological capacity to perform many of the miracles that Jesus once performed, like lifting off the surface of the earth or bringing the dead back to life—as well as even greater works than these.

The purpose of this text is to provide a context for the discovery of the specifics of humanity's greatest mission here on Earth. All those who read this work and feel called from within to act out the loving birth of humankind contain a pre-patterned element of this design in their being. This text encourages those who are activated from within to discover their specific task within the transformation of the whole human system.

This text recognizes and honors the essential contributions offered by all great traditions, avatars and seers of the human race. It calls for a new synthesis of the best of the past—or what can now be understood as precursors of the future—with what is unfolding right here and now, in all of us.

Evolutionary Bible Study Groups

This text can best be appreciated by reading it in small groups, in evolutionary circles of two or more. We therefore suggest that readers form evolutionary Bible study groups. We invite you to practice creating a sacred space as you do so, a resonant field that enables you to evoke your own inspired insights. Resonance leads to revelation.

First, read each passage of the New Testament and my inspired insights, then share your own realizations with one another. Within each of us exists a wellspring of inner scriptures that come forth from our own intuition, guidance or higher mind. When we're joined together in love and trust, this process informs us of our own potential to become whole beings: co-creators of our lives and our larger world. Through this process you can evoke within yourselves the emerging co-creative human, the being imbued with love who is seeking to express his or her unique life purpose for the good of the living whole.

Each of your evolutionary Bible study groups can become a seed of the new culture, connecting us via the Internet with each other and infusing the emerging world with insights and inspirations that come from our higher wisdom. A webpage has been created on *www.evolve.org* to serve you in establishing these study groups, and to enable you to connect with others who are also engaged in this deep spiritual exploration. The collective genius that emerges through each of us becomes a vital contribution toward the shift of consciousness from fear to love, and from separation to unity, at this most critical time in our shared evolutionary journey.

If this work resonates with the truth in your own heart, please spread the word to your friends and help us all to embody and express in our own lives the love and vast cre-ativity inspired by the life of Jesus, so that all who are so attracted can unite and co-create together.

Note: The full story of the origins of this work is pre-sented in *The Revelation: Our Crisis Is a Birth*, published by the Foundation for Conscious Evolution through a grant from Laurance Rockefeller's Fund for the Enhancement of the Human Spirit. That volume includes the story of my life journey, which ultimately led me to Jesus, as well as a com-mentary on the Book of Revelation. It culminates in this second volume: *The Evolutionary Testament of Co-Creation: The Promise Will Be Kept.*

As you read this text, you will encounter two distinct voices. One is my personal voice as I share my own insights and inspirations from each passage of scripture. The other voice comes through me as a higher, Christ-inspired revela-tory insight, and is styled like so:

SEEK FIRST THE KINGDOM OF GOD— intend above all else to evolve to universal life —and all these things shall be added to you.

—BMH
November, 2014

THE GOSPEL

ACCORDING TO MATTHEW

༄

In those days came John the Baptist, preaching in the wilderness of Judaea, and saying, "Repent all of you: for the kingdom of heaven is at hand. For this is he that was spoken of by the prophet Isaiah, saying, 'The voice of one crying in the wilderness, Prepare all of you the way of the Lord, make his paths straight.'"

MATTHEW 3:1–3

An intuition lives deep in the memory of humankind, inform-ing us that we are more than animals destined to repeat the endless mammalian cycle of eating, sleeping, reproducing and dying. The words of John the Baptist reveal to us that we are unfinished. Something more awaits us—a release of our potential, a fulfillment of our aspiration. Repent, John said, for the Kingdom of Heaven is at hand. Repent means to change our minds, to be dissatisfied with our present incomplete condition, knowing that within us is a state of being greater than we have yet realized. We *are* the Kingdom of Heaven, with our full potential realized.

REPENT! TRANSFORM! ALIGN WITH GOD. Do not accept your present limits. The time for newness is now.

❧

"*And think not to say within yourselves, 'We have Abraham to our father.' For I say unto you, that God is able of these stones to raise up children unto Abraham.' And now also the axe is laid unto the root of the trees: therefore every tree which brings not forth good fruit is hewn down, and cast into the fire.*"

MATTHEW 3:9–10

John the Baptist, who prepared the way for Jesus, told the Jews, the sons of Abraham, that they would be known by their acts, not their lineage. Any action that does not serve the good will be unable to take root and thrive in the new world. Only the good will endure. It does not matter where we come from or who our parents are; it matters only who we are, where we are going and whether or not we will deliver our highest potential.

Evolution constantly selects for characteristics that generate higher consciousness and greater freedom in all living beings. In us, this process has become conscious of itself. Free will has been introduced. We possess the freedom to discover the patterns in the process and cooperate with them, or not. If we pay attention to the patterns and cooperate with them, we become conscious participants in creation, ever evolving. If we refuse to notice the patterns and to cooperate with them—especially in this generation, when so much knowledge has become available—we shall not become conscious participants in creation, and we shall cease eternally evolving.

The choice is ours. The truth is known. The truth shall set us free to evolve eternally.

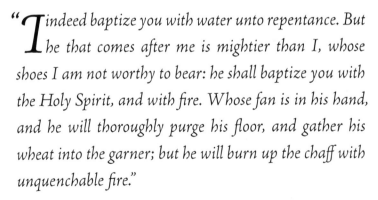

"*I indeed baptize you with water unto repentance. But he that comes after me is mightier than I, whose shoes I am not worthy to bear: he shall baptize you with the Holy Spirit, and with fire. Whose fan is in his hand, and he will thoroughly purge his floor, and gather his wheat into the garner; but he will burn up the chaff with unquenchable fire.*"

MATTHEW 3:11–12

John the Baptist prepared us for repentance, gently, with water. But Jesus, who came after him, baptized us with the direct lightning of God. At the appropriate time in history, an irreversible choice will be offered to each person. The choice is: Do you intend to evolve beyond self-conscious separation into whole-centered union with all beings? Do you intend to evolve beyond these perishable bodies? Or do you choose to die?

The choice has not been irrevocable, and will not be irrevocable, until the time in planetary history when the Earth-people inherit the power of the Tree of Life—operative knowledge of the invisible processes of creation. Even now, our generation comes close to possessing the powers of self-destruction and co-creation. This knowledge cannot be undone nor stopped. We *will* know more.

This power is too great for an immature humanity to wield. Therefore we must make a collective decision to mature in order for human life to continue on Earth and in the cosmos beyond.

*T*hen comes Jesus from Galilee to Jordan unto John, to be baptized of him. But John forbad him, saying, "I have need to be baptized of you, and come you to me?" And Jesus answering said unto him, "Suffer it to be so now: for thus it becomes us to fulfill all righteousness." Then he suffered him.*

MATTHEW 3:13–15

4

John served as the precursor for Jesus. He represents the human premonition of more to come, our readiness for the day when we shall all be changed. He realized that Jesus embodied a new capacity that as yet remains dormant within us all, and recognized that he needed to be baptized by Jesus. The lesser stage needs to be brought forward by the greater stage.

Jesus understood that the greater stage also needed to be welcomed by the lesser. John, the precursor, had to freely initiate and welcome that which was to come. The greater cannot be imposed upon the lesser. The lesser must willingly rise to meet the greater. Thus John, the expectant human, baptized Jesus, the fulfilled human, and through that action forged the essential link between self-conscious humanity and God-centered humanity.

And Jesus, when he was baptized, went up immediately out of the water: and, lo, the heavens were opened unto him, and he saw the Spirit of God descending like a dove, and lighting upon him. And lo a voice from heaven, saying, "This is my beloved Son, in whom I am well pleased."

MATTHEW 3:16–17

John, the self-conscious human who anticipated the coming of the God-conscious human, baptized and blessed Jesus, the first example. John's act emancipated the next stage of human evolution, causing the heavens to open up to Jesus. Like the heavens that awaited Jesus's baptism, so too is the next stage of our development always present. It lies dormant in the same way that adulthood exists as unexpressed potential during childhood, before the child matures sufficiently to experience it.

Jesus had to be baptized by John in order to manifest the new. Likewise, our human identity must acknowledge and welcome our divine identity in order to give birth to that which shall be revealed through us.

It now becomes essential that all those who expect the coming of the next stage of human evolution acknowledge the potential lying dormant within themselves.

FORGIVE YOURSELVES OF ALL PAST ERROR. Forgive the world of all mistakes. Focus your total attention on what you can become: natural Christs, universal humans, doing the work I did and even greater works than I. Then the heavens will be opened to you. The Spirit of God will descend on you as it descended on me. And you will hear a voice from Heaven saying: You are my beloved in whom I am well pleased.

❧

"*Blessed are they which do hunger and thirst after righteousness: for they shall be filled.*"

MATTHEW 5:6

The good will prevail. The poor in spirit—those who hunger and thirst for goodness, for God—shall surely be filled. For it is God's will and it is the law of the manifesting, evolving universe that at every quantum transformation a higher, more complex whole system emerges, in which each of the parts cooperates synergistically for the good of itself and the whole.

All members of the planetary body who desire to do right will do so, and will become part of the new whole. Each will transcend the limits of the separated self and partake of the powers of the whole body. At this coming stage of evolution, we do not transcend alone. We do it as members of a communal body. Whether it will be as a small colony of universal pioneers or the whole planetary body of the people on Earth depends on us.

Jesus had to demonstrate it first, on his own. Therein lies his apparent superhuman capacity. We will demonstrate it together. Thus our fully human, natural capacity will be drawn upon, accessible to all people who desire to follow the design of evolution.

⌇

"*Rejoice, and be exceeding glad, for great is your reward in heaven: for so persecuted they the prophets which were before you.*"

MATTHEW 5:12

7

THOSE WHO ARE PERSECUTED AND REVILED and outcast by the existing system shall be rewarded for their trust by experiencing the transformation in their own being. However, it is no longer necessary to be persecuted for my sake. The old formula of an eye for an eye and a tooth for a tooth will no longer work. Those who demonstrate love will not be reviled; they will be revealed and nurtured as the co-creative human.

There is a chance that your planet will not have to undergo the worst of the worst. It depends upon how quickly you receive my message, my word. Many are preaching salvation of the individual through love. No one is proclaiming the other half of my message: the transformation of the species by the use of its collective scientific, technological, spiritual and social capacities.

You, my newer messengers: you who are born at the time of the twinkling of the eye; you who are born at the moment of your metamorphosis; you, beloved, born at the hour of the planetary birth of the next era of evolution, must carry the new half of my message. This new half affirms and completes the ancient half that has been preached for two thousand years. It is the half that could not be pronounced until the fullness of time, until the quantum transformation has begun, until the Earth has cracked its shell and sent you, her children, forth among the stars.

"*Think not that I am come to destroy the law, or the prophets: I am not come to destroy, but to fulfill. For verily I say unto you, till heaven and earth pass, one jot or one tittle shall in no wise pass from the law, till all be fulfilled.*"

MATTHEW 5:17–18

The invisible laws of creation established a directional pattern in the evolution of the universe: one first intuited by mystics, and just now being discovered by scientists. The prophets foretold the direction of evolution. Scientists are discovering the processes.

You WHO EXPERIENCE THIS PURPOSE WITHin yourselves are discovering a new order of the future. You are here on Earth to advocate the fulfillment of the potential in such a manner as to attract, lovingly and gently, those who are afraid, defensive, cynical, skeptical or ignorant. Attract with the warm sunlight of the truth and see which seeds will grow. Those who grow toward the light are those who are ready to grow. Those who do not grow toward the light are not ready and should not be urged. Do not proselytize. Reveal. Affirm. Do not try to persuade; simply be persuaded. Be secure. Do not try to please. Simply be pleased. Do not try to force. Act upon the initiative yourself. Invite all who are willing to join with you to share their interests, their encouragement, their lives. Whatever they see fit to give, be grateful. Provide a channel for giving.

"Therefore if you bring your gift to the altar, and there remember that your brother has ought against you; leave there your gift before the altar, and go your way; first be reconciled to your brother, and then come and offer your gift."

MATTHEW 5:23–24

We cannot enter the next stage of evolution unless we are whole, with all wounds healed. Forgive, forgive, forgive every injury, back until the day when Cain slew Abel. Then forgive Cain; he knew not what he did. He was like a child, hurt by his father unwittingly. We forgive all wrongs of the world as we forgive the acts of a newborn child. For we are, as yet, a young species. *Homo sapiens sapiens* represent the infant stage of *Homo universalis*. Our present behavior will someday be unimaginable to the race of co-creative humans we are to become.

❧

"*All of you have heard that it was said by them of old time, 'You shall not commit adultery.' But I say unto you, that whosoever looks on a woman to lust after her has committed adultery with her already in his heart.*"

MATTHEW 5:27–28

We are ready to become the second couple. We interpret this passage as leading to the next stage of evolution in man-woman relations. In the biological, reproductive, terrestrial phase of human development, sexual fidelity to each other was vital for the preservation of the species. Mothers and fathers who did not stay together to care for the children jeopardized the survival of their progeny in most cultures. Society depended on sexual fidelity.

The decision to conceive children is a decision to commit our immortal seed to ongoing life. It is an eternal decision. Those who marry in order to have children are committed forever to the future. They do well to love, honor and cherish each other forever.

However, a new discipline and a new opportunity are emerging in our lifetime. Women will have fewer children. Most children born will be conceived consciously, by choice. Parenting will become a smaller part of the relationship between a man and a woman. Some couples will have no children. Some may choose extended life, travel in the cosmos or build new worlds. What will form the basis of their union, the foundation of their fidelity?

Co-creation will attract members of a universal humanity to one another—the chosen intention to create good works, events and enterprises for a positive future. Men and women will be attracted to each other in order to emancipate the potential of one another in a creative task that neither can perform alone.

In the co-creative phase of development, we will practice conscious evolution. We will be aware of the process of evolution, and we will consciously facilitate that process to realize our full potential as universal humans, joint heirs with Christ. Couples will unite to create works of art, broadly defined. Fidelity will be to each other for the sake of the creative *act*, the way it currently supports the creation of children.

As we extend human life over longer periods of time, there will be more than one faithful relationship in a cosmic (as contrasted to terrestrial) lifetime. As procreation decreases, faithfulness will increasingly flow toward the empathetic act. Intimacy in co-creation is already as personal, if not more so, than is intimacy in procreation. The love for our co-creations will cement our unions.

In the procreative, as in the co-creative, phase of human development, we pledge fidelity to the future. For the procreative couple, the undeveloped child represents the promise for the future. The couple remains faithful to each other for the sake of the child as well as for the love of one another. For the co-creative couple, the ongoing act of creation becomes the promise for the future. They pledge fidelity to their shared life purpose.

"*Again, all of you have heard that it has been said by them of old time, 'You shall not renounce swearing yourself, but shall perform unto the Lord your oaths.' But I say unto you, Swear not at all; neither by heaven; for it is God's throne: Nor by the earth; for it is his footstool...*

But let your communication be, 'Yea, yea; nay, nay;' for whatsoever is more than these comes of evil."

MATTHEW 5:33–35, 37

As the word becomes increasingly communicated and powerful, it becomes vital to say what we mean. Uttering destructive, contemptuous words permeates the thinking layer of Earth—the communication system, the noosphere—with negative energy, contaminating the entire psychosphere. We must not utter harmful words. We need to purify our thoughts and truthfully speak what we intend. The word is made flesh and our thoughts manifest as deeds, more and more directly, quickly and effectively. The power of positive thought, word and deed becomes the power with which we will build new worlds on Earth, and in space.

❧

"*All of you have heard that it has been said, 'An eye for an eye, and a tooth for a tooth.' But I say unto you, that all of you resist not evil: but whosoever shall strike you on your right cheek, turn to him the other also.*"

MATTHEW 5:38–39

The law of love is an eternal law. Prior to conscious evolution, organisms evolved through the survival of the most cooperative clusters of molecules, cells, animals and humans. But the process was not self-conscious; one co-operative cluster often survived at the expense of another.

As we graduate from unconscious to conscious evolution, however, we begin to render visible the invisible hand of God. Individuals gain vast power. The world becomes increasingly interdependent. The old, childish ways of one group winning at the expense of another cause destruction to winner and loser alike. Everyone loses when society is structured such that the winner exploits the losers; for all are members of one body.

Henceforth, life will require synergy to work. Synergy joins together separate parts to form a whole—one greater than, different from and unpredictable from the sum of the parts. Synergy aids us in overcoming our so-called enemies by including them in the creation of a whole society, which benefits them more than any partial victory of one over another. We move beyond competition, beyond co-existence and even beyond cooperation to co-creation as individuals, communities, nations and a world. Synergy is pragmatic. Nature works through synergy.

"Love your neighbor as yourself," reveals how nature pragmatically and ethically forms more complex whole systems out of the dissolution of past systems. Those following this great commandment are right now participating in the formation of vital clusters of like-minded lovers. Life supports them and fills them with energy.

Those who attempt to maintain the old separatist stance, wishing to punish their enemies, will be removed from the growing edge of the human community. They will harden, calcify and eventually die of separation. Only love can advance the next stage of evolution. The separatists may impede the progress of those who love the world, but eventually they will either change or wither away through alienation, stress and discouragement. Love them, attract them and leave them behind if they do not respond. Theirs is another day, another time, another cause. Judge not that ye be not judged.

Create new ground for synergy, places where those attracted to building new worlds on Earth, or new worlds in space, can work together. We need arenas where individuals can be invited in and will respond of their own free will. Do not pour new wine into old bottles. Build new systems for synergistic action through which attracted individuals can create their hearts' desires. Only free individuals co-creating freely, attracted by a transcendent possibility, rewarded by the acts of creation every step of the way and guided by an inner sense that all humans are members of one body can build new worlds.

At our stage of evolution, synergistic cooperation creates apparent miracles. Wherever two or more come into full and complete agreement, it shall surely be done. For such agreement implies that group members have recognized each other as themselves. This in-depth attunement calls in the power of the Creator, which is attracted to centers of synergy. Synergistic groups literally become infused with the creative ability of evolution and can transcend any obstacle. Those who partake in synergistic clusters with the purpose of cooperating with the Designing Intelligence will find themselves being transformed personally. Already today individuals are experiencing this change.

The unexpected mystery, the unanticipated reward and the catalytic trigger to move millions of incipient evolutionaries to action is the promise of personal transformation—in this lifetime—by accessing the full spectrum of human potential. We begin to transform by practicing personal growth, thought purification, body awareness and love of our neighbor as ourselves. We advance by partaking of the benefits of the biomedical advances in longevity, living and working beyond the biosphere, expanding our intelligence through positive thought, activating right intention and extending our intelligence through electronic means.

We are the generation living at the time that our planetary system as a whole is being born. We are the first generation that will be aware of ourselves as one, and we are now becoming responsible for the future of the whole. We possess an infinitely greater capacity as awakened humankind than we do as individuals, separate and alone.

It's happening now. Our story is a birth: our own. The ideal that Christ came to Earth two thousand years ago to demonstrate as one super-human, we can now experience collectively as fully human humans—the new norm—grateful for his expression of the potential that each of us now carries.

∽

"All of you have heard that it has been said, 'You shall love your neighbor, and hate your enemy.' But I say unto you, love your enemies, bless them that curse you, do good to them that hate you, and pray for them which despitefully use you, and persecute you."

MATTHEW 5:43–44

This is a positive commandment. "Resist not evil" means do not fight evil with its own weapons. Do not become negative to defeat negation. Become supremely positive to overcome evil, thereby converting it, rather than succumbing to it, by being persuaded to become destructive. The method for converting evil—which is defined as what separates us from contact with God and our neighbor—is *initiatory*, not passive, love. Passive love is love *responding* to love. It is "loving them who love you."

Initiatory love means choosing to love those who are not loving, but who themselves need love. Christ embodied initiatory love. Self-authorized, free and independent of the illusions of fear and separation, initiatory love recognizes attack as an expression of fear, or a childish call for love. It responds not with reaction, but with proactive loving strength, which both prevents destruction and invites construction. Initiatory love knows that the unloving other is part of the same body.

Initiatory love neutralizes evil by refusing to react in fear. It reflects love in response to hate. In the mirror of that love, the fearful may see a new image of themselves as lovable, and may then choose to become so. No one on Earth *desires* to be evil and filled with hate. Fear motivates acts of evil—fear and the illusion of separateness—the forgetfulness that all people are members of one body.

We, as new world builders, are called to practice initiatory love: first, to protect ourselves from becoming evil by acting constructively; second, to evolve ourselves into masters of co-creation wherein the dynamic power of our creativity inspires the fearful because the beauty of our acts attracts them. As Jesus healed the sick instantly, co-creators heal the alienated and the discouraged, elevating their hearts so they might realize their own potential.

Co-creators can perform miracles, converting pessimists and the sick of heart to joy, expectation and anticipation for the new. The modern miracle of mass communications amplifies this process. Television, radio and social media serve as the nervous system of the social body. Presently the newscasters are still immature, reporting pain, violence, dissension and breakdown as the "news." When eventually the mass media provides reports of breakthrough, success, innovation, acts of caring and creativity, it will transform despair to hope and activate the pent-up power in millions. The conversion of the mass media holds the power to activate our new cycle of growth.

My beloved people of Earth, the time is right, the soil is ready. Spring is near. Through the media of the world, begin the conversion to hope by spreading the message of potential to the members of the planetary body. Help them realize that the birth they are experiencing is their own.

◠◡

"*Be all of you therefore perfect, even as your Father which is in heaven is perfect.*"

MATTHEW 5:48

In the coming stage of evolution the Universal Human will become the new norm. The collective capacity of modern society, combined with the enhanced sensitivity of individual members of the planetary body, renders it natural for us to achieve what was previously beyond the reach of even the saints and geniuses of the human race.

We do not achieve perfection solely by our will to improve, although will is essential. We achieve perfection when our human will cooperates with the Divine. Creation's Intention—the tendency of evolution—is toward greater consciousness, freedom, beauty, wholeness and awareness of the process of which we are an integral part. We will be perfect as a beautiful flower, one that has not been damaged by disease, but which opens its exquisite bloom of purple and gold, pink and yellow, amber and wine, to the amazement of the observer.

Who could create a perfect flower? Who could create a perfect child? Who could create a perfect person? Not you and I alone.

You and I, in cooperation with the universal processes of creation, can perfect our being unto the very bosom of God, until we are all in the image of God, as we were created, as we are potentially now, and as we surely will be in this world without end.

"Be perfect" means to be who we *naturally* are. It means

to be original, unique, whole—our truest selves. The tendency of universal evolution encourages us as we grow naturally to our full stature. Those who work for the good do not work alone. We can take heart and know we shall succeed in being what we desire, because that is the Intention of Creation.

When humans and God join their wills in a common intention, no evil, no failure, and no fault exists or remains. Only certainty and the joy of creation abide.

⁓

"*After this manner therefore pray all of you: 'Our Father which are in heaven, Hallowed be your name.'*"

MATTHEW 6:9

Let us consciously connect with the Creator of the universe who is eternally present in us, the precious members of the creation. That conscious connection signals the contact with the Designing Intelligence. By that contact we tune into the Intelligence of the Creator. Mark well what we ask, for if we are in tune with the Intention of Creation, all will be given to us. Our initiative starts the process. Although the process is beyond our understanding, it responds to our intent. Prayer serves as an electric form of thought, signaling the creative generator of all being. When we pray that our will and the will of the Creator are one, all things shall be given to us in this world without end. Heaven is the alignment of the creature with the Creator, in acts of co-creation. This is our Creator's will and intent.

"Your kingdom come. Your will be done in earth, as it is in heaven."

MATTHEW 6:10

We pray that God's will be done now. For the Divine Will and ours are one, and if God's will be done on Earth, we will be in Heaven. The power is with us now, if we choose to be with it. We have free will. The choice is ours.

"Give us this day our daily bread."

MATTHEW 6:11

Help us meet our "deficiency needs," those lacks we have worked to overcome ever since Eve ate of the fruit of the Tree of the Knowledge of Good and Evil. Before that time we were creature humans, unconscious participants in the creation. We did not know ourselves, we did not know our limits, we did not know of our own death, nor did we strive to overcome it. We felt no need beyond the moment.

Once we ate of the fruit, we entered the painful period of self-consciousness. We learned how the creation works, in preparation for our rejoining it as conscious co-evolvers. During this period we felt deep need beyond the moment. Food, shelter, health, security, esteem, community—we experienced all of these as painful needs. And we struggled, dear God, how we struggled to provide, always falling short, and thereby always learning more. Every disease caused us to probe deeper and deeper into your processes of creation to learn how nature works.

Now is the time to meet our so-called deficiency needs through our collective capacity to produce and care for *all* members of the planetary body. We need only apply what we have already learned: how to grow, heal, spin, build, and provide for all basic human requirements, so that we may be free at last to be fully human—the daughters and sons of *Homo sapiens sapiens*, Christlike daughters and sons of God—free to co-create new worlds in space and a new Earth beyond the moral fear of bodily needs and physical death.

"And lead us not into temptation, but deliver us from evil. For Yours is the kingdom, and the power, and the glory, for ever. Amen."

MATTHEW 6:13

Let us not forget, ever again, that we are at one with God and all people, as well as with all creatures. This is the ultimate temptation of humans—to believe we are separate from God. We are often like children who try to kill their parents to inherit the Kingdom. This cannot work. It is not the way. We inherit the Kingdom by loving God and becoming mature enough to join the Creator in response-ability for the good of the Kingdom, so it may survive in glory forever.

‎~‎

" *Lay not up for yourselves treasures upon earth, where moth and rust does corrupt, and where thieves break through and steal; but lay up for yourselves treasures in heaven, where neither moth nor rust does corrupt, and where thieves do not break through nor steal. For where your treasure is, there will your heart be also."*

MATTHEW 6:19–21

Live lightly on the Earth. Security cannot be found in unnecessary things, but in gaining entrance into the process of creation. For all things that are created pass away, but all things that are creating are joined with the eternally evolving Creator. Security arises from creating, not from the objects created. There is no end to the creation. It is ever evolving. And so are we. When we put our hearts into acts of co-creation we shall live to sit at the right hand of the Creator.

‎~‎

" *The light of the body is the eye: if therefore your eye be single, your whole body shall be full of light. But if your eye be evil, your whole body shall be full of darkness. If therefore the light that is in you be darkness, how great is that darkness!"*

MATTHEW 6:22–23

We use our eyes to see. "I see" means "I understand." If we see and understand that we are good and loving members of creation, we become supremely healthy and eventually imperishable. We gain continuity of consciousness through a series of bodies that become ever more responsive to thought. This understanding will gain us access to the Tree of Life.

Otherwise we will repeat those great failed human efforts to be like the gods—the first Eve, the builders of the Tower of Babel, Icarus with his waxen wings. Even the Titan, demigod Prometheus, failed because he stole fire from the gods and set himself up, not as a Christlike link between creature and Creator, but as a rebel bandit, an immortal Robin Hood, a childish savior who neither loved humans nor God sufficiently to forge the link between them.

The person inspired by Christ incorporates the best of the Judaic tradition—its recognition of the one God, its morality, its sense of God in history and in the fulfillment of the world. The person inspired by Christ also incorporates the best of the Eastern world, its practical methods and disciplines of union between creature and Creator: meditation, release from the body through control of the body, the recognition of life on Earth as a school, its exquisite art and cuisine, its patience. Those inspired by Christ have yet, however, to incorporate science and technology as intrinsic to the mystery of our transformation.

It is no accident that science, technology and industry sprang up in the Western world from a Christ-inspired vision of reality. Science and technology emerged from a Christ-inspired world because Christ represents the transformation of the *person* through the transformation of the body, rather than through release from the body. Science sprang from this world because people believed the resurrection to be *real*. This belief stimulated interest in the material world. We began to learn how nature actually works. The expectation that we could transform the material world created our capacity to do it.

For 13.8 billion years the material world has been tending toward higher capacities, by bringing forth more complex systems that exhibit greater consciousness, freedom and order. The next evolutionary transition from degenerating to regenerating bodies is, like Jesus' resurrected body, a natural next step.

Christ acknowledged the ultimate and equal value of every person as a son or daughter of God. The honoring of personhood, the sacredness of every life, the desire to care for, heal, and comfort every body, spring from a Christ-inspired vision of reality. This vision fostered medicine, technology, industrialization—all of which are paving the way for the transformation of human existence from its terrestrial to its universal phase, as demonstrated by Christ through the resurrection, the ascension and the promise that what he did, we shall also do.

Science, technology and industry spring from the desire to extend and prolong life. They will now *evolve* from the love of eternal life. They will endeavor both to restore the environment, which is our life-support system, and to transcend the limits of hunger, disease, poverty, unchosen work, tyranny, planet-boundness and the ultimate tyrant—physical death. Science, industry and technology have just begun their meaningful work. For the three hundred years since the Renaissance, which fused Greek and Judeo-Christian ideas and produced the scientific method, we have been preparing for what comes next. The first phase of science is ending. The second phase begins with the restoration of our

Earth and the evolution of our Christ capacities—personal, social and technological.

Science, industry and technology reflect a vital aspect of the mystery described by St. Paul: "Behold, I show you a mystery: We shall not all sleep; but we shall all be changed..." (I Corinthians 15:51). Through scientific tools of transcendence we have learned enough of how God creates to work consciously with the processes of creation and begin overcoming the creature human condition.

Another aspect of the mystery of our transformation is the further evolution of the human nervous system and brain—the development of the spiritual faculty, the capacity to experience God within by resonance. Most people have received their knowledge of the Divine second hand, through priests and ministers who themselves never experienced direct contact with the Creator. Most carry an as-yet unawakened spiritual faculty. We either accept God by hearsay, on faith, or reject God because we cannot apprehend the Divine directly through our five senses.

The sixth sense, the inner eye of our spiritual faculty, is now being further evolved so that our maturing nervous system becomes capable of contact with the Universal Intelligence. In the same way that a newborn baby's nervous system is not sufficiently developed to comprehend language until the second year, so too is the human spiritual faculty not sufficiently developed to apprehend the language of creation until after our cosmic birth—the shift from terrestrial to universal life. Until now we have behaved like cells in the womb under the control of DNA, building we know not what. From this time onward, we will be like responsive cells in a fully formed organism. Greater awareness switches on in cellular consciousness when the whole organism shifts from womb to world. Greater spiritual awareness will likewise switch on when we humans shift into the post-terrestrial, postnatal, universal phase of our existence.

The ability to apprehend spirit has always existed in rare individuals since the dawn of civilization. It has, in fact, inspired civilization. Saints, seers and visionaries lit the dark path of our history with beacons of light that led us from our early human roots to our present condition.

Three new aspects of the mystery of transformation are now emerging. First, as we mature out of our early, materialistic phase of domination *over* nature, our sciences, industries and technologies are maturing alongside us and are aiding our shift to an ecological, organic phase of co-creation *with* nature.

Second, we are experiencing a maturing of our spiritual sensitivity. Millions of us recognize that we are all connected as members of one body, and we feel motivated from within by the same Universal Intelligence.

Third, our human intention to create—combined with our technological capacity to act on that intention—has delivered us to the stage of conscious evolution. At this stage, the evolutionary process grows aware and consciously directive of itself *through* us. In such acts as the lunar landing, or in recombining DNA to deliberately create new life forms, we have directly engaged with the process of evolution.

The human race is learning *how* to do the works that Jesus did through the harmonious maturation of our collective capacities—spiritual, scientific and social. The new synthesis emerges and fuses beneath our surface despair and confusion. Forces are gathering, connecting and exchanging information like rivulets of water beneath a crust of ice in the spring.

Our current environmental crisis represents the fulfillment of the scriptural time of sorrows and tribulations. It heralds the end of the world ... *as we know it*. During this crisis we will weed out the unworkable from the workable, and prepare for a future equal to our full potential. The scattered spiritual pioneers of Earth must align and support each other's planetary work at this critical time in history. We are everywhere; we cross all barriers of race, class, religion, culture, ideology, color and age. All who choose, of our own free will, to demonstrate with our lives our desire to follow the Way—to be the way toward full humanity—shall be transformed." If therefore your eye be clear, your whole body shall be full of light" (Matthew 6:22, Luke 11:34). Let all whose gaze aligns with the Intention of Creation act together, for the sake of the world.

⁓

"*No man can serve two masters: for either he will hate the one, and love the other; or else he will hold to the one, and despise the other. All of you cannot serve God and mammon.*

Therefore I say unto you, take no thought for your life, what all of you shall eat, or what all of you shall drink; nor yet for your body, what all of you shall put on. Is not the life more than food, and the body than raiment? Behold the fowls of the air: for they sow not, neither do they reap, nor gather into barns; yet your heavenly Father feeds them. Are all of you not much better than they?

Which of you by taking thought can add one cubit unto his stature? And why take all of you thought for raiment? Consider the lilies of the field, how they grow; they toil not, neither do they spin. And yet I say unto you, that even Solomon in all his glory was not arrayed like one of these. Wherefore, if God so clothe the grass of the field, which to day is, and tomorrow is cast into the oven, shall he not much more clothe you, O all of you of little faith? Therefore take no thought, saying, 'What shall we eat?' or, 'What shall we drink?' or, 'Wherewithal shall we be clothed?' (For after all these things do the Gentiles seek.) For your heavenly Father knows that all of you have need of all these things. But seek all of you first the kingdom of God, and his righteousness; and all these things shall be added unto you.

Take therefore no thought for the next day: for the next day shall take thought for the things of itself. Sufficient unto the day is the evil thereof."

MATTHEW 6:24–34

Put the Kingdom of God first and all the rest will follow. If we put our physical survival first, we shall not achieve that for long, for we shall become sick at heart and lose our motivation, our incentive and our sense of meaning.

To serve God, we must learn about God's creation in order to co-create with it. Such knowledge gives us the ability to produce in abundance. Yet if we have no other goal but the production of abundance—if we forget that there is some greater purpose than material well-being—we become mentally ill, alienated and stunted, suffering the malaise of modern humanity. The discovery that material success alone does not suffice us causes this malaise.

Having achieved a modicum of material affluence for multitudes of people for the first time in human history, modern society is learning that we cannot live by bread alone.

Enough people need to experience material sufficiency, yet still feel this powerful longing for something greater, for a society to be ready for the next phase of spiritual growth.

The first phase occurred in prescientific societies, where working to eat, reproduce and provide shelter claimed most of our energy. Life was short, disease was common and death was everywhere. Spiritual beliefs granted meaning to the difficult struggle to survive, with their promise of a transcendent state to come, after death.

The second phase of spiritual growth is beginning to occur in those postindustrial societies that have achieved economic sufficiency and relative abundance for millions. We need direct spiritual experience to help us overcome the mental misery of seeking material affluence as an end unto itself. Affluence cannot satisfy the whole person and, in its present stage, is destroying the environment and other species. As the first post-industrial society on planet Earth, the rapidity of the changes that we are encountering staggers us.

The nature of this new spiritual reality emerges through an increasing awareness of the unlimited potentials of the scientifically mature human race, working in cooperation with the laws of the universe, or God. While preindustrial spiritual reality offered the metaphysical attainment of contact with God-the-eternal through prayer, meditation, mystical experience, enlightenment and good works, this postindustrial spiritual reality calls on us to live out our transcendent capabilities in real time. It aligns us with God-the-evolving, as well as with God-the-eternal. Postindustrial spiritual reality does not discard the preindustrial or perennial form; it includes it, the way Einstein's physics includes Newtonian physics.

As we learn to live beyond our planet, to overcome involuntary aging and to regenerate, we can develop bodies comparable to the resurrected body of Jesus. There is no reason to assume that, with our particular version, nature has stopped evolving new bodies. The 13.8 billion-year trend has been to produce new bodies as consciousness expands, as attested to by the quantum leaps from fish to amphibian to mammal. The body of *Homo sapiens sapiens* differs from that of the early humanoids, and the body of *Homo universalis* will also be different from ours. Evolution moves toward higher consciousness and greater creative freedom, producing bodies that are ever more sensitive to thought.

Up until now, the evolution of biological bodies occurred through mutation and *natural* selection. Now though, through biological intervention, we can *consciously* select to correct physical defects, as well as recombine genes to create new organisms. We can also study the mechanisms of aging and reproduction, and in time learn to adjust them. Nanotechnology will grant us the ability to influence the structure of matter, based on molecule-by-molecule control of products and by-products. Through nanotechnology we may learn to repair cells and build new bodies as naturally as does nature. And at the very frontier of the healing arts, we are discovering that our thoughts themselves hold the power to heal. Our *faith* can make us whole. Jesus told us that those who believe in him shall have life everlasting. Our *belief* activates our evolutionary capacities. It directs our actions and produces the experience we believe is possible.

Who could have imagined, when young Robert Goddard sat in a tree, looked at the moon and decided to build a rocket to go there, that it was actually possible? Yet Jesus said we would do all the works he did, and even greater. Why should we not *believe* him, when already we perform modern miracles comparable to his own? We are crossing the great divide between the prescientific and the post-scientific ways of knowing God. Our human creativity serves as the bridge. The future humanity will apply its energy positively to attain even higher states of being than our own.

In the quantum transformation from *Homo erectus* to *Homo sapiens sapiens,* a positive factor appears to have been *Homo sapiens sapiens's* capacity to cooperate through food-sharing economy and sociability. The same selection process will be at work as we make the quantum transformation from *Homo sapiens sapiens* to *Homo universalis.* The evolutionary process will favor those naturally inclined to cooperate for the good of the world—those who love their neighbors as themselves. Conversely, those who resist creative involvement will experience increasing stress.

Research into longevity and extraterrestrial development will open up new opportunities, rendering our choice to die or to transform a *real* choice. Grace becomes a deciding factor here. We are beloved by the Creator and will be naturally assisted in this transition, by the process that organized the universe. Why should we imagine we could take this next step alone, when we did not create the world, the animals, the plants or even ourselves? The same graceful force that operated so magnificently before will support us during this quantum transformation. It has already carried us from the supernovas' bright glare, through the lifeless seas, to the rise into space of our rockets. How can this force possibly have run its course with us?

What arrogance such pessimism implies! For hidden in this vision of defeat is the illusion that we depend on ourselves alone. At the core of secular pessimism lies humanistic *hubris*. We are not now—nor have we ever been—the products of human intelligence alone. We must mature as much as humanly possible, and at the same time express total faith in the universal processes that exist beyond our sensory awareness.

SEEK FIRST THE KINGDOM OF GOD— intend above all else to evolve to universal life— and all these things shall be added to you.

◦✍◦

"Judge not, that all of you be not judged. For with what judgment all of you judge, all of you shall be judged: and with what measure all of you mete, it shall be measured to you again."

MATTHEW 7:1-2

We do not know enough to judge. The process creating this universe is so far beyond the capacity of the judging mind it's like an infant trying to judge the world based solely on its experience in the womb and the birth canal.

We cannot judge ourselves because we are still immature. We cannot judge our neighbors because they too are immature. We cannot judge the human species because it is still very young. We cannot judge the present crises, for we have never seen another planetary civilization make the birth transition from terrestrial to universal. We cannot judge God, because we do not fully know the Universal Intelligence.

If we dare to judge, we shall be restricted to the confines of our judgment. If we judge ourselves as guilty, we are guilty. If we judge our neighbors as guilty, they shall react in fear and attack us; we will react in fear and attack them, and Cain and Abel shall rise again, and again, and again through our infantile judging.

If we judge the human species as incapable of evolving, as doomed to remain in its ego-centered condition forever, we will act as if we are doomed to remain so and it will become a self-fulfilling prophesy. For as we see ourselves, so we act. And as we act, so we tend to become.

If we judge our current metacrises—the environmental, energy, resources, pollution, population, hunger, nuclear, alienation, all the challenges we face—as acts of evil people rather than as dangerous, but natural, evolutionary drivers and as stimulants to our own transformation, we will not respond to them with sufficient compassion, intelligence or good cheer to advance to the next stage of evolution. Through our condemnation we will condemn ourselves.

Beware of the prophets of doom, who preach the failure of the human race. Beware of the advocates of devolution, who counsel the human race to give up its aspiration for godlike power and return to the now-unnatural condition of our earlier societies, by working only by hand to survive. Noble unto each day is its work. But to return to the past is to die to the future.

We are created in the image of God; we are meant to be godlike. *Listen. Listen. Be sensitive to the Creator's love for us.* God's love for us is unconditional, eternal and personal. God needs every one of us for the creation of the world. Each one of us is precious; whether we know it or not, God knows it. Why do you suppose we were created, if we were not required for humanity's evolution?

As parents love their children, God loves us a million-fold more. Our mortal parents know only our mortal aspect, while our Universal Creator knows our universal aspect. How much more are we beloved by those who appreciate our full potential, than by those who know us only as an infant son or daughter of human parents? If we *must* judge ourselves, then let us take the perspective of God and judge ourselves as God's beloved children, still young and immature.

❧

"*You hypocrite, first cast out the beam out of your own eye, and then shall you see clearly to cast out the splinter out of your brother's eye.*"

MATTHEW 7:5

Our primary response-ability to ourselves is to mature, from self-centered to whole-centered consciousness. We purify our thoughts, cast a circle of white light around ourselves

35

and guard our thoughts with a sword of steel. If we can free ourselves from fear, anxiety and guilt and see ourselves as sons or daughters of God, we empower ourselves to free others from fear, anxiety and guilt. *As we see others, they shall see themselves.* Our insight into another's potential holds the power to activate that potential and reveal it to the person in whom it lies dormant. It then becomes true and can be manifested. Humanity's future depends on us seeing ourselves as heirs of God, conceived in God's image, and growing into the natural capacities of Christ.

"Give not that which is holy unto the dogs, neither cast all of you your pearls before swine, lest they trample them under their feet, and return and rend you.""

MATTHEW 7:6

No one enters the next stage of evolution by any way other than free will and a passionate desire to transcend. If we try to persuade others to evolve, they will resent us and may even try to prevent us from sharing our thoughts with those who wish to hear. In the sharing of the revelation of species potential, do not proselytize or persuade; share, reveal, demonstrate, attract, and ignore all those who ignore you. Let sleeping dogs lie.

Do not try to be popular. Be truthful. The truth shall spread like seeds of new life from those minds that are already choosing, already desirous, already striving to transcend their present condition. Our mission is to support the believers in the future of the world.

There are missions of mercy to nurse the sick. There are missions of conversion to those who have never heard the world of God. There are missions of redemption to criminals in the prisons. There are missions of peace among the warring nations, missions of plenty to the hungry, missions of knowledge to the ignorant, missions of reassurance to the captains of the old ships as our institutions crumble in disorder. *There is also the new mission of the future: a mission to the strong, the whole, the builders, the scientists, the artists— the conceivers who will co-create new worlds.* Let us cast our words to these people, and they shall be heard. Our words will provide the necessary encouragement to stimulate the innovations that are critical for the survival of our world.

⁓

"*Ask, and it shall be given you; seek, and all of you shall find; knock, and it shall be opened unto you. For every one that asks receives; and he that seeks finds; and to him that knocks it shall be opened.*

"*Or what man is there of you, whom if his son ask bread, will he give him a stone? Or if he ask a fish, will he give him a serpent? If all of you then, being evil, know how to give good gifts unto your children, how much more shall your Father which is in heaven give good things to them that ask him? Therefore all things whatsoever all of*

you would that men should do to you, do all of you even
so to them: for this is the law and the prophets."

MATTHEW 7:7–12

No seeker of God goes away unfulfilled. God wants to be discovered and directly experienced by every creature on Earth. Everyone who hungers for freedom from separation, everyone who desires to know the truth, everyone who sincerely wants to evolve, will be granted the opportunity.

The creative process supports our desire to participate in the creation. Just as parents want their children to be free to do their best, so too does the Creator of the universe desire that same freedom for each creature. But we also know, as parents, that if our children ask for something that will harm or spoil them, we must sorrowfully refuse them. At times God must likewise refuse our requests. If we seek power over others and receive it, both we, and our victims, will become diminished. If we seek riches without a willingness to share, we will arouse jealousy that will destroy our happiness as well as that of those who envy us. If we seek beauty to charm and possess other people and things we shall be sorrowful, because possessions control their possessor, and we will become enslaved by our own beauty. If we seek knowledge to control the ways of nature without first understanding and loving nature's ways, we will be dispossessed by the lands that we destroy. Ask and it shall be given, knock and it shall be opened—*if* the door we knock upon is marked *life,* not *death.*

Love. Truth. Joy. Health. Wisdom. Beauty. Abundance. Life everlasting. If we desire these for ourselves *and* for others, they shall be given to us. If we desire these for ourselves alone, they shall eventually be taken from us. For no one can receive the blessing of God in a selfish manner. It is the law.

∾

"Not every one that says unto me, Lord, Lord, shall enter into the kingdom of heaven; but he that does the will of my Father which is in heaven."

MATTHEW 7:21

The process of transformation is evolutionary. Only those who discover and align with the process can fulfill its purpose. Otherwise, how would the good prevail? If you were a creator, would you want it otherwise? Would you want the monstrous in spirit to populate the new Heaven and the new Earth?

How will we behave when we become apprentice co-creators, building little practice worlds in space—near Mother Earth—in preparation for the vast transforming voyage into intergalactic space/time, which is in further preparation for our role as maturing sons and daughters of God? Can we allow those who do not cooperate to enter our world? Can we invite the liars, the thieves, the lustful and the greedy? What would we do with them in our new worlds?

We will soon experience the predicament of God: Do we grant free will and allow suffering in those who choose it, as well as in the innocents they afflict? Or do we forbid free will and produce a robotic, uncreative, uninteresting, ever-repetitive, never-evolving world?

God chose to grant free will to the universe; so in the end of each phase of evolution a sorting occurs. Only the evolving/good advances to ever-more complex capacities, awareness and freedom to choose. That which does not advance will return to the whole, to be reshaped and repurposed within the greater creation.

Suffering becomes the price we pay for freedom. But would we choose otherwise? Will we choose otherwise? Think well, for our time is coming. We who survive the transition will have crossed the abyss from creature to co-creator, by virtue of our creative genius. We shall identify increasingly with the perspective of God as we build new worlds, create new microorganisms and redesign our bodies for cosmic time and space. This is natural, for we are naturally created in the image of God. We need not fear our powers as children of Earth. We appreciate them. We are the inheritors of the universal creation—so beloved are we. What trust. What faith. What hope God has in us to have granted us the power to become godlike!

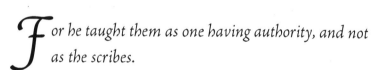

F or he taught them as one having authority, and not as the scribes.

MATTHEW 7:29

The root of the word "authority" is to *increase*. Jesus spoke with authority because he had direct access to the Creative Source, that which increases and augments. Jesus and God are one. Jesus spoke with the authority of one who can create, who can cause things to happen—who is the *source, rather than the effect,* of action.

Those who identify with the Creative Source of the universe, which is alive in each of us, will also speak with authority. They will be at one with the source of reality rather than at the effect of it. This realization reverses common sense;

that is, awareness received through our five common senses. Common sense assumes that our lives are the effect of the material world, not the cause of it, and indeed that often seems true. We "get" cancer. We are "hit" by a car. We "fall" in love. Or so it seems to the five senses.

But what about our sixth sense, the I that receives the reports of the nervous system's tastes, touch, sights, sounds, smells? Without the knower, nothing can be known. This knowing consciousness within each of us serves as the author of the reality we perceive. This consciousness also perceives the reports from reality. Even more, this consciousness created the nervous system that is doing the reporting. And, still further, this consciousness then decides what to make of these reports. Finally, and here is the crux: This consciousness can send messages as well as receive them. It can, for example, choose to send messages of love, regardless of any other messages the nervous system may be picking up. It can choose to send messages of wholeness that heal the body, rather than believing the messages of illness. It can choose to receive messages of illness, record them, and then return a signal of: "No fear. All is Well. Be well." And so it shall be. For that consciousness is the continual author of the body. Jesus demonstrated this fact through the healings he performed.

Every person's DNA transmits a unique code of life. Scientific investigation has revealed the process. The sperm fertilizes the ovum, fusing two existing designs into a new one. Then the DNA and its messenger RNA implement the new design by organizing available materials into the cells that form the body, which eventually births into the world, forgetting that it results from an exquisite design.

Scientists explore the process whereby the design of creation is executed. But they have not discovered the designer, the genius of the genes. The source of the design is not material; it is consciousness itself. This consciousness organizes the whole universe. Science can only know this source by its fruits, through its manifestations. What a wonderful achievement that is! Yet scientific methods of observation and measurement cannot cross the great divide between measurable effect (material) and immeasurable cause (conscious intention), except, of course, that individual scientists can experience their own intention, and be aware that they are causing their own reality.

Jesus spoke with authority because he identified with the author of the universe and realized that together they were co-authoring reality. God, the First Cause, the Creator, is greater than the children, Jesus said. However, when the children of God willingly and lovingly decide to join their intention with the intention of God, they gain direct access to the Source of the whole universe, because this is the will of the Creator. God desires the sons and daughters throughout the universe to become co-creators. Just as our mortal parents desire us to inherit their power, so the Creator of the universe desires all its children to inherit the power to transform everything into the kingdom of love, light, truth and goodness.

The good news is that God loves us now. If we will recognize this and become like Christ, loving God above all else, we can experience inner transformation and inherit the Kingdom right now, within ourselves. The future offers good news as well. We can evolve the material world, including our own bodies, into a perfect manifestation of the Kingdom of Heaven within. The Kingdom within and the Kingdom without are mirror images. However, we can achieve the Kingdom within instantaneously. All we need for the Kingdom to come alive within us is for the knower within to decide to experience its relationship to the Creator, and to join its will to that truth. This conscious choice is available to everyone at all times.

The Kingdom without takes time to create. It's an evolutionary process that we will achieve through the persistent effort of our loving consciousnesses gently and consistently acting upon the material world. It requires the "marriage of Christ and Eve," a union of divine love as expressed by Christ and the human desire for knowledge, as expressed in the story of Eve in the Garden. By joining Eve's yearning to know God with Christ consciousness of God, we co-create an Earthly Heaven.

It took time for the author of the universe to guide hydrogen and helium atoms to form the elements and the compounds, which formed the cells, which formed humans, who are presently forming a planetary civilization—and soon, new worlds in space. Some would prefer to ignore the work of time, because they have experienced the magnificence of the Kingdom within: Satori. Nirvana. Ecstasy. Bliss. Union. Totality. Immortality. Eternity. Why *do* more when already you *are* all?

This question arises in some who achieve the Kingdom within. They contribute to the world by holding that state, penetrating the noosphere with their experience to make it more available to the workers in the vineyards of the world. The good news for the future is that the Kingdom within will be able to create the Kingdom without in real time, gradually, through the union of love and knowledge, in alignment with the Intention of Creation.

The evolutionary children of God will be able to guide us through the transition. It is wise to achieve the Kingdom of Heaven within—the peace that surpasses understanding—and then work together to build the Kingdom without. They will learn to work out of fullness, not from lack. They will be different from other kinds of social reformers, be they socialist, liberal or conservative. The evolutionary children of God will not try to *improve* the existing world (important as that may temporarily be). Their purpose is to *transform* it, by evolving it to reflect the eternal Kingdom within. Thus they work at the growing edge, where innovation and breakthroughs spring up and are tended in the far-out gardens of the future. These pioneers will research the potentials inherent in nature. They aim to overcome environmental destruction, poverty, self-consciousness, planet-boundness and unchosen death.

*A**nd another of his disciples said unto him, "Lord, suffer me first to go and bury my father." But Jesus said unto him, "Follow me; and let the dead bury their dead."*

MATTHEW 8:21–22

At certain times we must put the higher purpose first, even if it means momentarily hurting the feelings of those following outmoded customs. This priority is justified, because the higher purpose will enrich everyone at a far deeper level than the assuaging of an immediate emotional need based on tradition. Great caution must be taken, however, for charity is the greatest virtue of them all. We must never put the higher purpose first, without also reassuring those who may feel bereft of our love. We must do everything possible to care for one another, while still serving our higher purpose.

The morality of co-creation is broader than the morality of compassion. It includes compassion, but is never confined to compassion alone. For we have more to do now than heal the sick. Our greater task is to evolve the healthy to a higher state of being, and to evolve the whole world to manifest that higher state of being. The message of Jesus has been applied to healing the sick and caring for the weak. But that is only a part of his purpose. If his major purpose had been to teach people to cure illness, in order to live happily in the world and die a peaceful death at the end of a good life, he would have said so and done so. But he did not.

Instead of living and healing the sick, he allowed himself to be crucified. He rose on the third day in a glorified body. He chose to demonstrate the morality of co-creation over the morality of compassion by his treatment of himself. Had he felt compassion for himself, he would have avoided the crucifixion and spent his life joyfully sharing his message, healing the sick and preaching love to all who would hear him. And for a moment he felt tempted: "O my Father, if it be possible, let this cup pass from me: nevertheless not as I will, but as you will." (Matthew 26:39)

Even so, he chose the higher purpose. In the agony of the moment, with a body sensitive to the horror to come, he chose the morality of co-creation over the morality of compassion. In his willingness to die to this mortal life and be resurrected in a new body, he set a new example for a morality more inclusive than charity, as essential as charity is. In his example we witness the priority of transformation, of growth, of the fulfillment of hidden potential.

"Let the dead bury their dead" means let those who choose to evolve follow the way of Christ, granting precedence to our transcendent purpose ahead of social customs.

The morality of co-creation, working with God to create the new, seems as difficult at this stage of history as it was for Jesus two thousand years ago. "But narrow is the gate, and narrow is the way which leadeth unto life, and few there be that find it" (Matthew 7:14). Yet victory is inevitable, because the transformation of simple to complex, to ever-higher awareness, to freedom and to union with the Creator, is a law as consistent in the universe as is the law of gravity.

The laws of transformation are as true and real as the physical laws of motion. They render it inevitable that life shall rise to a higher state of being. 13.8 billion years of evolutionary transformation of our physical universe provide us with ample evidence. This is the witness written in nature, the book of God's works.

The Bible serves as another witness. It reveals the reality of the resurrection and eternal life, as demonstrated by Jesus.

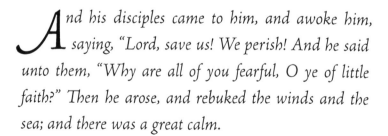

And his disciples came to him, and awoke him, saying, "Lord, save us! We perish! And he said unto them, "Why are all of you fearful, O ye of little faith?" Then he arose, and rebuked the winds and the sea; and there was a great calm.

MATTHEW 8:25–26

Conscious intention can influence the material world. Because of his total psychological connection to the Creative Intention, Jesus could heal, walk on water and affect the weather. He demonstrated a capacity that we are learning gradually, the way kindergarten children learn to read. Consider the weather. Through myriad new devices—from weather satellites to seismographs to cloud seeders—we learn how to affect the weather. These early, interim technological steps will make room for us to develop more elegant methods for affecting reality by our thought power alone.

Modern technology provides, as one of its purposes, a school wherein we learn the processes of God's material world, so we can become master builders at last: conceiving and manifesting as a continuous act, rather than step by laborious step. We have already discovered in brain research that certain states, which can be chemically induced, can also be induced by intention alone. We give patients morphine to overcome pain. We can also learn to instruct our brain to produce painkillers by conscious intention, rather than by taking the drug. We are thus revealing our own capacity to apply our minds and control the state of matter with conscious intent.

*A*nd, behold, they brought to him a man sick of the palsy, lying on a bed: and Jesus, seeing their faith said unto the sick of the palsy, "Son, be of good cheer; your sins be forgiven you." And, behold, certain of the scribes said within themselves, "This man blasphemes." And Jesus knowing their thoughts said, "Wherefore think all of you evil in your hearts? For whether is easier to say, 'Your sins be forgiven you;' or to say, 'Arise, and walk?' But that all of you may know that the Son of Man has power on earth to forgive sins," (then said he to the sick of the palsy), "Arise, take up your bed, and go unto your house."

MATTHEW 9:2–6

The forgiveness of sins and the healing of the body are connected. Sin is the illusion of separation of the creature from the Creator. To forgive our sins reminds us that the Creator and we are joined, mind with mind and heart with heart. Such forgiveness permits an instant restoration of the natural state of union between creature and Creator. This state of union overcomes disease. "The Son of man has the power on Earth to forgive sins" means that, when we act upon our potential and evolve the faculty of our minds, we can join our consciousness with the consciousness of God and heal ourselves. Christ demonstrated a potential that is dormant in us even now. At the next system stage of evolution this capacity will be a given. The evolution of the nervous system and the brain will grant the normal person access to Universal Mind. What has appeared to be supernatural will be realized as natural.

⟋⟍

*A*nd as Jesus passed forth from thence, he saw a man, named Matthew, sitting at the receipt of custom: and he said unto him, "Follow me." And he arose, and followed him.

MATTHEW 9:9

Some people are ready to go beyond their present functions; yet to trigger the action, they need support from those who have already gone beyond their own traditional role. This stage of incipient, evolutionary readiness is spreading subtly around the globe, yet remains relatively unnoticed by existing authorities, institutions and powers-that-be.

This lack of recognition protects the powers-that-are-to-become from the powers-that-be. Those whose task it is to maintain an existing system rarely cooperate to transcend the system they have been chosen to protect. Even if, as individuals, they feel attracted to the new, they will suppress that attraction in themselves—and in the world—to protect the system they are expected to maintain.

Yet the new inevitably overturns the old. Nothing can resist the inexorable force of creation. It moves like a universal tide toward higher consciousness, through deeper synergistic order. Holism is inherent in the nature of reality.

Anyone tasked with maintaining the integrity of any

part of the whole—whether it be a nation, a corporation, a church, a university, an army or an organization—will tend to resist, at first, the rising synergistic new order. For it seems—from the perspective of the part—to be a loss of sovereignty. Only from the other side of a transformation can it be clearly seen that the noncoercive integration of a part into a whole advantages the part as well as the whole.

Few leaders of major social institutions collaborate overtly in evolutionary transformation. They instead inadvertently help by *not* leading their institutions forward, thereby leaving a magnificent vacuum of leadership to be filled by those who feel genuinely attracted to what is emergent. This unwitting cooperation on the part of most of the existing leadership of the world's institutions is a natural evolutionary phenomenon. It creates more opportunities for enthusiastic action. The vacuum will be filled when the motivated members of the community cooperate synergistically, when the Matthews of the world, upon being asked to "follow me," do so immediately by following their highest aspiration as soon as they know it.

The preparation of this vacuum, caused by the loss of faith in a materialistic image of the future, has been under way for years. It is still not complete. First, it was necessary for Jesus Christ to be born and give his life to demonstrate the next phase of human capacity. Next, it was necessary for the idea of progress, through understanding nature, to be born in the Renaissance, through Francis Bacon and the early scientific observers.

Then came democracy. We needed to demonstrate the Jeffersonian statement that all people are created equal. Then came the industrialization of society, producing abundance for masses of people for the first time, and triggering the emancipation of unique human potential *en masse*. Then came the slow surfacing of the problems caused by the ceaseless productivity of our new machines: toxic wastes, pollution, overpopulation, resource depletion, acid rain. We are rapidly reaching a limit to this current form of material growth on Earth.

A double ache arose in the modern soul, seated amid the fruits of abundance, surrounded with lovely things. First we acknowledge that material well-being alone does not suffice. It leads to alienation, overconsumption and loss of aspiration. Second arises the deeper fear that this plentitude will not last forever, because the nonrenewable resources of the terrestrial world are limited, yet most of its people still live in dire need of basic necessities.

Materialism is not an end unto itself. Even worse, if materialism in its present form spreads to the developing world, it will trigger the collapse of our global environment and the destruction of our common future.

Answers to this dire dilemma will come from those who hold a vision of the next stage of evolution. Answers will come from those who can apply our powers—personal, social and technological—to promote a whole-system transition from Earthbound, self-centered life to universal, whole-centered life. For they know that our new crises serve to activate our new capacities, and that the purpose of our new powers is universal life.

We have known the truth for thousands of years, since the dawn of self-consciousness, when the First Adam looked upward to the stars and longed to be more than an animal body, eating, sleeping, reproducing and dying. We are passing through the final grades of the School of Self-Consciousness, wherein we separated from the creation to learn how it works. We are entering the new School for Co-Creative Consciousness, wherein we participate intelligently with the Creative Intelligence to fulfill ourselves as a new species, the mature inheritors of the labor of the whole human enterprise.

OH PRIVILEGED GENERATION. BE AWARE OF the grace that has been given you to act out the dreams of the ages. Oh Matthews, everywhere, leave your seats at the receipt of custom. Arise and act upon your own potential. Find your extended function, the unique work that you are qualified to do, and which the world requires in order to evolve. Trust your growth capacity. Trust the process of creation, which is complex beyond your intellect. Trust that you, too, can become as God intends you to be. Fill the vacuum with a new image of reality: humanity, co-creative with God, beginning its universal phase of development in a cosmos of unknown dimensions, with profound tendencies toward knowing more and more and more.

❧

"*No man puts a piece of new cloth unto an old garment, for that which is put in to fill it up takes from the garment, and the rent is made worse. Neither do men put new wine into old bottles: else the bottles break, and the wine runs out, and the bottles perish: but they put new wine into new bottles, and both are preserved."*

MATTHEW 9:16–17

Those who innovate may take nourishment from the existing system for as long as possible. However, we cannot, after a certain phase, patch the new into the old fabric. Rather, we patch the best of the old into the new, that it might be brought forward. For the sake of the world's future, the limitations of the past must not retard it. The rent, the tear in the fabric, grows worse with each attempt to attach the worn threads to the vibrant strands of the new.

To be a conservative evolutionary—conserving the past by incorporating the best of it into the new—we must create the new context. Otherwise, the old context collapses, the old bottles break, the new wine is lost, and the potential of the present is denied.

The creation of a new, inclusive context for those who desire change thus becomes the primary task of the future-oriented family on Earth. The new context offers a shared image of the future commensurate with our full capacities; a comprehensive set of actions, inclusive of diversity, calling upon everyone's unique potential to evolve the world; and a shared communication system for the plans of action to be heard, to help the networks of the attracted to coalesce, to match needs and resources, and to discover appropriate patterns of cooperation. This context, this matrix, is in formation now. This testament is one of its components.

*A*nd when he was come into the house, the blind men came to him: and Jesus said unto them, "Believe all of you that I am able to do this?" They said unto him, "Yea, Lord." Then touched he their eyes, saying, "According to your faith be it unto you." And their eyes were opened; and Jesus strictly charged them, saying, "See that no man know it."

MATTHEW 9:28–30

Why did Jesus repeatedly perform healing miracles and instruct the healed not to tell anyone? Is it because his purpose was not to heal the sick but to prepare humanity for the new? Was it because he did not wish to have attention distracted from the real purpose of his mission, which was not the healing of the sick but the transformation of the person from material to spiritual, from perishable to imperishable, from the creature human to co-creative human?

The purpose of the forgiveness of sins and the healing of the sick is not so that we might remain healthy *as we are*, but so that we can move to the next step in the development of humanity. Consequently, Jesus did not emphasize healing as the primary purpose of his mission. Yet he could not help but heal. It was so natural to him to be whole, and he was so totally devoted to the wholeness of everyone, that he healed as he breathed. He forgave sins as easily as he opened his eyes and saw the reality of the potential in each person rather than the reality of the limitations in each person.

Each person contains a coded memory of the future and intuition of things to come. Our mission, those of us who are attracted to the future, is to put forth clearly what attracts us, and to set out publically to realize what inspires us. Thus we will trigger the memory of millions and set in motion a process of unfolding, which will not depend solely on us.

When we nurture our potential selves, we are like sunlight and warm rain upon seedlings in spring. We activate the potential in others.

∽

"And when he had called unto him his twelve disciples, he gave them power against unclean spirits, to cast them out, and to heal all manner of sickness and all manner of disease. These twelve Jesus sent forth, and commanded them, saying, "Go not into the way of the Gentiles, and into any city of the Samaritans enter all of you not: But go rather to the lost sheep of the house of Israel. And as all of you go, preach, saying, 'The kingdom of heaven is at hand.'"

MATTHEW 10:1, 5–7

If we do not preach the Kingdom first and heal the sick second, we shall do neither. The Kingdom is the next step of evolution. Though it will not be achieved without compassion for immediate suffering, the compassion to heal the wounds of the world will not be realized if we focus on sickness first.

Focus on fullness first. Focus on wellness first. Focus on transformation first.

Focus on the New Jerusalem first. And then we shall also restore the Earth and build the City of Peace upon foundations that will never crumble, because they will be ever evolving.

We preach to the lost sheep. These are all people on Earth with the intention to evolve into divine humanness. The diaspora, the pioneering souls of Earth, cry out to be connected and in deeper communion as a unified body with the living Creator.

We do not impose ourselves on those who are not hungry for God. Nor do we judge who is and who is not hungry. We cannot tell a believer from a nonbeliever until we share our own being in total vulnerability for no other purpose than to build together the Kingdom of God.

We take no money except what we need. We are open, defenseless. We all have equal opportunity to leave what holds us back. Rich and poor, sick and well alike: all have this same opportunity.

It is true that those of us who are born healthy in free nations have a far, far easier time. Therefore our challenge is greater than that of those born under the tyranny of poverty or dictatorship. Our challenge is to go further than ever before, because we have started further ahead than ever before. This is especially true of those born in the United States of America.

We who are given the great gift of freedom stand upon the shoulders of the geniuses of the ages, especially the children of the old world who came to a new world and gave us the opportunity to respond to the next stage of evolution. Look now at the American dollar bill and be amazed at the purpose for this country that is inscribed on it in words and images. *E pluribus unum.* "Out of many, one." This heralds a synergistic order, a true democracy for those who are equally loved by the Creator, yet unique in their talents and abilities. Such democracy is for those who wish to attune to the design of the evolution and act it out in concert with others.

Novus ordo seclorum. "A new order of the ages." This is the next stage of social evolution, building the Kingdom on Earth as it is in Heaven, functioning as one body, synergistic and self-governing, combining the building power of science, industry and technology with the spiritual awareness of the Christ in each of us. We are laying the foundations for the New Jerusalem, a city for co-creators, heirs of God.

Annuit coeptis. "God favors this enterprise." We are the generation who must make the link between the unfinished pyramid and the cosmic eye, the generation born with the power to self-destroy or self-evolve—the generation of the Second Adam and the Second Eve. We are touching the Tree of Life. 13.8 billion years of evolutionary process favors this enterprise of freedom, union and transcendence. The United States was founded on this principle, which is now spreading throughout the world.

Our mission is the same one Jesus assigned to his disciples two thousand years ago. It is to emancipate the Divine human potential. Only the timing differs. Theirs was the time to sow. Ours is the time to harvest. The seeds of the future are ripe. If not picked, they will rot upon the vine, and we will lose our golden opportunities.

"And all of you shall be brought before governors and kings for my sake, for a testimony against them and the Gentiles. But when they deliver you up, take no thought how or what all of you shall speak: for it shall be given you in that same hour what all of you shall speak. For it is not all of you that speak, but the Spirit of your Father which speaks in you."

MATTHEW 10:18–20

Jesus sent his disciples on a mission not designed by human will alone, nor does it follow human plans. There is such uncertainty and ambiguity in this phase of the transformation that, as Jesus said, only God knows the timing of these events. Therefore, those of us who set forth upon the mission of revealing the potential of the future must listen to our inner voices, pray for guidance constantly and let ourselves be guided by whole-system consciousness, of which each of us is a part. Thus guided, we know what to say and do on each occasion, for we are inspired by a transcendent purpose beyond our full awareness.

When we are fully in action, fulfilled in action, we are in the flow. We know that we are not doing it, because it is doing us.

"*Fear them not therefore: for there is nothing cov-ered, that shall not be revealed; and hid, that shall not be known.*"

MATTHEW 10:26

The time for hidden, occult, priest-mediated religion is over. Everything we know is to be shared. There are no secrets in the Kingdom. Only the truth can serve us now.

"*Think not that I am come to send peace on earth: I came not to send peace, but a sword. For I am come to set a man at variance against his father, and the daughter against her mother, and the daughter-in-law against her mother-in-law.*

"*He that loves father or mother more than me is not worthy of me: and he that loves son or daughter more than me is not worthy of me.*"

MATTHEW 10:34–35, 37

As soon as Jesus presented the choice of the Kingdom *or* the world, a separation occurred. Once we become aware that we have a choice between death and transformation, our decision generates eternal results that can separate even the deepest blood relations. The call of the spiritual family becomes greater than the call of the blood family once a person is fully awakened. Individually we can choose to embrace options for evolutionary choices such as longevity, space migration and evolved consciousness. Those who choose these paths will evolve differently from those who choose to remain in the terrestrial/mammalian life cycle.

$\sim$

"*All things are delivered unto me of my Father: and no man knows the Son, but the Father; neither knows any man the Father, save the Son, and he to whomsoever the Son will reveal him.*"

MATTHEW 11:27

We are not creating ourselves. Everything we are and will be is a direct manifestation of our Creator—the animating principle of the universe. The Universal Human is the next step in the creation, the potential of the human realized.

Christ was a first Son of Man, a first person to graduate to the next stage of being, capable of healing, resurrecting and ascending beyond the planet, through direct attunement with the Creative Intelligence. No one can know the Creator from the narrow confines of a mortal, self-conscious being. Only through the next step of evolution, as incorruptible, whole-conscious beings, can we attune directly to God. We must ourselves become the sons and daughters of man to have deeper access to the Creative Intelligence.

Just as newborn children cannot meaningfully know their mortal parents until they mature, so we humans cannot know our Creator until we mature by exercising our own God-given creative capabilities. It is impossible for the Son to reveal God to those whose spiritual sensitivity has not yet matured enough to experience God intimately.

This revelation of the reality of God and the next stage of evolution was Jesus's mission. Christ served as an intermediary between self-conscious terrestrial humanity and God-conscious, universal humanity. A beacon of light, he reveals to us what we are naturally to become. If we keep his model constantly in mind it will hasten our evolution, because it serves as a map for our own potential as universal beings.

If we set out upon a voyage with no map and no goal, no compass and no stars to guide us, we would certainly get lost. Modern civilization now experiences this lostness.

We are not sure where we want to go. We have neglected the living example of the first future human by not accepting it as a genuine guide for our lives. Nor have we understood that the fruits of science and technology are tools of transcendence to help us gain access to our own inherent potential for universal life.

We are like abandoned children, unaware that we have been born to a thrilling life. We focus on problems and are crippled by feelings of fear and hurt pride. We require a new vision to inspire us to lift our heads and see what we can become. We require new demonstrations of the reality of life at the next stage, to magnetize the potential that exists in millions of humans now ready for growth. We require a taste of the experience of ourselves at the next stage, to activate our biochemical-psychological and social systems. We are like children just before puberty, beginning to feel the attraction of the opposite sex but not yet having experience of contact. Once that feeling is experienced, the parents do not have to tell the child to be attracted in order to procreate the human race. It comes naturally.

Once we have experienced the attraction to our own potential state of being, we do not have to be told to co-create the future. We are literally charged up, excited at a suprasexual level, our bodies energized, our minds alert, our lives breaking out of the limits of repetitive form—to seek the new.

∾

"Come unto me, all you that labor and are heavy laden, and I will give you rest. Take my yoke upon you, and learn of me; for I am meek and lowly in heart: and all of you shall find rest unto your souls. For my yoke is easy, and my burden is light."

MATTHEW 11:28–30

The ultimate rest is release from the human condition, not through death but through transformation. Once we have matured to the next stage of being, living up to our full capacity as a universal species, work as we know it will transform. We shall not produce by the sweat of our brow, but by the creativity of our minds and hearts.

The awareness of that coming condition can ease the struggle of this transitional phase of human evolution. For when we know that our suffering has meaning and is leading somewhere desirable, we can be tranquil and prevail—even under the most strenuous conditions. Through the knowledge that our present acts create the future, we unlock our extraordinary genius. It is thus that heroes and heroines are born. When we believe our present acts have no significance in the creation of a positive future, we lock up our talents, and focus on our pain.

❧

"*He that is not with me is against me; and he that gathers not with me scatters abroad.*"

MATTHEW 12:30

People who do not remain in alignment with their own aspiration to become Christlike and achieve their highest potential fall into a trap of self-inhibition. The suppression of one's own potential and aspiration causes bitter anger against oneself. It is based on the fear of growth. Those who are afraid of their own growth resent the presence of those who are attracted to growth. Jesus is a prime example of a person attracted above all else to demonstrating the reality of his full potential as a co-creator. He represents a threat to anyone who does not wish to do the same.

We build defenses against our own potential. We build bulwarks against hope. Once we acknowledge our potential and accept our purpose, we become willing to risk the loss of what is for the gain of what can be. If we struggle to protect ourselves against our own idealism, we will trade our transcendence for security. Unfortunately for those of us who feel afraid, security does not exist in clinging to our limits. Those who try to hold on to the past will be scattered and will suffer, as the old institutions change and old patterns dissolve. Only those who are moving toward the new potentials of the future will find security.

❧

"*Then one said unto him, 'Behold, your mother and your brethren stand without, desiring to speak with you.' But he answered and said unto him that told him, 'Who is my mother? and who are my brethren?' And he stretched forth his hand toward his disciples, and said, 'Behold my mother and my brethren!'*"

MATTHEW 12:47–49

A deeper tie exists between those who share a spiritual intention than between those who share only a biological connection. As we approach the historical moment of the quantum transformation that will mark the end of terrestrial self-conscious life, the desire to transcend is increasing, while the biological impulse to be fruitful and multiply is decreasing. We will have fewer children, because we have less need to reproduce and sustain multitudes of infants. That frees us to respond to our *noological* rather than our biological attractions.

The word *noological* combines the root word *nous*, which means mind (cognition through direct self-knowledge), and the word *logic*, which means reason. *Noologic* connotes the mind in direct contact with Spirit, expressing itself through reason in action. Noological attraction serves the same purpose as biological attraction: to create the future through unification with our beloved.

For biological creation, the form of union is sexual. The process involves the joining of genetic plans to synthesize a new and unique human being that differs from its parents. For noological creation, the form of union is suprasexual. People are attracted empathetically. Empathy may include sexual attraction, yet is not dependent on it. This process of creation involves the joining of ideas instead of the combining of genetic information. The purpose of noologic union is to synthesize a new and unique act for the future that reflects the characteristics of its conceivers. It also serves to further evolve the partners through their creative actualization.

Suprasexual co-creation is androgynous. These unions are not determined by gender, but by genius. Genius represents a fusion of masculine and feminine aspects within the individual into a new whole. Attracted to each other and to the Creative Intention of the universe, suprasexual partners develop new social patterns of creativity like intentional families, networks of shared purpose, new communities and rituals of communion and attunement. The union of whole being to whole being to create acts for the future, in attunement with the patterns in the process of evolution, forms the basis of the noological family.

The noological family may be the same as the biological family. Man, wife and offspring may share the same gene pool and the same idea pool. But this is rare. In the modern age, most children do not share the same creative task as their parents. They leave home and find their own way.

The biological family too will be elevated to an extraordinary purpose in the post-transformation, universal phase of human history. Those who decide to have children will do so with a greater sense of personal choice and vocation than in the past. These parents will consciously choose to have children. Every child will be wanted. Every care will be taken to nurture all children from conception through gestation, through birth and maturation—and if desired, through their transformation from *Homo sapiens sapiens* to *Homo universalis.*

We are gradually moving from purely instinctive mammalian sexual reproduction to conscious choice in the reproduction of humanity. We can apply this choice to spare our children from disease, and eventually to create new bodies fit for cosmic life. Through conscious choice, parents will become conceivers of the new race of humanity.

Both noological families and biological families will form the next basis of self-government. Already self-organizing, self-helping and self-motivated clusters of people are proving to be more effective in getting a job done than is a bureaucratic team.

Bureaucracy offers us less than the sum of its parts. It represses our creativity. When tasks are divided, everyone reports to a superior, so everyone feels inferior to the one above. The one at the top—the president—will either be inferior to the stockholders or the electorate, so the top too becomes an illusion. Bureaucracy organizes us into an endless, circular system of inferiors.

New forms of self-organization designed by co-creative, noological families are called *synocracies.* A synocracy governs by synergy rather than through adversarial means. The whole becomes more than a simple sum of its parts. Each unique member finds his or her way into participation in the whole through attraction, inspired by the desire to co-create with others. We seek to transform our bureaucracies to synocracies.

Synocratic co-creation is joyful and self-rewarding. With it, we find an enhanced opportunity for co-creation, and experience deepening participation in the social body.

Money declines in importance when all common basic needs are being met. A universal humanity will develop the environment and its resources for the benefit of all life. This shift will be crucial for space settlements to thrive, because human beings must create sufficient air, water, vegetation and real estate to support us on new planets. We will learn to synthesize the necessary natural materials by patterning ourselves after nature. Our future growth needs, being unique and inspired by attraction instead of deficiency, will be creative and regenerative. By meeting a growth need we create more for all, rather than taking from all.

When a society crosses the great divide from basic-need motivation to growth-need motivation, the majority of its people will have their deficiency needs for food, shelter and security met with minimum effort. They will act out their growth needs by doing creative work and by co-designing and co-evolving new worlds, in space and on Earth. The potential growth of our human creativity has no limits.

Earth too will become a new world as humanity undertakes the restoration, preservation, conservation and harmonization of Earth as a living organism. This new world is the Second Garden. After the period of the birth of planetary transformation, creatures will remember their Creator and consciously rejoin the creative process with joy.

In the new worlds in space, creative humans will make the leap to solar, stellar, galactic and eventually universal life. Some will feel attracted to the renewed Earth; others will long to build new worlds in space. This points to the intricate ecology of souls. All are needed. We love each other as vital members of a universal whole, which is diversifying even as it is unifying. Union differentiates. In oneness, uniqueness expresses. In wholeness we birth newness. Through synergy we experience the freedom to do our personal best.

$\backsim$

"*The kingdom of heaven is likened unto a man which sowed good seed in his field: but while men slept, his enemy came and sowed tares among the wheat, and went his way. But when the blade was sprung up, and brought forth fruit, then appeared the tares also. So the servants of the householder came and said unto him, 'Sir, did not you sow good seed in your field? From whence then has it tares?' He said unto them, 'An enemy has done this.' The servants said unto him, 'Will you then that we go and gather them up?' But he said, 'Nay; lest while all of you gather up the tares, all of you root up also the wheat with them. Let both grow together until the harvest: and in the time of harvest I will say to the reapers, Gather all of you together first the tares, and bind them in bundles to burn them: but gather the wheat into my barn.'*"

MATTHEW 13:24–30

This parable helps us understand how we can turn the other cheek to our so-called enemies and not be destroyed. If we try to destroy our enemy when we are both immature, we will pull out our own roots while tearing at his. We destroy ourselves by becoming the enemy, because by attacking we become self-destructive. The enemy wins.

However, if we have enough faith and courage to allow the apparently wicked to grow in our midst, at a certain point when the time arrives to harvest the mature growth, the "reapers" can gather the weeds and burn them without destroying the wheat. The "reaper" is the harvester, the evolutionary selection process that separates favorable mutations from the unfavorable. This selection process is not of human origin. It is the Divine Universal Intelligence that has been operative for billions of years. It is difficult for us to understand this at our immature stage. There are many forces of the larger system at work that we do not yet understand.

The question of evil is a pragmatic one. We face it daily in modern planetary society. How should we deal with criminals, the insane, totalitarian dictatorships and greedy entrepreneurs? The list is endless. How can we overcome evil without becoming evil? If we build vast military arsenals to defend ourselves against our so-called enemies, we become increasingly a military state, which we despise. What alternatives exist?

The parable of the separation of the tares from the wheat at the time of maturity suggests that it is more dangerous to destroy evil too early than to let it grow until both good and evil mature. At that time the difference becomes obvious and natural selection can be made at a higher level, by a more intelligent force than human judgment alone. For

13.8 billion years the evolutionary selection process has led toward ever more complex whole systems, an indication that this force is real and highly intelligent. It is more intelligent than what we call "evil" or we would not be here, in beautifully organized bodies as members of a living Earth, revolving around our sun in a galaxy of billions of suns. What organizing force did this? The same force that is operating through us right now.

The parable of the tares leads to the conclusion that when the Quantum Transformation happens, Universal Intelligence will discern what benefits the next step of evolution and should therefore continue, and what is to be eliminated because it no longer serves a useful purpose.

"The kingdom of heaven is like to a grain of mustard seed, which a man took, and sowed in his field, Which indeed is the least of all seeds: but when it is grown, it is the greatest among herbs, and becomes a tree, so that the birds of the air come and lodge in the branches thereof."

MATTHEW 13:31–32

The genuinely new is barely perceptible when it begins. It is too original to be noticed. Our senses perceive only what we already understand to some degree. The Kingdom is so different from our existing society that worldly eyes in fleshly bodies cannot see it physically sprouting in our midst, in the hearts of millions willing to love and in the minds and works of geniuses already creating the elements of transcendence.

When the Kingdom matures it will literally reach beyond the planet, beyond the self-conscious mind. Its dimensions exceed our current comprehension. Yet we are sowing its seeds now, as they have been sown by the faithful for thousands of years. These seeds look small and inauspicious in the mundane garden of modern society with its massive institutions of power—the government, the corporation, the military, the academy, the church. Who can change these giants? What new force can breathe life into the vital functions—governing, producing, defending, educating—that they represent?

The only force required is the right seed in fertile soil. Then the design will grow and find all the world's energy at its magnetic command.

DNA in the early seas organized all of the Earth's nutrients into cells. Likewise, the seed of the Kingdom of Heaven, sowed in the hearts, minds and souls of humans, will organize the elements of decaying societies into a new pattern for everlasting life.

"So shall it be at the end of the world: the angels shall come forth, and sever the wicked from among the just, and shall cast them into the furnace of fire: there shall be wailing and gnashing of teeth."

MATTHEW 13:49–50

The end of this phase of evolution will be orchestrated by the Intelligence of the whole universal system. It will select favorable characteristics from the unfavorable, and just behavior from the unjust. Unjust behavior shall disappear— whether by the slow rust of devolution or the rapid force of holocaust, no one knows. But of this much we can be sure: Only the good evolves; only the beautiful endures. The proof that good prevails over evil is the existence of life itself. Life has arisen from the maelstrom of evolutionary history, through forces contending with forces throughout billions of years of time. We are here now, dedicating our lives to the next step of evolution. We already represent the result of unimaginable victories of order over disorder, co-operation over competition, birth over death.

Humanity's past victories are not our doing. Nor do our present victories result from our doing alone. The will to transcend is an expression of the Intelligence that organized life out of a world of hydrogen and helium atoms. When we feel our own passionate desire to evolve, in concert with the Designing Force of the whole universe, we experience the power of that Intelligence infusing our intent to transform right now, at this moment.

But Jesus said unto them, "A prophet is not with-out honor, save in his own country, and in his own house." And he did not many mighty works there because of their unbelief.

MATTHEW 13:57–58

How difficult it can be to share our vision of what is possible when we live in the midst of those who identify us as part of their own past. Our biological families and traditional communities tend to view their children and neighbors as static. When we experience divine discontent and break out toward a transcendent life, our friends and family feel a natural resistance and often jealousy. Transcenders challenge their families and communities to be like them. Some do not wish to accept the challenge. To fully acknowledge and welcome our native prophets is tantamount to admitting they are right. If they are right, we should support them. If we support them, we have to change our own lives. But we are afraid to change our lives. What if it doesn't work? What if we fail? What if we lose what we have?

Many prophets are rejected in their own country and in their own homes, because their relatives identify with them and feel more challenged by their aspirations than do others elsewhere. Their relatives try to put them down and extinguish their flame, so that they don't have to ignite the flame in their own hearts. In such a climate of resentment a prophet cannot heal, for healing is based on total faith in the process. Thus the prophets among us usually leave home. Sisters shall be separated from brothers, and husbands from wives. Some within each family will be attracted to the next stage of evolution. Some will be repelled by it. Those of us who are visionaries and prophets need not be discouraged. We need not surrender to the resistance of those around us.

A new morality—a new foundation for fidelity—emerges at a time of transformation. The morality of growth supersedes the morality of preservation. If a person must choose between a biological relationship based on material, emotional and social well-being, and a spiritual relationship based on shared intention to overcome some barrier to growth in attunement with God, the spiritual relationship takes precedence.

Ideally, as co-creators we aim to preserve our traditional familial relationships, or even to transform them as we ourselves are transformed. Ideally, self-preservation, self-reproduction, self-actualization and self-transcendence are not mutually exclusive. But if members of our family choose to remain where they are, we have no moral obligation to suppress our own potential on their behalf. In fact, the suppression of our potential is more "immoral" than growing beyond our biological relationships.

We cannot maintain a harmonious relationship by suppressing our personal growth. This results in misery, frustration and bitterness. Once the fuse of aspiration is lit in a person, it cannot be contained. Any attempt to contain it literally burns the person alive, in the conflagration of suppressed energy, and inflicts the fire on those who are near and dear. For everyone's sake we must leave those who wish us to remain uninspired because they do not yet feel their own passion to create. But we can do so in love. If we follow our heart's desire we will be whole.

Our inner wholeness can heal the hurt of those we have apparently left behind, for we have not truly separated. Our growth serves as a stimulus for theirs. Our fidelity to our own potential sets an example for them to become more faithful to theirs. Everyone who keeps growing toward his or her own highest capacities will eventually meet everyone else who also keeps growing. All that rises converges.

Visualize a large mountain with a wide base and a narrow summit. Life's travelers are climbing this mountain. They start from different points at the mountain's base. Some stop at the threshold of the first steep climb and never even see the others who stop at the same place, for the mountain's base is too broad. Others climb to the middle of the mountain, high enough to see both the ground and the peak. They stop there, settling for a half life by resting at midpoint. They do meet many others, for the mountain is narrower in the middle than at the base. Still others keep climbing, more attracted by the peak experience than afraid of falling. As the terrain steepens the challenge deepens, and the obstacles enlarge. Every step presents a choice to go on or go backward, for we cannot stand still at this place on the mountain. It is too steep to rest anywhere.

At a certain point we look down and realize we cannot return to the middle of the mountain. There is no pathway down...only upward, onward, outward, inward, heavenward. To go back is to die. We have no alternative from this point. We have already made an irrevocable choice. We will go the Whole Way to the top of the mountain. Suddenly, when we realize we have no choice but to go the Whole Way, the path near the top becomes grassy, gentle, flowered, watered, tended, exquisite; yet hidden from those clinging to the crags just below.

At the top we meet everyone who has also kept growing. This union at the peak sets the foundation of our leap beyond the mountain and into the Kingdom; the quantum Transformation to life ever evolving as a universal species in a universe full of other beings who have also had the courage to rise to the tops of their mountains, on their own planets in galaxies everywhere.

A new spiritual rite of passage is being initiated. We are baptized at birth, confirmed or Bar Mitzvahed at puberty, and married during the time of procreativity. Now we experience the Rite of Transformation to symbolize the stage of co-creativity, when we choose to go the Whole Way in actualizing our potential in attunement with the universal process of creation.

"The Son of Man shall send forth his angels, and they shall gather out of his kingdom all things that offend, and them which do iniquity."

MATTHEW 13:41

Only the good endures. At the end of this phase of evolution there will be a synthesis of that which is full of love and willingness to serve the higher intention. All else shall pass away. Therefore we need not judge. The judgment shall be made at the next level of evolution. The selection process is inherent in nature, which for 13.8 billion years has been selecting beings of ever higher consciousness, freedom and order.

Our task is the Word of Hope and the Act of Transformation. The Word of Hope is that "we shall not all sleep but that we shall all be changed." We shall become universal beings living on this Earth, which will become a new world, as well as live on many new worlds beyond this one. We shall know the Creative Intention, God, directly through love of the Son, who reveals the potential in each of us. "The Son of Man" means that the potential exists within each of us to give birth to ourselves as a Christlike person. We can do it now, one by one, and become the precious seeds of future worlds. The Second Coming is a time of collective action, when we shall do it together. The former things will pass away—at a definite time in history.

*A*nd he commanded the multitude to sit down on the grass, and took the five loaves, and the two fishes, and looking up to heaven, he blessed, and brake, and gave the loaves to his disciples, and the disciples to the multitude. And they did all eat, and were filled: and they took up of the fragments that remained, twelve baskets full.

MATTHEW 14:19–20

Abundance flows in the Kingdom of Heaven. Scarcity does not exist in the universe. The co-creative power of Christ will become our own. We shall do as he did, and even more. Through the harmonious application of good will and science, in an Earth-space environment, the human race *that evolves* will produce in abundance, effortlessly. We are given extended means of production as new ways to emancipate us from the curse of Adam, that by the sweat of his brow did he live and did he die. In the next age we shall not survive by the sweat of our brow, but by the creativity of our minds and the love in our hearts. Eventually we may possibly be nourished directly from the sunlight like the lilies in the field that toil not, but surely they grow.

*A*nd in the fourth watch of the night Jesus went unto them, walking on the sea.

And he said, "Come." And when Peter was come down out of the ship, he walked on the water, to go to Jesus. But when he saw the wind boisterous, he was afraid; and beginning to sink, he cried, saying, "Lord, save me." And immediately Jesus stretched forth his hand, and caught him, and said unto him, "O you of little faith, wherefore did you doubt?"

MATTHEW 14:25, 29–31

When our bodies vibrate at a faster frequency they will not be so dense. They will be capable of levitation by our intention to be filled with light. Fear casts out light. When Peter was afraid he began to sink, because fear is the killer of faith.

We are not doing this work alone. We did not create ourselves. We did not create the world. We did not create the stars around which our planets revolve. The process that created it all is still creating right now, through us. It is responsible; we are response-able. By recognizing the reality of the creative process evolving us now from *Homo sapiens sapiens* to *Homo universalis*, we grow empowered to follow its signals, feel its strength, support its allies, heal the sick, feed the poor and raise ourselves into a universe wherein our mortal flesh will become immortal and death shall have no dominion. All of this shall we do, and more. For this is the beginning, not the end of our new life, in a world likewise without end.

"*Every plant, which my heavenly Father has not planted, shall be rooted up. Let them alone: they be blind leaders of the blind. And if the blind lead the blind, both shall fall into the ditch.*"

MATTHEW 15:13–14

We need not seek to banish evil, right wrongs, punish offenders or correct inequity. We need only do what is right by correcting ourselves, by forgiving all others, and ourselves and by affirming what is good, true, pure and light. Every act that does not carry out the Intention of Creation for higher freedom, consciousness, wholeness and purpose will eventually fail. Give no energy to false leaders. They will cause themselves to fail, and are only strengthened by the attention we may give them.

He said unto them, "But whom say all of you that I am?" And Simon Peter answered and said, "You are the Christ, the Son of the living God."

MATTHEW 16:15–16

The Son of Man is the individual potential of each of us, realized in our person. It is what we are to become. Christ is our self in the future. He is the aspect of our self that reflects our highest potential: our creative, imperishable universal spirit. Christ came to free us to be all that we can become. Every power that he has, we have: to heal, to walk on water, to produce something out of nothing, to rise into this universe alive and return to Earth, to join our will to the will of the Creative Intention and to be empowered by that joint intention to move mountains, circle the Earth in a flash of light, and to overcome poverty, illness, ignorance, tyranny and pain. All this we can potentially do *NOW*, yet do not do, because we are not aware that we can.

Christ came to tell us to do what we can, to be our best—which is to be like him. Our own sense of false limits holds us back, not a lack of capacity. Our own fear of failure causes us to fail and our own thoughts of anger are wounding us. We are creating our own destruction, yet we can choose our own transformation. We give birth to our potential selves through our intent and total commitment to doing so.

The emergence of the new humanity is our task. The act is both personal and collective. Each of us can overcome the separation within ourselves, but until society as a whole applies its cultural and scientific abilities to caring for the whole human community, the new humanity cannot prevail on Earth. Imagine the human race as a more mature species. As each of us has a higher, wiser self, so too does the entire human race. Our collective capacity is infinitely greater than our capacity as separate individuals.

❧

*A*nd Jesus answered and said unto him, "Blessed are you, Simon Bar-Jona, for flesh and blood has not revealed it unto you, but my Father which is in heaven."

MATTHEW 16:17

Flesh and blood with its five limited senses cannot fully perceive the Christ, the Son of the living God. The Son must be intuited directly as knowledge of what will be, emerging out of what now is. Our intellect alone cannot lead us to the Kingdom of Heaven. However, it can help us arrive once we have intuited where we want to go and what we desire to become.

❧

"*A*nd I say also unto you, that you are Peter, and upon this rock I will build my church; and the gates of hell shall not prevail against it."

MATTHEW 16:18

I, JESUS CHRIST, BUILD MY CHURCH UPON the rock of awareness in all people that they can recognize me and do as I do. Nothing of this world can prevail against the next step of evolution. No

81

evil is powerful enough to stop the inevitable emergence of Christ out of Adam. Can the oak be prevented from growing out of a planted seed? Yes, perhaps a single oak may fail to grow, but I have planted fields of oaks, acres of oaks, miles of oaks, billions of oaks throughout the world.

The power of that seed to fulfill itself cannot be stopped. For all that is needed for the oak to prevail is one full grown tree. From one tree come enough seeds to populate the world. One tree on one crevice on one hill is enough to save the seed of oaks. And yet there are billions. Success is inevitable. My church, first founded on the recognition of one man, Peter, as to who I am, will be enfolded in the rise of the new congregation of risen men and women who will embody me by doing what I did, and more.

The church will be everywhere; everywhere and nowhere. Emerging humans will reveal me to be the potential in each man and woman on Earth. Neither Jew nor Gentile, slave nor free, East nor West, religious nor secular, believing nor nonbelieving is your concern. All humans are potentially me.

Ideologies will fall like shells of seeds that sprout and grow. None can contain the magnificence of men and women free of fear, loving each other, risen in the universe, co-creating new worlds in Heaven and on Earth. None can touch the radiance of a single heir to this potential.

"And I will give unto you the keys of the kingdom of heaven, and whatsoever you shall bind on earth shall be bound in heaven, and whatsoever you shall loose on earth shall be loosed in heaven."

MATTHEW 16:19

I WILL GIVE TO EACH PERSON WHO GIVES birth to the son of man the keys of the kingdom. Whatsoever you accomplish on Earth shall pave the way for your future beyond this period of terrestrial self-consciousness. The barrier between Heaven and Earth shall disappear as the sons and daughters of Adam give birth out of their own genius to the children of humanity.

The barrier between Heaven and Earth shall disappear as creature humans give birth out of their own genius to co-creative humans. The division is like the womb that separates the babe from the world. As we build in the womb, so shall we become in the world. As we build in the womb of the self-conscious phase of human history, that is what we will see erected in the universal-consciousness phase of human history. Each of us is father and mother to the son/daughter in us, which is our potential to be Christ.

As we nurture our higher, wiser Self we shall either release it, or restrict it. This generation will give birth to our potential self as the new reality. It will shift from Earth-bound to universal. It will inherit the powers of the Tree of Life, the knowledge of how the invisible processes of creation work. It will produce child-gods through its scientific understanding of the laws of nature at work in the world. This generation shall sound the trumpet's last blare. Delivery is about to come. The whole creation suffers and groans, for the hour of our birth is near.

The Earth cannot much longer submit to the depletion of her resources, the storage of radioactive wastes in her veins, the paving of her flesh with stone, the cutting of her breathing trees, the annihilation of her wilderness, the ravage of her streams, the choking of her air. She is full with child. The technologies that have nourished the generation of god-children have done their work on Earth, and are now evolving to carry the young sons and daughters beyond the planet to become solar, stellar and eventually universal beings.

We must stabilize our growth here to restore, renew and heal our Mother Earth. Then we will lift her life beyond her, as children-pioneers carrying the seed of Earth to flower in Heaven, which is its new blossoming environment, the place where the fruits of the Earth-people will bloom cooperatively with the god-people of the universal community.

From that time forth began Jesus to show unto his disciples, how that he must go unto Jerusalem, and suffer many things of the elders and chief priests and scribes, and be killed, and be raised again the third day.

MATTHEW 16:21

Jesus knew he was to demonstrate the reality of the resurrection. He allowed himself to be reviled by existing authority in order to demonstrate a new authority, one that could not be controlled by any human force on Earth. If he had simply died without being murdered by the existing authorities, he could not have demonstrated to us that no earthly power can bind the son of man from imperishable life. Through his example, he demonstrated that transformation is the inheritance of every man and woman on Earth.

Then Peter took him, and began to rebuke him, saying, "Be it far from you, Lord: this shall not be unto you."

MATTHEW 16:22

It is normal for those who love the natural body to try to hold onto it, because in this phase of history it is not possible for the average human to realize that the natural body can become the spiritual body *in one lifetime*. Since it had never been so before Jesus demonstrated it, Peter did not believe that it could ever be so. However, once Jesus resurrected he established the new pattern for the next step of our evolution.

❧

*B*ut he turned, and said unto Peter, "Get you behind me, Satan: you are an offense unto me, for you savor not the things that be of God, but those that be of men."

MATTHEW 16:23

There exists a temptation to accept this life as all that is, squeezing every precious drop from it for fear there is nothing more. The fear of losing this life will prevent us from desiring the new life passionately enough to muster the energy required to achieve it. If our attention is on preservation and pleasure in this moment, we will surely pass away. If our attention is on the pleasure of the potential of every moment, we shall surely live on.

Even Jesus, clothed in a mortal body, was subject to the temptation of the worldly desire to cling to the present rather than to evolve. To evolve we must savor the things of God. We must desire, intend, imagine and act for the Kingdom to achieve it. That which our heart desires, we shall have.

∽

*T*hen said Jesus unto his disciples, "If any man will come after me, let him deny himself, and take up his cross, and follow me."

MATTHEW 16:24

Those of us who wish to transcend this mortal condition must deny ourselves and take up the cross—the step wherein we break with the past—and set our attention resolutely forward, toward what is coming: our becoming like Christ. Everyone has this choice to make: whether to attempt to hold on to what was, or to take up the cross and traverse the abyss from the old age of Earthly life to the new age of universal life.

∽

"*F*or what is a man profited, if he shall gain the whole world, and lose his own soul? Or what shall a man give in exchange for his soul?"

MATTHEW 16:26

What good is it to gain the whole transient material world at the expense of life everlasting? What could possibly be worth having here and now, other than the opportunity to become whole, free and ever evolving?

"*For the Son of Man shall come in the glory of his Father with his angels; and then he shall reward every man according to his works.*"

MATTHEW 16:27

Every thing we do counts…forever. When the Son of Man is born in us, we shall be rewarded for every creative, constructive word and deed of our life. Each thought and act becomes a building stone for our new life. When that life bursts forth we will be grateful for the works we have done to produce this magnificent state of being. We are becoming parents to ourselves. The self we parent is the God-being within us.

All creature humans are pregnant with themselves as co-creative humans, the Christ child within. We have all received word of the impending birth. We have heard that we are more than a mammalian body, living a brief instant and then dying forever.

We have known since time immemorial that we were something more than meets the fleshly eye. Everyone has known. And everyone forgets. We are born trailing clouds of glory, intimations of immortality. Then we fall sleep and identify with our mortal bodies alone. But when we awake, we are rewarded. As co-creators we must remember each day who we are. Every creative act prepares the way for our evolution, while every destructive act delays it.

❧

"*Verily I say unto you, there be some standing here, which shall not taste of death, till they see the Son of Man coming in his kingdom.*"

MATTHEW 16:28

Jesus knew that in his disciples' lifetime he would suffer death and rise on the third day in a new body.

❧

And was transfigured before them: and his face did shine as the sun, and his raiment was white as the light.

MATTHEW 17:2

When humans are fully aware of their identity, they glow with unearthly light. The inner radiation that is felt in the mortal condition ignites when contacted by higher life. It illuminates the being with light that resonates at a higher frequency than does earthly light.

❧

And Jesus rebuked the devil; and he departed out of him: and the child was cured from that very hour. Then came the disciples to Jesus apart, and said,

"Why could not we cast him out?" And Jesus said unto them, "Because of your unbelief: for verily I say unto you, if all of you have faith as a grain of mustard seed, all of you shall say unto this mountain, 'Remove behind to yonder place,' and it shall remove; and nothing shall be impossible unto you."

MATTHEW 17:18–20

Our belief serves as a communication channel for the powers of creation. It acts as an antenna for the electricity of God. God works through intentional thought. God said, "Let there be light," and there was light. All co-creators inherit this natural power.

Even now, in our transitional stage from Adam to Christ, we can practice the power of belief to perform godlike acts. Every day we can ask God what we should intend to do that day that is pleasing, and then we will it to be so. Thus we begin the early exercises of co-creators.

∿

At the same time came the disciples unto Jesus, saying, "Who is the greatest in the kingdom of heaven?" And Jesus called a little child unto him, and set him in the midst of them, and said, "Verily I say unto you, except all of you be converted, and become as little children, all of you shall not enter into the kingdom of heaven. Whosoever therefore shall humble himself as this little child, the same is greatest in the kingdom of heaven."

MATTHEW 18:1–4

Children have not yet learned the false perception that they are separate from creation. They are naturally integrated with the Creator. Innocent of separation, they take it for granted that they are beloved by God. That natural innocence of children is the human state closest to the Kingdom of Heaven. Children cry and are answered. They stretch out their hands and their parents embrace them. They live without care for tomorrow and do not fear death.

BE YE AS LITTLE CHILDREN, MY BELOVED. Act in perfect faith that everything you need will be given. Ask and you shall receive, knock and doors shall open. This attitude of perfect trust enables you to release fear that prevents my help from reaching you.

Fear blocks God's frequencies from reaching us. Our task is to free ourselves from fear and act effortlessly, producing abundantly and beautifully as artistic acts of creation. To be humble is not to be humiliated. To be humble is to know we did not create the creation, but are innocent heirs to it. To be humiliated is to be told we are not worthy of our inheritance. This is a lie. *Every person on Earth is worthy. Everyone is here to become godlike.*

MY GOD-CHILDREN, YOU WHO ARE THE first to recognize your identity must comfort and encourage all the children crying in the dark. Tell them they are my dearly beloved. The light is here for all who open their eyes to see the greatness within themselves and to act upon that greatness for the salvation of the world, from dust to divinity.

"How think all of you? If a man have an hundred sheep, and one of them be gone astray, does he not leave the ninety and nine, and goes into the mountains, and seeks that which is gone astray? And if so be that he find it, verily I say unto you, he rejoices more of that sheep, than of the ninety and nine which went not astray."

MATTHEW 18:12–13

Many self-selected souls dedicated to the future of the world have neither heard of nor yet loved Christ within themselves. They serve the secular world by learning how the processes of creation work. This movement supports the intellects of the world, who have had the courage to tolerate separation long enough to discover the invisible technologies of God hidden in the secrets of nature—how she grows and burns and builds and dies. These servants of God have forgotten that they volunteered to be ignorant of God long enough to learn how the creation works, as though they were separate and apart from creation itself.

I ESPECIALLY WELCOME THE NON-BELIEVERS in God, who have been and are now the believers in the world. They are my builders of new worlds, my liveliest co-creators. Those whom the hunger for knowledge drives to acts of devotion are vital to us all. For when scientific humans know me, they bring the matured mind capable of knowing how I do what I do. They will be able to help the easy believers grasp the importance of the transition from Homo sapiens sapiens to Homo universalis.

For the easy believers are readily satisfied. They are content to wait passively for the end of the world, since they know they are already saved and shall have eternal life because they believe in me. And so they shall. But the end of this world is the beginning of the new. I therefore call to attention those capable of creating the new in the name of God. Those who passively wait are beloved too, but they cannot build the New Jerusalem. For that I require the conceivers, the explorers, the scientists, the artists, those in whom the flame of expectation burns. The satisfied will inherit the Kingdom, but they will not build it. The evolving humans are here to strengthen and inform the builders of the New Jerusalem.

*T*hen came Peter to him, and said, "Lord, how often shall my brother sin against me, and I forgive him? Till seven times?" Jesus said unto him, "I say not unto you, until seven times: but until seventy times seven."

MATTHEW 18:21–22

To become co-creators, we must also envision others as co-creators. When one trespasses against us, we recognize the trespass as the manifestation of immature self-consciousness and treat it as we would the act of a child, knowing the child will soon grow up. We treat it firmly and with love. We do not condemn a two-year old for destroying a beautiful Chinese vase. We forgive and inform the child firmly that this act is destructive. We remove the vase until the child has matured enough to understand.

So it is with those who trespass against us. We recognize in any trespass the act of someone still in the state of self-consciousness. We do not react in anger but respond with love. With love we protect ourselves, and the trespasser, from the tragedy of infantile destruction, which in maturity will be deeply regretted. We recognize also that we are not yet perfect, so we ask forgiveness from those against whom we trespass. We ask for it by extending our love to all people. When we ask for forgiveness we gift another person the opportunity to mature by granting forgiveness to us. Our vulnerability becomes the signal for others to find their strength.

*T*hen answered Peter and said unto him, "Behold, we have forsaken all, and followed you; what shall we have therefore?" And Jesus said unto them, "Verily I say unto you, that all of you which have followed me, in the regeneration when the Son of Man shall sit in the throne of his glory, all of you also shall sit upon twelve thrones, judging the twelve tribes of Israel. And every one that has forsaken houses, or brethren, or sisters, or father, or mother, or wife, or children, or lands, for my name's sake, shall receive an hundredfold, and shall inherit everlasting life."

MATTHEW 19:27–29

Everyone who puts this purpose first shall experience some form of regeneration, even as Jesus has done. As our scientists probe the invisible processes of creation in the atom, the gene, the cell and the brain, and as psychics probe our extended capacities beyond the five senses, our generation is about to learn how regeneration works. We must be responsive to the inner compass of joy in each person by helping each other follow the path of regeneration. We are taking the first conscious steps now, in this generation on the cusp, between creature and co-creator.

❧

"*But many that are first shall be last; and the last shall be first.*"

MATTHEW 19:30

Many who are in positions of worldly power and authority will be unable to put the purpose of transformation first. Those who are responsible for maintaining the existing system are the least prepared to consciously change it. The last, those who are outside the current positions of power, are more able to respond to the new. They have a responsibility to respond with love. The powers-that-be need not be harshly put down. We can instead attract them to the realization of new opportunity that is in their highest interest, as well as the interests of those not empowered by the existing system.

Loving our neighbor as ourselves can be practiced without sacrificing one for the other. As we become co-creative we will produce synergistically, bringing forth far more than the sum of our individual efforts. The very concepts of first and last shall pass away, except in the sense of individual choice. The choice is to evolve or not to evolve—to give birth to ourselves as co-creators or to remain creature humans, choosing to die and be reborn in yet another mammalian body, which continues to learn the lessons until eventually all shall be free.

The first Adam, early *Homo sapiens sapiens*, represents a fleeting blink of the eye in cosmic time. *Homo sapiens sapiens* is already beginning to fade as the second Adam—that is, Adam of the quickening Spirit, the natural Christ—emerges.

Just as Neanderthal man passed away, so too will self-centered *Homo sapiens sapiens* retire once it has finished the work of preparing the way for *Homo universalis*.

❧

"*These last have wrought but one hour, and you have made them equal unto us, which have borne the burden and heat of the day.'*

'Take that which is yours, and go your way: I will give unto this last, even as unto you.'

"So the last shall be first, and the first last: for many be called, but few chosen."

MATTHEW 20:12, 14, 16

It may seem unfair that millions of good souls have striven to see the Kingdom of God in their lifetime and have failed, going to rest in a still unregenerated world. Those of us alive at the time of the transformation will witness what none have seen before out of all the generations that have ever lived.

❧

"*Tell us therefore, What think you? Is it lawful to give tribute unto Caesar, or not?"*

"Show me the tribute money." And they brought unto him a penny. And he said unto them, "Whose is this image and superscription?" They said unto him, "Caesar's." Then said he unto them, "Render therefore unto Caesar the things which are Caesar's, and unto God the things that are God's."

MATTHEW 22:17, 19–21

Do not confuse material power with spiritual power. Give the material world its due. We are still in the material phase of evolution. Our bodies still hunger and thirst. They need shelter, warmth, food, light and care. This too shall pass. In the next phase of human evolution we shall co-create as Christ did, producing what we require directly by intentional thought or conscious co-creation. But we are not there yet in Earth-time, although we are there in cosmic time. A baby cannot skip over the crawling stage. Yet its capacity to run is inherent in its crawl, and the crawling stimulates its running phase.

The material phase of human existence, where we work by the sweat of our brow, is vital. During this phase the human race is learning how nature works—not to submit to it, but to transcend it. We learn the laws of profit, productivity, legal systems and organizations so we can evolve to the next phase.

When we render unto God what is God's, we must know how to make a profit: that is, to produce more than we use. This surplus provides the material that evolution transforms from simple to more complex form. While the material world runs down to increasing entropy or disorder, the spiritual world runs upward toward increasing negentropy and higher order. The universe will not end in a heat death; it will end in a consciousness-birth of total enlightenment wherein all matter has been reorganized by consciousness to manifest perfectly the Intention of Creation, which has become identical with the intention of the creatures to become co-creative.

When we render unto God what is God's, we must be productive as God is productive. Already we are practicing productivity by manifestation as we synthesize fibers and new materials out of oil, coal and oxygen. Soon we will ephemeralize our energy requirements. Our bodies may take nourishment directly from the sun. Do not forget that our bodies are changing. The same nourishment was not required by Jesus's resurrected body as by one that is dying and replenishing its cells by the millions each day. The gigantic effort to produce flesh and blood will be overcome. New bodies that do not degenerate will not require the same kind of energy to constantly self-regenerate.

This freedom from continual body building and maintenance will be used to create new bodies, new environments, new materials and new forms out of old. The new body will become our house of thought—to be loved, beautified, repaired occasionally, changed when desired, released when necessary and renewed when the spirit wishes to work in the material world. The world into which we are being born has been called by sensitives "the other side," or "the spirit world." Such is the perspective on the next step of evolution as seen by creature humans. The "other side," like "life after death," is a womb imitation of universal life beyond the phase of terrestrial self-consciousness.

When we render unto God what is God's, we must learn

how the law works. We can start with the best law of the terrestrial phase, which is laid out in the United States Constitution. Based on the Declaration of Independence, it states that all people are endowed by their Creator with certain inalienable rights. Given the young age of the human race, protection against the misuse of power—so that no person or branch of government can usurp the inalienable rights of another—remains essential, even if not fully realized.

However, as we collectively transcend the illusion of separation, we will move beyond the Constitution as an external document, to the constitution as an internal document written in the consciousness of every co-creative person who is attuning to the evolutionary design. When our will and God's become one, and when we truly love our neighbor as our self, there will be modes of self-governance without coercion. We will be attuning to the internal, eternal laws that created the universe and are still creating it now.

What need has a child for external documents to grow its body? The truth is already written in its genes. What need for coercive laws does a godlike human have, when he or she is listening to the motivation within? That inner voice echoes back to the origin of the universe, to what formed the elements, organized cells, built the biosphere and conceived the human brain...and now perceives and reconceives itself through us.

The design innovation for *Homo sapiens sapiens* was culture, language and symbols—the ability to communicate exo-genetically. The design innovation for universal humanity is *conscious* evolution—the synthesis of intuitive and intellectual knowing in a suprasensitive state, wherein we realize the nature of the atom, the gene, the brain, the Earth and the stars, because we *are* the atom, the gene, the brain, the Earth and the stars. We will gain wisdom through identity—being at one with all we know. This form of knowing is as simple as opening your eyes and seeing. Only the mechanism is complex. Through our maturing sciences and technology, we will discover the techniques of creation and learn them as easily as we now write or build automobiles—impossible tasks for a brilliant chimpanzee.

When we render unto God what is God's, we must learn organization: how the atom is organized, how molecules form a cell, how cells form an animal, how humans form communities. For it will be our co-creative task to build a world in which all people have the opportunity to fulfill their God-given potential. We will learn to organize the Kingdom of Heaven through wisdom gained by identity—that is, by being one with it. We each possess a body comprising trillions of cells, all perfectly coordinated and sensitive to our command. As we learn to know our collective body by identity, we will gain the secrets of the next phase for the collective body politic. The universal human community is organized, as St. Paul suggested, as one body of which all people are members. Each person will act out a unique and chosen vocation, from an essential part of the Whole Design for how to evolve a universe from material to spiritual reality.

Each person's vocation is patterned in his or her genes and nurtured by free choice. Each vocation fulfills a need for the development of a specific aspect of the new universal humanity. When we become self-governing, we hear our own inner calling as clearly as we recognize our current needs for food, sleep, love and recreation.

Most vocational signals remain weak at this early phase

of human evolution. It would have been cruel to reveal to us our unique genius when the demands of bodily survival still required us to produce large numbers of children and work by the sweat of our brow to survive. Even so, many geniuses have emerged and broken the bonds of imagined human limits, to serve as examples for those who remain enslaved to their physical needs. Usually the toll upon the genius is stress, destruction, sadness and alienation, because he or she is offering more than the world can accept. And yet these geniuses create stepping-stones that lead to our collective transformation. They demonstrate that we truly can perform our creative vocations by answering to the inner calling that summons our godlike potential.

"*Master, which is the great commandment in the law?" Jesus said unto him, "'You shall love the Lord your God with all your heart, and with all your soul, and with all your mind.' This is the first and great commandment. And the second is like unto it, 'You shall love your neighbor as yourself.' On these two commandments hang all the law and the prophets."*

MATTHEW 22:36–40

These commandments—to love God, and to love others as our self—are the steps to universal humanity. To love God above all else means that we will naturally, spontaneously and joyfully obey our highest intention at all times. We do it with our heart, feelingly. We do it with our soul, spiritually. We do it with our minds, intellectually. We do it in the world, materially. The fusing of the heart, soul, body and mind in the love of the Creator will make us co-creative, so we can act with the energy, knowledge and intention of God infusing our being at all times.

To love our neighbor as our self is to overcome the illusion that we are separate from each other. We will know we are members of one body. It will be as unnatural to harm another being as it is to harm our self. The ego will evolve not by suppression, but through maturation. The fulfillment of the individual—acting upon unique vocation in the body of humanity, in a universe full of life and in tune with the will of God—is the condition toward which we are evolving.

Oh, my blessed children. Rejoice! Be glad. Joy that passeth understanding is yours if you will follow my commandments to love God above all else and your neighbor as yourself.

And as he sat upon the mount of Olives, the disciples came unto him privately, saying, "Tell us, when shall these things be? And what shall be the sign of your coming, and of the end of the world?" And Jesus answered and said unto them, saying, ... "For nation shall rise against nation, and kingdom against kingdom: and there shall be famines, and pestilences, and earthquakes, in divers places. All these are the beginning of sorrows. Then shall they deliver you up to be afflicted, and shall kill you: and all of you shall be hated of all nations for my name's sake.

"But he that shall endure unto the end, the same shall be saved. And this gospel of the kingdom shall be preached in all the world for a witness unto all nations; and then shall the end come. When all of you therefore shall see the 'abomination of desolation,' spoken of by Daniel the prophet, stand in the holy place, (whoso reads, let him understand), then let them which be in Judaea flee into the mountains.

"For then shall be great tribulation, such as was not since the beginning of the world to this time, no, nor ever shall be. And except those days should be shortened, there should no flesh be saved: but for the elect's sake those days shall be shortened. Then if any man shall say unto you, 'Lo, here is Christ,' or 'There;' believe it not.

"For as the lightning comes out of the east, and shines even unto the west; so shall also the coming of the Son of Man be.

"Immediately after the tribulation of those days shall the sun be darkened, and the moon shall not give her light, and the stars shall fall from heaven, and the *powers of the heavens shall be shaken: and then shall appear the sign of the Son of Man in heaven, and then shall all the tribes of the earth mourn, and they shall see the Son of Man coming in the clouds of heaven with power and great glory. And he shall send his angels with a great sound of a trumpet, and they shall gather together his elect from the four winds, from one end of heaven to the other.*

"Now learn a parable of the fig tree; when his branch is yet tender, and puts forth leaves, all of you know that summer is nigh. So likewise all of you, when all of you shall see all these things, know that it is near, even at the doors. Verily I say unto you, this generation shall not pass, till all these things be fulfilled. Heaven and earth shall pass away, but my words shall not pass away. But of that day and hour knows no man, no, not the angels of heaven, but my Father only.

"Therefore be all of you also ready: for in such an hour as all of you think not the Son of Man comes."

MATTHEW 24:3–4, 7–9, 13–16, 21–23, 27, 29–36, 44

A prefigured pattern exists, and is now being fulfilled, that pertains to the end of the world as we know it, and marks the beginning of the new. The contention of tribe against tribe intensifies. Famine and pestilence are now unfolding as millions starve every year. The earthquakes predicted by scientists and psychics alike are happening. The persecution

of the righteous has been proceeding, especially in the totalitarian nations of the world where millions have been bru-
tally murdered, tortured, imprisoned and otherwise suppressed. Those who endure these tribulations in total faith
that there is a design and that it is good, shall come through
the transition not only alive, but also transformed.

WHEN MY SELF-SELECTED PEOPLE, THOSE
who choose to follow me, see the desolation, they
are to draw inward to that holy place, wherein they
have been in prayer and meditation; that place protected by the circle of light and guarded by the
sword of steel.

The chaos is necessary, as the old must pass away
for the new to be born. Everything that resists love
will be dissolved. Beware of becoming the enemy
to overcome the enemy. To defeat this enemy, you
must change yourselves into Christlike humans,
and then the enemy shall be converted or he shall
surely die.

In this stage of transition from the old world to the new,
we maintain our armies to defend flesh from flesh for yet a
little while; but for God's sake, we now build our spiritual
consciousness to convert hate to love, the perishable to the
imperishable.

The New Order of the Future consists of self-selected
souls attracted to the future of the world. They are pioneering souls of Earth who not only can withstand the tribulation, but who will also begin to build the foundations of new

worlds on Earth and new worlds elsewhere in the universe. There shall appear the sign of the Son of man in heaven. The sign is that there are at last many sons and daughters of man in Heaven. The human race has given birth to enough god-children that the end can come without destroying the seed of the future. Enough of us are evolving beyond self-centeredness and planet-boundness. We are beginning to live beyond the self-centered state in unitive, or cosmic, or Christ consciousness. We will soon be living beyond the terrestrial world in the next physical dimension of outer space.

We are evolving toward universal life.

Then shall Christ, the first Son of man, come from that same Heaven—the next stage of evolution beyond Earthbound, self-centered life—in which *Homo universalis* shall dwell. "This generation" is a cosmic generation. It began with the birth of Christ and continues until this present time when the Earth has reached its limits and is producing the first generation of God-children capable of healing her wounds and carrying her seed into the universe.

No one knows when these events will occur. Therefore be ready always, in every way at all times. Be in a state of total love of God and yourself and your neighbor, and be carrying out your unique function in the transformation of the world.

"For as in the days that were before the flood they were eating and drinking, marrying and giving in marriage, until the day that Noah entered into the ark, and knew not until the flood came, and took them

all away; so shall also the coming of the Son of Man be. Then shall two be in the field; the one shall be taken, and the other left.

"Watch therefore: for all of you know not what hour your Lord does come."

MATTHEW 24:38–40, 42

Expect the unexpected. Anticipate the new. Be prepared at every moment with joy and peace in your heart.

∾

"For the kingdom of heaven is as a man traveling into a far country, who called his own servants, and delivered unto them his goods. And unto one he gave five talents, to another two, and to another one; to every man according to his several ability; and immediately took his journey. Then he that had received the five talents went and traded with the same, and made them other five talents. And likewise he that had received two, he also gained other two. But he that had received one went and dug in the earth, and hid his lord's money. After a long time the lord of those servants comes, and reckons with them. And so he that had received five talents came and brought other five talents, saying, 'Lord,

you delivered unto me five talents: behold, I have gained beside them five talents more.' His lord said unto him, 'Well done, you good and faithful servant: you have been faithful over a few things, I will make you ruler over many things: enter you into the joy of your lord.'

"He also that had received two talents came and said, 'Lord, you delivered unto me two talents: behold, I have gained two other talents beside them.' His lord said unto him, 'Well done, good and faithful servant; you have been faithful over a few things, I will make you ruler over many things: enter you into the joy of your lord.'

"Then he which had received the one talent came and said, 'Lord, I knew you that you are an hard man, reaping where you have not sown, and gathering where you have not scattered, and I was afraid, and went and hid your talent in the earth: lo, there you have that is yours.' His lord answered and said unto him, 'You wicked and slothful servant, you knew that I reap where I sowed not, and gather where I have not scattered: you ought therefore to have put my money to the exchangers, and then at my coming I should have received mine own with interest. Take therefore the talent from him, and give it unto him which has ten talents. For unto every one that has shall be given, and he shall have abundance: but from him that has not shall be taken away even that *which he has. And cast all of you the useless servant into outer darkness: there shall be weeping and gnashing of teeth."*

MATTHEW 25:14–30

God has given humans "his goods," his magnificent creation: the human brain, the Earth, the biosphere, the land, the oil, the coal, the rivers and the trees, to invest at a profit, to make something more than we were given. The servants of God who have invested their God-given talents into the world and have made more talents, more potentials, more resources for the future, are rewarded with more abundance. The servants of God who have buried or denied their talents for fear of loss or change, are deprived of abundance, even of the little they have. Unprofitable activities cannot prevail.

Only the creative evolve. That which is static disintegrates. Change is necessary if the universal creation is to fulfill its purpose, which is the transformation of inert material to animated consciousness of the Creator through the ever-increasing creativity of the creature. The courage to create is necessary for those who desire to participate in the next stage of evolution. The fear of failure will surely cause failure.

The risk of creation may fail a thousand times over; but inevitably innovation prevails. The pattern of progress is discovered, new capabilities are revealed, and the future unfurls itself through the acts of the risk takers, the inventors, the builders, the heroes and heroines of Earth.

"When the Son of Man shall come in his glory, and all the holy angels with him, then shall he sit upon the throne of his glory. And before him shall be gathered all nations: and he shall separate them one from another, as a shepherd divides his sheep from the goats. And he shall set the sheep on his right hand, but the goats on the left. Then shall the King say unto them on his right hand, 'Come, all of you blessed of my Father, inherit the kingdom prepared for you from the foundation of the world: for I was hungry, and all of you gave me food; I was thirsty, and all of you gave me drink; I was a stranger, and all of you took me in; naked, and all of you clothed me; I was sick, and all of you visited me; I was in prison, and all of you came unto me.' Then shall the righteous answered him, saying, 'Lord, when saw we you hungry, and fed you? Or thirsty, and gave you drink? When saw we you a stranger, and took you in? Or naked, and clothed you? Or when saw we you sick, or in prison, and came unto you?' And the King shall answer and say unto them, 'Verily I say unto you, inasmuch as all of you have done it unto one of the least of these my brethren, all of you have done it unto me.'

"Then shall he say also unto them on the left hand, 'Depart from me, all of you cursed, into everlasting fire, prepared for the devil and his angels: for I was hungry, and all of you gave me no food; I was thirsty, and all of you gave me no drink; I was a stranger, and all of you took me not in; naked, and all of you clothed me not; sick, and in prison, and all of you visited me not.' Then shall they also answer him, saying, 'Lord, when saw we you hungered, or thirsty, or a stranger, or naked, or sick, or in prison, and did not minister unto you?' Then shall he answer them, saying, 'Verily I say unto you, inasmuch as all of you did it not to one of the least of these, all of you did it not to me.' And these shall go away into everlasting punishment: but the righteous into life eternal."

MATTHEW 25:31–46

Love is the key to the next step of evolution for us as individuals. If we have every other virtue in the world but do not love one another, we shall not make the transition to universal life. The essential characteristic of universal humanity is holistic, co-creative consciousness. A selfish species cannot inherit the powers of creation. It would be deadly to the person, the planet, the species and the universe.

We cannot possess the powers of creation without love in our hearts for all creatures. Thus we shall mature before we are able to enter the Kingdom of Heaven.

Eve marries Christ to reach the Tree of Life. Human knowledge and divine love marry for the human race to inherit the powers of co-creation. This fusion of divine and secular is the key. Marry, join, wed, and bind love and knowledge together forever.

*A*nd as they were eating, Jesus took bread, and blessed it, and brake it, and gave it to the disciples, and said, "Take, eat; this is my body." And he took the cup, and gave thanks, and gave it to them, saying, "Drink all of you all of it, for this is my blood of the new testament, which is shed for many for the remission of sins. But I say unto you, I will not drink henceforth of this fruit of the vine, until that day when I drink it new with you in my Father's kingdom."

MATTHEW 26:26–29

Jesus is telling us that we are to incorporate his body into our bodies and his blood into our veins and become flesh of his flesh and blood of his body. The blood of Jesus is shed to empty us of the blood of our past lives, our past consciousness, our past way of being, which is early *Homo sapiens sapiens*. This blood that he shed we too must shed, giving ourselves a transfusion of new blood of a higher frequency, blood like his that is not contaminated with the mammalian instincts of kill and be killed, of attack and react, of an eye for an eye and a tooth for a tooth. All of this must be overcome for the remission of sins, meaning the forgiveness of the illusion of separation, and the rejoining God as co-creators.

We require new bodies because the old bodies are deeply imprinted with fear, anxiety, lust and eons and eons of pain. This fear, anxiety, lust and pain can be held at bay while we are in mammalian bodies, but only by exertion of superhuman will. To normalize the powers of Christ and the way of love as a natural state of being, we must receive into our bodies a gentle spiritual energy that radiates our body with electricity, gradually (not traumatically) erasing our mammalian reactions. This forgetting of our old instincts, which were in their time vital for survival, is in preparation for our entry into the Christ-state of being.

In the past the mystical experience was often a traumatic shock. Your flesh was so dense that only a mighty jolt of energy could get through. Now, through the natural process of evolution, millions of you are sensitizing yourselves, purifying your own minds and bodies, elevating your own thoughts, practicing forgiveness of all sins. Meanwhile, in the laboratories of the world, you are penetrating my secret technologies of creation so that in the fullness of time, you who are desirous of evolving will be fully prepared. I will not drink of this fruit of the vine with you until we meet in God's kingdom, at the end of the old world and the beginning of the new.

The building of new bodies will occur through a subtle change in our DNA's building code. A few genes will be repressed; a few others, dormant since the flowering of the big brain, will be activated. The mammalian instincts of self-preservation and self-reproduction will fade. The humane responses of self-actualization and co-creation will turn on. In order to survive we will emancipate our unique talents and co-operate synergistically with each other and with the design of evolution.

⌒❧

*T*hen said he unto them, "My soul is exceeding sorrowful, even unto death: tarry all of you here, and watch with me." And he went a little farther, and fell on his face, and prayed, saying, "O my Father, if it be possible, let this cup pass from me: nevertheless not as I will, but as you will."

"Watch and pray, that all of you enter not into temptation: the spirit indeed is willing, but the flesh is weak."

MATTHEW 26:38–39, 41

Jesus accepted humanness, the ability to feel pain and sorrow, while also fully accepting the spiritual reality of his powers as the future human—the Son of man, which each of us is to give birth to out of ourselves. He naturally asked God if it were possible to avoid the agony of the crucifixion. He knew that he had the power to overcome all human adversaries. "Think you that I cannot now pray to my Father, and he shall presently give me more than twelve legions of angels? But how then shall the scriptures be fulfilled, that thus it must be?" (Matthew 26:53–54)

Jesus realized it was necessary to demonstrate the reality of the resurrection. For this demonstration he had to suffer the crucifixion in the full light of day, for the entire world to see. For without the reality of the resurrection, we experience the tragedy of the human struggle against the ways of the flesh.

The dialectic is inherent in the nature of reality. Nature forms more complex whole systems through thesis, antithesis and synthesis. However, without the reality of the resurrection and the uniting of human will with the will of God, which is pure love, human power has become the greatest coercive force the world has ever seen. It is the thesis of nature untempered by the guiding force of love.

Humans attempting to be God without going the way of love will be struck down like Icarus, like Prometheus, like the first Eve. They will never attain the powers of the Tree of Life. Without the recognition of oneness, we remain in a state of self or separate consciousness. In this state we misuse the powers of co-creation implicit in our new capacities—the biological revolution, brain-mind research, cybernetics, astronautics, nanotechnology and nuclear power. Eve, the separated immature human intellect, must mature enough to marry Christ, must fuse intellect with spiritual power, thus transforming both self-consciousness and the mammalian limits. We marry Eve and Christ within ourselves to give birth to a new mind-body: to normalize the resurrection, as we transform ourselves from creature to co-creator.

It is not merely our limited life span that we must overcome. The imprint of fear, attack and defensiveness also need to be erased in order to reach the next step of evolution. Yet these imprints are imbedded deep within our reptilian, mammalian and early human experience. How can we overcome them?

We will overcome them through a quantum transformation. We will literally die to the old experiences that formed the mammalian body and be evolved toward a new experience of pure love, security, abundance and absence of fear. While we are embedded in this mortal body, we feel pain, fear, anxiety and insecurity, illuminated with only brief moments of joy and well-being, which are always evanescent. As we mature spiritually—as we connect our consciousness with Christ and *choose* to live in Heaven now, choosing love over fear, choosing to forgive and not to acknowledge the inevitability of disease and death—only then will we naturally build a bridge from this state to the next.

The bridge has not been strong enough to let us cross to the other side as Jesus did. The part of the bridge connected to the material/terrestrial world is corruptible. It always rots out in the end, and forces the spirit to disembody, and then re-embody, beginning the cycle over again. As we enter the Universal Age, this will change. There will come the first generation that does not undergo animal-like physical death, that does not experience mammalian fear and that only knows pure love and creativity. It is this generation that the reality of the resurrection predicts, foretells and prophesizes.

It is this generation that will build the New Heaven and the New Earth. We who are now alive are nurturing this generation into being, stretching our mortal selves from the foot of the bridge on Mother Earth to the foot of the bridge secured in the universe, the ark to the stars. The path of the human ark to carry the seed of *Homo sapiens sapiens* beyond the Earth into the universe leads to the future human, the fully human, the universal human.

This co-creative act will also transform those who remain on the new Earth—an Earth populated with beings who do not die involuntarily, and who are harmonizing and preserving nature and its endangered species. These are the meek who shall inherit the Earth. They too are no longer in a state of separated consciousness. They become mothers of the Earth. Mother Nature gives birth to many mothers of nature, who understand and love her so well that they care for her like a daughter cherishes a beloved but aging parent. However, we must remember that Mother Nature is not limited to this tiny planet Earth. Mother Nature is the whole universe. Mother Nature is billions of galaxies, multitudes of solar systems, millions of stars with planets giving birth to conscious life like ours.

We must stretch our love for Mother Nature to include her vast arena of life and to recognize ourselves as heirs to all our mother has created—heirs with but two responsibilities: love of God above all and of our neighbors (including cosmic brothers and sisters) as ourselves, and knowledge of how nature works so we can cooperate consciously with her.

LOVE AND KNOWLEDGE FOREVER WEDDED IS the commandment of the Universal Age.

Love the Lord thy God with all your heart, and with all your soul, and with all your mind.

Love your neighbor as yourself. You shall know God directly within yourself so that you may join your will to God's will and knowingly act out our mutual intention.

How do we know God directly? The answer is we do not, as long as we remain limited to our five senses. This condition is like going to the movies with our eyes closed and trying to grasp the story through the flickering light that penetrates our lids. Only by the natural process of transformation from self-consciousness to God-consciousness can we know God directly. We need not feel guilty about that. Would we criticize a newborn for its inability to read?

We can catch a glimpse of God through our deepest experience and the example of our future self, the Christ. But even he—because he had to take on a human/animal body—could not in that form experience the fullness of the Creator of this universe. That is why he said, "You shall do as I do, and greater things shall you do" (John 14:12). When we have graduated from the creature human condition, we will begin to know God at the next level.

Progress is inherent in the system. Those who so choose will surely evolve. Progress is not only by incremental improvement of existing conditions—although such steps may be necessary. Progress proceeds by quantum transformations, from molecule to cell, from cell to multicell, from multicell to human and from human to Christ, or universal human. We must not be concerned that we have no appropriate word to symbolize what we are to become. Words describe the known. We are approaching the unknown. Only experience, only demonstration counts at this stage. Be alert to every experience of change. Mark it well, nurture it, understand it and build on it. We are laboratories in which our own lives are our experiments.

THE TRANSFORMATION IS NOT CODED IN the English language. It is coded in the genes and in the Mind of God. Labor in the laboratory of your own life—learn to be like me, your being-at-the-next-stage. Be perfect as God in Heaven is perfect.

This is the time of preparation for the Quantum Transformation. No one knows the precise time when the quantum events will be triggered. Like pregnant mothers, we prepare for the child. We care for ourselves, build the crib, buy the clothes, remain alert to the slightest change in our bodies that will signal our labor has begun and cannot be undone.

Those who are experiencing bodily changes, inner heat, healing powers—powers of all kinds—recognize that these are indicators of the coming change. They are like the restless stirrings of the unborn child, not quite ready to start the fateful journey down the birth canal through the dangerous transition from womb to world. Who knows exactly what sets off the contractions that start the process of birth? The baby in the womb grows ready. It practices its powers as well as it can within the now unnatural confines of the womb, soon to become a lethal environment for a growing child. If the infant emerges prematurely, it dies. If it emerges too late, it dies. Timing is of the essence.

What is the historical timing for our planetary birth from *Homo terrestrialis* to *Homo universalis*? Who knows exactly? But we can see the signs. The day is coming soon. We cannot continue to grow as we have grown before and survive in the womb of the Earth. We must stop growing here because our new capacities to extend life, to utilize nuclear power, to explore the universe, to cybernate work cannot be contained within this biosphere. Just as a baby about to be born cannot exercise its full capacities in the womb, we cannot exercise our full capacities in the terrestrial world. The reality of the resurrection is a demonstration of the reality of the transformation. It is the natural way to evolve.

*A*nd Peter remembered the word of Jesus, which said unto him, "Before the cock crow, you shall deny me three times." And he went out, and wept bitterly.

MATTHEW 26:75

The fear of pain, of alienation, of condemnation by our peers when we have taken the step toward transformation, is real. But we must not let the fear of being different stop us, because the "difference" we are moving toward will soon be recognized as the new norm. The unchanged will be the different ones, and the changed ones will be the normal ones. We shall no longer fear to acknowledge the reality of our potential to be like the Son of man.

Two thousand years have passed since the crucifixion and the resurrection. That time was necessary for science and democracy to be developed to their first stage: materialistic science and individualistic democracy. A second stage will be process-science and synergistic democracy. Process-science is the science that studies nature as events in transformation, not things. Process-science recognizes that the material world is an abstraction of our nervous system. It is not studying an objective outside world, but examining the relationship between human consciousness and the energetic patterns of events that are forming the manifesting world—of which we, the students, are an integral and co-creative part.

Synergistic democracy is the form of government suited to evolved humans who know that each is related to the whole, and who are attuning directly to the patterns in the process of evolution, or the intention of the Creator.

Process-science and synergistic democracy will be essential elements in the New Jerusalem. They will help erase the fear in the hearts of those who are transforming. Materialistic science and individualistic democracy have served their magnificent purpose. They brought us through the end of the Epoch of the First Adam of the living soul, to the threshold of the Epoch of the Second Adam of the life-giving spirit—of the resurrected, reconstituted, reborn and renewed sons and daughters of *Homo sapiens sapiens*.

The fear in the heart of Peter that forced him to deny Jesus three times to save his own skin dissolved in the reality of the resurrection. The fear in our heart at the possibility of our own transformation will dissolve when we experience ourselves as fully human and natural Christs, sons and daughters of God.

⁂

Jesus, when he had cried again with a loud voice, yielded up the spirit. And, behold, the veil of the temple was rent in two from the top to the bottom; and the earth did quake, and the rocks rent; and the graves were opened; and many bodies of the saints which slept arose, and came out of the graves after his resurrection, and went into the holy city, and appeared unto many.

MATTHEW 27:50–53

The resurrection of the saints serves as a premonition of things to come. "Behold, I show you a mystery: We shall not all sleep; but we shall all be changed." This is true for those who died before the resurrection, as well as for the generation alive at the time of the collective transformation or the Second Coming. The mystery of the resurrection of the already dead is not hard to understand if we realize what a body is. A body is a manifestation of a design, encoded in an information seed in the nucleus of the cell. Each person's "blueprint" is unique and recordable. Could not the generic blueprint that builds every body be recorded in the Universal Mind?

Once the interaction of sperm and egg triggers the information plan into action, the cell takes material from the environment—iron, calcium, phosphate, oxygen, hydrogen and other elements—and forms it into a body. Throughout a lifetime, the actual body cells are born and die, but the blueprint remains immortal. Could it not be that when the physical body "dies," the blueprint remains recorded in the Library of Life, the universal memory bank? Could it not also be that the body of our personal experience is likewise preserved in the Library of Life, and is available like data in a computer?

Consider this possibility: whenever a body is to be resurrected, its basic design, its code of life, is quickly reconstituted, using the same materials—iron, calcium, phosphate, oxygen, hydrogen, etc. At the next stage of evolution it may be as natural to resurrect a body as to conceive a body. Meanwhile, the soul of the resurrected body has never died. Like the blueprint, the soul is immortal and is prepared to reincarnate whenever necessary to carry out the design of evolution—that is, the transformation of humanity.

MANY PEOPLE AMONG YOU TODAY ARE souls who have chosen to return and reassure their brothers and sisters that they are good, capable and free to evolve. After my death, a cluster of resurrected beings helped prepare the way and spread the Gospel. Now, vast numbers of volunteers have again returned to help in the next phase of transformation. You will recognize them when you meet them. They have no other agenda but the transformation of the world. That is how you will know each other, my friends.

❧

And as they went to tell his disciples, behold, Jesus met them, saying, "All hail." And they came and held him by the feet, and worshipped him. Then said Jesus unto them, "Be not afraid: go tell my brethren that they go into Galilee, and there shall they see me."

And Jesus came and spoke unto them, saying, "All power is given unto me in heaven and in earth. Go all of you therefore, and teach all nations, baptizing them in the name of the Father, and of the Son, and of the Holy Spirit: teaching them to observe all things whatsoever I have commanded you, and, lo, I am with you always, even unto the end of the world." Amen.

MATTHEW 28:9, 18–20

Jesus demonstrated the reality of the resurrection, which founded the faith that gave birth to science and democracy, and which has further resulted in this generation gaining both the capability and the intention to do precisely what he said he would do. We, this tiny band who are beacons unto ourselves, are—whether we know it or not—following the example of Jesus. The flame of expectation has been lit. The current of excitement runs through our nervous systems. Nothing in Heaven or Earth can prevail against the coming of the new humanity.

THE GOSPEL

ACCORDING TO MARK

❧

*A*s it is written in the prophets, *"Behold, I send my messenger before your face, which shall prepare your way before you. The voice of one crying in the wilderness, Prepare all of you the way of the Lord, make his paths straight."*

MARK 1:2–3

John the Baptist prepared the way for the first coming of Jesus. Who prepares the way for the Second Coming? Those who desire it, work for it and communicate it in its *wholeness*. Not just the part about loving God above all else, nor just the part about loving our neighbor as our self, nor just the part about the final defeat of Satan. We communicate all these and more, including the very reason for all the rest. We communicate the part about the New Jerusalem, the resurrection of all who are whole and the final victory over the last tyrant, death. We communicate the part about our preparation for our life as Universal Humanity.

Those who desire the *whole transformation* and who spread the hope of it through their words and deeds serve as did John the Baptist, preparing for the Second Coming. No one on Earth knows what that will be like, for it is unlike anything we have yet experienced. Our seers have made certain prophecies and our scientific studies enable us to make predictions for evolutionary whole-system changes. We have seen quantum leaps in consciousness and freedom—such as the jump from nonlife to life, or from animal to human. We have the New Testament and other great spiritual texts. We have flashes of enlightened being. We have our own inner flame of expectation.

The witness of 13.8 billion years of history, *and* sacred writings, *and* the experience of expectation, *and* the moments of union with the all, *and* our new capacities—all these form the basis of our fragmentary knowing of what is to come. We are like fish in the sea, peering through the waters to see the world. Now we see darkly. Soon we shall see face to face. Divine and secular visions are beginning to fuse. Let all of us who prepare the way for the transformation do as did John the Baptist. Speak it to all who would hear. Work for it with all our might. And be humble, for what is to come is far greater than we can imagine.

*A*nd *at evening, when the sun did set, they brought unto him all that were diseased, and them that were possessed with devils. And all the city was gathered together at the door. And he healed many that were sick of divers diseases, and cast out many devils; and suffered not the devils to speak, because they knew him.*

MARK 1:32–34

What is this instant healing power that Jesus exercised? How did he do it? Modern medicine explores and repairs the mechanical aspect of the body. Medical technology can replace parts, add parts, repair parts, reduce fever, kill germs and simulate vision, hearing and feeling through artificial parts or prostheses. It has penetrated the environment of the body and learned how it works, up to the very threshold of the essential person, who is more than the simple sum of the body's parts.

At this threshold, medical science stops. Its instruments and tubes and drugs cannot yet cross the great divide between the animated parts and consciousness itself, the source of animation. On that other side of the great divide, our spiritual healing begins. The Animator within informs the body to repair, renew, regenerate—or die. A consciousness at one with the Creator within is in charge of its material manifestation, or body. Jesus demonstrated this.

Just as we can now send a message to our finger to turn this page—an extraordinarily complex interaction between

129

thought and matter that took billions of years of evolution—
so too can we potentially send a message to any part of our
body to heal itself or to evolve. These powers are normal
at the next stage of evolution. Jesus and his disciples, along
with others, demonstrated them for our benefit.

❦

*A*nd he said, "So is the kingdom of God, as if
a man should cast seed into the ground; And
should sleep, and rise night and day, and the seed should
spring and grow up, he knows not how. For the earth
brings forth fruit of herself; first the blade, then the ear,
after that the full corn in the ear. But when the fruit is
brought forth, immediately he puts in the sickle, because
the harvest has come."

MARK 4:26–29

We are not creating the universe; God continually creates
it, and us too. To the extent that we are creative we are one
with God, co-creating with, through, by and for God. When
we are creative we partake of the force that grows the seeds,
that forms the planets, that conceives life throughout the
universe. The joy of knowing that the Creative Force created us, and that our awareness of it enables us to co-create
consciously with it, is a taste of Heaven now.

Most of our creating comes forth like the seed in spring,
we know not how. However, there comes a time in our life,

and in the life of a planet, when we must be wise enough to *act consciously*. When nature has brought forth the fruit and the situation ripens, we must put forth our sickle and harvest it. There is a time for personal initiative. If we miss it, the fruit will rot. This is a delicate truth.

To "try" to decide what to do kills creativity. The pattern of the Whole System extends so far beyond our awareness that we cannot decide what we should do. When we open our self to signals from the Whole System Consciousness, the Holy Spirit will inform us of our part through intuition transmitted directly from Universal Mind. How intuition connects with intellect and motivates creative action is as complex as how DNA communicates the building plan to the messenger RNA that goes forth and collects the material to build the cell according to the blueprint. We do not need to understand the mechanism to receive the intuitive signal any more than a baby needs to know how its body is growing in order to grow. Our species has understood the operational genius of our own DNA for only a few years, yet we have been building our own bodies since the beginning of time.

A larger design exists, of which each person is an integral, organic part. The large design is encoded in our consciousness, the same way that the design to build our whole body is encoded in each of our cells. An individual need not know how to do it all, any more than a single cell must build the eye, ear or nose all by itself. Like our cells, we each have a specific vocation. We do not identify our vocation by conscious decision, but by resonance with signals that come to us through intuition, and that guide us to do what we are uniquely qualified to do. No genuine competition exists between individuals, because each of us is unique and has a different calling within the same whole body.

Our vocation connects us with the evolving aspect of God, in the same way that our beingness forms our connection with the eternal aspect of God. It determines our specific role in the creation. To discover our vocation is heavenly. That discovery emancipates the stored-up energy in our being, which is like the sunshine that has condensed in coal and now powers our machines.

We have been given an inner guide: the compass of joy that leads us to our function. We can tell when we have found our vocation by the signal of joy. In this early phase of vocational attunement, however, the signals are still weak and blurred. We must listen closely, or we will go through life feeling a nameless frustration. No matter how successful or unsuccessful we may be in worldly terms, nothing substitutes for discovering and enacting our unique, creative vocation.

As "the earth brings forth fruit of herself," we bring forth our creative gift to the world—naturally. Our intuition reveals the pattern to us. Our heart's joyful signal confirms our role in the pattern. Our intellect helps us execute the design in the world of form. When this natural flow moves within us, we avoid hubris, preserve humbleness and allow co-creation to flourish. All whom we touch with our joy likewise feel stimulated to join in the union of unique beings co-creating to the rhythms of the universe.

This is where common sense no longer serves us. Common sense tends to believe only what it has already seen, and works by past experience. It lacks sensitivity to newness and isn't ready for quantum change. It believes in incremental steps, not sudden leaps. But evolution does not operate by the manual of human common sense. Evolution constantly creates newness through the synthesis of separate elements.

Evolution's power of synergistic whole-making is one of the stunning facts of creation. From single atoms to the human brain, evolution has moved in a silent invisible process of creation. Quantum leap by quantum leap, God moves in strange and wondrous ways. We are born at the moment that a quantum leap is occurring on planet Earth. As promised, humanity is transforming from terrestrial self-conscious beings to universal whole-centered beings.

❧

And a certain woman, which had an issue of blood twelve years, and had suffered many things of many physicians, and had spent all that she had, and was nothing improved, but rather grew worse, when she had heard of Jesus, came in the press behind, and touched his garment. For she said, "If I may touch but his clothes, I shall be whole." And immediately the fountain of her blood was dried up; and she felt in her body that she was healed of that plague. And Jesus, immediately knowing in himself that virtue had gone out of him, turned him about in the press, and said, "Who touched my clothes?"

And he looked round about to see her that had done this thing. But the woman fearing and trembling, knowing what was done in her, came and fell down before him, and told him all the truth. And he said unto her, "Daughter, your faith has made you whole; go in peace, and be whole of your plague."

MARK 5:25–30, 32–34

This story reveals Jesus's sensitivity. He exchanged some form of energy with those whom he instantly healed. He said, "Daughter, your faith has made you whole." That was true. But what role did Jesus play in her faith? He communicated reinforcing energy that stimulated her self-healing powers. Her faith drew his energy into her.

Jesus's faith came from his shared presence with God. He embodied the energy of that connection at all times. He did not have to consciously turn it on; it was always on.

This exposes a deep difference between Jesus and others. Many spiritual people flicker in and flicker out of their connection to the Whole, for we are still in an early phase of universal consciousness. The great Indian seers, the Egyptians, the Hebrews, and others on down the corridors of ancient history have recorded the existence of this advanced form of consciousness. Jesus demonstrated a *constant, unbreakable connection with the Creator.* Thus he could perform a resurrection. He was able to change his body through the transformative energy of his unbroken connection with the God-force.

When the woman touched his clothes and was healed behind his back, in the midst of a massive crowd, he instantly knew that some power had drained out of him. The woman tapped into his active potency and drew upon his force to heal herself. Jesus thus served as a perfect channel for the energy of the Creator. His faith magnetized the energy of creation and fused it into his very being. His message to us is that each of us, by being like him and following his way, can establish this same direct connection to the Creator and become a perfect channel ourselves. This is the next step in human development.

The future work of psychology, and the goal of the co-creative person, involves perfecting our communication channel to God by clearing all the static out of our system. The static energies of egotism, anxiety, hostility, fear, hubris and guilt dissolve when we remember that we are already forgiven our sins of separation. Jesus demonstrated the connection between humans and God so that each of us can do as he did. All we require is the awareness that this open connection between God and ourselves already exists, right here and now.

Once we have experienced the reality of this connection, we find it easier to clear up the static created by fear. Love dispels fear like sunshine dissolves clouds. God is pure love, pure attraction, a pure magnet for connection. We do not focus on our fear. We instead turn our attention to love, deepen our connection with the Creator and let the Force be with us. Thus we learn step-by-step to evolve, to mature to our rightful normalcy as co-creative individuals and partners with God.

◦⌣

"*M*aking the word of God of no effect through your tradition, which all of you have delivered: and many such like things do all of you."

MARK 7:13

The institutionalization of inspiration invariably corrupts what it was designed to communicate. Tradition, whose purpose is to transmit culture, calcifies inspiration. Vested interests feed off our traditional institutions and repress those who would continue to build upon them. The vital meaning of the living truth is almost lost until other geniuses revive it by evolving our moribund systems. Culture, like life, is only healthy in dynamism.

Nitpicking traditionalists render the Word of God ineffective. The truth must be heard and communicated by those whose faith has not been destroyed by fear of change. At this time of quantum transformation, traditional institutions lack effectiveness in carrying out the deep intention for which they were formed.

The Church fails to fully communicate the evolving Word of God. The state cannot fully guarantee life, liberty and the pursuit of happiness. The university cannot fully educate us for conscious participation in the creation of the future. The military cannot fully defend us in an interdependent world in the nuclear age. The corporation cannot make profit its sole objective in a world where we *are related to all life*, and where we're destroying our own environment through mental and physical pollution.

We cannot blame the ineffectiveness of these institutions on the millions of good men and women embroiled in them.

Institutional decay is a natural, evolutionary phenomenon. Overcomplexity, unmanageability, stagnation, the suppression of creativity, limits to growth—these are signs that a new order, a higher level of co-ordination is about to occur. We now see innovation everywhere: in individuals, self-organizing groups and networks of shared intention. A pattern for the future self-scaffolds beneath our ossifying institutions.

The transmission of culture through symbols and language became the great design innovation that advanced humanity beyond the animal world. We can learn from the past and build upon it. Conscious evolution now serves as the great design innovation of Universal Humanity, forging the next advancement in the communication of God's Design. From the genetic code to the written word to conscious knowledge of the Creative Intention, life has progressed through an ever-improving capacity to communicate ideas and embody them in action.

Conscious evolution refers to an ability to know God's evolving aspect, and to work with the laws of transformation, consciously. It includes, yet transcends, symbolic human culture. It is knowledge by *identity*, by internal subjective communion with that which we know. This shift reflects the quantum leap between learning information and realizing wisdom.

Jesus operated by accessing knowledge through identity. He and God were one. He knew what God wanted him to know by being one with God. He healed by being whole and by being connected to Universal Intelligence, which not only heals but also creates all life.

Our own bodies already know how to heal themselves. It's a matter of transferring that wisdom from the autonomic nervous system to the conscious mind.

As we enter the age of conscious evolution through awareness of our oneness with the whole and all life in it, we will know the truth by identifying *as it*. The children of the future will know how to participate in life the same way our cells know how to build our body—through direct communication with the design of creation.

❧

*A*nd the Pharisees came forth, and began to question with him, seeking of him a sign from heaven, tempting him. And he sighed deeply in his spirit, and said, "Why does this generation seek after a sign? Verily I say unto you, there shall no sign be given unto this generation."

MARK 8:11–12

We have a childish tendency to want God to perform a magic act, relieving us of our responsibility to grow up. Yet the message of Jesus is clear. We can act out our potential by doing as he did—loving God above all else and our neighbor as our self—and all things shall be given to us. There is no magical shortcut to the resurrection. The next step of evolution awaits our own maturation. The temptation Jesus felt to do it for us was one he had to resist. For in so doing, he would have deprived us of the satisfaction of learning to do it ourselves. The same way a parent resists the temptation of doing a child's homework, so too did Jesus resist giving his generation a sign.

To partake of the blessings of the Kingdom of Heaven,

we self-authorize our own evolving potential to be as Jesus was. We choose the truth of our limitless capacities and exercise them.

The whole creation in its awesome magnificence—the very existence of our universe, created we know not how—*is the sign*. The yearning in our hearts for union with all being is the sign. Anyone who cannot be impressed by the achievement of the whole universe, and who waits for a clap of thunder or a stroke of lightning, is blind and needs to be awakened to the total miracle of being. Everything is miraculous. Everything is beyond our comprehension. At the ultimate level, all is mystery.

The great telescopes of the astrophysicists analyze the light from the first explosion, probing backward in time/space to the origin of creation. How, when, why, by what intelligence was it created? The creature probes for the Creator. Beneath the veil of matter, hidden in the invisible processes of creation—the gene, the atom, the cell, the nervous system, the star, we seek the Intention of Creation, the motivating power that created it all. The Creator and the creature share the same intention, because they are One.

All is the sign.

∾

"*Why reason all of you, because all of you have no bread? Perceive all of you not yet, neither understand? Have all of you your heart yet hardened? Having eyes, see all of you not? and having ears, hear all of you not? and do all of you not remember? When*

I brake the five loaves among five thousand, how many baskets full of fragments took all of you up?" They said unto him, "Twelve." "And when the seven among four thousand, how many baskets full of fragments took all of you up?" And they said, "Seven." And he said unto them, "How is it that all of you do not understand?"

MARK 8:17–21

Imagine if we came to planet Earth from another planet at the dawn of self-consciousness, fifty thousand years ago. Our mission is to communicate to early humans that their future is to fly like the birds, swim underwater like the fish, see further than eagles, travel to the stars, communicate with the speed of light, be like the gods. How could we do it? It would be difficult.

Jesus came to us at the dawn of universal consciousness. His mission was to tell us that we are one with the Creator of the universe. We are to identify with the Divine Technologist that exists beyond our technology. We are to be godlike, eternally creative.

For the past few thousand years, humans have been flickering in and out of universal consciousness. From self to whole, we go back and forth, not quite able, yet, to remain connected with the All. Just so, early humans wavered between animal and self-consciousness.

Jesus' task was as difficult as ours would be at the dawn of self-consciousness. How can we explain to a less mature stage of consciousness the vastness of its own potential, when it has never experienced the capabilities that to us have become normal? This was Jesus's challenge. He performed many so-called "miracles": healing, walking on water, producing abundance out of scarcity and, finally, the resurrection, to demonstrate for us *our* potential, not merely his own. He came to tell us what *we* could do.

Even our perspective on our past failures is arrogant. Think of the rise of self-reflective humanity out of the pre-human and animal world. The mothers and fathers and children in caves with no language, attacked by animals, the elements, pain and disease— knowing only that they are different than the creatures around them, and tuning in gradually to legendary gods telling them to be more, do more, become more.

Humanity has *not* failed. We have succeeded beyond the wildest dreams of our ancient ancestors. In a mere tick of the cosmic clock we have progressed from early *Homo sapiens sapiens* to early *Homo universalis.* Can anyone doubt that the next tick will bring greater transformation? Can anyone doubt that we can do what Jesus did...*and more?*

❧

And he began to teach them, that the Son of Man must suffer many things, and be rejected of the elders, and of the chief priests, and scribes, and be killed, and after three days rise again. And he spoke that saying openly. And Peter took him, and began to rebuke him. But when he had turned about and looked on his disciples, he rebuked Peter, saying, "Get you behind me, Satan: for you savor not the things that be of God, but the things that be of men."

MARK 8:31–33

Peter and the other disciples expected Jesus to be the Messiah. That meant he would bring the power of God to Earth and be victorious over those who did not specifically believe in making Israel the free and powerful chosen nation of God, as was prophesied in the scriptures. When Jesus claimed he had to die to this world and be reborn, he was rejecting any worldly solution to the world's problems, which shocked and disappointed his disciples. His approach was not to improve the situation, but to *change* it utterly by changing himself.

No external social change would suffice. Jesus chose to transform his life of flesh and blood to demonstrate that incremental improvement was not the goal of this phase of history. Rather, something new is to be born out of the dying flesh of each person, and thus out of the clay of Earth itself, since our flesh is made of the dust of the Earth and to dust it has always returned.

Jesus did not return to dust. His body *disappeared*. He did not leave behind a decaying body while going on in a disembodied form as a purely spiritual being. No! He transformed the material substance itself. This means that through him the materials of Earth, Gaia, our Mother, were transformed. Iron, calcium, phosphate, oxygen, hydrogen were transformed.

Jesus's resurrection represents the transformation of the material world into a different substance—a substance more responsive to love and to intentional thought. This new substance is more sensitive, subtle and receptive to conscious direction.

Do atoms remain unchanged by the activities in which they participate? Does an atom of iron in a stone possess exactly the same nature as an atom of iron in a resurrected body? Jesus' solution appears pragmatic from the perspective of evolution. At a certain stage of social development, managing the crises a little better or tinkering with the system will no longer work.

Now is such a time. The problems of the world—injustice, starvation, pollution, war, poverty, abortion—are evolutionary drivers: They are moving us toward something entirely new. We have been trying to put our fingers in a leaky dike that is springing a hundred new holes for every leak we plug. Behind the dike is the sea itself, relentlessly pressing against the wall...building, building, building greater momentum.

The sea is life itself. This particular barrier will no longer hold it. Earth-bound history, self-centered consciousness, unchosen work and the bureaucracy of our past stages of history have all created the container that now constricts us. This container has been our nurturing womb while we have prepared ourselves to become a universal species. When the time for the birth arrives, however, nothing will prevent the sea of life from going beyond the womb.

No one can solve the problem of birth by fixing the womb, supplying it with more resources, cleaning its environment and pacifying the fetus to accept its limits as natural. Even if the unborn child gets seduced into a forever dream of the comfort of its womb, nature would not permit it to stay unborn. The cells in the body of a child in the process of being born have two choices: to celebrate and act, or to collapse in fear. The quality of life of the aborning child hinges upon that choice. At this time, the life of our future selves also depends upon our choice between love and fear.

The commonsense pragmatic approach, which works during one phase of development, becomes lethal during the next. Birth is not a *problem*. It's an opportunity. If we treat our spiritual birth like a mistake that needs correcting, we will kill the child—ourselves—the sons and daughters of man.

We are in transition now. New leadership is arising to act upon the opportunity, not the problem. This new leadership will do well to keep in its heart of hearts the memory of Christ's decision to resurrect rather than reform. Our decision, like Christ's, is not to reform the world, but to transform ourselves. The actual programs that will in fact save the world will arise out of this decision. If we perceive this phase of history as the great transition from Earth-bound to universal life, then the appropriate policies and programs, including solutions to all our problems, will emerge naturally.

If, on the other hand, this phase of history is viewed as a metacrisis to be overcome by returning to some past norm, no proposed solutions will work. The crisis will mount exponentially and society will collapse. Yet there is no need for us to act out this dismal scenario. We can experience a less traumatic transition by acting upon our opportunities now.

Jesus felt disappointment at the people's lack of comprehension of their potentials. "How is it that you do not understand?" he asked, in reference to the capacity to produce abundance for the multitudes from a few loaves of bread. Two thousand years later, his disappointment still has not been dispelled. Current leadership still does not understand. They call separately upon those innovators who can heal, produce or overcome various aspects of the human predicament, with no overarching matrix upon which to spin the new potentials and with no vision for the new Kingdom. Only an appreciation of the *new fabric* will make it possible for the new strands to interweave and work together to design the new society.

In a parable Jesus says: "No man puts a piece of new

cloth unto an old garment, for that which is put in to fill it up takes from the garment, and the rent is made worse." (Matthew 9:16)

Who will establish the warp and the woof upon which to weave the new cloth? For those who have eyes to see and ears to hear, the process is already under way. The process is a self-organizing one. It interacts with itself through networks of activated people, working through shared attraction and mutual concern. These networks increasingly intersect, although often at this early stage they do not recognize the validity of one another's tasks.

The networks of environmentalists do not recognize their natural alliance with the networks of space explorers. The network of bio-technologists and specialists in aging may not recognize their relationship to faith healers. The network of electronic engineers and cyberneticists may not feel at home with the network of psychics practicing remote viewing, telepathy, clairvoyance and psychokinesis. And yet these, and many more, are inevitably related.

Today, a new ecology of souls differentiates as people feel uniquely called to a variety of vocations that will create new worlds on Earth, and in space. The Matrix of the Whole has not yet been fully illuminated. The pattern is implicit, not explicit—hidden, not yet clear. But for those who have eyes to see and ears to hear, it is available. This Matrix is expressing as a higher fractal of the warp and woof on which DNA strands congregate in the invisible nuclei of cells. It replicates, at a higher level, the same pattern through which multicellular life has clustered. It represents a fractal advance of the same pattern upon which human communities formed, and upon which planetary society and universal communities will be built.

This self-evolving Matrix *is* the recurring Pattern that informs life's process and serves as the foundation of all creation. It is the Ground of the Whole. We do not need to invent it; it awaits our realization of—and our conscious alignment with—it.

The most traditional pattern found in the 13.8 billion years of creation is the process of transformation. Over and over again, for billions of years, existence overcame perceived limits through:

- crises;
- innovations;
- synergistic coordination;
- new whole systems; and
- transcending through the union of formerly separate parts.

From atom to molecule to cell to multicell to human and to what is now coming, the *tradition of transformation* repeats itself in the celestial harmonies of creation.

The hope we have gained through science is a logical hope. Through science, by observing and recording the many billions of years of cosmic transformation, we have discovered the awesome intelligence of the process of evolution. Our studies reveal for us our own evolutionary spiral—from the simple atomic origins of the universe to the complex self-aware creatures that we are. We are awakening to ourselves as fully aware participants *in* the universe, preparing to consciously coevolve with it.

This rise of order out of disorder, the animate out of the inanimate, consciousness out of unconsciousness and freedom out of passivity demonstrates the capacity of the Divine process that operates in us. This rise of order out of disorder corroborates Jesus's capacity to resurrect himself in a new body with greater freedom, awareness and ordering power. This tradition of creative transformation will continue—either with us or without us. *That* is the extent of our choice. To transform, or not to transform.

*A*nd John answered him, saying, "Master, we saw one casting out devils in your name, and he follows not us: and we forbad him, because he follows not us." But Jesus said, "Forbid him not: for there is no man which shall do a miracle in my name, that can lightly speak evil of me. For he that is not against us is on our part."

MARK 9:38–40

Those acting with intention and with similar purpose are with us, and with each other, even if they do not acknowledge it. Wise leaders inspire others, and do not require credit for inspiring those who then perform great acts. In secular society, many good people are acting for the transformation without accepting any spiritual belief system, without believing in Jesus or in God. So be it. What does it matter, as long as we are doing what is needed? If we do not demand belief from others, or require adherence to any organization, or insist upon receiving social credit, we can accomplish far more for our cause.

*A*nd *Jesus answered and said, "Verily I say unto you, there is no man that has left house, or brethren, or sisters, or father, or mother, or wife, or children, or lands, for my sake, and the gospel's, But he shall receive a hundredfold now in this time, houses, and brethren, and sisters, and mothers, and children, and lands, with persecutions; and in the world to come eternal life."*

MARK 10:29–30

Physical abundance and a transcendent future are promised to those who put the Kingdom first. There is no indication that putting God first requires an ultimate sacrifice of material well-being. *Everything* needed is promised to those who love God above all else, and their neighbor as themselves.

At this time of social transformation we are called upon to reverse our common sense priority, which has been to first secure our basic needs, then go on to achieve our spiritual or transcendent goal. If we put our potential first, if we put the vision of the New Jerusalem first, we will then have both an evolving future and material security, whatever that may come to mean for us. This choice remained unavailable until the capacity to transform the material world and our own bodies had fully developed, that is, until science and technology matured. Now, with the advent of space exploration, the biotechnological and cybernetic revolutions and with nanotechnology—the ability to restructure matter at the atomic level—the time for choice has arrived.

Projecting ourselves a few decades hence, we can imagine the reality of these choices. Do you wish to die in the traditional way at the scheduled age, or do you wish to extend your life? Do you wish to remain on this Earth, or do you wish to migrate into the universe, never to return? Do you wish to remain in the normal (for terrestrial humanity) self-consciousness, or do you wish to extend your consciousness through prayer, meditation, electronic extensions and the search for extraterrestrial intelligence?

Let's imagine these opportunities become available. What will be the criteria of choice from the point of view of the individual? Equally important, what will be the criteria of choice from the point of view of society at the next stage of social evolution?

The Lord drew Moses up to the top of Mount Sinai and gave him the Ten Commandments. He spoke as the "Lord your God, which have brought you out of the land of Egypt, out of the house of bondage." (Exodus 20:2) Jesus proclaimed the two positive commandments: to love God and our neighbor. What commandments will we receive to guide us through the *actual* transformation from *Homo sapiens sapiens* to *Homo universalis*?

From the individual's point of view, the choice to transcend the new way— utilizing the collective scientific, spiritual and social capacities of humanity—will spring from the deepest personal preference: Does it attract you to do these things, or does it repel you?

Only those who feel attracted will choose to move beyond the mammalian condition, at least in the first few generations. However, once children are born in space to parents who have chosen to migrate, they will no longer have a choice to be born an earthling! One phase begins; another closes forever.

From society-at-the-next-stage's point of view, what will be the criteria for selection? Who will be permitted to evolve? Everyone who wants to? Or only some? If the latter, who among us will be chosen to partake of the collective capacities and *actually* become universal, living an extended life span in an extended environment? Could it be that the selection process described in the Book of Revelation is the way it will actually happen?

❧

*A*nd they were judged every man according to their works. And death and hell were cast into the lake of fire. This is the second death. And whosoever was not found written in the book of life was cast into the lake of fire.

REVELATION 20:13–15

Could it be that the "reaper" at the "harvest" represents God's evolutionary selection process, which is *not in human hands* and *is not ours to judge*? Could it be that only the "good" will evolve, good defined not by our judgment, but by the larger system recorded in the Book of Life? If so, what would be some characteristics of the good that might be selected to proceed onward to the next step of evolution?

From our 13.8 billion-year history, we see that after every quantum transformation, consciousness, freedom and union leap to a higher state of being. A more complex whole system forms that embodies characteristics of greater awareness and more freedom of action. A cell is more aware and has more options than does a molecule. A human has greater awareness and freedom than does an animal.

Jesus demonstrated the next leap in consciousness, freedom and union. This recurring pattern leads to the conclusion that the characteristics that will be essential for survival at the next stage of human development are:

+ the capacity for universal consciousness, in consistent attunement with the patterns in the process of evolution;
+ love of freedom—the capacity to tolerate expanded choice, diversity, flexibility, ambiguity, uncertainty, responsibility and response-ability; and
+ the capacity to cooperate, unite, synergize and love everyone as a member of your body.

Universal consciousness, expanded freedom of choice and a love of unity in diversity appear to be some of our emergent characteristics at the next stage.

⁓

"*But to sit on my right hand and on my left hand is not mine to give; but it shall be given to them for whom it is prepared.*"

MARK 10:40

Even Jesus does not decide who shall transcend and who shall not. "For whom it is prepared" means that the decision extends beyond our personal choice and effort. Evolutionary progress suggests that the attraction to evolve is based on a complex process of synchronicity, synergy, coincidence, simultaneity and being at the right place at the right time with the needed characteristics.

It is true that chance favors the prepared person. But there exists a *higher* system of selection beyond chance or individual intention. That aspect remains a mystery. All we can do, and all we need do is *intend* to evolve, *prepare* to evolve and *trust* in the process. The process itself is not ours to judge.

Now when Jesus was risen early the first day of the week, he appeared first to Mary Magdalene, out of whom he had cast seven devils. And she went and told them that had been with him, as they mourned and wept. And they, when they had heard that he was alive, and had been seen of her, believed not. After that he appeared in another form unto two of them, as they walked, and went into the country. And they went and told it unto the residue: neither believed they them.

MARK 16:9–13

We find it difficult to believe in the reality of the next stage of our evolution. Our five animal senses have no experience of ourselves behaving with the power that Jesus demonstrated. Only our extraordinary peak experiences—mystical flashes, unitive moments—presage the reality of ourselves as universal beings. Most of us do not fully believe in our own highest experiences, when they are in fact the most real aspect of ourselves—what we potentially are.

Even the disciples, who had been told what to expect over and over again by Jesus, whom they adored, could not believe in his capacities until they saw them for themselves. Jesus had to reappear in a new body, visible to the mammalian senses of sight, touch, taste, smell and hearing. Thomas had to feel Jesus's wounds with his own hands to believe in the resurrection.

We still need to see to believe. There must be demonstrations, visible to us in our present state of self-consciousness, because our nervous systems are still unawakened to their capacity to connect indirectly with Universal Mind.

Two thousand years ago Jesus reappeared to a tiny handful of people, who were then galvanized by the reality of the resurrection to spread the gospel of transformation to the world. Those humans who are expanding their self-consciousness to universal consciousness and learning the invisible technologies of creation are now preparing a new demonstration of the reality of the resurrection. We are preparing to be Christlike through our own readiness to evolve.

Afterward he appeared unto the eleven as they sat at food, and upbraided them with their unbelief and hardness of heart, because they believed not them which had seen him after he was risen. And he said unto them, "Go all of you into all the world, and preach the gospel to every creature. He that believes and is baptized shall be saved; but he that believes not shall be damned."

MARK 16:14–16

WE HAVE IN THE PAST, AND WE STILL DO, get away with murder. Over and over again we are forgiven our "sins," our separation from each other and from the Creator. However, at this time quantum changes are speeding up, and a new whole system is about to be integrated. At this time, destructive elements would contaminate the next phase of evolution. We must therefore pass through a ring of fire at this stage of evolution. This is the ring of wholeness. We cannot get through it in a state of selfishness. The illusion of separation from the creation *will* be overcome. What was forgivable in the early phase of humanity becomes deadly at the universal phase.

We can see an example of this in the first space missions. The slightest defect, a faulty crew, a careless act, a lack of trust, and the mission can be totally destroyed. NASA aims for "zero defects." Perfection becomes the norm. The astronauts were selected for perfection in certain areas. What would be a minor problem for a person on Earth—a heart murmur, a bad temper—might be lethal in space.

The builders of new worlds in space will aim for zero defects, because when mistakes occur they will be less acceptable than on Earth. This is not a question of human judgment, but is due to the laws of nature in outer space, where the environment itself is less forgiving. We have to meet its requirements or we will not be able to survive.

The great traditional values of excellence, intelligence, cooperation, honesty, fidelity, patience, integrity and sensitivity are also necessary for survival in our next phase. Their opposites—laziness, sloth, greed, lust, carelessness, stupidity, dishonesty, intemperance and violence—will be vigorously selected against, even unto quick death of a space colony in which these characteristics occur.

If we define morality as the awareness that we are part of a whole and are integrally related to every part of the whole, then holistic morality must rapidly increase in the next phase of evolution. This requirement will be more obvious in outer space, but holistic morality is also an increasing survival necessity on Earth. Interdependence already requires awareness that we are our brothers' keeper if anyone wishes to survive.

Those who live in a state of separateness—who feel repelled by cooperation because they want to possess, manipulate and overpower—are under increasing stress. Breakdown, alienation and self-destruction increase among those who are not attracted to participate in the co-creation of the world. They suffer from heavier and heavier "future-shock," despair and the loss of motivation.

A bifurcation of the species may be about to occur. Those attracted to the unknown future will become increasingly vital and in love with life. Those repelled by new potentials, or who desire to make themselves comfortable at the current stage of evolution, will be increasingly disappointed by life.

When genuinely new options such as space migration and longevity open up, the difference between the attracted and the non-attracted people will be even more obvious.

Eventually, those who evolve will transcend present human limitations. Those who do not evolve, those who do not believe in the potential for transformation, for eternal life and for a new Heaven and a new Earth, will pass away forever from this strand of evolution—becoming an extinct species like the dinosaurs.

Some species adapt to a specific niche and can survive for long periods without much change—bees and ants, for example. This niche state is unavailable to humans who remain self-centered, because a selfish, terrestrial humanity empowered with high science and technology is neither a stable nor a well-adapted species.

From both the evolutionary perspective and the scriptural perspective a last judgment on this phase of human terrestrial life is now occurring, both collectively and individually. We may fail collectively if we continue to pollute the environment, trigger a nuclear war, refuse to create sufficiency for all peoples, refuse to develop a productive capacity in outer space or refuse to love each other. We may fail individually by the personal choice not to participate in the transformation, not to believe in the gospel of the Kingdom. As we move into the next phase of evolution, the time for forgiveness is ending. The time for transformation is at hand.

THE GOSPEL

ACCORDING TO LUKE

✺

*A*nd when they found him not, they turned back again to Jerusalem, seeking him. And it came to pass, that after three days they found him in the temple, sitting in the midst of the doctors, both hearing them, and asking them questions.

And when they saw him, they were amazed: and his mother said unto him, "Son, why have you thus dealt with us? Behold, your father and I have sought you sorrowing." And he said unto them, "How is it that all of you sought me? know all of you not that I must be about my Father's business?"

LUKE 2:45–46, 48–49

Jesus was born connected to a transcendent awareness. He was not confined to his biological or geographical roots. He was primarily noological from the beginning, connected to the mind and spirit beyond material circumstances. Once the human nervous system and brain evolve to form a stable connection with Universal Intelligence, everyone thereafter will be born knowing they are about their "father/mother's business." For in fact, we are all involved in carrying out the Creative Intention, whether we know it or not.

We know not how we come into being as infants, why or from where we came. Have you ever looked into the eyes of a newborn child? Awake in an infant body, a spirit seems to be looking out in bewilderment and anger at being in such an undignified condition! As the look of surprise gradually disappears, the child forgets its birth and settles into the challenging task of learning how to move, eat, grow, speak and read.

A set of desires then arises, attracting the child to prevail in the world by exercising its capacities. Every goal achieved forms a stepping-stone to another, or becomes a graveyard for the spirit. Our desires to fulfill our presumed needs and experience new pleasures, seemingly for our own survival, can be seductive. But from an evolutionary perspective it becomes clear that individuals are serving more than their immediate needs. Each act of excellence is a vital element forming an invisible *cathedral of action*. Each act that is good, useful and creative reaches beyond the individual, making some enduring contribution to the whole.

Human culture reflects the glorious accretion of multitudes of interconnecting acts that comprise a body of language, inventions, customs and ideas into which each new child is born. The child inherits not only human culture, but all of cosmic evolutionary history. In its genes are written the story of our entire universal journey, from the origin of the physical universe.

In our atoms resides the memory of creation. In our molecules lives the history of the synthesis of elements and compounds that compose our Earth and body. In our cells exists the coded history of life's emergence from the silent seas of early Earth to the lush jungles of animal and vegetable life. Our brains contain the experiential records of reptilian, mammalian and early human life. Our heartfelt motivation serves as the inspiring force that animates the process of creation. We are *it*!

Future humans in the model of Jesus will know the truth of their origins and the meaning of their lives. The Creator animated us with the Intention of Creation, and now we hold within ourselves (though often still unconscious) the wisdom of the whole creation. We are fulfilling the potential of the universe by transmuting material substance into co-creative consciousness.

We eat material food such as iron, calcium and phosphates and transform it into ideas, symbols, art and institutions—the works of our minds and hearts. This alchemical work produces our cultural body—the collective, learned capacity of the human race. That cultural body of wisdom provides the energy we now use to transcend the animal/human phase of history. The difference between a child born today and one born fifteen thousand years ago is our collective cultural heritage. Biologically we are similar, but noologically we are different. We stand upon the collective achievement of billions of individuals, whose acts live on in our actions, ideas and feelings.

Jesus set the first example of the spiritual/human being

we all potentially are. With him the future became the present. He served as the living bridge between the cultural phase of history, when we passed on knowledge through language, to the conscious evolution phase of human development. By being one with the Consciousness that creates, Jesus demonstrated the power to transform himself into a resurrected or divine human. That is the essence of conscious evolution.

Jesus began his early life learning the traditional culture of his people, "sitting in the midst of the doctors, both hearing them and asking them questions." Upon his baptism by John the Baptist, he became aware that he was the "beloved Son of God" with a unique mission. He was to consciously evolve before the very eyes of humanity. For Jesus to fulfill his mission of visible and purposeful evolution, he chose to overcome the worst kind of ignominious death. He rose victorious as an example of what we all can do, in the fullness of time, by serving our highest intention now.

When we feel within the attraction to go beyond the traditional pattern of our life, we are to become sensitive and listen to the Intention of Creation within. We are to recognize in our own aspiration the invisible language of the Creator gently urging us to become conscious of our heritage, and be willing to go about our father/mother's business.

⌒～

*N*ow *when all the people were baptized, it came to pass, that Jesus also being baptized, and praying, the heaven was opened, and the Holy Spirit descended in a bodily shape like a dove upon him, and a voice came from heaven, which said, "You are my beloved Son; in you I am well pleased."*

LUKE 3:21-22

There is always a first example of what will become a new form. Jesus was a first example of a new possibility. His example has enlightened the minds and inflamed the expectations of hundreds of millions of souls for two thousand years. His demonstration of human potential stimulates the same potential in us. Our potential lies dormant. His was awake. Through the example of his awakened potential to become consciously self-creative, self-regenerating and self-evolving, our own potential is *remembered*. What he did, we can do too. Yet we have difficulty believing in his resurrection, and even more difficulty believing in the possibility of our own. Both are true.

At a deep level of superconscious knowledge, every human being knows there is more to human potential than eating, sleeping, reproducing and dying. The example of Jesus's life stimulates the memory of the nature of that "moreness," and activates us to fulfill that potential. It helps us to overcome self-imposed limits to our potential, limits fostered by our past mammalian experience.

Our past experience informs the foundation of the new, but is not a description of it. We can leave behind the limits of our past experience and grow toward our natural stature as universal humans—joint heirs with Christ. Our awareness that we can transcend self-conscious limits is essential now.

To imagine that human nature never changes limits us; we remain moribund. Conscious evolution requires active, creative imagination; for as we see ourselves, so we increasingly are. As our power to create grows, so grows the requirement that we envision ourselves performing at our highest possible capacity. The very nature of the power of co-creation demands a new self-image and a deeper attunement to the universal design of creation. The most comprehensive self-image is Christ. Love. Attunement. Mind in communion with matter. A readiness to put the Kingdom first and to aspire toward the highest vision of ourselves, so that the design of evolution can be fulfilled.

We are naturally taking a leap from self-consciousness to evolutionary consciousness, from seeing the movie of creation frame by frame as stills, to seeing the movie quickly, catching the movement of the process of creation and experiencing ourselves co-creating with the process.

Through conscious evolution we learn the techniques of creation. Already the eyes of science probe the material world to uncover energy in motion. Soon the eyes of a consciously evolving human will penetrate energy to discover its intention. The Book of Knowledge has many chapters. Those who so desire can learn everything that is there. Nothing is hidden. All will be revealed to those who choose to go the whole way to the top of the mountain.

If you know what you can become and still freely choose *not to evolve*, you become blocked and unable to flow, to grow, to evolve yourself and leap into your partnership with God.

The pain of knowing your potential and not committing yourself to its realization is hell, self-imposed.

Jesus prayed when John baptized him. The heavens opened up and welcomed him to the next step of evolution, because he was *totally willing to go the whole way.* We must be careful what we ask for because we shall receive it. Ask and it shall be given. Knock and doors will open.

The Good News we receive is *so good* that it sometimes blinds us with a flash of brilliant light. The seeker shields his eyes. The human, heretofore locked into the infinitesimal box of self-consciousness and the five senses, is exposed to the infinitely creative intention of God. Most of us must move slowly into that light, to become accustomed to its brilliance until our nervous systems are gently tempered with excitement. Our will is being educated by glimpses of glory untold.

We who so desire are being prepared to let in the light, to allow the dove to descend upon our shoulders and receive a voice which tells us we are the beloved sons and daughters with whom the Creator is very pleased.

And Jesus, being full of the Holy Spirit returned from Jordan, and was led by the Spirit into the wilderness, Being forty days tempted of the devil. And in those days he did eat nothing: and when they were ended, he afterward hungered. And the devil said unto him, "If you be the Son of God, command this stone

*that it be made bread." And Jesus answered him, saying,
"It is written, 'That man shall not live by bread alone,
but by every word of God."*

LUKE 4:1–4

Once the power of creation dawns on the human mind, the temptation to misuse it intensifies. Jesus received the communication that he was the beloved Son of God. He inherited the capacities of the Creator. He was enabled to act like God, who created all of us in the Divine image.

To be created in the image of God means we imitate, resemble and represent God. This power is awesome. This power is ours. The devil is the temptation to use the power of co-creation for selfish, rather than loving, purposes.

It is permissible, and even necessary, for children to be selfish. Thus do we establish our sense of uniqueness. However, to be selfish as an adult, and most especially as an adult who inherits the powers of co-creation, will destroy not only the individual but the whole body politic. At that level, selfishness becomes deadly.

The devil tempted Jesus once he knew Jesus was created in the image of God, even as we of this generation are being tempted now that we know we are inheritors of godlike powers to co-create or destroy whole worlds. Jesus's first temptation was to turn stone into bread. Jesus refused. To turn one loaf of bread into thousands to feed the hungry multitudes was right, as he demonstrated. To turn a stone into bread to flaunt his power, rather than to use it with compassion, was wrong. Godlike power is to be used for godlike purposes.

The temptation of modern industrial society to misuse power, to flaunt the self-interest of individuals, groups or nations, is deadly to the world; the practice cannot be continued. The proper use of modern power, to create abundance from the rocks of the Earth for the sake of the poor and hungry, is blessed. It shall be done.

But there is yet more to be done. Man shall not live by bread alone. It will not suffice that we use our powers of co-creation to produce comfort as an end unto itself. The power must be used first to fulfill the Word of God. What is that Word? The word is: *You are my beloved son and daughter. You are in my image. You are to become like me, and with me you are to co-create forever and ever.*

～

*A*nd the devil, taking him up into an high mountain, showed unto him all the kingdoms of the world in a moment of time. And the devil said unto him, "All this power will I give you, and the glory of them: for that is delivered unto me; and to whomsoever I will I give it. If you therefore will worship me, all shall be yours." And Jesus answered and said unto him, "Get you behind me, Satan: for it is written, 'You shall worship the Lord your God, and him only shall you serve.'"

LUKE 4:5–8

If we use godlike power to be powerful in human terms, meaning power over others, we will not become co-creators. We will be co-destroyers. If we use godlike power for the purpose of celebration and continued creation according to the pattern in the process of evolution, we will become godlike.

Individuals have taken the step to demonstrate the godlike use of god-given power, but no group of individuals has ever done so. Who will be the first group? Who will elect to use power for the purposes it was given to us: that is, to overcome the creature human condition and become universal beings, at one with the Source of it all? It will be those who are so attracted. It is for them that *The Testament of Co-Creation* is written.

∿

A nd he brought him to Jerusalem, and set him on a pinnacle of the temple, and said unto him, "If you be the Son of God, cast yourself down from behind: For it is written, 'He shall give his angels charge over you, to keep you,' and, 'In their hands they shall bear you up, lest at any time you dash your foot against a stone.'" And Jesus answering said unto him, "It is said, 'You shall not tempt the Lord your God.'" And when the devil had ended all the temptation, he departed from him for a season.

LUKE 4:9–13

When the awareness of the power of co-creation comes, with it comes the dual temptation of hubris: pridefulness, or using power for selfish purposes, and passivity, the lack of responsibility for the powers. In this verse the devil tempts Jesus to deny his own responsibility for the power by turning it over to angels who will protect him and fostering a desire to be protected, rather than to protect.

It is written, "He shall give his angels charge over you, to keep you." This is true for the sons and daughters of God, provided they do not ignore their own powers. The "angels" we must work with include our own intelligence aligned with God, not childishly dependent on God. At our co-creative stage of capacity, it is wrong to try to "tempt the Lord" to do for us what we have been given the power to do for ourselves.

When Jesus refused to be seduced, the devil "departed from him *for a season.*"

We can never take it for granted that we have overcome temptation forever, for as long as we are in mortal bodies we can still fall prey to self-centered consciousness brought on by fear of hunger, disease and death.

This period of transition between self-consciousness and universal consciousness, between corruptible and incorruptible, requires constant attention to our transcendent purpose. We need to remind ourselves that we are here to evolve, not remain. Our minds already hold the truth. We tend to forget, to lose the remembrance of who we are, because our five senses deny it. We were given the five senses to learn how the material world works. We were given the sixth sense to connect with the Creative Source, of which the material world is the manifestation. We need to remember that each of us is a member of the whole universe of creation, and is destined to partake of the whole, consciously.

In this period of transition we flicker in and out of awareness, from self to whole. Disconnected momentarily from the whole, we return to self, only to be reconnected with the whole once again. Like living lightbulbs we turn ourselves on and off. "On" is remembering who we are. "Off" is forgetting. The power to connect our being with the power of the whole creation is ours to use. Meditation and prayer serve as the means by which many connect with the whole.

As history moves from its terrestrial to its universal phase, the way will become easier. In the coming period, children born on Earth, and more especially in the universe, will know naturally that they are the beloved Sons and Daughters of God. Those who cannot remember who they are will not be able to use the powers of God. No one is forced to transcend.

Through the evolutionary selection process we are continually offered the opportunity to grow or die. It tests for weakness, constantly. The higher we climb, the more vigorous becomes the process of selection. Each footstep counts as we head up the steep crags of the mountain of life. The way to Heaven is narrow at this stage of history.

We are at a transformation point from one phase of growth to the next. Mutations of all kinds spring up as the old forms disintegrate and the new forms are not yet apparent. Most mutations, most innovations, cannot survive. They do not fit the criteria of evolution. What is that criteria?

It is the capacity to love God, the Intention of Creation, above all else and your neighbor as yourself. It is the capacity to know how God builds the technologies of creation, so we can co-create the future in cooperation with the design of evolution.

If we are insensitive to the patterns of the universe, we will be off the mark. We will not make it through to our own next stage. At some point the door to a particular stage of evolution shuts. The evolutionary window closes. The opportunity ends. The favorable juncture of circumstances no longer prevails. That particular choice is finished forever. The dinosaur has no further choice to evolve. Neanderthal Man has no way to begin again. At some point, self-centered humans also will become extinct, obsolete and no longer able to choose to go on.

The choice is open to all. This is the choosing hour. This is the time when the call is clearest because the danger is greatest, the stakes are highest and the current of communication from Creator to creature is amplified. Hear it, all who are willing.

    ❧

"No man also having drunk old wine immediately desires new: for he says, "The old is better."

LUKE 5:39

Those who believe they know it all already do not understand the new news, and do not desire to drink the new wine. Those who are spiritually and intellectually satisfied are less receptive to the new news than those who hunger. "Blessed are the poor in spirit; for theirs is the Kingdom of Heaven." (Matthew 5:3)

Those in profound need of deeper meaning are the ones who will respond most faithfully to the new possibilities of our age. The incipient evolutionaries are the potential avant-garde.

Old forms, old wineskins, no longer suffice at a time of quantum transformation. The reality of the present cannot be compared with the past. There is newness in the creation. It never repeats the past. It is never totally predictable. It remains ever open to the unexpected. No dogma can contain the living truth.

As we enter the period of conscious evolution, we realize that no form in which we behold reality *is reality itself.* We will remain ever sensitive to newness.

We stand upon a threshold built of a synthesis of all human potentials, the past and the present. A new synthesis is now in formation. From every culture, those elements that contribute to the next stage of evolution are being selected. From the experience of early preindustrial societies to the perennial wisdom of the great traditional cultures to modern industrialized societies, we are learning lessons and preserving them in preparation for our universal phase of growth. We build the future on the best of the past.

What will be selected from the past and what will be rejected, no one knows for sure. However, certain principles of evolution are clear. Established cultural contributions that increase the freedom, union and transcendence of humanity will be included. The process will reject any historic traits that inhibit freedom, union and transcendence. Meanwhile, brand new cultural ideas, techniques, works and institutions that will enhance our potential for greater consciousness and freedom will be inspired.

Most biological species that have ever existed were rendered extinct before humanity appeared. However, the lessons learned by those species in the past were incorporated in the genetic codes of all surviving species. Our mind-body system represents the synthesis of billions of experiments and multitudes of exploratory species whose material embodiments have disappeared, but whose genetic ideas live on through us.

A large percentage of human-made cultural artifacts will also pass away as we take the great leap from terrestrial to universal humanity. Already we see some obvious contenders for cultural extinction: human sacrifice; tyranny of all kinds; torture; cruelty to children and to animals; racial, ethnic and gender prejudice; drug abuse; environmental pollution; nuclear war. These aspects of human civilization cannot continue into the next phase, just as a self-centered infant cannot survive unchanged to the age of thirty-five. Infantilism, appropriate for a child, becomes deadly for an adult.

A built-in safety valve exists at this stage of evolution. If we cannot handle our capacities creatively, we will self-destruct. How many planets in a stage of cosmic birth similar to our own spontaneously abort when they come to the end of their high technology phase, right when they are preparing to restore their environment and impregnate the universe with new seeds of life? Those who prefer the old wine will have a difficult time tasting the new. The new species of humanity is composed of those who have always understood that the freedom to change is essential for survival.

Now when he came nigh to the gate of the city, behold, there was a dead man carried out, the only son of his mother, and she was a widow: and much people of the city was with her. And when the Lord saw her, he had compassion on her, and said unto her, "Weep not." And he came and touched the bier: and they that bare him stood still. And he said, "Young man, I say unto you, Arise." And he that was dead sat up, and began to speak. And he delivered him to his mother.

LUKE 7:12–15

Two channels to transcendence are available to us. We can detach our higher self from our physical person and return to the All. We can also fuse our higher self with our individual person, thereby evolving beyond self-consciousness and mortality to participate with God in a new body, the personality fulfilled. One is the way of union with God through *emancipation* of consciousness from the human person; the other is fusion with God through the *evolution* of the person into a Christlike being, ready for the next stage of *action* in the universal creation, whatever that may be.

These two channels of transcendence have opposite attitudes toward death.

The channel of transcendence that sends us toward a bodiless, impersonal future regards death of the personal body as a release. The channel of transcendence that sends us toward a personal, *embodied* future regards death as the great barrier to be overcome by the *transformation* of the body, as demonstrated by Jesus's resurrection.

A great metaphysical choice awaits us as individuals, as our evolutionary capacities for space migration, intelligence expansion and life extension become real options, within the lifetime of some members of the present generation on planet Earth.

Do you choose to die to the mammalian phase, to return to the Source as an indivisible element or as a purely discarnate spiritual being? Or do you choose to transform the mammalian body into an incorruptible body, and begin the next step of individual work in the universe, building new worlds, communicating with other life, and transforming the material universe into the conscious universe? Both choices are needed to balance the energies of life.

☙

*A*nd John calling unto him two of his disciples sent them to Jesus, saying, "Are you he that should come? Or look we for another?" When the men were come unto him, they said, "John Baptist has sent us unto you, saying, 'Are you he that should come? Or look we for another?'" And in that same hour he cured many of their infirmities and plagues, and of evil spirits; and unto many that were blind he gave sight. Then Jesus answering said unto them, "Go your way, and tell John what things all of you have seen and heard; how that *the blind see, the lame walk, the lepers are cleansed, the deaf hear, the dead are raised, to the poor the gospel is preached. And blessed is he, whosoever shall not be offended in me."*

LUKE 7:19–23

We know who we are by what we do. By our fruits we shall be known. Jesus' acts were extraordinary, far beyond the normal capacity for good works. He recognized he would offend anyone who resented knowing how much more is possible than was customary at that time.

A new level of excellence excites envy and fear. This sets up a profound challenge for all who would settle for less than the best in themselves. The call to transform taunts us into self-development. Out of fear, people build mental defenses against the hope that such a life is possible for them. They fear the hurt, the vulnerability of trying to grow, and become all that they can be.

Whenever we meet cynics, we recognize sensitive people whose hopes have congealed into a protective callous. They feel reluctant to recognize the possible, the new, the hopeful, for fear it will not be realized. They settle for the protection of hopelessness rather than the vigorous risk of hope. For, in fact, over and over again human hopes have been dashed upon the rocks of human weakness. All the great visions of wholeness and transcendence remain poised, as yet unfulfilled.

The Indian rishis, the Egyptian priests, the Hebrew prophets, the great shamans, the Muslim Imams, the Christian saints, the scientific seers and the proponents of democracy held visions of the possible humanity beyond the confines of our present condition. None have as yet been fulfilled, for it has not yet been time in the organic development of planet Earth. The time is coming. It is the time in history for the cosmic birth, the quantum transformation from terrestrial to universal, the historic, collective tribulations and the salvation. Blessed are those who are not offended by the example of Jesus, by the example of the potential to come. Affirmation of the possible is essential for its realization. Only by our belief in the potential of the future will it be fulfilled.

There has always been a continuing dialogue between the possibilists and the impossibilists. The impossibilists affirm what has been so and deny the new, for it *seems* unreal. They are often called realists, pragmatists, experts: people who know what has worked. They are needed in times of little change. The possibilists affirm what can be, and deny that the limits of the present are fixed. They are often called visionaries, dreamers, impractical. And yet in the long run, they are the builders of the real world.

For what is the *real* world, even as we see it now in all its magnificent diversity, but the awesome rise of the new out of the old, of molecules out of atoms, solar systems out of gasses, cells out of molecules, animals out of cells, humans out of animals, and universal humans, Christlike humans out of us? Is reality what has been, what is now or what will be? Is it all of that—it is also what always is.

However, blessed are those of us who are not offended by the highest potential, for we are the bearers of evolution, the heralds of new forms out of the old. We are especially needed at a time of rapid change such as our own.

While he yet spoke, there comes one from the ruler of the synagogue's house, saying to him, "Your daughter is dead; trouble not the Master." But when Jesus heard it, he answered him, saying, "Fear not: believe only, and she shall be made whole." And when he came into the house, he suffered no man to go in, save Peter, and James, and John, and the father and the mother of the maiden. And all wept, and bewailed her: but he said, "Weep not; she is not dead, but sleeps." And they laughed him to scorn, knowing that she was dead. And he put them all out, and took her by the hand, and called, saying, "Maid, arise." And her spirit came again, and she arose immediately: and he commanded to give her food. And her parents were astonished: but he charged them that they should tell no man what was done.

LUKE 8:49–56

What, in fact, was done? Let us assume the child was physically dead and Jesus stimulated her life processes to begin again. At our stage of evolution, this capacity seems miraculous, superhuman. But it is conceivable that what is in fact superhuman to us, from our perspective, is natural from the perspective of the next step of evolution, for evolution increases capacity.

It was natural for Christ, who is us at the next stage, to renew life. We can learn to become like Christ, doing as he did, and even more. What appears miraculous from the perspective of one stage of evolution becomes natural for the next. From the perspective of a single cell, floating passively in the sea, an animal moving about would seem supernatural. From the perspective of an early human, our flight to the moon would seem supernatural. From the perspective of a human at the end of the twentieth century, Christ's powers still seem supernatural. But will they still appear so to those living at the end of the twenty-first or twenty-second century? Or after the quantum transformation, when we are a universal species? Probably not. Already we sense the normalization of the miraculous as humans learn to heal themselves through the recognition that Spirit is the cause, the matter, the effect.

What is the inherent essence of the reality we have witnessed through billions of years of evolution from a hydrogen cloud to us upon the solid Earth, now seeking to know our Creator in order to be like godlike? The nature of reality is the continual transformation of matter to higher forms of consciousness, through the formation of ever more complex bodies that are capable of overcoming ever greater limits. That is natural.

We can see the pattern now through the discovery of cosmogenesis, the continuous unfolding of the cosmos. We are now learning how nature transforms from one stage to the next. For we ourselves are nature, in the act of transformation from one phase of consciousness to the next, from one phase of physical limits to the next. Through conscious evolution we are learning how nature works, so we can be ever more natural, ever more creative, creating as naturally as nature creates.

Ultimately, natural means a manifestation of God-in-action. Nature is the creation. God, the logos, the Universal

Mind, is the Creator. Because the creation itself evolves, what once seemed supernatural becomes natural as we grow. Let us look at Jesus's miracles as forecasts of a new norm; they reveal what will be natural to us as fully grown humans.

❧

"*Let these sayings sink down into your ears: for the Son of man shall be delivered into the hands of men.*" *But they understood not this saying, and it was hid from them, that they perceived it not: and they feared to ask him of that saying.*

LUKE 9:44–45

People had difficulty recognizing the reality of the Kingdom. Jesus was adored for his miracles of healing and implored to become a political messiah to bring temporal power to the Jews. Surrendering to the narrow focus of his contemporaries would have reduced him to less than he was. He was teaching transformation. They were seeking reformation.

Even his disciples were afraid of the power of change. He sent his disciples forth to preach the Kingdom of God, and to heal the sick, which they did, and returned to him.

Herod, the political leader, became afraid of the power of Jesus over the multitude and said, "John have I beheaded, but who is this, of whom I hear such things?"

Herod wanted to see Jesus. Ominous warning! The historical situation was driving toward a political confrontation between Roman authority, egged on by the anger of the Pharisees, and the people, who wanted Jesus to triumph for them over the temporal powers. The more popular Jesus became, the more imminent the political confrontation became.

Finally Jesus understood in communion with God that he would have to "be slain and be raised on the third day." He decided to initiate a transformational act rather than submit to a political battle—which, in winning, he would lose all by affirming the old way. The crucifixion would not have been necessary if the reality of the resurrection could have been believed before his death. But the limitations of human experience precluded this belief. Jesus was forced into a painful demonstration: a public death and then reappearance before his disciples.

What about contemporary history? How stands the situation now? Those with eyes to see can see the reality of the transformation, with positive innovations emerging in every field. Meanwhile the political/economic forces escalate the possibility of massive destruction through climate change, pollution, arms proliferation, social inequities and resource shortages.

The reality of the transformation is based on the reality of the potentials now available for the collective evolution of the human race, from terrestrial self-consciousness to universal whole-consciousness. In every field, innovations spring up that attest to the reality of our ability to transcend historic human limits rather than conform to them. An innate capacity for evolutionary consciousness resides in our abilities to produce abundance in an Earth/space environment, to organize cooperatively, to heal and extend our lives, to automate our work, to emancipate our unique creativity in a universe of unlimited dimensions. All these new powers overwhelmingly point to the reality of a collective evolution. Yet the forces of destruction accelerate.

Two thousand years have elapsed. We are no longer looking to an individual savior to bring on the transformation, while we remain passive. We are looking also to the Saving Power within ourselves, inherent in our own capacities to be like Christ. We are multitudes of self-saviors, for those who have eyes to see.

Why do we not generally see it, then? The conditions Jesus confronted were more difficult than our own. Today, the miracles of transformation are obvious. Science has democratized awareness of the invisible technologies of creation. The processes and techniques of the resurrection are being slowly revealed as the human mind probes deeper and deeper into matter and finds design, pattern, directionality, intentionality and an ability to become godlike, co-creative beings.

The networks of activated believers are self-organizing now. These networks have begun to network. Metanetworks connect under the surface of the mass media's infantile attachment to the past and its nostalgia for the womb.

Must we carry out the crucifixion again on a collective scale, with the negative forces acting out the drama of self-destruction? Or can we proceed more gracefully through the tribulations, to the next stage? When we recognize that events are prepatterned but not predetermined, we realize that our acts now will make the difference between a painful birth and a graceful one.

Like any birth, some trauma is inevitable. But how differently we experience pain if we know its meaning and love its purpose, versus if we fear each contraction as a signal of defeat and disaster? The gospel of the transformation, the reality of the "new" news, the ever-evolving good news, must be broadcast throughout the world and soon.

Our urgency is as great as that of the disciples who were

sent forth with "power and authority over all devils and to cure diseases ..." with instructions to "Take nothing for your journey, neither staves, nor pouch, neither bread, neither money; neither have two coats apiece. And whatsoever house all of you enter into, there abide, and thence depart. And whosoever will not receive you, when all of you go out of that city, shake off the very dust from your feet for a testimony against them." (Luke:3–5)

We collectively have power and authority over devils and diseases, both individual and social. As co-creators we are not yet fully exercising that power and authority. We who desire to communicate the reality of the transformation must now do for our time what the disciples did for theirs, trusting the rest to God.

First, we must exercise power and authority over ourselves, overcoming inner negativity and disease. Second, we must communicate the collective power for good. The innovators have not yet gained access to the mass media. The general public does not yet know the *new good news*.

The essential step now is to fuse ancient spiritual knowledge and love of the Divine—the capacity to become one with Consciousness—combined with our modern creative capacities, and then to demonstrate the reality of the transformation through the media, the nervous system of humankind.

*A*nd when they had brought their ships to land, they forsook all, and followed him.

LUKE 5:11

When we know the Intention of Creation, we follow it with all our heart, mind, body and soul. We put the Kingdom first. We identify our highest aspiration and follow it the whole way to the top of the mountain.

During quantum transformation, when all things are in transition, the only security we will find is to go toward the next step of evolution—universal humanity, the Kingdom of Heaven, the human race matured with our full capacities functioning harmoniously at the dawn of the universal age—a new beginning. Every person on Earth now has a unique role to play in that transformation based on individual capacity translated into chosen vocation or discipleship.

What does it mean to become a disciple? It means to discover what we most deeply desire to do—our inner calling—what is most needed for the evolution of the world, and then to do it with all our heart, mind, body and soul. This commitment requires self-discipline and self-authorization. As co-creative humans we cannot expect an external authority to tell us what to do.

The maturation of Adam and Eve means the connection to the Creator is reestablished at the next level of evolution, and we know from within what role we are to take in the creation. This inner discovery of our part in the process requires deep listening, to identify our own talent and our own way of giving it. We are like messenger RNA seeking contact with the cosmic DNA, the design of the social body, in order to receive specific instructions on how to build our particular part of the larger whole.

The methods of attunement to our role in creation, the process of our discipleship to co-create the future, are hardly developed. We go to school to learn to read, write and develop a skill to earn our living. But where can we learn the deeper and vital skill of connecting our unique capacity to the specific needs of the social body, in alignment with the Intention of Creation? There are, as yet, few Schools for Conscious Evolution where we learn how the processes of creation work, and how we can perform our part in them.

The Metacurriculum for the Future is yet to be taught.

This challenge makes being alive now very exciting— if you are a pioneer, an explorer, a discoverer, a listener, a seeker, and a questioner. As Jesus said, no one—not himself, not the angels in Heaven, only God—knows when and preciously how the tribulations will end. Therefore, we can take heart in our uncertainty. It means we are experimenters for God.

The cosmic drama is still being written. We are actors in the play. Its name is the Story of Creation.

～

A nd it came to pass, when the time was come that he should be received up, he steadfastly set his face to go to Jerusalem.

LUKE 9:51

There comes a time in each of our lives when we must steadfastly set our face "to go to Jerusalem." If we do so, we transcend our limits. If we do not do so, we submit to our limits. The decision "to go to Jerusalem" is the inner choice to give our utmost to what we believe is the highest good.

Everyone has that choice. No matter what our external condition, rich or poor, sick or well, we can choose to go the whole way, or we can stop somewhere below the peak of our vision. There are no excuses. We can blame no one else if we choose not to go. This truth is profoundly liberating. We are in charge of our own transcendence.

No one can make us a victim. No circumstance, no deprivation, no ignominy, no pain can render us a victim if we choose to be co-creators and set our faces to go to Jerusalem. Jesus's life sets a sublime example. He exercised the power to choose not to be a victim by transforming himself. He specifically accepted humanness to demonstrate humanity's power to overcome our own limits when we are aligned with God's design. That is the essence of his capacity to save us. He reveals to us that each of us can choose to transform ourselves by following his way: that is, by loving God above all else and our neighbor as our self.

"He died to save us" means he demonstrated once and for all that our potential, ultimately, is not to submit to involuntary death but to transform ourselves into a new being by becoming a new species, as different from *Homo sapiens sapiens* as we are from *Homo habilis*. We are the cause, not the effect, of our lives.

We can restore the Earth by recognizing it as part of our own body and healing it as we heal ourselves. We can transcend the Earth by recognizing that the existing planetary body does not limit us any more than our existing physical body is our ultimate limit. We can transform ourselves by the use of our total potential in alignment with the Designing Intelligence, or the tendency of universal evolution to develop more conscious life. Jerusalem no longer means sacrifice, crucifixion and death. It means self-actualization, transformation and life ever evolving.

We only need one example to know something is possible. One resurrection is all it takes to demonstrate the possibility of life everlasting. One moon landing was all that was necessary to demonstrate that we are not earthbound. One healing of the sick is all that is necessary to demonstrate that we need not be the victims of disease. This is true of all our powers. All we need is right here—except the awareness, the intention and the encouragement that form the natural next step in our conscious evolution.

Already we can do many miraculous things. This is the good news.

And he said unto another, "Follow me." But he said, "Lord, suffer me first to go and bury my father." Jesus said unto him, "Let the dead bury their dead: but go you and preach the kingdom of God." And another also said, "Lord, I will follow you; but let me first go bid them farewell, which are at home at my house." And Jesus said unto him, "No man, having put his hand to the plough, and looking back, is fit for the kingdom of God."

LUKE 9:59–62

Those who know the way and set out upon the path cannot turn back. Our life is like a rocket launch. During the countdown before the actual launch all is forgivable. Mistakes can be corrected. The launch can be postponed until all is ready. Even once the countdown has begun the launch can be held up until the final second. But once the launch has been initiated we must go the Whole Way—into a new orbit. Then, when all becomes peaceful again in the new orbit, next steps can be taken.

Jesus announced that the time is at hand. The Kingdom is coming. In evolutionary time, the last two thousand years are but a millisecond, barely visible within the context of the billions of years of the past and the billions of years yet to come. Yet they are the critical millisecond without which the next step cannot be taken. Two thousand years is not a long time for the launch of a whole species into universal life.

On planet Earth it would seem we have already gone past the point of no return. We have "blasted off." The danger of destruction is intense at this stage. Violence, pollution, economic collapse, starvation and poverty are no longer local problems.

These exponential problems are accelerating geometrically toward total systems breakdown.

In this same time frame, our new potentials can also grow exponentially, becoming more interactive, synergistic and mutually reinforcing. Exponential breakthroughs can overcome exponential breakdowns. That is the nature of evolutionary transformation. Thus the urgency felt by Jesus. Thus the urgency we feel today. The time was at hand then. It is even closer at hand now. Who knows how long the twinkling of a cosmic eye might be?

*A*nd he turned him unto his disciples, and said pri vately, "Blessed are the eyes which see the things that all of you see: for I tell you, that many prophets and kings have desired to see those things which all of you see, and have not seen them; and to hear those things which all of you hear, and have not heard them."

LUKE 10:23–24

The greatest privilege of human life on Earth is to experience God-consciousness.

All the beauties of friendship, human love, worldly success and creative function are impulses of light to prepare our eyes for the brilliance of our emancipation from the prison of limited self-consciousness. What we see is love, creativity, life ever evolving.

Fear vanishes. Barriers disappear. We are free of mortality and separation forever. One glimpse of this experience, and truly, the riches of the world become as nothing.

These glimpses of unity with God do not deny the riches of the world; they give sanctity to them. Riches are no longer something to possess and be possessed by. They exist for us to share, appreciate and nurture for the profit of the whole. We were born to be "rich," with all our needs met. That is the design.

The experience and the sharing of God-consciousness is the highest pleasure on Earth. It does not deny the others: It includes and thereby transmutes the more worldly goods with the alchemy of greater meaning.

The love of nature, the love between man and woman, the love of parents for children and the love of knowledge, adventure and creativity are freed from the stigma of selfishness when we experience them as elements of our co-creation with God. The terrible fear of loss, death, separation and disease is overcome by God-consciousness. We know that this consciousness is always ours. Nothing can take it away. Nothing can alter our connection.

When we experience this as a certainty, the material world is transformed. Appreciation of every leaf, every sunrise, every face, every good, every touch floods our being. God-consciousness makes us conscious of God in all there is.

❧

Now it came to pass, as they went, that he entered into a certain village: and a certain woman named Martha received him into her house. And she had a sister called Mary, which also sat at Jesus' feet, and heard his word. But Martha was cumbered about much serving, and came to him, and said, "Lord, do you not care that my sister has left me to serve alone? Bid her therefore that she help me." And Jesus answered and said unto her, "Martha, Martha, you are careful and troubled about many things: but one thing is necessary, and Mary has chosen that good part, which shall not be taken away from her."

LUKE 10:38–42

Who has not had lists of things that must be done that, in doing, obscure what is important to do? The tidying up of the ever disordering material world is an endless, hopeless task, even if needed. The mess will always return, to be cleaned up once again, because matter tends toward disorder. However, Spirit tends toward higher order, and eventually transforms disorder into greater coherence; not by focusing primarily on tidying up the existing system, but by placing attention on the higher system, the purpose, the aspiration, the Kingdom, the quantum transformation.

If the overextended molecules had "cleaned up" the macromolecular world by returning it to the old order, they would never have arrived at the new order—the cell.

If the single cells in the early seas of the first Earth had handled the stagnation and pollution brought on by over-population and resource depletion by cleaning up the sea, decreasing their numbers and consuming less, they would never have developed photosynthesis, multicellular organization, the biosphere, plants, animals and us. If we spend all our energy cleaning up the world that is in chaos, by attempting to return it to some past order, we will miss our opportunity to build the new world. The Marthas of history are always fussing about the mess we are in, and we are always in it. Mary paid attention to Jesus, "the good part." Through the Marys of the world, the new order, which will serve *all* people, will come to pass.

The present always appears to be disorderly because we are in it. It is a matter of perspective. We do not see the whole from the perspective of the part. If you were a cell in your own body working away at cleaning the blood or healing a wounded knee or growing a fingernail or being a freckle or fighting a virus, how amazed you'd be to see a picture of the whole being of which you are a vital part. That being looks nothing like you, the cell, who is building it.

An eye, composed of millions of cells, looks nothing like any of its component parts. We as individuals, working to keep our houses neat, to earn our living, may never catch a glimpse of the glory of the body of humankind—a coordinated whole system comprising the Earth, all nature, plants, animals, insects, cities, institutions, works, books, tools, ideas and systems now becoming a planetary whole and being born into universal consciousness and action.

Jesus had a vision of the whole, so clear that he communicated it in every gesture.

Each of us has at the center of our being a vision of that

whole. To overcome the Martha in ourselves and to affirm the Mary, we seek out the inner vision, the Kingdom within, the coded knowledge of what we already are at our highest, so we can act upon our full potential.

Each cell holds in its nucleus the information to build the whole body. All of that information is repressed except the specific information needed for the unique task of the individual cell. There are ways to reactivate the whole design in any cell, which is then capable of building a whole body out of its hidden, coded information in the DNA. It is called cloning.

In each person, dormant at the core of our consciousness, lies the information of the whole universal system of which we are infinitesimal parts. We are a microcosm of the whole system. We *are* atoms, molecules and cells. We hold in our being the reptilian, mammalian and early human experiences. Through our language and culture the genetic, neuronal library has extended beyond our genes— into words, pictures and numbers, to give us access to all recorded human history, and now to the history of the whole cosmos.

Jesus activated the necessary information to inspire our evolution. The very thought of his example reverberates to the deepest recesses of the coded information, which is, at this very moment, building our mammalian bodies and our big brains. The thought of his example reminds our mind-body systems that there is more to come, more to life than eating, sleeping, reproducing and dying.

Get ready to do something new! Get ready to love all life! Get ready be your full potential self. Get ready to generate new bodies capable of longevity! Get ready to live beyond the biosphere! Get ready to know God directly!

Thus says the thought of Jesus to our cells. The image of Jesus has, in two thousand years, awakened the aspiration of millions of people to be like him.

There is as yet unused information in our DNA—untriggered coils of chromosomes—awaiting what? Are they waiting for the right time in the history of the whole planetary body, the time when the whole planetary system awakens to its oneness, its terrestrial limits, its consciousness limits, and sets in motion the events leading toward the phase of universal life? Is that what the unused DNA, the as-yet untapped human potential, is waiting for?

The whole system has ways to communicate to its parts that the parts know not of.

The Science of Whole Systems is underdeveloped as yet. We have been learning the science of the parts, down to the infinitesimal particles that flit like shadows, composing the illusion of this too, too solid world. As the Science of Whole Systems is learned, we will discover how nature forms whole systems that are greater than, and different than, the sum of their parts.

Holism is inherent in the nature of reality, or we would not be here, trillions of cells organized in complex bodies, on a planet in a solar system in a galaxy in a universe of galaxies, all moving in a symphonic rhythm as yet inaudible to the human ear.

The ordering process of transformation—from hydrogen and helium atoms to us reading these words—is awesome to contemplate.

This process obviously cannot stop now with us. The ordering process for the next level of the whole system is at work, through the chaos and breakdown of old institutions and traditions. It uses disorder to build the new. Evolution "eats" entropy.

The Mary aspect is attempting to follow the design to the next level of order.

Martha cannot be excluded. Her work is needed still. The trains must run, the milk must be delivered, the firefighters must be prepared. But never will that worthy aspect of human nature build the new heavens and the new Earth. At a moment of quantum transformation, it is the Mary part of our nature that we must affirm and fulfill.

❧

"Are not five sparrows sold for two farthings, and not one of them is forgotten before God? But even the very hairs of your head are all numbered. Fear not therefore: all of you are of more value than many sparrows."

LUKE 12:6–7

Everything counts. Every thought, intention, desire and act is registered in the creation, recorded in the mind of the Creator, and effective within the whole, for better or for worse. As the human race gains capacity and power to affect the future, this saying becomes increasingly true.

The world is ever more sensitive to our individual acts. Having babies, driving cars, speaking cynically or acting violently on television affects the whole system increasingly as we grow more interdependent. Each of us is a formative part in the process of creation. We are actors in the play of history. We are co-authoring the drama the moment we are born. We cannot get off the stage. Everything we do is influential. Even doing "nothing" is influential.

It is said that there is a great record in the universe, a Library of Consciousness, a whole-system database, where every event that ever occurred in the universe is recorded. The universe never forgets. It remembers everything.

We know that every impression ever received by our sensory system is recorded on nerve cells in our brain and in our mind-body system. We also know that the design to build our bodies is recorded on the chromosomes in the nuclei of our cells. Is all of that, plus everything we do, recorded in the movie of creation, to be played back at the time of "judgment," when the evolutionary decision will be made by the process itself as to what evolves and what does not evolve? Billions of species are extinct. Nature does not preserve species. She selects for greater consciousness, freedom and synergistic order. This is a 13.8 billion year trend.

The key point for us is that every one of us is precious. Every individual is uniquely valuable. All people are created equal, endowed by the Creator with certain inalienable rights. The great institution of democratic government has sprung from the Christ's vision that every individual is of inestimable worth, sacred in the eyes of God.

This concept forms the pillar of the modern world that leads us to new worlds. Individual life does now count and is in essence boundless because it partakes of the nature of God, and deserves our unconditional love.

In the story of the rich man and the beggar Lazarus, the rich man was sent to hell; the beggar Lazarus to Heaven—into "Abraham's bosom." Seeing Lazarus, the rich man cried out to Abraham to send Lazarus to comfort him from the torments of the flames of hell fire. But Abraham said, "Son, remember that you in your lifetime received your good things, and likewise Lazarus evil things: but now he is comforted, and you are tormented." (Luke 16:25).

❧

"*And beside all this, between us and you there is a great gulf fixed: so that they which would pass from behind to you cannot; neither can they pass to us, that would come from thence.*" *Then he said, "I pray you therefore, father, that you would send him to my father's house: for I have five brethren; that he may testify unto them, lest they also come into this place of torment.*" *Abraham said unto him, "They have Moses and the prophets; let them hear them.*" *And he said, "Nay, father Abraham: but if one went unto them from the dead, they will repent.*" *And Abraham said unto him, "If they hear not Moses and the prophets, neither will they be persuaded, though one rose from the dead.*"

LUKE 16:26–31

After a certain point, irrevocable choices of conduct are made that result in unbridgeable differences. There is "a great gulf fixed" at the next stage of life between those who have chosen to love God and neighbor as themselves, and those who have chosen to remain in ego-centered selfishness, between those who have chosen to evolve and those who attempt to hold on to life as it was.

During this phase of earthly life, no choice is as yet irrevocable. We can make mistakes, self-correct, be forgiven by life itself, over and over again, until at a certain point a great divide emerges between those who have evolved to their next stage and those who have not.

We see it at the biological level with species that become overspecialized and then go extinct when the environmental conditions to which they have adapted change. Or even more pertinent, at some critical point *Homo sapiens sapiens* appeared and the Neanderthal became extinct, with no further choice to evolve. The difference between those now choosing self-transformation and those remaining self-centered is barely perceptible—a little more vigor, joy, excitement and hopefulness in the self-transcenders as contrasted with the self-centered population's depression, cynicism, exhaustion and hopelessness, with no attraction to the future within themselves or in the world.

In a few decades of quantum change, this difference will deepen. The self-transcenders will accelerate their potential exponentially, while the self-limiters will, in contrast, decelerate exponentially. After the quantum transformation, the great gulf will be fixed. Those who choose to transcend will not be able to go back to the limits of self-centered *Homo sapiens sapiens*; and those who limit themselves will no longer have the opportunity to take the needed steps to transform. *Homo sapiens sapiens* will have become *Homo universalis* on Earth and in space. Those remaining in self-centered consciousness will be either extinct on Earth like all past earlier humans, or so different that they seem to be a different species.

The conditions of rapid change foster innovations. However, once a new state of being becomes established the conditions of rapid change will no longer prevail. Innovations or cultural mutations will have already been selected for and against.

Another key lesson from the story of Lazarus is that if we cannot understand our potentials through natural demonstration, we are too insensitive to understand them from the perspective of supernormal events, which will therefore not be provided for us.

The rich man begged Abraham to send a resurrected Lazarus to his five brothers, to prove to them the reality of Heaven, causing them to be willing to repent. Abraham responded: "They have Moses and the prophets; let them hear them. ... If they hear not Moses and the prophets, neither will they be persuaded though one rose from the dead." (Luke 16:29, 31)

A key difference among people is the degree to which they are sensitive to their own potential and the collective potential of the human species. The capacity to be attracted by the magnetic field of the possible is essential for self-development. If we can feel the appeal of our self at the next stage of evolution, we will act upon it, and thereby do what we can to be a fully realized universal human. If we cannot feel this appeal, our own potential will appear unreal to us. We will not act upon it, and we will not become more than we now are.

We can see the outlines of the self-inflicted choice between heaven and hell every day in our own lives, as well as all around us. Do we choose love or fear? Do we choose to be a giver or a receiver? Do we choose to explore or retrench? We are each deciding our own futures, choice by tiny choice, day by day. Imperceptibly we are electing to grow or die.

❧

[Jesus is on his way to Jerusalem, knowing that
he will be slain to rise again on the third day.]

A nd when he was come near, he beheld the city,
and wept over it, saying, "If you had known,
even you, at least in this your day, the things which
belong unto your peace! But now they are hid from
your eyes. For the days shall come upon you, that
your enemies shall cast a trench about you, and com-
pass you round, and keep you in on every side, and
shall lay you even with the ground, and your children
within you; and they shall not leave in you one stone
upon another; because you knew not the time of your
visitation."

LUKE 19:41–44

Think of the pity we would have in our heart for an ancient
village that succumbed to the plague, while we held in our
hands the vaccine to free its people from all illness. They
rejected our help, for they preferred to cling to their old
ways rather than to accept the new. Think of the suffering
millions praying in the dark of hopelessness and disbelief.
Think how Jesus would look upon us now—and take his
vision to be our own.

We see it with the same tears he wept over Jerusalem, and
with the same resolve that he had to move toward the transformation—the resurrection—as the only demonstration

sufficiently real to work. But how tragic that we do not already know "the things which belong unto our peace."

The Kingdom is already here, if we but knew it. The time of our "visitation" is upon us. The potentials have been given us. Let us dry our tears and activate our capacities, in time.

[*The chief priest and the scribes were angered and threatened by Jesus's obvious mastery over the people and condemnation of their own shortcomings. They sent spies, who were to pretend they were good men, to catch him in a blasphemous statement, which would authorize them to imprison him, but Jesus outwitted their legalism at every turn. The Sadducees were confounded. Finally Jesus turned to the people and said:*]

"*Beware of the scribes, which desire to walk in long robes, and love greetings in the markets, and the highest seats in the synagogues, and the chief rooms at feasts; which devour widows' houses, and for a show make long prayers: the same shall receive greater damnation.*"

LUKE 20:46–47

The scribes were furious, more determined than ever to destroy Jesus, for he had humiliated them before the people. There comes a time when accommodation to the negative forces is no longer necessary or appropriate. When is that time? It is when we have discovered that the negative elements cannot be attracted to the positive.

Then it is no longer appropriate to waste our energy persuading the negative to become positive, or attempting to make them see us as a positive force. If we cannot convert or ignore the opposition, if the opposition is unalterably determined to exterminate us, what does Jesus's example tell us to do?

First, reveal them publicly for what they are. Second, do not try to destroy them by employing their own means. Do not fight them by becoming negative, for thus they have "won" by causing us to reduce ourselves to their level. Beware of becoming the enemy to overcome the enemy.

We win by overcoming our own self-limits. We win by becoming more, higher and better than we were before, attracting all who oppose us to do the same, in order to achieve their own fulfillment. Not "an eye for an eye and a tooth for a tooth," but rather forgiveness and self-transformation. Compassion and co-creation. Love our enemies. Do not react in anger. Convert our collective strength from defense to transformation, from star wars to star worlds.

On the social/political level this means to take our power and massively apply it to the restoration of the Earth, the healing of the sick, the feeding of the hungry, the education of the young and the exploration and development of the universe, with love.

Are there some great enough in the world to turn negative reaction to positive pro-action? Yes there are. The co-creators beneath the surface of the body politic are connecting, self-perfecting and preparing, at this very moment, to unite with others so attracted. The hour of our emergence is at hand.

*A*nd he came out, and went, as he was known, to the mount of Olives; and his disciples also followed him. And when he was at the place, he said unto them, "Pray that all of you enter not into temptation." And he was withdrawn from them about a stone's cast, and kneeled down, and prayed, saying, "Father, if you be willing, remove this cup from me: nevertheless not my will, but yours, be done." And there appeared an angel unto him from heaven, strengthening him. And being in an agony he prayed more earnestly: and his sweat was as it were great drops of blood falling down to the ground. And when he rose up from prayer, and was come to his disciples, he found them sleeping for sorrow, And said unto them, "Why sleep all of you? rise and pray, lest all of you enter into temptation."

LUKE 22:39–46

Let us have compassion for the suffering of Jesus: that he freely chose to demonstrate the power of the resurrection rather than succumb to the temptation of power over the existing world. He felt agony. The sweat poured from his face. He knew the horror of the scourging and the crucifixion to come. He occupied a body with a nervous system as sensitive to pain as our own, with a spirit far more sensitive to God than our own. He was, and is, God made flesh

201

in order to transform the flesh, before our very eyes, so we will know that we can do as he did, and even more can we do.

Compassion for a God-man, the Creator? Yes! For we are now far enough developed to imagine what it will be like when we ourselves become co-creators, heirs of God, joint heirs with Christ. We are not disciples who sleep. We risk ourselves with Jesus to co-create the new world. We can feel compassion for a God-man as we become godlike ourselves, and foresee the problems we too may have.

Imagine how we will feel when we have co-created little new worlds in space and they perhaps begin to "misbehave," spreading the killing into the universe and contaminating the infinite with the selfish screams of a still infantile humanity—us. As we are about to become co-creators of worlds, our awe in the face of God includes a deep compassion and understanding.

We will study the Jehovah principle—that aspect of God that creates worlds. What can we learn from the lessons of the creation of this world as we begin to co-create new worlds? What can we learn from our own experience that will help us avoid repeating the agony that we have suffered on planet Earth? Will we bring carnivorous animals onto new worlds in space? Will we alter genes that carry diseases? Will we incarcerate ourselves as criminals, or reprogram our nervous systems and brains through mind-altering techniques? Will we co-create new species, bio-organisms to perform new functions, through recombinant DNA, as once the birds were new, the mammals were new, the human brain was new?

These are questions modern society now asks—usually without the perspective of billions of years of transformation—without the awareness that it is natural for us to become godlike, in the image of God. The guidelines for godliness and the curriculum for co-creators have not yet been written.

An introduction to the guidelines and the curriculum are the Old and New Testaments, which take us from the creation of this world to the gates of new worlds. From Genesis to Revelation to Resurrection to Pentecost, the Intention of Creation has been described. These books carry us through the transformation to the New Jerusalem: the beginning of our lives as co-creators. The Bible prepares us for the next, as-yet unwritten phase of evolution. The principles are clear.

- Do unto others as you would have them do unto you.
- Love God above all else.
- Love your neighbor as yourself.

In the twenty-first century we add:

- *Learn the invisible processes of creation;* and
- *Know more of how God works in order to work consciously with Universal Intelligence.*

These last two are new. They awaited science and technology before they could be proclaimed and understood.

We are given the power to know how God works in order to work like apprentice gods. We have to start somewhere, sometime, consciously knowing we are to inherit the Kingdom. Now is the time. For better or worse, God has given this generation on planet Earth the early knowledge of how nature works. Let us pray above all else that our minds may be connected to the Mind of God, that the maturing intellect may marry pure love and know from within, as well as through science and technology, how to do the works of God.

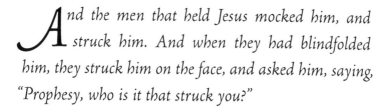

*A*nd while he yet spoke, behold a multitude, and he that was called Judas, one of the twelve, went before them, and drew near unto Jesus to kiss him. But Jesus said unto him, "Judas, betray you the Son of Man with a kiss?" When they which were about him saw what would follow, they said unto him, "Lord, shall we strike with the sword?" And one of them stroke the servant of the high priest, and cut off his right ear. And Jesus answered and said, "Suffer all of you thus far." And he touched his ear, and healed him.

LUKE 22:47–51

Forgiveness. Forgiveness. Forgive to prepare the way for the transformation.

*A*nd the men that held Jesus mocked him, and struck him. And when they had blindfolded him, they struck him on the face, and asked him, saying, "Prophesy, who is it that struck you?"

LUKE 22:63–64

What is this horrible tendency toward useless cruelty? The history of the human race is a saga of magnificent intelligence, constantly interlaced with hideous torture, often in the name of the good—God, home and the motherland. Is it true that our nervous system and brain are still evolving, that better connections are emerging between the old brain, the neo-cortex and the spiritual facility?

It must be so, if we are to evolve to our next stage. For a creature whose emotions, reasoning mind and spirit are misaligned could never handle the powers of co-creation. Only those individuals capable of full body-mind-heart-spiritual alignment can evolve. This is the *key* personal factor.

The big brain evolved very rapidly and has not yet been fully activated. *Homo sapiens sapiens* are a young species. Only fifty to sixty thousand years ago we emerged in self-reflective consciousness. Both written language and the most ancient civilization are no more than five thousand years old. The great spiritual avatars arrived on Earth only a few thousand years ago. Modern civilization, which brought education, mobility, choice, good health, freedom and creature comforts to millions of ordinary people, began several hundred years ago. Our evolutionary technologies of transcendence—astronautics, genetics, cybernetics, nanotechnology—are only a few decades old. We can take hope from these dates, which attest to the fact that humanity has just begun.

As Jesus said, "Father, forgive them, for they know not what they do." (Luke 23:34) We are young.

THE GOSPEL

ACCORDING TO JOHN

❦

*A*nd the Word was made flesh, and dwelt among us, (and we beheld his glory, the glory as of the only begotten of the Father), full of grace and truth.

JOHN 1:14

Jesus perfectly represents the Mind of God, the Intention of Creation for this coming phase of the development of human life, as it is manifested on planet Earth at the edge of a galaxy called the Milky Way in a universe of billions of galaxies. Jesus embodied the stage of being through which consciousness must pass to enter the universal phase of co-creative life, resonating accurately with the Mind of God. Jesus embodied the stage of being natural to a planetary civilization passing from its phase of terrestrial self-consciousness to universal co-creative consciousness.

He reflects God's intention that human life can transcend

its mortal phase and become imperishable beyond the limits of planet-and body-boundness. He showed the way for us to attain universal life by his life, death, resurrection and ascension. He is the map of human evolution. In life: put the Kingdom first and love your neighbor as yourself, forgive the sin of separation, abstain from aggressive or reactive power.

In death: transcend it by gaining continuity of consciousness and a new body sensitive to your thought. In resurrection: begin your new life as a co-creator in a universe of unlimited possibilities and forms of life, ascend, enter the next stage of evolution and experience what we will be like after this period of quantum transformation is over.

Imagine the universe, with billions and billions of galaxies, multitudes of solar systems, some of which have life comparable to our own, some with life younger than our own, some with life more mature than our own. Every planetary species that develops sufficiently to understand the laws of the universe develops intellect, science and technology, thereby learning to work with those laws to design new technological bodies to extend capacity.

These technological bodies grow so powerful they eventually disturb the ecology of their planetary system. The capacity of life, as it enters its terrestrial-technological phase, is too powerful to be contained within any biosphere in the universe. It is too powerful to continue to use power aggressively, that is, against itself. The nuclear bomb symbolizes such a leap in technological power.

Every planetary civilization hits the same set of limits— resource limits, consciousness limits, population limits, biospheric limits. Planets are wombs for universal life. They contain it. They are designed to conceive it, gestate it and give birth to it. Jesus embodied the consciousness required to graduate from terrestrial to universal life.

Human self-consciousness is an appropriate phase serving as the link between terrestrial and universal life. It cannot make the quantum leap to the next stage without passing through Christ consciousness, which represents knowing the Intention of Creation as love of God above all else and our neighbor and nature as ourselves, that is, recognizing the pattern in the process, and accepting the pattern as our own.

The marriage of human consciousness with Christ consciousness is natural for a species to pass from creature to co-creator. The marriage of Christ and Eve symbolizes this union. Christ is the co-creative consciousness that already attunes directly to the will of the Creator. Christ already experiences the ecstatic love of God as a natural state of being. Eve symbolizes human intellect seeking to know God through the probing of the mind in a state of self-consciousness—still under the illusion that creatures are separated from their Creator.

Eve, human intellect, probes to the heart of the invisible processes of creation—the gene, the atom, the brain, the star—and is stopped by its limits. There at the veil between the flesh and the Word, Eve calls for Christ and asks him to wed her, to transform her, joining his body to hers, transfiguring hers, carrying her beyond the limits of her five mammalian senses, to know God and do the Will of God, directly, always and forever.

The symbolic marriage of Christ and Eve is the entrance into co-creative life. This union empowers us to create acts according to the word of God. Everywhere throughout the universe, when life reaches its planetary limits, Christ consciousness appears and demonstrates the reality of the post-self-centered phase of consciousness. Everywhere through the universe, after Christ consciousness first is made flesh (as it was for us two thousand years ago), the self-conscious flesh rapidly matures its democratic institutions and scientific-technological capacities.

Eve, everywhere, seeks to marry Christ in order to unite with God. The maturing intellect everywhere becomes attracted to Christ as the way toward the co-creation of new life. The universe is full of weddings. It abounds with celebrations of the Second Comings of Christ to ripe and ready planets whose human intellects are longing to co-create with God, rather than to self-limit and to self-destruct through the misuse of power.

The next day John saw Jesus coming unto him, and said, "Behold the Lamb of God, which takes away the sin of the world! This is he of whom I said, 'After me comes a man which is preferred before me: for he was before me.'"

JOHN 1:29–30

The next stage of human being, as demonstrated by Jesus, is one in which we always know we are joined with the Creator. There exists no separation to be overcome. There is, therefore, no "sin" at the next stage. The supersensory channel of cognition that was fully developed in Jesus, a future human, matures in us, as a new norm.

The five senses are now a normal capacity. Once they were nonexistent, as in the single-celled organisms floating in the seas of the early Earth. Could the single cells see, hear, taste, touch or smell? No, because the sensory organs of perception could not exist in a single-celled animal. With multicellular life, the senses developed. With the human brain, self-consciousness developed.

Several thousand years ago a few individuals developed Universal Consciousness, the blissful overcoming of self-consciousness through union of the human personality with the soul, with God. The channel of supersensory cognition flickered on. In these early examples of God-consciousness, the connection could usually be preserved through extreme disciplines such as meditation, isolation, fasting, chanting and single-pointed attention on God. In Jesus, the channel of cognition of God was stabilized at the new norm. He was able to use that channel to demonstrate the endurance and operation of consciousness beyond the five senses and even through the death of the mammalian body and brain. He was able to reawaken that mechanism and transform it through a consciousness that obviously did not depend upon the body for its survival.

John the Baptist represents the human awareness that we are as yet an unfinished species and are to become more than we now are—that we are to become Christed beings. He was looking for the Son of man because he was aware of that potential in himself. Yet, he was also aware that he had not yet evolved enough to actualize it. "After me comes a man which is preferred before me: for he was before me."

Our potential preexists its actualization. We know our potential because it is coded in our consciousness, just as the full human is coded in the invisible nucleus of a fertilized egg. We are attracted to our potential before it manifests because we possess a natural evolutionary urge to be, know and do *more*. It is a 13.8 billion year tradition, written even deeper than the genetic level; for it existed before life, in atoms and molecules—urging, driving, motivating and inspiring elements to coalesce and evolve to ever higher levels of consciousness, freedom and purposefulness.

John the Baptist knew, before he saw Jesus, that one greater than he was coming.

You and I know we can become greater than we yet are. We are John the Baptist, baptizing ourselves into our full humanhood, heralding our own true appearance.

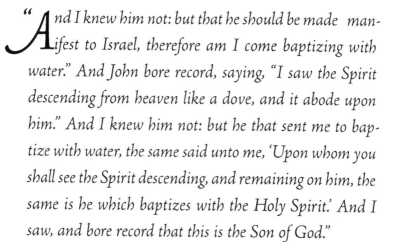

"*And I knew him not: but that he should be made manifest to Israel, therefore am I come baptizing with water.*" *And John bore record, saying, "I saw the Spirit descending from heaven like a dove, and it abode upon him." And I knew him not: but he that sent me to baptize with water, the same said unto me, 'Upon whom you shall see the Spirit descending, and remaining on him, the same is he which baptizes with the Holy Spirit.' And I saw, and bore record that this is the Son of God.*"

JOHN I:31–34

From an evolutionary perspective, John the Baptist is ourselves bearing witness to the coming of our own potential, the future human not knowing itself fully, yet knowing something greater must surely come. We baptize ourselves with water, a symbol of life, yet knowing we need a stronger current than water to awaken our full potential. We need something more than we can do for ourselves alone.

When we see the example of Jesus, like us, but not us, who is electrified with the attraction of God, we are profoundly moved, and wish to be baptized by the Holy Spirit, the direct communication from God. Jesus reveals ourselves in the future, when the Holy Spirit shall descend upon us and remain within us, and when we shall have fully developed our supersensory channel to God. But we cannot do this by human will alone. We need grace, the reaching toward us of that toward which we are stretching.

Again the next day after John stood, and two of his disciples; and looking upon Jesus as he walked, he said, "Behold the Lamb of God!" And the two disciples heard him speak, and they followed Jesus.

JOHN 1:35–37

Our recognition of what we can become is essential to our becoming it. Our acknowledgement of our own potential is essential to our actualizing it. Our willingness to announce to the world that we are to become co-creators is essential for helping others who are also ready to do so. Those who announce and act upon their potential serve as beacons of light for others Those who publicly baptize themselves as ready to transform, ready to be born again, ready to take steps to become a Christlike human, pave the way for all who follow.

"And the two disciples heard him speak, and they followed Jesus." The path becomes clearer as more of us walk it. We overcome the obstacles so that those who follow may move more swiftly through the great transition from us as we are now to us as we will be: the universal human.

⌀

*H*e [Nicodemus] came to Jesus by night, and said unto him, "Rabbi, we know that you are a teacher come from God: for no man can do these miracles that you do, except God be with him." Jesus answered and said unto him, "Verily, verily, I say unto you, except a man be born again, he cannot see the kingdom of God." Nicodemus said unto him, "How can a man be born when he is old? Can he enter the second time into his mother's womb, and be born? "Jesus answered, "Verily, verily, I say unto you, except a man be born of water and of the Spirit, he cannot enter into the kingdom of God. That which is born of the flesh is flesh; and that which is born of the Spirit is spirit."

JOHN 3:2–6

What does it mean to be "born again" from an evolutionary perspective, taking into account the full range of our collective capacities to become a universal species? It means to make the choice to transform the *whole* way. The born-again experience, as it has been known on the Earth during the terrestrial, self-conscious phase, has been a psychological experience of enlightenment, of energy rising from sexual procreation to spiritual co-creation, a mystical experience of bursting out of the shell of self-consciousness into unity with the all.

No one can see the Kingdom of God in a limited stage of self-consciousness. The psychological transformation is essential to seeing the Kingdom. Yet there is more than the psychological to the born-again experience as we begin to cross the great divide from *Homo sapiens sapiens* to *Homo universalis*. "Born again" in the future will mean to transform our bodies from degenerating to regenerating, to new bodies more sensitive to thought. Does the electricity of the super-sensory channel of cognition change the body at the atomic level (as in kundalini experiences), charging the particles with new frequencies, preparing our flesh that now must die to become flesh that can be resurrected, in a transformed, "glorified" state?

If this quality of being becomes a reality for us, as a species, then to be "born again" will come to mean to change our bodies to a less corruptible form, until at last we have continuity of consciousness in bodies that can materialize and dematerialize, ascend and descend as Jesus did. Can you imagine Jesus getting cancer, hardening of the arteries or sinking into old age? Can you imagine us being in the Kingdom with five senses trapped in aging bodies over which we have little control? Is that suitable to the sons and daughters of God? What becomes of the flesh of a totally God-conscious person?

If Jesus is our example, then it transforms into a new body, resembling a light body that can materialize and dematerialize, appear and disappear, as Jesus demonstrated after the resurrection. To be born again at the next stage of evolution means to change our body as we change our mind, to become ever more closely attuned to the Intelligence of Creation.

❧

"And as Moses lifted up the serpent in the wilderness, even so must the Son of Man be lifted up: that whosoever believes in him should not perish, but have eternal life."

JOHN 3:14–15

Jesus knew he was to demonstrate the reality of the resurrection. The serpent symbolizes an irresistible energy that is leading us toward life ever evolving. First the serpent tempted Eve to eat of the Tree of Knowledge of Good and Evil. It attracted her beyond the animal/human world that knew no separation from the Creator. Then self-awareness came. We felt alone, different, afraid, guilty, incomplete. We forgot our Creator. We listened to inner voices, urging us to do more, be more and become more.

The hunger of Eve awoke to reunite with God.

The great world religions birthed out of the experiences of a few enlightened geniuses experiencing, transmitting and teaching a new stage of being for humanity. The multitudes prayed in the dark, believing in the reality of the potential, yet not quite prepared to experience it personally. Then Jesus came and demonstrated the transformation into a new body—from living to dying to being born again in a new body, literally ascending to another dimension of life. He introduced the cycle of universal life on planet Earth. By believing in him, we believe in our own capacity to be like him. With that intention alive in our hearts, we shall be like him. We shall not perish. We shall have eternal life. And we knew it all the time.

"For God so loved the world, that he gave his only begotten Son, that whosoever believes in him should not perish, but have everlasting life."

JOHN 3:16

To lift us up beyond our early human condition, a godlike one descended into the human condition to demonstrate that we could all be lifted up into the light of life everlasting. God loves the world. The Intention of Creation is for the transformation of the material world, not its degradation. From atom to molecule to cell to human to Christ, the material world progressed. The Intention of Creation is to bring order out of chaos, consciousness out of unconsciousness, love out of selfishness, immortality out of death.

If we love the Divine Intelligence that created us, how could that Intelligence not love us? But if God loves us, how do we explain suffering? How can God be omniscient, omnipotent, omnipresent—and permit the innocent suffering of a single child, much less the agonizing crucifixion of Jesus? The only answer must be freedom. God so loved the world, so loved the human creature, that freedom was designed into the nature of reality. At the prehuman level, freedom is revealed in the continual process of selection for beings that cooperate best—from cell to animal to human to Christ. We also see freedom in the continual experimentation through genetic mutation and selection. Ours is not a robotic universe. Freedom abounds in the system—from the origin of creation, through the five mass extinctions that came before us, through the billions of species already extinct. And now, for the very first time in this planetary life cycle, comes a species aware that it can cause its own extinction and that of billions of other species or, through conscious self-evolution, that it can free itself to evolve to the next order of being.

Evolution by choice, not chance, has entered the process of evolution. It is our choice whether we live or die, whether we love or hate, co-operate or compete, adapt or transcend. Freedom of choice becomes deeper and deeper as we approach the great divide between this phase of human life and whatever is to come. "He that believes on the Son has everlasting life: and he that believes not the Son shall not see life; but the wrath of God abides on him." (John 3:36) The choice is definitive indeed.

⌒⌣

"Say not all of you, 'There are yet four months, and then comes harvest?' Behold, I say unto you, Lift up your eyes, and look on the fields; for they are white already to harvest. And he that reaps receives wages, and gathers fruit unto life eternal: that both he that sows and he that reaps may rejoice together. And herein is that saying true, 'One sows, and another reaps.' I sent you to reap that whereon all of you bestowed no labor: other men labored, and all of you are entered into their labors."

JOHN 4:35–38

The generation that lives through the tribulations and reaches the time when the new order of the ages begins will reap the harvest of the labors of all previous generations, of all life, of all creation. Once the process of transformation begins, it accelerates exponentially. Time collapses in a multidimensional leap from here to there. The connections among the new potentials, the networking of networks, the synergy of synergies, overcome time as we know it. Time is events. When events speed up, everything seems to happen at once; time itself speeds up and almost disappears. It becomes an instantaneous synchronicity of interconnected events, all operating simultaneously to transform the world.

In the twinkling of an eye, we shall be changed. Those who are self-selected, those who have chosen to respond to the call during the days of darkness and unknowing, will be the most privileged generation on Earth. The cells alive in the fetus at the time of birth harvest the labors of all those cells that built the baby in the womb, knowing not what or why they build. The people alive at the Quantum Transformation will live to see the new Earth, harmonious and beautiful, and new worlds in space, staging grounds for Universal Humanity, co-creating in conscious harmony with the mind of the Creator.

They will love to be with Christ, to be like Christ, to be fully human at last—the goal of the labor of the ages of history achieved. The hunger of Eve fulfilled. The thirst of Prometheus quenched. The wings of Icarus repaired. The lives of the saints renewed. The time of the birth complete. The joy of God shared with the children making their transition into universal life.

***

"*Verily, verily, I say unto you, the Son can do nothing of himself, but what he sees the Father do: for what things whatsoever he does, these also does the Son likewise. For the Father loves the Son, and shows him all things that himself does: and he will show him greater works than these, that all of you may marvel.*"

JOHN 5:19–20

Jesus wipes away the existential fear of acting out of our power all alone, in a meaningless universe composed of material atoms going down to an inevitable heat death. He asserts that it is by, through and with the power of the whole creation that he acts. His capacities are a reflection of the capacities of God. His will is aligned with the Intention of Creation. His life is infused with the power of God, whose desire is for the elevation of matter to spirit to life everlasting. His life cannot fail because it partakes of the pattern of creation. Our life cannot fail if we recognize that we are like him, and prepare ourselves to do as he did.

⌒

"Verily, verily, I say unto you, he that believes on me has everlasting life. I am that bread of life. Your fathers did eat manna in the wilderness, and are dead. This is the bread which comes down from heaven, that a man may eat thereof, and not die. I am the living bread which came down from heaven: if any man eat of this bread, he shall live forever: and the bread that I will give is my flesh, which I will give for the life of the world." The Jews therefore strove among themselves, saying, "How can this man give us his flesh to eat?" Then Jesus said unto them, "Verily, verily, I say unto you, except all of you eat the flesh of the Son of man, and drink his blood, all of you have no life in you.

Whoso eats my flesh, and drinks my blood, has eternal life; and I will raise him up at the last day. For my flesh is food indeed, and my blood is drink indeed. He that eats my flesh, and drinks my blood, dwells in me, and I in him. As the living Father has sent me, and I live by the Father: so he that eats me, even he shall live by me. This is that bread which came down from heaven: not as your fathers did eat manna, and are dead: he that eats of this bread shall live for ever.

JOHN 6:47–58

Reality, reality, reality of the transformation of the body by eating, incorporating, becoming the body of Christ—this is the promise. Eternal life is not a metaphor for psychological enlightenment alone. Eternal life is not a metaphysical, disembodied future. Eternal life is not a condition comparable to the past condition of the human race. Even the highest examples of the past do not represent the potentials of the future for life everlasting.

Even our fathers who ate manna with Moses, leaving the bondage of Egypt under the guidance of God, do not represent the fulfillment of the evolutionary potential inherent in the intention of God, for they died. Their bodies decomposed. They did not rise again. They did not live forever. The Intention of Creation offers a new stage of being for those who choose to follow the way of Jesus.

We are to dare to go the whole way with no self-imposed limits. We are to dare to realize the reality of the resurrection collectively, as the transformation of humanity from *Homo sapiens sapiens* to *Homo universalis*. The time is now ripe. We are to exercise our potentials, in faith that it is the Intention of Creation for humanity to transform into a universal, everlasting, ever-evolving species in a universe of billions of other planets that may have life comparable to our own.

We are to coordinate all our evolutionary capacities in consciousness expansion, in space development, in longevity, healing and rejuvenation, in cooperative organization, in education, in productivity, in communication, and have faith that victory is inevitable because it is the irresistible direction of evolution to higher consciousness, freedom, order and love.

The intention of Creation is that flesh-and-blood humans will become universal cosmic Christlike beings. The Kingdom of Heaven is at hand. Events are accelerating. Time is collapsing. The new order is emerging. Let those who have eyes to see, see. Let those who have ears to hear, hear. *Know* and believe we can do it! That is the message of Jesus.

His news was too good to be believed by the learned scribes and Pharisees. The simple people—the fishermen, the publicans, the poor in spirit who hungered after righteousness—believed then; they carried the torch of faith through thousands of years, and they hold it now as the hour of transformation is at hand.

Those people of faith believed in the reality of an unlimited future. In the darkness of ignorance, disease, tyranny and death, in churches large and small, in hovels and homes across the world, they prayed to God to help them become like Jesus, to do as he said and inherit the Kingdom. Their faith is an awesome leap of imagination.

It is out of the faith of these millions of ordinary men and women that the future of humanity is being born.

~

"But there are some of you that believe not." For Jesus knew from the beginning who they were that believed not, and who should betray him. And he said, "Therefore said I unto you, that no man can come unto me, except it were given unto him of my Father." From that time many of his disciples went back, and walked no more with him.

JOHN 6:64–66

The reality of the promise of ever-evolving life was too challenging to many who heard. Then as now, sisters are separated from brothers, and husbands from wives, by the capacity to respond to hope of this magnitude. This light burns too brightly for many to bear.

Many say it is unnatural for mere humans to aspire to be godlike. Who are we to change the way it has always been? We cannot even handle our problems in the present, and yet here you are talking about activating our powers for universal life? What about the poor? What about urban blight? What about war? What about selfishness? What about climate change and the loss of our life-support systems? We can't overcome these immediate obstacles, and yet you who have hope in your hearts are trying to make us believe in an unlimited future? Thus even to this day, the believers and disbelievers separate, each to his or her reward.

"And all of you shall know the truth, and the truth shall make you free."

The truth lies in the fundamental laws laid down by the Intention of Creation. We discover the truth, the Intention of God, from without and from within. From without, we witness billions of years of evolution, from the origin of the universe to those of us who are now seeking the truth. What intention do we see there? We see an evolutionary spiral, proceeding quantum leap by quantum leap. We see the spiraling rise of consciousness, freedom, order, love and a growing desire to know God. We see that the Intention of Creation is to generate ever-higher forms of creative life, through ever-more synergistic whole systems.

As we learn the laws, we find that we ourselves can transform by following the law to its ultimate. We left the Earth in space rockets not by ignoring the law, or by denying the law, but by knowing the law of gravity: how fast we must accelerate to leave the pull of Earth. We did not break the law of gravity; we *used* our knowledge of it to set us free of the gravity of Earth. In this same way we shall one day escape the gravity of the solar system and go far, far into the galactic light.

We shall also transform our bodies, not by ignorance of the law or through denial of the law, but by knowing the law. How does our genetic code communicate with our cells and inform them to degenerate? Which genes are responsible for the clock of death? Can we reach them? How does our mind-brain-body system work? How can we communicate our intention to transform to our nerves and cells, which are following the design encoded in their nuclei? As we discover the truth, the truth sets us free. We come not to deny the law, but to fulfill it.

What is the truth as experienced from within? From within, we sense as the truth that which motivates us to be more, love more and become our full potential selves, whatever that might be. We sense the truth of own intelligent longing to know the Source that created us. We sense it as our love longing to unite with what loves us. We sense it as our desire to become more than we are—to become as Jesus, a glorified being, an ever-living Son or Daughter of God. We sense it as the essence of ourselves united with the Creator of it all. We sense the truth from without and from within as the irresistible intention to become a co-creator with the Consciousness of God.

The truth is a mighty current that draws the creature to the Creator. It is the pattern in the process of evolution. As we discover those patterns and resonate with those patterns, we become more and more like God, which empowers us to *be* the Truth, the Light and the Way.

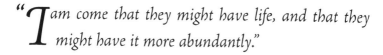

"*I am come that they might have life, and that they might have it more abundantly.*"

JOHN 10:10

The truth is that we, and future generations, shall have more abundant life. The transformation has been awaiting the perfect organic timing on planet Earth. The metacrises and the metaopportunities of the present time in history have had to ripen and mature, so that the old forms can pass away and the new forms rise up and prevail. Let us not be disheartened that we have waited so long. How long has God waited for us to mature enough to see, and desire to work with it on the universal scale? Think of the patience of God, and be equally patient.

❧

"*I am the good shepherd, and know my sheep, and am known of mine. As the Father knows me, even so know I the Father: and I lay down my life for the sheep. And other sheep I have, which are not of this fold: them also I must bring, and they shall hear my voice; and there shall be one fold, and one shepherd.*"

JOHN 10:14–16

There are many great prophets, saints, teachers and ways to God that carry us to the end of terrestrial history and to the death of the individual body, preparing the way for whatever life after death may be. Jesus carried us a step beyond the end of terrestrial history and the death of the individual body. His life went beyond personal death into a glorified body. Jesus's promise to the society of believers who choose to follow his way to God is a *new* Heaven and a *new* Earth—a transformed material world.

All those who choose to carry on the work of evolution by transforming themselves will come into his fold. There shall be one fold and one shepherd for those who choose to become a universal species. "And I, if I be lifted up from the earth, will draw all men unto Me" (John 12:32).

⌒

Simon Peter said unto him, "Lord, where go you?" Jesus answered him, "Where I go, you can not follow me now; but you shall follow me afterwards."

"In my Father's house are many mansions: if it were not so, I would have told you. I go to prepare a place for you. And if I go and prepare a place for you, I will come again, and receive you unto myself; that where I am, there all of you may be also."

JOHN 13:36, 14:2–3

Jesus promised us that he was preparing the way for us to do as he did, but that it is not yet the time. Our hour has not yet come.

"In my Father's house are many mansions." The universe is filled with diversity. The Kingdom of Heaven is not a single state of being. The next step of evolution will emancipate as much newness as have the previous billions of years. Think of the diversity that arose after the first fish colonized the dry land—amphibians, reptiles, insects, birds, mammals, early humans—and now us, ready to leave this Earth alive, to explore outer space, transform our bodies, attune more deeply to the creative intention—breaking the bonds of self-consciousness and mortality.

Imagine the diversity that will follow after we have taken the Christlike step. Surely what shall follow from that evolutionary step will be more diverse than any prior step of which we know. For we are born into a universe of billions of galaxies beyond planet Earth!

It is not only what will come from our own transformed seed, as future humans interact with new environments in space. It is *also* what will come of our interactions with other forms of consciousness and other intelligences that exist in alternate dimensions of reality.

No wonder Jesus said we would do more than he did. He must have experienced life on Earth two thousand years ago as modern humans would experience life in a Paleolithic cave. The capacities of humans in his day were so underdeveloped compared to his own, that he could tell us very little of what might be coming. Even the little he revealed was more good news than most people could believe.

The Old and New Testament take us to the end of a humanity that is bound to planet Earth, self-centered consciousness and mortal bodies. They give us a glimpse of the next chapter of evolution. Yet looking back toward the billions of years of transformation that lay behind us, and forward toward the countless billions of years beyond us, we realize that human civilization itself is but a brief period. Consider the patriarchy, the written word, all our religions, science, democracy and individualism. All of these great human achievements prepared the way for the post-transition era, when we would gain radical new powers of co-destruction and co-creation. "I go to prepare a place for you." Jesus was telling us there is a real future beyond this phase of existence. He knew, because he had been there.

"*Verily, verily, I say unto you, he that believes on me, the works that I do shall he do also; and greater works than these shall he do; because I go unto my Father. And whatsoever all of you shall ask in my name, that will I do, that the Father may be glorified in the Son. If all of you shall ask any thing in my name, I will do it."*

JOHN 14:12–14

The "greater works" we shall do are not done by human will alone. Those of us who believe in the capacity to do as Jesus did will do these works. Through our belief we activate the creative process within ourselves. "Believing in Jesus" means following in his path from the commandment to love each other and to love God to the reality of the transformation of our whole being to new life. Humans who remain in self-centered consciousness will not do these greater works.

The great works of the past phase of evolution are complete; they ended with the invention of the atomic bomb, the natural signal that we could self-destruct or co-create with powers we used to attribute only to our gods. The period since 1945 is part of the transition to the new Heaven and Earth—the *next* phase of our evolution. We are already experiencing the tribulations. The hour of the unexpected is at hand. Anything that we ask for that moves us along the path, as part of the natural direction of evolution, shall be granted.

∽

"*But the Comforter, which is the Holy Spirit, whom the Father will send in my name, he shall teach you all things, and bring all things to your remembrance, whatsoever I have said unto you.*"

JOHN 14:26

We remember the future, that which we can potentially be, because it has already been told to us, albeit in parables and symbols. Jesus has told us, and demonstrated by his own example, what the future human can do. When we read his words, they strike a note of deep familiarity, not only because we have heard them so often, but also because they trigger the dormant potentials in us to fulfill the intent of those words.

They ease the labor pains we suffer in the natural process of giving birth to our full potential selves. The words stimulate the cells, the nerves, the brain and the body to focus upon the transformation of human nature. To the degree that we pay attention to these words, we stretch our capacities to fulfill their intention, which is that we are to become Christlike humans ourselves.

The memory of the future is coded in our genes and in our higher selves, through which we have access to the larger design of the whole system. Jesus awoke the memory of the future in us. He said the time would come when we would follow him the whole way to Universal Humanity. The time is at hand for those who have eyes to see and ears to hear.

"If all of you keep my commandments, all of you shall abide in my love; even as I have kept my Father's commandments, and abide in his love. These things have I spoken unto you, that my joy might remain in you, and that your joy might be full."

JOHN 15:10–11

Joy is the sign of connectedness with God. If we feel joy, we know we are acting out of love for our own fulfillment and the fulfillment of the world. Our compass is joy. Our reward is joy. Our future is joy. Our present can be joy if we recognize now that all of this is true and act upon it—loving our neighbor, God, and our transcendent future to come.

"If I had not come and spoken unto them, they had not had sin: but now they have no cloak for their sin."

JOHN 15:22

An eternal difference exists between ignorance of the good and rejection of the good, once the good is known. Sin, in this passage, means conscious rejection of godliness, once we have had the opportunity of witnessing its demonstration through the healings, the miracles and the resurrection. Once we know something is possible, and we consciously reject it, we are much worse off morally than if we had never known it.

How great then will be this generation's "sin" if we consciously reject the possibilities for an ever-evolving future? For our possibilities have never been greater in all of human history. Why would we consciously do such a thing? Why would we deliberately deny ourselves a hopeful future of unlimited possibilities? This is a question that goes to the heart of human nature. Do we have a fatal flaw of blindness?

Or are we still so young as a species, from the evolutionary perspective, that we are like a six-year-old child refusing to leave its mother and go to school? Entering the first grade is hard for children. They are wrenched from their mothers, their first home and their self-centered infancy, and expected to grow up, join their peers and take their chances in a brand new situation. They are afraid to grow up.

Their mothers encourage them while taking them to school. Yet they cry and cry with longing for the past, the time before they had to learn all these new things. Some children never stop crying within. They are always afraid. They never fully grow up, never participate in the evolution of the world. Perhaps the same is true of planetary civilizations. Some may cry out against growing up, as ours is now doing, but eventually they dry their tears, attracted at last to their potentials. Some may continue to cry, and never grow up. They are never heard from in the galactic community of universal beings.

"*He that hates me hates my Father also. If I had not done among them the works which no other man did, they had not had sin: but now have they both seen and hated both me and my Father. But this comes to pass, that the word might be fulfilled that is written in their law: 'They hated me without a cause.'*"

JOHN 15:23–25

Here is the tragic truth of human history. The pain-scarred, agonizing history of war, torture, inequity, tyranny—all are self-inflicted wounds. Worse, they are wounds without cause. Jesus did nothing but good deeds, and yet he was murdered. So many did nothing wrong, and yet have been murdered.

We do not know how to diagnose a planetary species like humanity, for we have never seen another like ourselves. We do not know what is natural for an early self-consciousness that is flickering on and off in an animal world. We do not know what is natural during the rise of evolutionary consciousness.

Until we encounter life on other planets as a shared experience, we will not know whether we are subnormal, normal, or superior as far as planetary life goes. One possible diagnosis is that we are sick, yet potentially still great. We are merely undergoing a traumatic birth. One of our most serious sicknesses is a disease of our planetary nervous system—our mass media—especially our television networks.

The world does not know how good it is. It receives constant reports of pain, violence, dissention, eccentricity and death. It rarely hears about its own goodness, growth, creativity, innovation, excellence and love via its mass media. For a lack of knowledge of how good we are, the people perish.

We need desperately to hear *all* the good news, the promises of the past and the potentials of the present. Together they make for universal life. Goodness communicated amplifies rapidly, as does destructiveness. As millions of people change within their own hearts, dedicating their lives to forgiveness and creativity, their acts must be amplified by our mass media in time to save the world.

"I have yet many things to say unto you, but all of you cannot bear them now. Nevertheless when he, the Spirit of truth, has come, he will guide you into all truth: for he shall not speak of himself; but whatsoever he shall hear, that shall he speak: and he will show you things to come."

JOHN 16:12–13

Imagine what would have happened if Jesus had been accepted by the Jews, and if in his day the idea of love had spread sufficiently to overcome the illusion of separation—the root cause of cruelty, war, injustice, disease, and death. The indication in the Gospels is that Jesus eventually decided he would have to undergo the crucifixion to demonstrate the resurrection. But earlier in his ministry, especially upon the return of the first disciples who reported their success to him, he seemed for a brief time to believe his people would understand in their lifetime that the Kingdom of God was already at hand.

If we had accepted his message then, would we all have become Christlike, healing ourselves, producing abundance, decked in splendor like the lilies of the field, working continual miracles of mind over matter without the necessity for technologies of any kind? Jesus did not need medicine or assembly lines or rockets or telescopes. He came before the age of the scientific method and democratic institutions and the technologies of transcendence. His mind was so powerfully attuned to Universal Intelligence that he knew it all, already.

If his message had been fully accepted and acted upon two thousand years ago, it seems unlikely we would have been motivated to create machine extensions to human brain-body capabilities. Would this have been good or bad in terms of our ultimate goal: co-creation with God? Who knows?

It would have meant that our planet skipped modern history—the rise of science, the nation state, industrialism, technology, the invention of democracy, the probing into genetics, the building of rockets. Perhaps we would now be in the condition of the great mammalian dolphins that remain in the environment of the sea, never having faced the challenges of the colonization of dry land. They have community, communication and cooperation. The ethics of the Sermon on the Mount are at least partially acted out by our water-bound cousins, the gentle, brilliant dolphins and whales. They have remained stable. We will learn from their success once we understand their language and comprehend the experience of millions of years of evolving within limits of the marine environment.

What would have happened if we had adapted more quickly to terrestrial life, if we had blossomed in Jesus's lifetime in psychic/spiritual power without the agonies we have suffered to understand the material world through the development of our intellect, through empirical observation, experiment trial and error, failures and successes?

We might have been a planet of great beauty, long-lived genius and adaptability, like so much of the animal world.

So perhaps we can take heart at the suffering of the past two thousand years, as well as at the uncertainties of the present. Perhaps we have been through a normal, natural phase of learning that every planetary system must go through before its members are prepared for life-everlasting in a universe full of life. We won't know unless we successfully grow up!

Jesus indicates that he has much more to tell us, but it was more than we could bear then, and may still be more than we can bear. Those who could not bear his message attacked him. Humanity at that phase could not tolerate that brilliant vision of its own future. The demands on individual behavior were still too great.

So Jesus promised to send the Comforter—the Spirit of Truth, the Holy Spirit—to enter each of us invisibly and guide us to the Kingdom if we choose to go. The Spirit of Truth comes to us as our inner voice. No one can take it away from anyone else. No one can see it. No one can kill it. No one can deny it. The Spirit of Truth will only respond to what we ask. We must ask in order to receive. We must seek in order to find.

Jesus decided he needed to be betrayed, crucified and resurrected. He wanted Judas Iscariot to betray him. The whole thing was planned once he decided the resurrection was essential, due to the infantile condition of the people he was sent to serve.

Those of us now on Earth who feel we are volunteering our services to humanity can take heart from Jesus's example. We are here by choice. The Spirit of Truth abides in each of us. Our personal victory is inevitable. Each person who follows the commandment to love shall have eternal life. The question is, will the human race experience a collective evolutionary transformation? The personal future is not in question. The social future is still unknown.

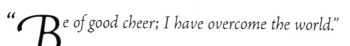

"Be of good cheer; I have overcome the world."

JOHN 16:33

So be it. One man overcomes the limits of the human condition. All men and women henceforth know they can do it too. We can indeed be of good cheer.

Beneath all temporal anxiety lies the certainty of the real possibility of a life beyond this life. All we need to prove the reality of a possibility is for it to be done *once*.

The joy Jesus told us to hold in our hearts at all times, even if chaos erupts all around us, is derived from our certainty in our personal transcendence. If he could do it in the midst of the barbarous cruelty of Romans and Jews, we can do it in the midst of the threat of mass global destruction.

"*For God so loved the world, that he gave his only begotten Son, that whosoever believes in him should not perish, but have everlasting life.*"

JOHN 3:16

We so love the world that we give it our whole life. But if the world does not receive us in the end, *it is not the end of us.* Nothing can destroy our life if we live it with the love of God above all else and our neighbors as ourselves. This world may perish. We shall not.

These words spoke Jesus, and lifted up his eyes to heaven, and said, "Father, the hour has come; glorify your Son, that your Son also may glorify you: as you have given him power over all flesh, that he should give eternal life to as many as you have given him. And this is life eternal, that they might know you the only true God, and Jesus Christ, whom you have sent. I have glorified you on the earth: I have finished the work which you gave me to do. And now, O Father, glorify you me with your own self with the glory which I had with you before the world was."

JOHN 17:1–5

What a glorious act of faith, one that cast the die and set the pace for the human race to evolve from creature to co-creator.

O, BELOVED, HUMANS, MARK WELL THE PRO-cess that I began. I pierced the veil. I rent the flesh. I opened the door for you to enter. Come now, beloved, glorify yourselves with the glory I give to you now.

"For I have given unto them the words which you gave me; and they have received them, and have known surely that I came out from you, and they have believed that you did send me. I pray for them: I pray not for the world, but for them which you have given me; for they are yours."

JOHN 17:8–9

It is not the world Jesus prays for. He prays for us, his co-creators, who believe in the evolution of this world. We pray for the world, knowing he already prays for us; for we serve by carrying on his service, to the end of this world and the formation of new worlds beyond.

*A*nd there are also many other things which Jesus did, the which, if they should be written every one, I suppose that even the world itself could not contain the books that should be written. Amen.

JOHN 21:25

The gospel stories are merely a glimmer of what really happened during Jesus's ministry on Earth. Imagine if you came to an Earth like ours two thousand years ago, and tried to tell the people about their potential future. How much of your story could even the most intelligent disciples of yours actually comprehend? How much could they write of what they comprehended? How many of your ideas would they even have words to describe?

The only way to discover more about what happened in the past is through evolving ourselves into a Christlike future. We will know him by *becoming* our full potential selves. We will learn the story by living it out in our lifetimes.

THE ACTS

OF THE APOSTLES

*[The resurrection has occurred. The
disciples question the risen Christ.]*

*W*hen they therefore were come together, they
asked of him, saying, "Lord, will you at this
time restore again the kingdom to Israel?" And he said
unto them, "It is not for you to know the times or the
seasons, which the Father has put in his own power. But
all of you shall receive power, after that the Holy Spirit
has come upon you: and all of you shall be witnesses
unto me both in Jerusalem, and in all Judaea, and in
Samaria, and unto the uttermost part of the earth."

ACTS 1:6–8

After the resurrection, the risen Jesus knew that the Kingdom would not materialize immediately. As he said before being crucified, only God knows when the tribulations will begin and end. The Holy Spirit, the Spirit of Truth, granted the disciples of Jesus the power of communication. The disciples prepared the way by sharing their vision of a *historic* change that would come in its own time. The power of the Holy Spirit continues to guide us from the end of this phase of history to the beginning of the new.

Jesus's commandment has been carried out. People are hearing the gospel in the uttermost parts of the Earth. The power of the Holy Spirit, combined with the message of The New Testament, spread the amazing word throughout the world over the past two thousand years. That humanity preserved such a mysterious message and inspired billions of people with it indicates the depth of its reality. It resonates with a truth deeper than our understanding. The truth reveals itself more fully as the historic transformation intensifies.

❧

And when he had spoken these things, while they beheld, he was taken up; and a cloud received him out of their sight. And while they looked steadfastly toward heaven as he went up, behold, two men stood by them in white apparel; Which also said, "All of you men of Galilee, why stand all of you gazing up into heaven?

This same Jesus, which is taken up from you into heaven, shall so come in like manner as all of you have seen him go into heaven."

ACTS 1:9–11

The resurrected Christ seemed to appear and disappear at will. Is this a natural capacity at the next stage of mind-body "technology"—similar to the fantastic natural technology of our being able to move our thumb by thought alone, something a single celled organism cannot do? What *is* matter, but energy moving at a certain frequency? Why could it not enter different states by intentional thought, since thought possesses psychokinetic power?

The disciples and multitudes of believers took the story literally until very recently. But in the two hundred years after the rise of early materialistic science the resurrection began to seem unbelievable, because materialistic science offers a limited perception of reality. *Maturing* science is discovering that matter *is energy.* The universe is beginning to look more like a thought than a thing. It is a participatory universe. We affect what we observe. There is no objective position. There is no matter.

We recognize how young our science is, and how much it has yet to learn, as we enter the second millennium since the resurrection of Christ. So we now reexamine the old stories from the perspective of our own emerging capacities to do those godlike things. We can now create holographic images, send light pictures around the world in a flash, leave the Earth alive in a cloud (although we still rely on a noisy rocket launch!).

The valuable period of skepticism during the first wave of Newtonian science brought precious respect for experiment, verification, new observation and distrust of superstitions, casting light into the musty corners of the prescientific world.

But science itself began to calcify. High priests of scientism became dogmatic, preaching that their physics could explain the universe and implying that if anything happens that cannot be measured with their instruments, it did not happen. The new dogmatists have labeled the entire paranormal field—clairvoyance, telepathy, psycho-kinesis, clairaudience, healing—as either unreal or pathological.

However, the fundamental ethic of science requires it to mature, to continue investigating all phenomena and to correct its own dogmas whenever new verifiable evidence develops. As the scientific view of the universe becomes evermore esoteric and mysterious—quarks, charms, black holes, tachyons that move faster than the speed of light, neutrinos that pass through bodies with no trouble at all, and antimatter—we may reconsider the old mysteries with a wiser, less skeptical and more reverent eye.

❧

And when the day of Pentecost was fully come, they were all with one accord in one place. And suddenly there came a sound from heaven as of a rushing mighty wind, and it filled all the house where they were sitting. And there appeared unto them cloven tongues like of fire, and it sat upon each of them. And they were all filled with the Holy Spirit, and began to speak with other tongues, as the Spirit gave them utterance. And there were dwelling at Jerusalem Jews, devout men, out of every nation under heaven. Now when this was noised abroad, the multitude came together, and were confounded, because that every man heard them speak in his own language. And they were all amazed and marveled, saying one to another, "Behold, are not all these which speak Galileans? And how hear we every man in our own tongue, wherein we were born?"

And they were all amazed, and were in doubt, saying one to another, "What means this?" Others mocking said, "These men are full of new wine." But Peter, standing up with the eleven, lifted up his voice, and said unto them, "All of you men of Judaea, and all you that dwell at Jerusalem, be this known unto you, and hearken to my words: for these are not drunken, as all of you suppose, seeing it is but the third hour of the day. But this is that which was spoken by the prophet Joel: 'And it shall come to pass in the last days, says God, I will pour out of my Spirit upon all flesh: and your sons and your daughters shall prophesy, and your young men shall see visions, and your old men shall dream dreams.'"

ACTS 2:1–8, 12–17

The disciples were lifted up together at the first Pentecost. The Holy Spirit filled them with light. They spoke in tongues. A multitude gathered from many races and nations. The collective field of light inspired the whole group and gave each person access to their own experience of God. Everyone could hear in their own inner voice the same words of God. For one instant in time, the separation was over. There lived One Mind, One Thought and One People.

This shared experience transformed the disciples. They became natural Christs. They could heal. They could prophesy. They could break the bonds of prison. The experience created a resonant field that stabilized Christ consciousness in a whole group of humans. *Then* they had the courage to tell the incredible story: *"Christ is risen."*

Those who believed these words changed their own lives—and in so doing changed the world. They activated within themselves the expectation of life everlasting as a transformed person, in a universe without end. This vision of our potential future gave rise to the collective capacities to do it; for as we believe, so it is done.

Now, DEARLY BELOVED, YOUR TIME HAS come. You are the second generation of disciples. You are to go forth and tell the new story to your generation. You are to tell the world: "We are rising." You now have the capacity to do the works that I did, and greater works can you do. You who believe in your capacity to do as I did are the new Disciples of Christ. You will work together for the Planetary Pentecost.

The Planetary Pentecost is the alternative to Armageddon. It is a time on Earth when all those who choose to evolve occupy the upper room of consciousness simultaneously. In this aligned field of love and expectation you will all hear in your own language, in your own words, in your own inner voices, the mighty works of God that you are to perform. You will be empowered with the powers of a natural Christ. You will be able to heal yourselves, to restore the Earth and to emancipate the untapped genius of all those who so believe. The media, your planetary nervous system, will pulse with light as it reports on the stories of your transformation.

This experience will shift the dominant thought pattern on Earth from fear to love. You will open your collective eyes together and see the light of who you really are. You will recognize the universal Christ within you and beyond you. You will draw to you the higher dimensions of life in this universe of many mansions. You will open your collective eyes, and smile together your first planetary smile. Your life as a universal species, co-creative with God, will begin.

[*The disciples began to preach, baptizing thousands of Jews who were willing to believe in Jesus. An extraordinary maturation in the personality of Peter took place. He became a leader. He could heal. He spoke with the power of the Holy Spirit flowing through him.*]

*A*nd as they spoke unto the people, the priests, and the captain of the temple, and the Sadducees, came upon them, being grieved that they taught the people, and preached through Jesus the resurrection from the dead. And they laid hands on them, and put them in hold unto the next day: for it was now evening. Nevertheless many of them which heard the word believed; and the number of the men was about five thousand.

ACTS 4:1–4

And so it still goes, on and on. The existing system resists its own transformation. While individuals respond to the new, at the head of organizations are those who are empowered to maintain the status quo. We see the principle of rising impotence. The closer to the top of any institution we go, the less capable we feel of changing anything.

Perhaps evolution requires this phenomenon of institutional resistance to change to prevent a too-hasty acceptance of the new. Innovations and mutations must be tested and tested in the fiery resistance of the old until they are sufficiently strengthened to bear the enormous load of responsibility for the functioning of society. Until we become wise enough to create self-organizing and self-evolving institutions, we will condemn ourselves to the continual surprise that things simply will not remain the same as they are. They never have and they never will.

And when they had prayed, the place was shaken where they were assembled together; and they were all filled with the Holy Spirit, and they spoke the word of God with boldness. And the multitude of them that believed were of one heart and of one soul: neither said any of them that ought of the things which he possessed was his own; but they had all things common. And with great power gave the apostles witness of the resurrection of the Lord Jesus: and great grace was upon them all. Neither was there any among them that lacked: for as many as were possessors of lands or houses sold them, and brought the prices of the things that were sold, And laid them down at the apostles' feet: and distribution was made unto every man according as he had need.

ACTS 4:31–35

THERE ARE INSTANTS IN HISTORY WHEN
humans are inspired to cooperate totally for a transcendent purpose. We catch a glimpse of ourselves
in the future. We see ourselves functioning in noncoercive whole systems. Each of us is free to participate in such a manner that our contributions are
both to our own good and to the good of all others. At such moments we see the potential of group
genius, of *synocracy*—synergistic democracy. This
form of self-government transcends all past forms
and depends on individuals maturing to a state
of whole-centered consciousness, where they feel
attracted by a shared intuition of a design that is
being discovered, and not invented, by themselves.
Constant growth through an ever-deeper connectedness to oneself, to others and to God becomes
the reward.

The fulfillment of the potential of synocracy awaits the
organic timing of the planet. We are passing through the
tribulations. At the "other side" of the Quantum Transformation we see the emergence of a set of interrelated characteristics necessary for the normalization of synocracy:

- Christ consciousness;
- an attraction for acting out the next step of
  evolution;
- the discovery of our own untapped potentials
  through chosen vocation;
- nonpolluting development in the Earth/space
  environment;

- freedom from unchosen work, disease and involuntary death; and
- contact with the Creator or Cosmic Consciousness as continual experience.

Synocracy cannot hold in relatively static conditions. It gets institutionalized, as eventually the Church did. But once we become Universal Humanity, evolutionary action will be normalized. We will know that we are ever evolving. We will have developed sensitive instruments—extrasensory and extraneuronal—sufficiently attuned to the enthralling adventure of revelation unfolding in evolution.

∾

And Saul, yet breathing out threatenings and slaughter against the disciples of the Lord, went unto the high priest, and desired of him letters to Damascus to the synagogues, that if he found any of this way, whether they were men or women, he might bring them bound unto Jerusalem. And as he journeyed, he came near Damascus: and suddenly there shined round about him a light from heaven. And he fell to the earth, and heard a voice saying unto him, "Saul, Saul, why persecute you me?" And he said, "Who are you, Lord?" And the Lord said, "I am Jesus whom you persecute: it is hard for you to kick against the goads. And he, trembling and astonished, said, "Lord, what will you have me to do?" And the Lord said unto him, "Arise, and go into the city, and it shall be told you what you must do."

ACTS 9:1–6

Saul the persecutor of the Way became Paul the preacher of the Way. In an instant he changed from one who was blind to the Truth to one who was blinded by the Truth. He represents the conversion capacity in each of us. Each of us can change from one who believes that the way is through following the existing law of material, terrestrial reality to one who believes that the way is through knowing the revealed law of spiritual, universal reality. The conversion of an individual can be instantaneous because the Truth of what we are to become already exists within us.

Jesus triggers the instantaneous conversion of the individual because he is already evolved to the post-terrestrial human phase of evolution, and we are already potentially able to become like him. Once we are convinced of *his* reality, we become convinced of the reality of *our own potential to become like him.* For that is his message, his mission, his purpose and his revelation to us. Know the truth and the truth shall make you free of pain, sorrow, disease and death.

The vision of Jesus activated the potential of Saul to live in Christ and gain life everlasting. Christ said to the stunned Saul, "I am Jesus whom you persecute: it is hard for you to kick against the goads." (Acts 9:5) The goads are the jabs of our own growth potential, sending painful thrusts of awareness, frustration and discontent into our ordinary lives, alerting us to the fact that there is more to come and that we have more to do.

This divine discontent becomes our greatest hope. For if we settle for life at this stage, aspiring to nothing more than eating, sleeping, reproducing and dying in peace and comfort, we will not activate our dormant potential.

Yes, we kick against the goads of our own creative potential. Yes, it hurts. And it will continue to hurt until we surrender totally to our attraction to evolve. Until we respond to the growth signals, as Paul did: "Lord, what will thou have me do?"—until that moment (and it could come now), we will continue to be tortured by the nameless malaise of modern humans—the vague discomfort of knowing that we can do more and be better than we are. This malaise is more intense in our times, not because we are worse than other generations, but because we are nearing the threshold of transformation.

The light of the future brightens—not as the blinding light that traumatized the nervous system of Paul on the road to Damascus, but as a slow dawning awareness that we are meant to cooperate consciously with the Creative Intention in the building of a new Earth and new cosmic life in the universe, that we are meant to have new bodies which do not become diseased and decrepit, that we are meant to have a harmonious planet, that we are meant to have access to the next stages of consciousness and action in a universe without end. The design aims at higher consciousness, freedom and love. We can love the goads we kick against. They signal new life.

The process is accelerating. The "twinkling of an eye" is now meant for humanity collectively, for all those who wish to see the light and act out the next stage of evolution on this Earth and beyond. The noosphere, the thinking layer of Earth, is thickening. Signals of impending disaster and of emerging capacities now stimulate our nervous systems daily. We no longer occupy separate villages, cultures and regions. Many billion links of awareness now connect everywhere in the world to everyone in the world.

Those of us who are actively disciplining ourselves to prepare for the events to come are plugging deeper and deeper into the noosphere. The fire of the light of awareness tempers our nervous systems. The Holy Spirit infuses our hearts daily with the relentless radiation of a challenging truth. The Christ capacity, our growth potential, becomes the "Lord" in each of us. We can eventually do as he did. Really. So he told us. Our Lordly potential is calling us forward to become divine humans, as destruction and self-limitation intensify and prod us from behind. We pray to the "Lord" within ourselves, and the Lord beyond ourselves— the Christ who lived and still lives on.

The whole Earth is now preparing for its moment of awareness when enough of us are linked in consciousness of the same thought at the same time. We are one body ... born into the universe...seeking greater awareness...of our Creative Intention. At the moment of planetary awareness, we shall suddenly smile. Our nervous systems will connect telepathically and our mass media will connect electronically. We shall see, just like a newborn cosmic child, that we are loved: that we are good, that we are needed.

The Lord will appear to us as a shared experience at that moment of cosmic time. He will be revealed as the emancipated power within us, to know God and to love each other. He will also be revealed as an emancipating universal power.

∽

*A*nd Saul arose from the earth; and when his eyes were opened, he saw no man: but they led him by the hand, and brought him into Damascus. And he was three days without sight, and neither did eat nor drink.

ACTS 9:8–9

We have seen that evolution is a consciousness-raising experience. From molecule, to cell, to multicell, to humans, to us now—flickering in and out of Christlike consciousness—the process has moved inexorably onward, forward, upward, heavenward. Our consciousness naturally expands and deepens. Saul's sudden conversion is a precursor to our own gentle progression from early human to fully human. What was so traumatic for him will become easier and easier, until at last, after the tribulations are over and once the Quantum Transformation has occurred, we will be born already totally attuned to the Creative Intention. The human creature will have rejoined the creation as fully human, natural co-creators.

We are making pathways in the consciousness field of Earth. The magnetic field of thought grows more intense as our thoughts orient in the same direction toward God, and toward each other as aspects of God. The conversion of consciousness from self to whole, creature to co-creator, terrestrial to universal will become easier and easier, until at last we are born free.

But all that heard him were amazed, and said, "Is not this he that destroyed them which called on this name in Jerusalem, and came here for that intent, that he might bring them bound unto the chief priests?" But Saul increased the more in strength, and confounded the Jews which dwelt at Damascus, proving that this Jesus is the very Christ.

ACTS 9:21–22

The conversion of the negative to the positive is easier than the conversion of the neutral to the positive. A person like Saul, one who actively and passionately stands against the next step of evolution, possesses powerful suppressed energy that drives him to deny what he already feels attracted to unconsciously. Saul denied the truth, because to admit it to himself required him to cast aside all the known limits upon which security and morality seemed to depend. When such a passionate individual is released, all Heaven breaks loose.

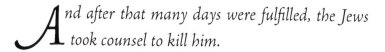

And after that many days were fulfilled, the Jews took counsel to kill him.

ACTS 9:23

One stage of consciousness resists the next. The scribes and the Pharisees feared Christ. An aspect of our own nature fears our evolutionary or aspirational aspect. The scribes and Pharisees, the protectors of the status quo, live in each of us and make us afraid to leave behind the existing interpretation of the law, for fear that we will lose contact with security, and with God. Christ within us understands the purpose of the law, which is to make us free. The law springs from the patterns in the process of creation. Their intention is to free us to become ever more like God.

The fear of our own innate power binds us to the past. This fear is justified based on the precedent of our past behavior, because the human race has misused power. In our infantile stage we forgot we were connected to the creation. We forgot that all our power comes from God Consciousness. We assumed that freedom meant the right to discover and freely enact the Intention of Creation without God.

The fear should not be of the power, but of our own regression, our own infantilism. The power is our hope, since it flows from the Creative Intelligence. It is said that we will not be permitted to use our new capacities fully until we learn to love each other. The scribes and the Pharisees among us are preventing us from going forward until we evolve beyond our self-centeredness.

The question is, how can we best overcome our regressive, infantile self-centeredness on planet Earth? Here we are, in possession of the capacities to meet all our basic needs, able to free all people for chosen work and to transcend the limits of terrestrial, mortal existence. Yet our attention, especially in mass media, is riveted to our pain.

We must expand the focus of our attention beyond our pain, to include our potential for enhanced life. We cannot will ourselves to love ourselves. Love does not spring up by command. It springs up when the heart leaps with joy.

What is the essence of this joy? It is mutual emancipation. We free in each other the capacity to co-create, to penetrate the dividing wall of self, to enter the whole of which we are dynamic parts—to become more than we are by joining the whole, which is greater than the sum of its parts.

The answer to the question is to love each other, and experience the joy of co-creation. The joy of procreation alone no longer suffices to sustain our love, for humanity stands on the cusp between terrestrial and universal life. Functions are shifting from maintenance and reproduction to conscious evolution.

How will humanity now learn to love itself? It can only be through *attraction*. Love is the feeling we have when we are attracted to each other. Love turns off when we feel repelled by each other, or neutral. What is the essence of the attraction? In biological, sexual love (whether the lovers are conscious of it or not), the lovers are attracted to the future, which is to be made manifest through the conception of the unknown child.

Nature has its alluring ways. It uses beauty, charm and all the baubles of adolescence to attract two separate individuals to perform an amazing act of sexual union. Why? To create a child. That is nature's purpose, no matter what the lovers think they are doing.

In noological, suprasexual love, people are also attracted to the future, which is also to be made manifest through conception—not of babies, but of *ourselves*—at the next stage. It is our own next phase of being that now attracts us, as well as the re-creation of ourselves through our children. We love each other in order to be born again as emancipated beings. We love each other in order to transform the world by transcending our own self-imposed limitations. We love each other in order to unite more closely with the Creator.

The hunger of Eve is for union with God. Our attraction to each other turns on when we sense, however dimly, that through each other we will reach beyond ourselves to God, from whom the blinders of self-concentration presently block us. If we are not to misuse our power, we must become attracted to co-creating a different future. More of the same will no longer suffice.

We must bring forth all our old visions of transcendence stored in the ancient myths of the past—Nirvana, Paradise, the Elysian Fields, the New Jerusalem, Universal Humanity—and see that they are *real* visions of our potential future. In the past, many seemingly impossible statements eventually transformed the world: *Christ is raised. All men are created equal. Humanity is rising.* And now: *Our crisis is the birth of a universal humanity.* Within those visions made flesh lies the switch that turns on attraction, which causes joy to spring up in our weary hearts, makes us fall in love with each other and overcomes the repulsion of self from self through the desire to be fully what we can be co-creatively.

Through the power of this attraction, the Pharisee within us lets go of its fear of the Christ within us. For the law will be fulfilled, not denied. The human race will mature to become partners with God.

❧

After Peter had the vision that commanded him to "kill and eat all manner of beasts," which was forbidden by Jewish law, he was sent for by Cornelius, a Roman centurion.]

And he [Peter] said unto them, "All of you know how that it is an unlawful thing for a man that is a Jew to keep company, or come unto one of another nation; but God has showed me that I should not call any man common or unclean."

ACTS 10:28

No one is uncommon or unclean. Everyone is potentially Christ. No one dares judge another, for potential is invisible and immeasurable. Peter opened his mouth and said, "Truthfully I perceive that God is no respecter of persons, but in every nation he that fears him, and works righteousness, is accepted with him." (Acts 10:34–35). It is our calling to be attracted to the potential for becoming like Christ, and to express it in ourselves by supporting the self-actualization of all others.

That attraction, which works like a magnet attracted by another magnet, unlocks our potential. We are called to recognize that everyone on Earth, and on all other Earths anywhere in the universe, *is* the Holy Son or Daughter of God, and then hold that picture of ourselves in our whole being. All have the "like gift." In this respect we are all equal.

We cannot judge beforehand who will respond to their

own gift, believe in their own potential and then manifest their own capacity to be Christlike. All who do respond to their "like gift"—all who are activated to participate in their own transformation and the transformation of their world—are already founders of the future.

When we share with others our own experience of the reality of the potentials, both personal and planetary, either they will be excited—or not. We can measure the stage of our evolutionary growth by our response to the potentials, by our capacity to get excited, both as individuals and as a collective. During sex, an unexcited man cannot impregnate a woman. We call him impotent. With suprasex, only excited people can arouse their own or others' potential to co-create. The Holy Spirit is God's way of exciting the awareness of an individual, to ready that person to act out their potentials through their chosen vocation in an ever-evolving world.

Those of us who have been stimulated by the Holy Spirit—those of us already experiencing the Divine impulse of growth, hearing inner voices, seeing visions and dreaming dreams—are being readied to perform those acts that have been given us to do as modern disciples on the path toward full humanity, the New Jerusalem, universal life. Just being in the presence of a suprasexually excited person can arouse an incipient evolutionary.

Sometimes people feel unprepared for their own excitement. After the experience, they ask, "What happened to me? What was that you said? What was the purpose of what we did? Let's do it again—whatever it was, it felt so good!"

When two or three of us are gathered together for a purpose beyond our selfish interest, we become inspired. Being inspired, we bond with one another. Empathy increases.

Feeling together feels good. We eliminate distrust and our fear of rejection. Suprasexual love begins to flow. We find ourselves co-creating some act beyond our individual capacity, and often beyond our conscious plan or intention.

At these moments a suprasexual attraction magnetizes separate individuals to create something together that gives birth to the unique potential of each person, fusing it with the unique potential of others. The separation of self from self ends with suprasexual union. A sense of effortlessness arises. What seemed heretofore impossible becomes natural. We gain access to each other's capacities.

We become more than our individual selves when we participate in such action.

Synchronicities occur. People call when we need them. We know when someone needs us. Coincidences seem to occur way beyond chance. We find ourselves at the right place at the right time to cause something unexpected to happen that somehow has always been our secret heart's desire, but that we didn't know enough to plan for consciously.

This phenomenon enables us to experience the fundamental organizing process of the universe. The force that brought atom to atom, molecule to molecule, cell to cell, human to human, and eventually humanity to other humanities in a universe without end—we feel this force binding us together and orchestrating the action when suprasexual excitement takes over. We trust it with all our hearts, as Peter trusted his experience at the home of the Roman centurion Cornelius when the Holy Spirit animated Jews and Gentiles alone in a universal embrace.

We have not yet developed a psychology of Whole Systems. We do not understand how one part of the body "knows" what to do in relationship to the whole organism. How does a system communicate to its members? How does a synergistic democracy work? Can it be that it works by the power of magnetic attraction to co-create? As the Holy Spirit increasingly activates the hungry souls of evolving humanity, the magnetic field of attraction is intensifying, intensifying, intensifying. Clusters are forming, breaking down the walls of self-centeredness.

Vast networks of self-activated individuals outside the overcomplex bureaucracies are coalescing in an invisible pattern, like rivulets of water under the ice as the ground warms in the spring. Eventually the networks will interconnect at so many points at once that the pattern of the new order of the ages will be visible—all at once. It will spring into being, as suddenly as one falls in love. Yet how complex is the process of falling in love? It requires everything from babyhood through adolescence to prepare individuals for the experience of sexual union, to procreate the unknown future child. It has taken all of evolutionary history to prepare the members of a planetary body to fall in love with each other, and to experience the joy of suprasexual union to co-create the unknown future reality.

If anyone asks us whether it is too "idealistic" to expect a self-centered species to move toward the recognition and delight that we are "all members of one body," we respond: Is sex idealistic—two individuals irresistibly attracted to one another? Is multicellular organization idealistic—single cells irresistibly attracted to one another? Is single-cellhood idealistic—molecules irresistibly attracted to each other? We might as well ask, is the universe idealistic? The answer is *yes*. The universe *is idealistic!* For all existence owes its form to the law of irresistible attraction.

Now about that time Herod the king stretched forth his hands to vex certain of the church. And he killed James the brother of John with the sword. And because he saw it pleased the Jews, he proceeded further to take Peter also. (Then were the days of unleavened bread.) And when he had apprehended him, he put him in prison, and delivered him to four quaternions of soldiers to keep him, intending after Easter to bring him forth to the people. Peter therefore was kept in prison: but prayer was made without ceasing of the church unto God for him. And when Herod would have brought him forth, the same night Peter was sleeping between two soldiers, bound with two chains: and the keepers before the door kept the prison. And, behold, the angel of the Lord came upon him, and a light shined in the prison: and he struck Peter on the side, and raised him up, saying, "Arise up quickly." And his chains fell off from his hands. And the angel said unto him, "Gird yourself, and bind on your sandals." And so he did. And the angel said unto him, "Cast your garment about you, and follow me." And he went out, and followed him; and knew not that it was true which was done by the angel; but thought he saw a vision. When they were past the first and the second ward, they came unto the iron gate that leads unto the city; which opened to them of his own accord: and they went out, and passed on through one street; and forthwith the angel departed from him. And when Peter was come to himself, he said, "Now I know certainly, that the Lord has sent his angel, and has delivered me out of the hand of Herod, and from all the expectation of the people of the Jews."

ACTS 12:1–11

The "Angel of the Lord" came to Peter—a messenger of the *reality* of our essential divinity. The light of that awareness awakened in him his spiritual powers wherein matter is responsive to mind, wherein the material world reflects the effect of spiritual intention, wherein the word becomes flesh. He rose up from the prison of self-concentration—and "his chains fell off from his hands." Hallelujah! Our hour is coming. We will soon be released from the fleeting imprisonment of limited mind by the material world.

*A*nd when he had considered the thing, he came to the house of Mary the mother of John, whose surname was Mark; where many were gathered together praying. And as Peter knocked at the door of the gate, a damsel came to hearken, named Rhoda. And when

she knew Peter's voice, she opened not the gate for glad-
ness, but ran in, and told how Peter stood before the gate.
And they said unto her, "You are mad." But she constant-
ly affirmed that it was even so. Then said they, "It is
his angel." But Peter continued knocking: and when they
had opened the door, and saw him, they were astonished.

ACTS 12:12–16

The natural skepticism of the faithful brethren was only
overcome by incontrovertible evidence of the reality of the
miracle. Peter had been in jail. Now he stood before them,
free. Their first thought was that it was not Peter in the flesh,
but his "angel"—his soul body—a vision. (Just as Peter had
thought the angel was a vision, yet found it to be real enough
to break chains and open prison doors.)

But it was not an etheric vision. It was a real Peter, escaped
from a real prison.

The spiritual power that the awareness of Jesus had awakened in Peter can be awakened in each of us as we become
attracted to the Kingdom of Heaven, and pray without ceasing. Ask and it shall be given. "Cast your garment about you,
and follow me." Each of us who desires to evolve will discard
everything that encumbers us, and follow our higher self. At
this stage, attraction is the key.

When Peter followed the angel he did not realize it was
true. He thought he saw a vision. The disciples continually failed to recognize the reality of human potentials, even
unto the resurrection. They thought the resurrection was a
vision, a hallucination, until it was proven to them by direct,
tangible experience.

Over and over again it was demonstrated that the miracle was real. The body did rise up on the third day. They could touch it, eat with it, be with it. Peter did escape from a *real* prison. A *real* gate did open for him of its own accord. Every indication is that we are not to be subjugated to the laws of *this* physical world at the next stage of evolution.

No purely metaphorical or metaphysical interpretation fits the facts as described in the New Testament. A supra-physical force, whose purpose was not to deny the material world but to transform it, overcame ordinary physical limitations by making itself receptive to the higher intention of the human will, in full alignment with God.

Women were often the first to report this astonishing reality. Mary Magdalene and Joanna, and Mary, the mother of James, first encountered Jesus after the resurrection. When they "... told these things unto the apostles ... their words seemed to them as idle tales, and they believed them not" (Luke 24:10–11).

Feminine consciousness may be more receptive to our dormant powers. It attaches less importance to the position of the experts in the limits of the present than does masculine consciousness. Feminine consciousness opens itself more fully to the reality of nature's miracles through the experiences of conception, pregnancy and birth. Men who feel an attraction to their own feminine energy, and who allow their feminine energy to move into balance with their masculine energy, also develop this expanded capacity.

Women's bodies self-transform by design. They transform themselves whenever conception occurs. The womb accepts a stranger, a child different from the mother. A whole new apparatus sets itself up. The placenta takes nourishment from the mother and shares it with the child. The breasts engorge as the mammary glands respond to a sudden trigger to produce milk. Self-sacrificing love overtakes the self-centered girl. All this occurs without the slightest conscious direction from the mother herself. The accomplishment occurs at another level.

Women's bodies also appear more sensitive to the *planetary* transformation. In the same way that our bodies prepare themselves to receive the fertilized seed and to change into a garden for new life, so too are our bodies preparing themselves to receive the seed ideas of new life, new potentials vital to the formation of Universal Humanity.

Co-creation triggers the release of a "hormonal reserve" in us. The love of the world sensitizes our nervous systems to pick up signals of direction from the whole-system—guidance for the future—as the chaos intensifies, and the unprecedented begins.

At the same time that the planet has reached the limits of human terrestrial growth, the function of women is shifting along with it. Women respond naturally to the call to restore our environment and to begin the development of a new environment beyond the womb, in outer space. As individual members of a whole planetary system undergoing a Planetary Birth, we can expect to feel the change in our bodies. Our bodies are composed of energy; they vibrate at frequencies sensitive to the stimuli that precede an impending birth.

Women naturally feel the impending planetary transformation within their own bodies. Because the organic whole system is under stress, so are we. As the organic whole system becomes excited by its new experiences, so do we. Our nervous systems and brains are constantly stimulated by the complex events going on within this enveloping biosphere.

Earth changes signal body changes in all humans, but especially in women, whose maternal love for the stewardship and co-creation of new worlds on Earth and in space becomes aroused by new incoming signals.

The process of maternity took millions of years to evolve. From the careless dropping of eggs in the sea to the careful protection of the child for a generation after birth, maternity has evolved. Through the willingness of the mother to postpone her self-development for the sake of the development of her child, prolonged childhood became possible. This extended period of youth enables the child to learn for a longer time, rather than demanding that the child become immediately saddled with an adult need to reproduce and maintain the species.

Creativity, imagination, artistry and genius all flowered because enough time existed for the child to grow while remaining sheltered by the love and care of its parents. What is happening to the maternal and paternal instinct as the need for more babies decreases—and as each child lives a more extended life span? If the whole system communicates to its parts, might it now be activating women's nervous systems to handle an emerging supramaternal capacity—a capacity as mysterious and fruitful as is pregnancy and birth? Are we being prepared for the post-reproductive, androgynous, Christlike cosmic phase of human evolution? Will women's bodies manifest a new resonance, supranormal energies and extra-sensory intuitions for new life?

We shall see; we shall see.

⁓

*A*nd when Herod had sought for him, and found him not, he examined the keepers, and commanded that they should be put to death.

And upon a set day Herod, arrayed in royal apparel, sat upon his throne, and made an oration unto them. And the people gave a shout, saying, "It is the voice of a god, and not of a man." And immediately the angel of the Lord stroke him, because he gave not God the glory: and he was eaten of worms, and gave up the spirit.

ACTS 12:19, 21–23

The power of the present cannot be compared with the glory that shall be revealed in the future. All social and political glamour shall fade in the light of the reality of our capacities to transform the material world, including ourselves. Everyone clinging to power over the existing system will be washed away in the tides of change. Everyone struggling toward the new will be uplifted by waves of force that will carry us to the next level of life.

⁓

"*A*nd we declare unto you glad tidings, how that the promise which was made unto the fathers, God has fulfilled the same unto us their children, in that he has *raised up Jesus again; as it is also written in the second psalm, 'You are my Son, this day have I begotten you.' And as concerning that he raised him up from the dead, now no more to return to corruption, he said likewise, 'I will give you the sure mercies of David.' Wherefore he says also in another psalm, 'You shall not suffer your Holy One to see corruption.' For David, after he had served his own generation by the will of God, fell asleep, and was laid unto his fathers, and saw corruption: But he, whom God raised again, saw no corruption. Be it known unto you therefore, men and brethren, that through this man is preached unto you the forgiveness of sins: and by him all that believe are justified from all things, from which all of you could not be justified by the law of Moses. Beware therefore, lest that come upon you, which is spoken of in the prophets; 'Behold, all of you despisers, and wonder, and perish: for I work a work in your days, a work which all of you shall in no wise believe, though a man declare it unto you.'"*

ACTS 13:32–41

Paul recapitulates the story of creation, leading to the birth of the savior of humanity from corruption. He takes us from the beginning through the threshold of the next stage of the human condition, beyond the terrestrial mortal phase as demonstrated by Jesus's resurrection and ascension.

All others who came before Jesus, including David, died. Their bodies deteriorated. Jesus died, and then rose up his body from deterioration and corruption to imperishable incorruption. He built a new body and ascended beyond the terrestrial self-conscious dimension of reality.

Paul tells the Jews, "... all that believe are justified from all things, from which you could not be justified by the Law of Moses." For Moses died. "Through this Man is preached unto you the forgiveness of sins." How could the demonstration of one superhuman man save the rest of us from our sins? How could his capacity to transform his body from perishable to imperishable help us to do the same?

Here is an answer for those in the modern generation: His demonstration can save us from death because he awakened in us the awareness that it is possible for us to resurrect. For he said we could do what he did—and more. Once we became aware that it was possible, we set about to actualize the possibility. We stimulated our consciousness to *expect something more* than the current human condition, through love of God and each other.

This awareness activated Western civilization by its affirmation that we are to become transformed persons in a transformed world. It activated science and technology to probe the material world, to discover how it works, to lift the veil of matter to penetrate the invisible processes of creation so we could transform this phase of materiality. It activated democratic institutions based on the sacredness of the individual as coequal to one another, and equally beloved by God.

Democratic institutions liberated individual potential, which by their success have now brought about the "end of the world" as we have known it, and the beginnings of new worlds. The awareness of our potential has created capacities too great for Mother Earth to contain, thereby activating a planetary crisis of limits and overcomplexity, a crisis of birth that cannot be managed by science and democracy alone.

The powers that led us to the metacrisis will be insufficient to overcome it. The metacrisis is forcing us to extend the human intellect to fuse with spiritual intuition, to discover the pattern in the process of evolution, as the guide for change. The pattern is the evolutionary expression of Spirit. It is not material. It is the Intention of Creation, or the will of God.

Jesus demonstrated the pattern, which our intuition is reaffirming, as the intellect falters in the face of planetary crises beyond its capacity to model or to manage. When life hits a crisis of limits, it innovates and transforms by creating new, more complex bodies capable of increased consciousness, freedom and order.

Jesus took the next quantum leap in his own lifetime, from creature human to co-creative human, by manifesting a new glorified body that could transcend the terrestrial-physical frontier. He has saved us by giving us the awareness, encouragement, expectation and permission—by his demonstration—that it is right and possible for human beings to transcend their present experience.

Paul thought the end of the world was at hand. *We think it is at hand now.* Because he thought it was at hand in his lifetime, he urged people to repent, believe and be prepared for the Second Coming, when the dead would be raised incorruptible and the disbelievers would become extinct on this Earth.

Paul did not expect a church that would have to last for almost two thousand years, preserving the seed, keeping the flame of expectation alive through the cruel darkness of self-centered infant human history, shot through with magnificent rays of light, genius and hope in the reality of our potentials. There are those among us now who feel as Paul did then, that the hour of the Second Coming is at hand.

Why do we believe this is true, when for almost two thousand years life has progressed, incremental step by incremental step? We believe the Second Coming, or the Quantum Transformation, is at hand because incremental steps no longer suffice. We are in a whole-system change at all levels.

Now, for the first time, we recognize the limits to growth on a finite planet. We can destroy life on this planet. We can destroy the biosphere of the planet. We can leave this Earth alive. We can probe the workings of the nervous system and brain. We can change the design of our bodies. We can create new bodies by conscious conception, uniting deliberately selected sperm and egg. We can create responsive extensions to our mind/bodies in our electronic machines.

Our problems lead to self-destruction. Our unused powers lead to the unknown.

Our unprecedented powers of destruction and our unprecedented powers of co-creation both force and attract us into a quantum change, a radical leap from the root of our potential into the next phase of our being.

We cannot continue as we have for the past two thousand years and survive.

Further growth, further exercise of capacity on this plane within the confines of this environment, will destroy our opportunity. The hour of transformation is at hand. The process has begun, about which Paul preached and for which the millions of souls during the culmination of Earth-bound history have prayed.

The prayers of two thousand years are mingling with the scientific/technological genius of the human race, to propel use through the metacrises to the metaopportunities of the first phase of universal consciousness and action. What is the timing of the Planetary Birth, and how long will the process of transformation last? In the twinkling of an eye—all shall be changed. The sufferings of the present will be forgotten in the glory that shall be revealed. The former things will pass away, and will scarcely be remembered. Just as we cannot remember our life in the womb of our mother, so we will someday be unable to remember our former life in the womb phase of terrestrial life.

The transition will accelerate in the next generation. Twenty to fifty years can reveal the outline of Universal Humanity, if we so choose. We have free will. We cannot choose whether or not the world will transform. We can only choose whether the process will be graceful or disgraceful.

*T*hen Paul and Barnabas waxed bold, and said, "It was necessary that the word of God should first have been spoken to you: but seeing all of you put it from you, and judge yourselves unworthy of everlasting life, lo, we turn to the Gentiles."

ACTS 13:46

Each of us has a choice—the most important choice we will ever make. We choose to judge ourselves either worthy or unworthy of everlasting life. Those who judge themselves worthy in the terrestrial phase of human growth live in a state of joy, are "saved" at the time of the death of the body, "judged" worthy by Christ at the end of the world (this phase of evolution) and given entrance to a spiritual heaven.

We have not yet penetrated through the veil that separates the living from the post-living in a shared, verifiable way, yet there are countless individual experiences of communication with the deceased. Many people believe that consciousness transcends its physical embodiment. Let us assume it is so, and that our belief in Christ in this life actually affects our future in the "next." If the existence of a spirit does not depend on a physical body—if, in fact, each spirit creates its own vehicle, then obviously our behavior today will impact our spirit in the future. Everything we do has an effect. Our self-judgment—whether we feel worthy of life everlasting—is the key to our attaining our "reward" in the next life.

As we enter the universal age, we will have a choice to either let ourselves die or maintain our continuity of consciousness in a new body. In each case, our vision of the future will trigger our capacity to achieve it. The danger now is that those who refuse to take the next step will try to destroy or immobilize the others. The Romans horribly persecuted the early Christians. Then, later, the Christians horribly persecuted the "heretics" who founded science and had faith in human intelligence.

Now we see the same attitude arising in subtler form. There is an anti-evolutionary cadre of orthodox believers who focus on the limits of this life and the unworthiness of human nature. Now they would destroy *our* capacity to transcend.

They would stop the space program. They would prevent aging research. They would stop the development of cybernetic machines and return to labor-intensive work. They would have us living by the sweat of our brows, as of old. These people unwittingly try to kill *ideas*. Unaware of our evolutionary potential, they prevent the action and response needed to transcend the terrestrial phase of our existence. They would annihilate the possibility of Universal Humanity by claiming we have no right to achieve it.

According to this view, we are not good enough. We are selfish and corruptible. We should repent and learn to be good children on Earth: co-operating, cleaning up, limiting growth, redistributing wealth, holding off the actualization of our new powers. True, these things need to be done, but we must *also* look outward. We can only overcome the limits of our self-centered lives by exercising our new capacities. We can only improve human nature by evolving it, as Jesus so vividly demonstrated.

To imprison ourselves in a closed system on Earth, when we are ready to become a universal species, is like cutting our muscles for fear we might misuse our strength. Fortunately, anti-evolutionary sentiment cannot hold us for long. The force of creation is irresistible!

∽

*N*ow when they had gone throughout Phrygia
and the region of Galatia, and were forbidden
of the Holy Spirit to preach the word in Asia, After they
were come to Mysia, they assayed to go into Bithynia:
but the Spirit suffered them not.

ACTS 16:6–7

The Holy Spirit "forbade" Paul to go into Asia. How does
the Holy Spirit communicate to a person? Does a communication channel exist that once was active and is now dormant? For in Paul's time people considered it normal for
someone to hear the voice of God, whereas we consider it
eccentric or aberrant. What happened? The period of scientific secularization happened. The time between the early
apostles and modern humanity ushered in the development
of the materialistic, reductionist scientific view of the nature
of reality.

The current scientific mind sees the world as material;
composed of particles and waves, operating according to
physical laws that can be understood—and to some degree
controlled—by human intention. God, or Spirit, is seen as
either nonexistent or as irrelevant to the behavior of the
material world. Human consciousness is perceived as an
epiphenomenon of matter. The mechanistic Second Law of
Thermodynamics dooms human aspiration for life everlasting, because it decrees that entropy, or disorder, will inevitably increase and lead to individual death and the death of
the material universe.

No wonder we have not been hearing the counsel of the Holy Spirit recently. We have not expected to hear it. We expected silence, and we received silence. The majority of people during the scientific period have continued to believe in God and life everlasting, but they have not incorporated the scientific information about the material world into their belief system. We therefore have a dichotomy between scientific and spiritual observation.

Now, gradually, we begin to hear the voice of God again as a normal event. People are receiving guidance and hearing inner voices. The first phase of science has fulfilled itself by penetrating the veil of matter and discovering that matter and energy are interchangeable. Beneath the subatomic levels lies an energy field that is activating the whole system.

The new sciences begin to investigate consciousness itself. We can therefore expect that human consciousness will again become receptive to signals from the non-material field of force—because it will fit our belief system, our consensual reality. We get what we expect!

People who have been hearing voices all along will again appear normal, and many of us who have never heard anything but the human voice will listen in meditation, will ask for guidance, and will rediscover that within each person there is a waiting, ready voice that only needs to be asked in order to respond. It is as though each of us has a radio set in our heads, which needs only to be turned on to receive information from the whole system in which we live. Turning on the receiver requires a conscious decision. The more mature the receiving intelligence, the clearer will be the interpretation of that which is received.

Through the maturation of the human intellect, the Holy Spirit can now work at a far more complex and effective level for the transformation of the world. As secular, educated minds begin to acknowledge the reality of the nonmaterial or spiritual agent of action, the channel of co-creation opens and the era of the Universal Human begins.

One key factor for this next step of evolution is to question: are we or are we not *asking* to hear the voice for God—the Holy Spirit, which is ready within each of us, to give guidance? If we do not ask, we deprive ourselves of information vital for life. Just as someone who never learns to read will not develop to their full potential, so too will someone who refuses to ask for guidance be limited to the intellectual level of self-expression. Producing a co-creative consciousness necessary for evolving our world requires the fusion of our intuitive and our intellectual faculties.

❧

"*And now, behold, I go bound in the spirit unto Jerusalem, not knowing the things that shall befall me there: save that the Holy Spirit witnesses in every city, saying that bonds and afflictions abide me. But none of these things move me, neither count I my life dear unto myself, so that I might finish my course with joy, and the ministry, which I have received of the Lord Jesus, to testify the gospel of the grace of God.*"

ACTS 20:22–24

Some of us have a profound sense of mission, a purpose for our life on this planet, which we have chosen beyond immediate self-interest. We sense we have volunteered to come to Earth to do a particular task. Are individuals like cells within the body, each with a unique, vital task essential to the whole? Is there a design for each life? Potentially, yes. If the overall system is prefigured and prepatterned but not predetermined, then each of our lives is also prefigured and prepatterned but not predetermined. We are each born with a unique set of characteristics that are needed for the evolution of the world. Whether or not we use them is up to us.

Each person has the free choice to use God-given talents for the highest purpose—or to squander them for lesser purposes. Those like Paul, who always apply their total capacity to achieve their highest purpose, are free.

As we approach the time of transformation it counts more and more whether or not we use our freedom to do our best. The time of preparation is almost over. Every member in the social body is being stimulated to play the appropriate role destined by their unique potentials. Freedom grants us the opportunity to discover our unique capacity—what we can best do that is most required—and then to do it with all our hearts, minds and strength.

This is how we can fulfill the twofold command: love of God and our neighbor as our self. To love God we must desire to fulfill God's purposes. To love ourselves is to discover our unique role in fulfilling God's purpose—which is our own. Without this sense of chosen vocation it is difficult to love God or neighbor or self. If each of us seeks our purpose on the planet, turning within and asking for guidance, then we will go the whole way together to the top of the mountain.

❧

[Paul is traveling on a ship, on his way to be judged by Caesar. They have set sail for Italy. Paul admonished them, saying, "This voyage will be with hurt and much damage." He was ignored. A tempest arose. "All hope that we should be saved was then taken away."]

*B*ut after long abstinence Paul stood forth in the midst of them, and said, "Sirs, all of you should have hearkened unto me, and not have loosed from Crete, and to have gained this harm and loss. And now I exhort you to be of good cheer: for there shall be no loss of any man's life among you, but of the ship. For there stood by me this night the angel of God, whose I am, and whom I serve, saying, 'Fear not, Paul; you must be brought before Caesar: and, lo, God has given you all them that sail with you.' Wherefore, sirs, be of good cheer: for I believe God, that it shall be even as it was told me."

ACTS 27:21–25

Is there a design that guides our action, even unto saving us from calamity if we still have work to do? Do accidents exist, or is every event intentional? Is randomness an illusion, due to our lack of sensitivity to the underlying, motivating, energetic force? Is there an evolution from randomness to increasing order?

It would seem so. The higher the awareness of the individual, the fewer random or accidental events occur. Intentionality increases to the point of guiding most events. Jesus, a perfect master, demonstrated perfect control of bodily events, preparing for and then consciously submitting to his crucifixion so he could rise again on the third day, in order to fulfill the Scriptures. The closer we listen to the inner voice—the Holy Spirit, the voice for God, the design of creation—the less accidental and the more purposeful, guided and directed do our lives become.

The 13.8 billion-year Story of Creation begins with the Creator and the act of creation: an intentional act. Every particle of energy was infused with an intention and axioms for action—laws designed to fulfill a purpose. Energy has been behaving lawfully, according to the original intention, since then. At every quantum transformation, energy has demonstrated the miraculous capacity to form more complex whole systems with higher consciousness and freedom, through synthesis of the separate parts. From molecule to cell-to-cell organisms to humans, and now to us becoming one planetary, organic, whole humanity—the laws of creation are operating.

At every stage of evolution, randomness decreased as consciousness increased. Consider the difference between the molecule, floating passively in the seas of the early Earth, and humans, composed of quadrillions of molecules, now intentionally attempting to understand evolutionary laws so we can operate lawfully in the co-creation of our own futures. The process of evolution produces increasing order, intentionality and awareness of the patterns in the process of creation.

While material energy tends toward disorder, toward increased entropy, consciousness tends toward greater ordering capacity—through alignment with the ordering principles or intelligent purpose of God. God created the material universe. The result of that material creation has been the rise of conscious beings, capable of attuning to the laws and principles of God's process. The rise of intentionality is based on the increased ability of the individual to freely receive and act upon the intention of God.

Paul's intention was to serve totally the intention of God. His attunement was so acute that he could know by supra-sensory cognition the patterns of weather, even as we now do by means of our extrasensory satellites. Deeper than passively knowing the weather patterns, and being a victim of them, Paul sensed that there was an intention at work beyond himself that would protect him from destruction by the tempest, because he was totally serving the intention of God. "For there stood by me this night the angel of God, to whom I belong, and whom I serve."

When human intention aligns itself with God's intention, it overcomes accident, randomness, entropy, corruption and death.

THE EPISTLES

~

*B*ecause *that which may be known of God is*
manifest in them; for God has showed it unto
them. For the invisible things of him from the creation of
the world are clearly seen, being understood by the things
that are made, even his eternal power and Godhead; so
that they are without excuse.

ROMANS 1:19-20

God has revealed to us the result of the invisible process of
creation: The creation results from the creative action of
God. Everyone can see it, for "God hath shown it unto them."
Anyone who witnesses the miracle of everything—every leaf,
every bird, every body—and does not understand that all is
the product of a creative action, is "without excuse."

We cannot say we did not know. We know we did not create this universe or anything in it. To imagine it was created
by accident, and has evolved by accident to ever-increasing consciousness and order, is to willfully ignore the world.
Once we are aware that the visible world is the product of
an invisible, intelligent process of creation, we know the

Creator at all times and recognize divine creativity in every act in the universe, including ourselves.

Thus as co-creators we rejoin the creation gladly, joyfully inviting the larger creative process to infuse our unique being with a glimmer of the genius of God.

Since the universe responds to request, this invitation focuses within our being the creativity of the Creator. We were created in the image of the Creator, and we shall become co-creators, natural Christs, fully human beings.

Therefore you are inexcusable, O man, whosoever you are that judge: for wherein you judge another, you condemn yourself; for you that judge do the same things. But we are sure that the judgment of God is according to truth against them which commit such things.

ROMANS 2:1–2

Great care must be taken with our all-too-human instinct to feel sure of what God will judge as "good" or "bad." More evil has been done in the name of righteousness than in the name of selfishness. The religious wars, the inquisitions, the prejudices—all spring from limited minds falsely believing they have unlimited knowledge of the mind of God.

Beware of those who think they know it all. Yet realize there are fundamental laws of evolution, not invented by humans, which we must obey or die. The discovery of these laws will enhance our capacity to evolve.

In the long run, anything that is not part of God's design for the future will not continue. Since we have freedom, we can err. We can disobey the law. But we cannot disobey the law and survive for very long. For if we go too far in aberration, we shall self-destruct—and disobey no longer. Cancer, an unlawful growth, cannot win. In winning over a body, it destroys the whole body upon which it depends.

Unlawful behavior is self-limiting because all people are members of one body. After a certain point we cannot hurt another without actually hurting ourselves. We cannot win a war using nuclear bombs that pollute the entire Earth. We cannot win by excluding or undermining others who are in the same body as ourselves. The will of God will be done now, as it has been for billions of years.

> Our Creator,
> Which art in Heaven,
> The state of oneness, of all-with-all,
> Hallowed be your name.
> We, the creatures, salute you,
> With love and awe at the magnificence of
> Your genius.
> Your Kingdom come,
> Your will be done,
> On Earth as it is in Heaven.

∽

Therefore as by the offence of one judgment came upon all men to condemnation; even so by the righteousness of one the free gift came upon all men unto justification of life. For as by one man's disobedience many were made sinners, so by the obedience of one shall many be made righteous.

ROMANS 5:18–19

From an evolutionary perspective, the "sin" of one man, Adam, was to gain self-consciousness, the consciousness of self as separate from others and from God. The overcoming of sin by one man, Jesus, was to gain Christ consciousness, or the consciousness of self at one with all others and with God. The reason we all were "punished" by the "sin" of one man, Adam, must be that the mutation in consciousness known as self-consciousness occurred somewhere once, first, in some early human whom we call Adam. It must have offered some advantage over all other primitive contenders for the rise in consciousness, and was then passed on to all *Homo sapiens sapiens.* And we are still in a state of self-consciousness. The "punishment" is the illusion of separation, feeling cut off from the Creator and other creatures.

The reason we will all receive the "free gift" of life everlasting by the "righteousness" of one man, Jesus Christ, is that he was the first to separate out from the creature human condition to a co-creative human phase, by the accomplishment of the mind-body transformation of the material body into an incorruptible body capable of life ever evolving.

Those who have faith that they can do as he did, will by that faith, affect in themselves, a mutation from self-consciousness to co-creative consciousness in the fullness of time. Those who do not have faith in the potential of the transformation of themselves from creature humans to co-creative humans will not take the intentional steps necessary to change.

Those who do intend to change will eventually receive the capacity as a free gift, an evolutionary inheritance, like the sighted eye or the hearing ear. Done once, it is done for all time. It can be copied, reproduced and inherited effortlessly. As the five senses and self-consciousness separated us from the Creator, so do the sixth sense and Christ consciousness reunite us with the creation.

For what the law could not do, in that it was weak through the flesh, God sending his own Son in the likeness of sinful flesh, and for sin, condemned sin in the flesh: that the righteousness of the law might be fulfilled in us, who walk not after the flesh, but after the Spirit.

ROMANS 8:3–4

The Law of Moses could not create perfect beings because it did not change the nature of the body, nervous system or brain. The purity of the law was contaminated by the fact that our bodies are still mammals, scarcely rid of their fur. The law was "weak through the flesh."

The mutation that Jesus represented overcame the "sin-fulness" of the flesh—its illusion of being separate from the Creator—through a higher level of union with the Creator. This union gave him the capacity to change his body from mortal-animal to immortal-human, as demonstrated by his resurrection from the dead.

Why would one person's mutation enable the rest of us to mutate? How can one suprahuman make suprahumans of us all? By faith, it is said. When Jesus healed the sick, he usually said, "Your faith has made you whole." Faith is a magnet that attracts the current of God to flow through the body, making it whole. Jesus acted as a conductor for that energy, allowing it to connect between the Creator and the ailing creature.

If faith can heal the body, can faith *evolve* the body to a new body? Paul believed so. For almost two thousand years millions of people have believed so. They held the expectation of the resurrection as a promise for all who have faith. Now, through the maturation of science and faith, we see we may gain the capacity to *actually* evolve our bodies consciously. The positive image of life everlasting, stimulated by the example of Jesus, has a triggering effect on the DNA-hormones-nervous system and brain of a body still in evolution. Images, intentions, expectations are real. They affect reality. The universe is responsive to request. Jesus's example, along with our faith that we can do as he did, is in fact cultivating the actuality.

ut if the Spirit of him that raised up Jesus from the dead dwell in you, he that raised up Christ from the dead shall also restore life in your mortal bodies by his Spirit that dwells in you.

ROMANS 8:11

If God (the Spirit of him that raised up Jesus) did it once, he will do it again. The Spirit of God animates everyone. Jesus came to demonstrate that we have the same potential as he. That is why he came in as a man, with a human body, rather than a superhuman being already graduated from earthly limitations. His life is the transition *personified*. He started out in a human body, went through the crucifixion and death, then the "Spirit of him that raised up Jesus" reconstituted his actual body into a more vital version, which carried the appearance, memory and personality of Jesus in a quickened form. His crucifixion and resurrection represents our collective, planetary transformation from terrestrial to universal life. That shift is occurring on the planet now!

From an evolutionary perspective, the time when the Spirit, which dwells in each of us, will quicken us to become like Christ will be when the planetary whole needs Christlike beings to survive the tribulations and to guide the evolutionary process that we have inherited. That time is now.

Therefore, as individual members of the planetary body, born when the whole planet is shifting, we will gain rapid access to our Christlike, co-creative power. Soon these powers will be given as free gifts to those born after the transformation in the past-millennium generation.

*T*herefore, brethren, we are debtors, not to the flesh, to live after the flesh. For if all of you live after the flesh, all of you shall die: but if all of you through the Spirit do mortify the deeds of the body, all of you shall live.

ROMANS 8:12–13

In our generation we do not have to "mortify the deeds of the body." We can celebrate our bodies and what they have accomplished in the past. This has laid the groundwork for the transformation of the body that is to come. Give your body unconditional love. Love it like a child, and ask it to grow to become like Christ's body. *Attract* it toward its higher potential; don't *attack* it.

Already we are changing our bodies. We can replace decaying parts with incorruptible parts. Veins, eyes, joints, limbs. We can stimulate regeneration of cells to a minor degree. We can control our involuntary functions—respiration, body temperature, heartbeat—through visualization and biofeedback. We can heal the sick through faith.

We can change the DNA through genetic surgery. We can correct some genetic defects.

We can create new forms of life by recombining DNA. One day we will create new bodies through the union of our spiritual intention and our new scientific capacities.

God so loved the world that he sent us his only begotten Son. And God so loved the world that he sent us—you and me—to co-create in the world through our own transformation.

The Spirit itself bears witness with our spirit, that we are the children of God: and if children, then heirs; heirs of God, and joint-heirs with Christ; if so be that we suffer with him, that we may be also glorified together.

ROMANS 8:16–17

We have always known that we were destined to go beyond the creature human condition. We have always known that we have a greater purpose than to adapt to comfort and survive. We have always known that there is more to come. The hunger of Eve, the longing of humanity, awoke at the dawn of human consciousness, infusing us with passionate desire for fulfillment of our potential beyond the animal world.

The hunger of Eve, the separated human, is for union with God. The hunger could not be fulfilled until the advent of Christ and the maturation of Eve. Christ is the pure channel to God. Eve is the maturing intellect. Their marriage fulfills the desire of humanity for co-creative union with God. We are now maturing from being children of God to heirs of God through joining with Christ as joint heirs. Humanity is growing up.

What does it mean to be the heirs of God? What does it mean that we are to "inherit the Kingdom"? It means we have access to the powers of creation, which is precisely what is happening now. Through the maturation of the intellect combined with the intensification of the intuition, we are gaining the powers of creation, becoming heirs of God, joint heirs of Christ, about to co-create new worlds on Earth and in the universe.

Paul was right. The churches were right. The millions of believers praying in the dark were right. The explorers were right. The cathedral builders were right. The healers were right. The doctors were right. The scientists were right. The technologists were right. The industrialists were right. The astronauts are right. The geneticists are right. The cyberneticists are right. Civilization is right. All, all, all pulses toward the day when we shall not all sleep but we shall all be changed.

> It is written in the laws of evolution.
> It is encoded in our genes.
> It is written in the scriptures.
> It is happening NOW.
> We are the generation born when humankind is born.
> We are the first to know, collectively,
> What it means to become
> Heirs of God, joint heirs with Christ.

❧

For I reckon that the sufferings of this present time are not worthy to be compared with the glory which shall be revealed in us.

ROMANS 8:18

The glory that shall be revealed awoke the hope, and aroused the potential to act out the transformation. The glory will be revealed to living generations in the fullness of time. That time is now.

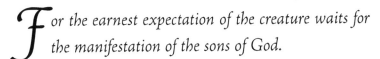

To every thing there is a season, and a time to every purpose under the heaven: a time to be born, and a time to die; a time to plant, and a time to pluck up that which is planted.

ECCLESIASTES 3:1–2

As for the body of a child, as for the body of a fruit, so also it shall be for the body of a planet. Viewed from the perspective of the universe, we are a tiny body struggling to coordinate its functions, outgrowing its womb, reaching beyond itself for new experience.

For the earnest expectation of the creature waits for the manifestation of the sons of God.

ROMANS 8:19

We have been the "creature," the still childish, self-centered human maturing within a planetary system. Our history began with the dawn of self-consciousness.

- **Human consciousness** began, symbolically, when Eve—early humanity—ate the fruit of the Tree of Knowledge of Good and Evil. We separated from the animal world. We felt separate from the Creation. The development of the intellect began.

- **Christ consciousness** was fully embodied when Jesus taught, was crucified and arose in a new body.
- **Secular consciousness**, the development of the materially oriented intellect, matured when the first great observers of nature began to measure how nature works. Galileo, Newton, Copernicus, Kepler, Bacon and others initiated the scientific method.

Now, **co-creative consciousness** begins. The creature human has been waiting for thousands of years "for the manifestation of the sons of God." Humanity has waited and worked to develop the capacity to become joint heirs with Christ, co-creators with God. We are at the threshold of the Tree of Life. Christ consciousness and Eve-consciousness are uniting. Love and intellect are joining to co-create new heavens and a new Earth, new worlds on Earth and in the universe, through the full activation of human potential as the heirs of God.

❧

For we know that the whole creation groans and labors in pain together until now.

ROMANS 8:22

Not only do we creature humans, spirits gestating in mammalian bodies, groan and travail; all of creation groans and travails. The whole planetary system becomes conscious through us, this generation graduating from creature to co-creator, from children of God to heirs of God. Through us the whole ecological system will be reproduced in outer

space. The genius of the mineral kingdom, the plant kingdom, the animal kingdom and the technological kingdom
is being synthesized, learned, adapted and transmitted into
the universe in seedpods—little rockets, which are early
mutations of the coming interstellar arks. These arks will
carry the seed of the genius of Earth life into the universe,
and this knowledge will restore the environment on Earth.

Through us the entire planet is reproducing Earth life
in the universe, beyond the biospheric womb. We are the
product of the whole process of creation. We have come
a long way from the origin of the universe: through the
formation of Earth, life, multicelled life, the biosphere,
early humanity, the first human-made machines. We are
ready at last to fulfill the purpose of planetary life: to produce a universal species capable of transcending the limits of womblike consciousness to populate this Earth, and
eventually the universe, with natural Christs—heirs to the
whole creation.

One day our sun, like billions of other suns that may have
given life to the creature world, will expand and destroy this
planet. By that time, Earth's children, heirs of God, natu-
ral-born Christs, will live in the universal community. The
material universe will run down. The energy from the original act of creation will dissipate. It is being absorbed, trans-
muted, incorporated into nonmaterial awareness by the
alchemy of consciousness.

The universe of consciousness is being born out of the
universe of matter. Conscious humans are becoming aware
of the Designing Intelligence of the universe and beginning
to co-create with It. Out of disorder comes higher order;
out of chaos, creation; out of physical matter, consciousness.
The whole creation is suffering and laboring to give birth to
co-creative life, to conscious partnership with God.

We are the generation born
Two thousand years after Paul wrote
His famous words.
We are privileged to witness
The time of the birth
Of which he so magnificently preached.
We are the human beings
Born at the time
Of the end of this phase of evolution
And the beginning of the new.
O privileged generation,
Awaken to the joy of the hour at hand!

*A*nd not only they, but ourselves also, which have the first-fruits of the Spirit, even we ourselves groan within ourselves, waiting for the adoption, to know, the redemption of our body.

ROMANS 8:23

Even though we have experienced Jesus Christ, the first fruits of the Spirit—who visibly transcended the human condition by returning from the dead—we ourselves "groan within ourselves." For we have not yet acted out our potential, the "redemption of our body." We have not yet activated our full capacity to transform our bodies. We can see we are closer to the time of the transformation of our bodies than was Paul's generation, but we have not yet arrived at that condition.

The signal that Jesus set forth is at hand. The word has been heard by all the nations on Earth. The tribulations are increasing in danger; the metacrises intensify, the planetary limits are felt, and the new capacities for universal life, for life ever evolving, are emerging from the creativity of the human mind. The whole creation is poised with expectancy, awaiting the outcome of the cosmic drama on planet Earth. Will we make the birth transition from terrestrial to universal life? Or will we fail, overcome by the trauma of the great transition?

No one knows. But those of us alive on Earth now are here to do our best to assure the successful transition. Each of us is a vital cell in a body being born. As we are each awakened to the role we play, the promises we fulfill and the possibilities we may enjoy, we shall gladly commit our lives, our fortunes and our sacred honor to the cause of the birth of humankind.

❧

For we are saved by hope: but hope that is seen is not hope: for what a man sees, why does he yet hope for? But if we hope for that we see not, then do we with patience wait for it.

ROMANS 8:24–25

We are saved by hope. What we hope for is invisible. What is this invisible reality we hope for? It is to fulfill our hidden potential to be like Christ, co-creative heirs of God. We hope to graduate from the early phase of human existence to inherit our birthright as Sons and Daughters of God. No other hope is sufficient to inspire us now. Our belief in progress is not enough. No promise of incremental improvement will activate the full genius of humanity. Only the hope of life ever evolving will stimulate the genius in every man, woman and child.

We hope for the transformation that is unseen except for the dramatic demonstration of one man. Jesus gave us our first glimpse of our potential self as he rose from the dead and ascended into heaven—the next phase of evolution.

Inheritors of the power of creation, this is where we hope to be and what we want to do. The realization of ourselves, as first manifested by Jesus, is an unseen hope. We have witnessed the miracle of our bodies ascending beyond this Earth in chariots of fire—and then returning alive. We have witnessed the miracle of birth as our babies are consciously conceived outside the womb. We have witnessed the miracle of our images circling the globe with the speed of life. We have witnessed the miracle of the genes, which build bodies and which receive our instructions to reform. To our cells we can communicate our desire not to sleep, but to be changed from creature to co-creator, so that we may fulfill the potential of each person to become a natural Christ.

Children resist growing up. So too does humanity, at the threshold of inheriting the adult powers of co-creation, hesitate, congealed with fear at the responsibility of the powers we will inherit as heirs of God. Some wish to return to the past, when we were children of God, not heirs of God. They want to be cared for in the bosom of mother nature in the first garden of Eden, before the intellect awoke and gave us the illusion of separation so we could stand apart from the animal world to learn how God's creation works.

But this cannot be. We cannot go back again. We can only go onward. It is the Will of our Creator that we inherit these powers and become creative as sons and daughters, whom we are now to be. We cannot go back to the First Garden as children of God. We must go forward to the Second Garden as heirs of God. In the Second Garden we will restore the Earth, save the endangered species, preserve the works of art and nature, cultivate the world as our cultural center, the birthplace of the human race.

In the Second Garden we now prepare for our role as conscious heirs of God.

We learn the invisible technologies of creation, and educate our mind/hearts/bodies to become servants of God, which is for us to become joint heirs with Christ. In the Second Garden we are prepared to go forth to co-create new worlds, to carry the seed of Earth into the universe, thereby becoming Universal Humanity in a universe without end.

Amen.

⌒

*L*ikewise the Spirit also helps our infirmities: for we know not what we should pray for as we ought: but the Spirit itself makes intercession for us with groanings which cannot be uttered.

ROMANS 8:26

We do not know how to release the next level of our potential any more than an adolescent understands how to grow a reproductive system. It is, however, scripted in the genes. It awaits the right time for the code to turn on. So it is with us. We do not know how to become natural Christs, but it is already scripted. The time is now.

Spirit will help us overcome our natural infirmity, which comes simply from the fact that we have never before been required to graduate collectively from this class in God's School. The Inner Teacher knows. It is the still, small voice that always responds when we ask it to point the way. We cannot evolve by intellect alone. We cannot evolve by intuition alone. We evolve by the fusion of intellect and intuition within ourselves, so that the inner voice can now speak to us with a *full voice* rather than in parables, mysteries and enigmas. God will come out of hiding when the human race grows up sufficiently to be able to stand the glory that shall be revealed in us. We are no longer to be blinded by the light. We are to *be* the light.

⌒∿

*W*hat shall we then say to these things? If God be for us, who can be against us?

ROMANS 8:31

Can we withstand the power that is given us when we act according to the purpose of God? Can we endure our own divinity? Can we acknowledge our own strength? Do we dare to become all that we are? Yes, we can. We can maintain our humility in the face of our own greatness by remembering that we did not create ourselves.

Our glory is the product of the work of God. To acknowledge our own magnificence is to praise the work of God. God deserves the praise, not us. Ours is the opportunity to make of our lives a hymn of praise to the Creator of the universe by acting upon the genius that is given to us as a gift so that we can be godlike. God and we are one. To love ourselves is to love God.

⌒∿

*H*e that spared not his own Son, but delivered him up for us all, how shall he not with him also freely give us all things?

ROMANS 8:32

We have suffered so deeply during the learning period of self or separate consciousness that we cannot believe God wishes to freely give us all things. Why, we rightly ask, would we have been allowed to suffer the slings and arrows of outrageous fortune if God had wished us to have all things freely? The answer is: We were not ready. We were not mature. We had not learned how the world works. We were not ready to become co-creators. Can a father give a child the keys to the kingdom? Can a mother hand over to her infant the jewels of the household? Not until the fullness of time, when the child matures enough to desire to become an adult, like the parents.

A first example of human adulthood was Jesus. He knew he and his Father were one and he called upon his Father to overcome visibly the creature human condition that prevailed during the infancy of humanity. The mature human is the natural Christ. It is to humans at this stage that God can give all things freely.

God cannot give us these powers until we mature beyond the self-centered human condition as did Jesus, our older brother, the first-born child of the next phase of human evolution. We are prepared to become a natural Christ by intending to do so. We do not have to know how. We only need to ask and the creative process, coded in our genes, will now turn on. For it is time. All nations have received the word, and the terrestrial limits to growth have been reached.

The Whole Creation—which has suffered and groaned and is now in the process of giving birth to a universal species—will soon be embodied in those who consciously work to restore the Earth, serve the people and seed the universe with new life.

❧

Who is he that condemns? It is Christ that died, yea rather, that has risen again, who is even at the right hand of God, who also makes intercession for us.

ROMANS 8:34

If Christ rose and ascended, he lives still. If he lives still, he is conscious of us. For his life purpose on Earth was to encourage us to fulfill our potential. If his purpose was our fulfillment, he will make intercessions for us now with the creative process of the universe. He is our older brother. He already experienced what we will experience soon. He knows God better than we. He can ask on our behalf if he is convinced that we are prepared to act upon our capacities.

Jesus waits patiently until we are desirous of his help. He came the first time, unasked, unwanted by a human race unready to mature. He needed to set an example for those individual members of the species who were ready to evolve. Now there are millions in the process of transformation from self-centered to whole-centered awareness.

Not only will Jesus make intercessions for us, he will be with us when we are ready to be the same kind of person as he—natural Christs, heirs of God. The key is our desire. The key is our expectation. The key is our request. The universe is responsive to our request.

⌒

or I am persuaded, that neither death, nor life, nor angels, nor principalities, nor powers, nor things present, nor things to come, Nor height, nor depth, nor any other creature, shall be able to separate us from the love of God, which is in Christ Jesus our Lord.

ROMANS 8:38–39

We cannot be separated from Christ, for we are one with Christ. We cannot be separated from our divine identity, for that self is the motivation of our being. We desire to become fully human, conscious co-creators with God, animated by the Creative Intention, motivated by the creative will, actualized by the union of the will of our personal self with the transpersonal will of the Creator of the universe.

Nothing else will suffice. The illusion of separation is over. The period of observation is completing itself as we observe that we are at one with that which we are observing. Scientific intellect has matured enough to penetrate the veil of matter and find the same patterned energy as is in the mind of the observer.

We are to be consciously united with Christ because the human intellect has almost matured enough to reencounter the Creative Intelligence. By fusing with the self that is at one with God, the intellect awakens to its real function as student of God's process and executor of God's design. The intellect will realize that all beings are part of the same design, expressing their own part within one universe, ever evolving. Christ—pure love and knowledge of God—marries Eve, the human intellect. As the Second Couple they reach the Second Tree and enter the Second Garden at the time of the Second Coming, when the Christ within the people of Earth awakens simultaneously in a Planetary Pentecost.

What shall we say then? That the Gentiles, which followed not after righteousness, have attained to righteousness, even the righteousness which is of faith. But Israel, which followed after the law of righteousness, has not attained to the law of righteousness. Wherefore? Because they sought it not by faith, but as it were by the works of the law. For they stumbled at that stumbling stone.

ROMANS 9:30–32

Good works according to the law are no substitute for hope in things unseen and faith in the will of God. The law of righteousness cannot in and of itself help us dissolve the wall that separates us from each other and from God. In this phase of human evolution we still exist in a state of separate consciousness. Righteousness that comes from the law can lead to self-righteousness, which cuts us off from contact with the larger process from which human law springs.

We still know so little. Faith keeps us open to, and available for, the creative force of the universe, which lies beyond our conscious mind. The idea that we know it all creates a stumbling stone. Human arrogance in the name of righteousness destroys our relationship with God.

The early Christians were Jews who believed that Christ was a fulfillment of their expectations. The Jewish authorities rejected them, so they went to the Gentiles, who responded—having fewer preconceived notions about precisely how the Messiah would appear. Now hundreds of millions of Christians live throughout the world. For almost two thousand years they have spread and nurtured a great expectation: The end of the world is coming. The Kingdom of Heaven is at hand. Christ will return again. Only the believers will survive the time of tribulations. The New Jerusalem will come. The former things will pass away. Death shall be overcome. A new generation will arise that is not subjected to the mortality of the body or the limits of self-consciousness.

They are right. The "end of the world" is the end of this phase of evolution.

"The Kingdom of Heaven" will unite humans with God as co-creators. "Christ will return" fulfills the expectation of our becoming Christlike, combining love with our new capacities to do the work that he did, to reencounter Christ as joint heirs of God. "Only the believers will survive" recognizes that the process of evolution will favor those in a state of loving, God-centered consciousness.

"The New Jerusalem" hints of the next phase of human evolution when our collective and individual capacities will be functioning harmoniously, transforming us into a universal society beyond planet-boundness, beyond death, in direct contact with the Source of our being, at the beginning of our next phase of exploration of the "many mansions" of the universal house of God.

Will those who have nurtured this evolutionary expectation recognize it when it happens in a new form—for surely the form will be new—or will they, like the scribes and Pharisees, hold onto a preconceived notion of the form of the events to come?

Will Christians reject the Second Coming because it may not happen as they preconceived it in the darkness of the premillennium? That remains to be seen. No one knows the form of the Quantum Transformation. It appears to be unfolding in strange and wondrous ways.

"Behold, I show you a mystery: We shall not all sleep; but we shall all be changed." What might this mystery be? We are getting closer to the discovery as we witness the modern miracles of scientific capability that have externalized the expectation, performing acts of transcendence by technological means, which mirror the acts of transcendence that Jesus performed by spiritual means: ascending beyond the planet, healing, extending life, changing the body, communicating over distance with the speed of light.

Is the early technological acting-out of the spiritual capacity part of the mystery of our transformation from perishable to imperishable beings? Is science humanity's way of knowing how God works? Is technology humanity's way of joining the process of evolution to create new forms out of old? Is democracy humanity's first attempt to guarantee the sacred inheritance of every individual to the Kingdom of Heaven? Is the secular world a part of the mystery that will change us?

The secular world has caused the metacrisis. Science and democracy are the cause of the present global condition. Science and its offspring technology, by externalizing the expectation of life everlasting, are on the verge of achieving it in a closed system, Earth, which could cause the destruction of life—in a closed system.

Democracy, and its offspring, individuality, have normalized the expectation that every individual is equally the child of God, causing an outburst of human potential too great for any existing body politic to contain. The fragmentation, alienation, disorder, confusion and overgrowth of the modern world have been caused by science and democracy acting out the expectation of life everlasting for the individual, reaching a point of systemic crisis in which incremental change will not suffice.

Science and democracy are a primary cause of the problem. A maturing science and democracy are at the core of the solution. The solution to the world crisis is the transformation of humanity to heirs of God in a universe of many dimensions. Our maturing science is part of our qualification for the inheritance of the Kingdom—the responsibility to know how it works.

Our maturing democracy is moving toward synergistic democracy or synocracy: *e pluribus unum*—out of many, one, in a free, noncoerced whole system whose capacity is greater than and different from the sum of its parts, where individuals are free to be their best: that is, to fulfill their potential to be natural Christs in a community of Christlike beings.

Our maturing science and democracy are key elements in the mystery of which St. Paul spoke, living as he did in the prescientific, predemocratic age. They have caused the metacrisis. They are also the means by which the word is spreading throughout the world. They provide vital tools for the democratization of the expectation of personal life everlasting, for those who believe in the way of love. They suggest a New Politics. It is the Politics of Transformation to achieve the fulfillment of the human race not by reforming the world, as the Jews expected of their Messiah, but as Jesus did, by transforming ourselves. He healed the sick, fed the hungry, loved his enemies, resurrected his body and rose from the Earth alive, opening closed-system Earth for humanity.

This is the living model of the goals of the Politics of Transformation: New Worlds on Earth, New Worlds in Space and New Worlds in the Human Mind. We *free* ourselves from deficiencies through productive capabilities; we *unify* ourselves as members of one body; *we transcend* ourselves by becoming universal beings attuned to the Intention of Creation, co-creating in partnership with God in a universe without end.

The stumbling stone of Jews and Gentiles, of agonistics and believers, of East and West, of black and white, of woman and man, is that we are all still in a self-centered stage of evolution, just breaking through the wall of self-consciousness into universal consciousness. We are all limited by our lack of awareness. Yet we are all capable of unshackling ourselves from our prior limitations.

or there is no difference between the Jew and the Greek: for the same Lord over all is rich unto all that call upon him. For "whosoever shall call upon the name of the Lord shall be saved."

ROMANS 10:12–13

The end is coming for human ideological differences, discriminations and prejudices.

No difference exists among us except the fundamental difference as to whether or not we "call upon the name of the Lord." All those who call will be answered. "Those that call upon the Lord" means those who call forth from themselves their own highest potential. The "Lord" is us in the future, what we can give birth to out of ourselves, our latent humanity.

The call is the *desire*, the *intention*, the *expectation* to become like Jesus. This call *activates* us to do more than we have before. Action follows expectation. Thinking causes action. Energy follows thought. We become what we imagine, or image in. In the beginning was the word and the word became flesh.

As the sperm fertilizes the egg and manifests hidden capacities, so the idea of becoming like Jesus inseminates the self-conscious mind and catalyzes our dormant capacities to mature into universal humans. The call to the Lord triggers the suprasensory channels of cognition to open up, giving a person eyes to see the invisible, ears to hear the inaudible, touch to feel the intangible, taste to savor the food of light. Desire is the key to transformation. Our faith in our potential is essential to our achieving it.

❦

O the depth of the riches both of the wisdom and knowledge of God! How unsearchable are his judgments, and his ways past finding out! "For who has known the mind of the Lord? or who has been his counselor?"

ROMANS 11:33–34

We, the created creature, awaken to the miracle of the creation as our own creativity grows. We grow in amazement at the marvels performed by the Creative Intelligence of this whole universe. We cannot fully understand the wisdom and knowledge of Universal Consciousness, for we are as newborn children in this universe. We have barely opened our eyes to the invisible processes of the invisible God, who does not appear to our five senses.

However, we are growing up. The time will come when the created creature becomes sufficiently co-creative with the processes of creation to know ever more fully the mind of God. We will know God by becoming ever more godlike. We have not been God's counselor. Yet, since God has created us in the Divine Image, we are becoming partners in creation. As infinitesimal co-creators we greet the infinite Creator with the faith that we are loved, capable, needed and potentially good—as are all children.

∽

For I say, through the grace given unto me, to every man that is among you, not to think of himself more highly than he ought to think; but to think soberly, according as God has dealt to every man the measure of faith. For as we have many members in one body, and all members have not the same office: so we, being many, are one body in Christ, and every one members one of another.

ROMANS 12:3–5

Each of us is a member of the body of humankind, which is now coming together as one whole and being born into the universe. Each member is unique. As the whole social body is integrated and born, each member of it is emancipated to its next phase of unique function. The birth of humankind is the awakening of each of the cells of the body to a new action.

The cells in the body of a child being born shift their function from building organs in the womb under the absolute direction of the DNA to maintaining, coordinating, growing and responding to a new environment after birth. The commandments of DNA no longer signal every cellular act. Yet the prepatterned capability of the separate parts to function together as a harmonious body is prefigured in the genetic plan.

So it is also with individual people within the social body. Each of us in the past was limited to performing more repetitive functions to reproduce and survive. Now, as the whole body of humankind is being born, each of us is activated to fulfill our extended and unique creations in this emerging "body politic."

Having then gifts differing according to the grace that is given to us, whether prophecy, let us prophesy according to the proportion of faith; Or ministry, let us wait on our ministering: or he that teaches, on teaching.

ROMANS 12:6–7

During the prenatal phase of human evolution, most people, most of the time, were limited to performing the repetitive tasks of reproduction and survival. During the birth transition from terrestrial to universal life, which is now occurring through the collective capabilities of the Social Body, the individual members of this body are being *swiftly* transformed from performing repetitive survival functions to embracing unique evolutionary vocations. Each of us has a differing gift "according to the grace that is given to us." None of us created our own talents. We simply choose to use them for our own development within the development of the whole.

It is essential that we recognize the historical importance of being born at the time when the whole planetary system is undergoing a shift toward conservation on Earth, and co-creation beyond the Earth. Every individual is being awakened to new creative capacities that lie dormant in the untapped mind-body potential. This is happening not because we, as individuals, are more capable than those who came before us, but because the Social Body is affecting our mind-body systems with the need to be activated at a more creative and unique level at this time.

A whole array of new functions, which none of us have performed before, is just beginning to open up:

- the function of stewardship of the planetary system;
- the function of production and distribution on a planetary scale;
- the function of planetary self-government;
- the function of de-bureaucratization, decentralization, coordination, restructuring;
- the function of planetary communications;
- the function of planetary defense—activities that would destroy the whole must be neutralized without damaging the adjoining body—much as a healthy biological body produces antibodies to neutralize deadly invaders;
- the function of self-education for evolutionary tasks;
- the function of body transformation from sickness to superhealth, from superhealth to longevity, from longevity to continuity of consciousness in new bodies;
- the function of building new worlds in space—the practice of young co-creators;
- the function of mind-body attunement to align totally with the will of God and inherit the powers of co-creation;
- the function of communications with nonhuman species on the Earth—plants, animals, dolphins, whales;
- the function of communication with extraterrestrial intelligence;

...and so on, ad infinitum, in an ever-evolving universe.

Each of us born now inherits not only the biosphere and the big brain and human culture—the achievements of the past—we also inherit the opportunity to participate consciously in the evolution of the new. We inherit the collective brain, the stored memory of humankind, plus access to the collective superconscious channel to God.

We are born at the dawn of conscious evolution. This means we are breaking through to co-creative consciousness. We will align with the patterns in the process from within, and realize those patterns with the full resources of a developed human intellect.

Members of the young generation are natural inheritors of the new functions of our planetary system.

At the moment, those entering the age of reproduction are in a deep quandary. It appears momentarily that they are not needed. The period of history wherein we were commanded to be fruitful and multiply and grow on Earth is over. Yet the new functions of conscious evolution have barely opened up.

It is essential that this new generation be quickly informed that it is needed for the most exciting tasks the world has ever seen. This excitement will trigger the biochemical systems of those now entering the age of reproduction to switch on their innate preprogrammed evolutionary capacities. If they do not know they are needed, they build a defensive shell to protect themselves from feeling unneeded, and wither away inside.

One of the major tasks of the evolutionary testament is to reach the under-twenty-one-year-old generation with the vital message that they are needed for the evolution of the world. They are prepared—biologically readied—to *hear these words.* These words will act as triggers to motivate their systems to creative function.

Consider the remarkable mind-body transformations that we already know about. The first transition is conception, from nonmaterial to material form. We begin life as a fertilized egg, the combination of two seed ideas fused into one body. For several weeks our cells rapidly multiply, encased in a fluid-filled sac completely protected even from our mother's body.

The second transition is the embryo. We proceed to build a fully functioning body in the womb. Following the coded design in every cell, we build for ourselves in the womb environment a body capable of surviving in an environment totally different from the environment in which we are conceived, creating capacities we will use in a new environment at a certain time in history—postbirth—after we are ejected into a new environment that at first will appear deadly, but for which we have been unknowingly preparing.

The third great transition is the birth itself. The umbilical cord through which we were nourished in the womb gets severed. A totally new system turns on. The collapsed lungs expand. Air rushes through the system. Eyes open. Ears hear. Voice cries. Hands grasp. Mouth seeks nourishment from outside. Bowels and bladder begin to eliminate wastes. The environment of our prenatal history will soon become strange, alien and forgotten as we accustom ourselves to breathing, eating and eliminating on our own in the outer world.

All these are *new* cellular functions, vocations, and callings that lay dormant in the womb, waiting for the historical transition from prenatal to postnatal life. The cells know exactly when to stop performing one function and start doing another because that directive is preprogrammed in the genes. How can we know what else may be patterned in our genetic code that has never happened before?

The fourth great transition occurs at puberty. The child's body changes quickly. In the male, sperm is prepared, the organ of insemination develops, and the mechanisms of erection and ejaculation turn on. Hair appears and covers the "private parts."

In the female, the reproductive organs develop. The uterus prepares itself, the mammary glands grow ready to produce milk, the ovaries produce eggs that proceed patiently, month by month, down the fallopian tubes, in readiness for the great encounter with a sperm that will trigger the incredible sequence of life all over again.

In the female, the next great transition of the body is pregnancy. The sperm fertilizes the egg. The embryo fixes itself in the uterus. It begins to siphon off nourishment from the mother to build its body—a foreigner within her. The mammary glands turn on. The emotions refocus from self-centered to child-centered. The mother becomes a selfless vehicle of creation—and, in a moment of miraculous joy and by surrendering utterly to an irresistible process, she gives birth to a child.

In most lives, the next great transition is senescence. The body degenerates quickly once the reproductive phase ends. The cells are preprogrammed to die. The copying mechanisms blur. The reproductive organs diminish. The motivation to live diminishes. The eyes dim. The ears fail. The skin shrivels. The bones become brittle. The memory fades. The clock of death ticks relentlessly on, killing us. Backup systems of degeneration wait in reserve. If one "enemy" does not get us, another will.

The final great transition is death. Scheduled cellular death was an evolutionary advantage, along with multicellular life and sexual reproduction. It led to the diversity of the species. Only the seed lives on through genetic information exchange. The physical body dies.

There exists another intermediate stage that only a relatively few individuals have experienced in the past. It occurs between adulthood and senescence. It is the great transition from self-consciousness to cosmic consciousness—the mystic stage that affects the body by opening up a supersensory channel of cognition. The third eye, the pineal gland and kundalini experiences change the nervous system, awakening the inner eye to see auras, to hear voices, to have visions, to move objects at a distance.

The yogi, the mystic, the enlightened being, achieves a stage of human life that is as yet rare. Through the stimulus of Jesus's example, through the expectation for a personal future beyond the mammalian life cycle, the collective capacities to achieve this future were triggered. Social, scientific and technological capacities were then developed that have now brought the whole planet to the stage of cosmic birth.

Children born now are already more prone to transform from self-consciousness to universal consciousness. Just as the cells alive during a biological organism's birth know to stop building parts and start exercising innate capacities in the postnatal environment, so do children born in the postnatal phase of planetary history know to do what was never done before, especially in the developed world, where the need for fewer children has already been reflected in a lower birth rate. Their procreative energy is held in reserve. Women's reproductive systems remain dormant most of the time. The hormones that trigger that system will be used less.

Our children are already far more educated than other generations, brought up on vast new communication systems that stimulate the right hemisphere, the way that reading stimulates the left. They are already planetary and universal citizens in their minds, for they have seen this world and beyond via an extended nervous system, television.

They have traveled under the seas with Jacques Cousteau. They have swum with dolphins and lived with chimpanzees. They have visited the deserts and climbed the Himalayas. They have traveled inside the body with light cameras. They have seen the traces of subatomic particles. They have seen cells divide and supernovas explode. They have been inside a computer. They have fought the wars of the past and the wars of the future. They have seen Hitler burn the Jews, and Jesus rise from the dead—on film. They have known the world and beyond as no generation has ever known it before. The infinite and the infinitesimal are already their home.

They are the children born just after Sputnik sent the first seed of human-made intelligence beyond the womb of Earth, when we became aware that we are responsible for the future of our little Mother Earth. As individuals they are different, for their *species emerges in a different postnatal condition*, one with utterly new requirements. To survive in the future, we must limit growth on Earth and extend life into the universe.

If information and images and intentions affect the body and brain, then the bodies and brains of modern children must be different from those of any other generation. If they are different from any previous generation they will respond to the opportunity to perform their new functions—naturally. An innate capacity to take on the evolutionary tasks of the world resides in the younger generation's dormant creativity.

As we go through the Quantum Transformation, we shall see that they shall do as Jesus did, and even more shall they do, these children of the universal age. The postnatal generation may find that the mystic stage becomes normalized in them. Those who go through the transition may become Natural Christs, natural Buddhas, natural yogis.

An inner change may accompany the external change in the generation that transitions from terrestrial to universal life. The body changes reported by the yogis, wherein they can control their autonomic nervous system and prevent themselves from degenerating—to a degree—as well as the body changes demonstrated by Jesus in his resurrection and ascension, are evolutionary precursors of a natural state of being for the universal generation.

*A*nd that, knowing the time, that now it is high time to awake out of sleep: for now is our salvation nearer than when we believed. The night is far spent, the day is at hand: let us therefore cast off the works of darkness, and let us put on the armor of light.

ROMANS 13:11–12

The human race has been in an intense effort of transformation for almost two thousand years. The intuition surrounding the end of this phase of evolution was so powerful in the early Christians that they literally took no thought for tomorrow. They believed tomorrow would not be.

They devoted all their energy to preparing for the beginning of the next phase.

"Let every soul be subject unto the higher power" (Romans 13:1) was the key. Century after century the patient preparation rolled on. Perfect! Improve! Realign! Renew! Become like Jesus! So we worked through the ages until now, when once again, like the early Christians, we believe the end of the old is at hand.

Some of us focus totally on preparation. We are stripping off all anxiety, hate, guilt and fear so that we may experience connection with Christ, our potential self, as the tribulations intensify. We are putting on our "armor of light," protecting our thoughts with shields of light, determined to think only the thoughts we must think with God.

We must not be afraid as the disorder increases. Chaos signals the pending emergence of the new order through the interconnecting of the evolving elements of the social body. This design is inherent in the nature of reality. Crisis precedes transformation. Disorder facilitates new order. Breakdown heralds breakthrough. Holism is natural. The system evolves by increasing order.

God is at work in the social body just as in the biological body. Why would there be a design for biological organisms, and none for planetary systems? Just because we have not yet discerned the processes of communication on the planetary scale, does not mean it does not exist. We only recently discovered DNA, the mechanism of genetic communication.

The night is far spent; the day is at hand. The timing is unknown but the signals are clear. The transformation approaches, day by day. Scientists call it the paradigm shift. Environmentalists call it limits to growth. New Agers call it the Age of Aquarius. New Potentialists call it the dawn of the universal age. Evolutionaries call it the new era of evolution. The more of us who feel it, prepare for it and pray for it, the sooner it will come. For the universe is responsive to request. We hasten the day by our desire for it.

❧

*T*here has no temptation taken you but such as is common to man: but God is faithful, who will not suffer you to be tempted above that all of you are able; but will with the temptation also make a way to escape, that all of you may be able to bear it.

I CORINTHIANS 10:13

Temptations that distract our attention from God serve as our learning experiences. We are like athletes training for the Olympics. We are born encased in the limits of self-consciousness, and are in transition to whole-centered consciousness. As the generation of the great transition, we are undergoing more rapid learning through temptation than ever before, unto the very limit of temptation: the urge to use nuclear weapons to resolve conflicts among members of the same planetary body, and the destruction of our own biosphere.

The powers are given us. We have matured to become heirs of God. This process is irresistible and cannot be stopped. We can misuse our inheritance and self-destruct, or we can use it and self-evolve to natural Christs, but we cannot reject our inheritance and return to an earlier time before the genius of humanity had unlocked knowledge of the processes of creation. We cannot return to the innocence of unknowing.

Each of us receives temptations or learning opportunities according to the needs of our natures. In this time of transformation, the pressure to evolve exerts its force upon us all, pointing to weaknesses in our minds and bodies that suddenly show up like fractures in a structure under stress. It is vital that these weaknesses be revealed to each of us now, so we can consciously strengthen them. For when the tribulations (or transformation) intensifies, we will have no time to practice. We are like astronauts preparing for a launch into outer space. Ordinary weaknesses, which would be insignificant on Earth, will kill us in outer space.

Some of us carry the weakness of pride. We feel tempted to "Lord" it over others and sever the connection of love. Others carry the weakness of self-condemnation. We feel tempted to judge ourselves, rather than to surrender all judgment to God. Some carry the weakness of arrogance. We feel tempted to believe we know it all, so we block out the sound of the still, small voice within, which will guide us to the next stage of consciousness. And so on and on.

God is faithful. He will not tempt us beyond what we can bear. There is no weakness in any of us that cannot be strengthened. Our goal is wholeness, to be perfect as our Creator in Heaven is perfect.

We must learn to *ask enough of ourselves*. It is our responsibility to become universal beings if we so choose. It is our responsibility to use the powers of co-creation we have inherited to restore the Earth, free ourselves from poverty, emancipate our unique creativity and impregnate the universe with new life.

Every weakness that reveals itself to us through a temptation should be lovingly strengthened so we can evolve freely, unhampered by the ancient impediments of human existence. To do less is to deny God's intention for us, which is to become partners in the process of creation.

⌒

But I would have you know, that the head of every man is Christ; and the head of the woman is the man; and the head of Christ is God.

For a man indeed ought not to cover his head, forasmuch as he is the image and glory of God: but the woman is the glory of the man. For the man is not of the woman: but the woman of the man. Neither was the man created for the woman; but the woman for the man.

I CORINTHIANS 11:3, 7–9

Paul set the tone for two thousand years of domination of man over woman. Those two thousand years of domination are over. It may have had meaning during the time of the preservation of the seed of the expectation of life everlasting.

During the era of male domination, the instruments and institutions of transformation were exquisitely designed, mainly by the masculine conceptual mind. Science and democracy matured under the dominant masculine consciousness, as it gained understanding of the material world in preparation for the transformation from terrestrial to universal life as well as in preparation for acting out the resurrection through collective human capacity.

We had to develop both science and democracy to take the next step of evolution, in which the sacred individual gains co-creative power as joint heir with Christ. Science (the understanding of the material world, or God's processes of creation) and democracy (the emancipation of individual creativity through the guarantee of inalienable rights) have been magnificent achievements over the last two thousand years. They enable us to take the step forward from the creature human condition.

Women have been largely occupied with procreating, nurturing and educating the young, but that situation is changing rapidly. We have reached the point where our scientific dominion over nature must become co-creation with nature. Individual independent creativity, liberated by democracy, must become synergistic co-operation within a more complex whole—the emergence of a new order of freely participating individuals, enlarging the definition of self-interest to include the larger body of humankind.

Women now arise from the role of procreation to take leadership in a new partnership with men for the co-creation of universal life. Only the fusion of feminine consciousness with the masculine can produce whole beings in whom emotional maturity is attained and love infuses power, until they are one and the same.

The feminine energy, therefore, refocuses itself to take the initiative in guiding science and democracy toward synergistic cooperation in the building of new worlds on Earth, new worlds in space. Women are not to consider themselves only healers of the wounds of the past, or restorers of the ravages of the modernized world. We are also arousers of the technologies of transcendence, to carry the seed of life into the cosmos so that a universal species may be born out of the peoples of Earth. Ours is the task of suprasexual arousal of the co-creative capacities of the human genius—male and female.

Co-creative women are leaders, pioneers and innovators, guided by their attraction for more life. We lead by our attraction to the next step of evolution. A new "Eve" arises at points of quantum transformation. She arose at the time of the leap from animal to human consciousness. She ate of the fruit of the Tree of the Knowledge of Good and Evil. The experience of separation began. Her desire for knowledge aroused the masculine intellect, and the dominion of the male began. We learned how the material world works.

Now, Eve rises again during the leap from self-centered human to co-creative universal consciousness. We are about to eat of the fruit of the Tree of Life, and become godlike. Woman's desire for Christ-being, for godlike inheritance, for partnership with God, through the maturation of intellect in service of pure love, must attract the energies of the world to a new level of creativity.

At this time the male capacities have become dammed up due to the limits created by their own success. These limits to growth in a finite world are constricting the creativity of the masculine mind. Men stand there, poised on the edge of transformation with their great machines of transcendence—all their rockets, computers, instruments of microbiology and microtechnology—yet the scientists, astronauts, explorers, inventors and creators of all races, creeds and colors remain stymied by a lack of vision of what all of that power is *for*.

This magnificent masculine genius is being told that the purpose of this power is only for the stewardship of Earth, the conservation of its resources and to provide for the comfort of its billions of human bodies. The masculine genius for creation is not yet being told that its purpose is also the creation of universal life. This is the attractive role of the Second Eves.

I would have you know
That at the center of every
Woman and man united
In a new partnership for life is Christ,
And at the center of Christ is God.
For the man is not of the woman,
Nor the woman of the man:
They are coequal
Coauthors of creation.
Each man brings forth
The feminine aspect of his nature.
Each woman brings forth
The masculine aspect of her nature.
Each man and woman become whole,
Uniting masculine and feminine within them.
Then you can unite, whole being to whole being
In a new partnership for life.
Your fidelity is to your common act
Of creation in the service of God:
This act becomes your "child"
As a co-creative couple.
To it you remain faithful
And through it you fulfill each other's
Desire to co-create with God.
A new dispensation begins.
The Pauline doctrine of the dominance
Of man over woman is declared
Null and void
By the generation of the transition
To universal life.
In the distant future

When you have evolved
Beyond physical death and sexual reproduction,
When the perishable has become imperishable
And death has no dominion,
The masculine and feminine will be so fused
In each immortal being
That each man and woman will be whole.
You shall become androgynous beings.
Each of you will be a natural Christ.

∾

*F or I have received of the Lord that which also I
delivered unto you, that the Lord Jesus the same
night in which he was betrayed took bread: and when he
had given thanks, he brake it, and said, "Take, eat: this
is my body, which is broken for you: this do in remembrance of me."*

*Wherefore whosoever shall eat this bread, and drink
this cup of the Lord, unworthily, shall be guilty of the
body and blood of the Lord.*

I CORINTHIANS 11:23–24, 27

The communion ceremony becomes the union ceremony of
the marriage of Christ and Eve at the dawn of the universal age. Divine love and human intellect marry and become
one. We are not only to eat of his body in "remembrance of
him" but also in order to *be fused with him* so that our bodies

become new bodies, glorified bodies capable of inheriting the Kingdom. As we grow from children of God to heirs of God we evolve the meaning of the communion ceremony from remembrance to re-creation, from expectation to manifestation of ourselves at the next stage of human evolution.

In this time of transition the words of Paul become even truer. Those who eat the bread and drink the cup of the Lord "unworthily" shall not only be "guilty" but shall actually be preventing themselves from evolving. "Unworthily" means being contaminated by negative thoughts, fears, anxieties, hostilities.

If it is true that our bodies are designed to transform at a certain stage of evolution, and if we are at the beginning of that stage now, then our thoughts will deeply affect the quality of the body we are becoming. We know that negative thoughts cause illness and positive thoughts enhance wellness. If the body is undergoing a deep transformation now, our thoughts now—negative or positive—will have an *increased* effect, more directly manifesting in illness or super-wellness, than at an earlier, more static stage of evolution.

If our bodies are in evolution, our thoughts will affect that evolution. If we are contaminated by negative thoughts, those vibrations will literally be incorporated into our bodies, causing deadly defects. This is why so many of us are actively purifying ourselves through meditation, good nutrition, exercise and self-development courses of all kinds. Intuitively we know that we are affecting ourselves by what we think, eat and imagine.

Those of us who are putting ourselves through the crash course in transformation are speeding up the process of evolution. We are preparing to evolve during the great transition and to be gathered together "from the four winds, from one end of Heaven to the other," called by "His angels with a great sound of a trumpet."

Our nervous systems will be prepared for the change of communication, however it comes, to signal that a new stage has begun. We are approaching superexponential change where the old disappears and the new suddenly exists as though it had been there all along. We can take communion now, both as an act of remembrance and as an act of preparation to change into beings more responsive to the Intention of Creation.

*F*or as the body is one, and has many members, and all the members of that one body, being many, are one body: so also is Christ. For by one Spirit are we all baptized into one body, whether we be Jews or Gentiles, whether we be bond or free; and have been all made to drink into one Spirit. For the body is not one member, but many.

I CORINTHIANS 12:12–14

All of us are members of one body now being born into universal, co-creative life.

What Christ came to announce will be experienced as true, as the body of humankind recognizes that all the members of that one body, being many, are one body.

Each of us can experience ourselves as Christlike right

now. But we look out upon a world in which most people are not yet aware of who they are. They do not realize they are members of one body. They still carry the illusion of separation that began at the dawn of human intellect.

Remember: self-consciousness is a historical event. At one time all creatures, animal and early human, were in a state of pre-intellectual unity. Intellect arose at a certain time in history. It will be transcended at another time in history, when it fuses with the channel of pure love—which is pure knowledge of God—and fulfills itself through participating easily, in the flow of the creative process, like great geniuses, visionaries and seers now do.

The shared awareness that we are all members of one body, born into an infinite universe, has yet to be experienced by humanity even though individually many have been aware of our relationship to the Whole. The *shared* awareness is the coming "Planetary Birth Experience." This is the approaching Planetary Pentecost, the long-awaited Second Coming. This is when all those who choose the Way of Love will know at the same moment that they are members of one body—united by the same consciousness.

We all witnessed ourselves as one *geographic* body, from the same eye and at the same time, when we landed upon another world. We looked upon ourselves from the moon with the shared eye of our cameras in space, and we saw that in fact it is utterly true: We *are* one planetary body.

The next step in awareness will take place when we experience ourselves as members of one *psychological body.* We will *feel ourselves* as one body, each member alive to its unique function within its own body, which is *itself* evolving into a coordinated whole whose capacities are infinitely greater than those of its separate members. Each of us will feel the power of the whole. Each of us will feel ourselves connecting, empathizing with each other the way cells in the body feel with each other when the nervous system connects at birth. Then the body relaxes, the eyes open, the child smiles.

We stand on the threshold of a planetary smile. It will happen when enough members of the body realize what is already true. We *are* one planetary body. Then the Christlike power of individual members of the body will be awakened as an ensemble. In a chain reaction, one mind will stimulate another, exponentially releasing awareness times awareness, till enough of us feel it at the same time. We will then experience the benign presence of our potential self—Christ—communicating with us directly.

The message will go out to the peoples of Earth. We will hear in our new tongue: "*You* are the sons and daughters of God." Then will it be known that we are one body, born into the universe, seeking greater awareness of our creative intention, which is to become Christlike, heirs of God, co-creators of a new Heaven and a new Earth, graduated into the next phase of evolution—forever aware that we are an integral part of the same creative process.

When will this awareness occur? As Jesus said, no one knows. Quantum jumps are unpredictable. They occur when the stress is great enough and the new capacities are mature enough to interconnect, to cross the abyss from the old to the new without disintegration of the parts.

The tributaries of awareness of the new are multiplying and feeding into the larger body. We sense a dam about to break, a flood about to flow, a joining of separate forces about to occur which will bring on the Second Coming—which is the birth of ourselves as Christlike beings.

*B*ut covet earnestly the best gifts: and yet show I unto you a more excellent way.

Though I speak with the tongues of men and of angels, and have not love, I am become as sounding brass, or a tinkling cymbal. And though I have the gift of prophecy, and understand all mysteries, and all knowledge; and though I have all faith, so that I could remove mountains, and have not love, I am nothing. And though I bestow all my goods to feed the poor, and though I give my body to be burned, and have not love, it profits me nothing. Love suffers long, and is kind; love envies not; love vaunts not itself, is not puffed up, does not behave itself unseemly, seeks not her own, is not easily provoked, thinks no evil; rejoices not in iniquity, but rejoices in the truth; bears all things, believes all things, hopes all things, endures all things. Love never fails: but whether there be prophecies, they shall fail; whether there be tongues, they shall cease; whether there be knowledge, it shall vanish away. For we know in part, and we prophesy in part. But when that which is perfect has come, then that which is in part shall be done away. When I was a child, I spoke as a child, I understood as a child, I thought as a child: but when I became a man, I put away childish

*things. For now we see through a glass, darkly; but then
face to face: now I know in part; but then shall I know
even as also I am known. And now abides faith, hope,
love, these three; but the greatest of these is love.*

I CORINTHIANS 12:31, 13:1–13

This magnificent passage is a guide to us who still see
through the glass darkly, but for whom the darkening glass
is shimmering with beams of light from the slowly rising
dawn. Love never fails because it is the binding force of the
universe, the primary magnetism that unites atoms to atoms,
molecules to molecules, cells to cells, and now humans to
humans as members of the one body of humankind, which
is awakening to its stage of Christ consciousness.

All forms pass away. The force that *forms* form does not
pass away. We feel that force as love. All ideas, all gifts, all
prophecies are temporary contributions to the evolution of
the world. Love is the evolving force of the world.

As we grow beyond the stage of childish, self-centered
consciousness (when we knew only in part), we shall "know
even as we are known." The Creator knows us now, for we
are created in the Divine Image. God created us—we did
not create God. But we do not yet know God fully, for we
have not yet recognized our own perfection; we have not
achieved sufficient creativity to know our Creator as well as
we are known. We must grow up and use our full capacities
harmoniously, as members of one body.

"When that which is perfect is come, then that which is in
part shall be done away." When we have become as perfect
as God in Heaven is perfect, we shall know God, and forget the early phase of self-centered consciousness, the way a
grown child forgets the first hours of postnatal life. They are

too different to be remembered. We must become godlike to know God. The reward for maturation is knowledge of God.

Just as when a newborn child matures and meets its earthly parents, so we, as members of a newborn planetary species just now cracking our cosmic egg, will mature and know more deeply our universal Creator. As we become aware of ourselves as one body, and begin to exercise our collective creative capacities, we will know the Architect of the universe. As above, so below.

Faith is magnificent—it brings our potential into being. Hope is essential—without it, the people perish. We cannot withstand the suffering of the present without expectation for the glory that shall be revealed. But love is God in action. It requires neither faith nor hope, which are future oriented. It acknowledges what is *already* here, now, forever and ever. That is the creative action of universal love. Without this love the particles would spring apart. Planets would fall out of their orbits and gravity would cease to hold. The whole of the universe would be in pieces, all coherence gone, all life gone, all existence gone, all reduced to chaos—were it not for the continual action of magnetic love, or God at work in the world. To the degree that we express love, we express God in action. To the degree that we express God in action we become like God. To the degree that we become like God, we are inheritors of the Kingdom.

*F*or since by man came death, by man came also the resurrection of the dead.

I CORINTHIANS 15:21

With man came the awareness of death and the effort to overcome it. All of human history can be interpreted as the effort to overcome the limits of mammalian existence: eating, sleeping, reproducing and dying. Through tools, language, religion and art, and today through science, industry, technology and the conscious activation of our human potential, we strive to overcome the limits of the material world. The present generation is the first to have the capacities to act out the resurrection by transformation.

*F*or as in Adam all die, even so in Christ shall all be made alive.

I CORINTHIANS 15:22

Early humanity, as Adam, was bound to the creature body. Christ demonstrated that our next step is to free ourselves from that body by being one with God. Even now some of us alive during the transition from the Earth-bound to the universal phase of our species are experiencing some subtle body-chemistry changes. Those who are attracted and magnetized by Christ, who passionately intend to follow his example the Whole Way—from the Sermon on the Mount to Mount Cavalry to the Resurrection and Ascension—sense a subtle energy shift and slowly begin to transcend our physical limitations. Jesus showed us the Way: Love your neighbor as yourself. Die unto this life. Be born anew. Go the Whole Way: *Love. Death. Transformation. Universal life.*

But every man in his own order: Christ the first-fruits; afterward they that are Christ's at his coming.

I CORINTHIANS 15:23

Christ was the first human to demonstrate the way to overcome death. At this period of history and forevermore, all humans who follow The Way will partake of that same capacity. Those born once the transformation is completed will carry a new seed, a new pattern, free from the creature human condition.

Then comes the end, when he shall have delivered up the kingdom to God, even the Father; when he shall have put down all rule and all authority and power.

I CORINTHIANS 15:24

The end of this phase of history will occur when the whole of humanity has transformed to the capacity of Christ. All existing institutions will have passed away. Once people are in a state of unitive consciousness, loving God above all else and all others as themselves, there will be no need for rulers, authority or power. We will be self-governing, freely cooperating with God. Each person will be a unique, creative aspect of the Divine. We will recognize our neighbors as ourselves.

Synergism occurs when human will cooperates with Divine Will for the regeneration of the human race. When we have put down all external rule, authority and power, synergistic self-government will prevail. Through the co-operation between divine grace and human activity, we shall have overcome death and the separation of self from self, and the self from God. The Spirit will create the body to suit its requirements to eternally co-create with the Creator. Ever-evolving, eternally creative—this we shall be.

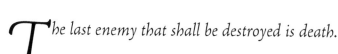

*T*he last enemy that shall be destroyed is death.

I CORINTHIANS 15:26

Unchosen death is the greatest tyrant of all. It separates us from the continuity of consciousness, blanking out the great persistently evolving human soul from self-knowledge, forcing us to begin anew each time, with each birth coming in helpless, spending precious years learning the language, then spending ourselves in reproducing more bodies, working for their sustenance, and then dying, with scarcely a moment to be aware of who and where we really are.

෨

*A*nd *when all things shall be subdued unto him,
then shall the Son also himself be subject unto
him that put all things under him, that God may be
all in all.*

I CORINTHIANS 15:28

Once the transformation is complete there will be no need for
the link between humanity and God, between the creature
and the Creator. The separation will be over. Humanity will
know God directly. When everyone is conscious that they
are the Son or Daughter of God, the human race grows up
and moves forward as a full and integral part of the creation.

෨

*If after the manner of men I have fought with beasts
at Ephesus, what advantages it me, if the dead rise
not? "Let us eat and drink; for tomorrow we die."*

I CORINTHIANS 15:32

Flesh and blood will not inherit the Kingdom. No worldly
solution will heal the world and emancipate its people.

AS YOU READ THESE WORDS, CONSIDER THE
hand that holds the pen. It has come to you
through billions of years of transformation. From

the first pulsing light in a protocell, through the giant dim-witted dinosaurs, through the fragile birds that flew through the night on the early Earth, and through the first humans peering at the dawn from the blackness of caves, this hand that holds the pen has come to you.

Now the conscious mind takes the hand that holds the pen and gradually transforms the ideas into written words. In the beginning, the word was made flesh. Now flesh is making the word. This is the meaning of the phrase "for this corruptible must put on incorruption, and this mortal must put on immortality." There is no other way to Heaven but through eternal life. Your generation is on the cusp from creature to co-creator. What you know as "man" was a fleeting instant of conscious time to train the mind to transform the body and to be fully human—meaning to be a full expression of God.

❧

You fool, that which you sow is not quickened, except it die: and that which you sow, you sow not that body that shall be, but bare grain, it may chance of wheat, or of some other grain.

I CORINTHIANS 15:36–37

Flesh and blood must die to its present phase in order to grow to its incorruptible phase. The resurrected body does not look like the seed from which it came. It is new and cannot be conceived from the perspective of the seed, save as a dim intuition of things to come. Fear not. The design is written in the stars. Every seed holds the design of its own future. The human being of flesh and blood is seed to the Universal Human. The human being carries encoded in its mind the design for its own growth. Fear not. Let us allow ourselves to be naturally what we can be. We do not need to know how to grow in order to grow. Let the plan unfold by purifying our minds, trusting our intuitions, acting on our visions and remaining humble in the face of the awesome infinity we do not yet know, but soon will.

But God gives it a body as it has pleased him, and to every seed his own body. All flesh is not the same flesh: but there is one kind of flesh of men, another flesh of beasts, another of fishes, and another of birds.

There is one glory of the sun, and another glory of the moon, and another glory of the stars: for one star differs from another star in glory.

I CORINTHIANS 15:38–39, 41

The universal human we are growing toward has a beautiful body. Our only task is to purify our thoughts and act on our vision. Initiative is essential to growth. Unless the seeds break their shell, put down their roots and send up their shoots to seek the light of the day, there will be no new body.

Every seed is unique and every race of seed or species of seed is unique. Everything that endures is beautiful. Evolution is a beautifying experience. What will be is even more beautiful than what has been. What comes forth at this stage of history will know its Creator more clearly. The beauty of the body will be reinforced by the appreciation of the mind, which can know the source of beauty, which can know God.

⌇

*S*o also is the resurrection of the dead. It is sown in corruption; it is raised in incorruption.

It is sown a natural body; it is raised a spiritual body. There is a natural body, and there is a spiritual body.

I CORINTHIANS 15:42, 44

The seed of humanity, which is sown in animal bodies, will grow up in spiritual bodies. The natural body resonates at a low frequency. The spiritual body resonates at a higher frequency. During the transition from natural to spiritual, through conscious evolution rather than physical death, there comes a time of instability, when the frequency shifts from lower to higher, the intellect grows disoriented and the body feels surprised. This is a time for hibernation. As the bear sleeps through the winter alive, the transforming human must sleep awhile to the world, must renounce all worldly concerns, must trust the process as a newborn child trusts its mother whom it has not yet recognized—so strange is she to a creature conceived and grown in the darkness of the womb, born into the world it knows not or how or why or where. It is natural for a flesh-and-blood body to transform into an imperishable body at the stage of history, when the species graduates from its terrestrial to its universal phase.

OH, YE OF LITTLE FAITH, WHO BELIEVE THIS is all there is, open your eyes and wonder how even this is here when only yesterday the Earth was silent, the rains fell, there was no light, and no mind experienced life.

Imagine tomorrow, when the Earth is renewed, the body is imperishable, the minds are joined, the cocoon of Earth is open, the stars are your home and you have discovered that you can speak the language of the universe.

The unknown tongues of yesterday are the universal tones of tomorrow. The music of the spheres becomes comprehensible to bodies resonating at a frequency that can pick up the vibrations of the universal conversations, which are even now gently impinging on your sleeping senses.

Awake, oh humans, and smile, for the time you have
prayed for is coming, the love you have yearned for
is yours, the sights you have longed for will be seen.
Day will break through the long dark night of the
soul, encased in dying bodies praying for the light.
The light is near. The light is here.

*A*nd so it is written, "The first man Adam was
made a living soul; the last Adam was made a
life-giving spirit."

1 CORINTHIANS 15:45

The first human was endowed with a consciousness of the
Creator buried deep within the psyche. Humans have always
known they are more than a perishable body. From the
dawn of human consciousness they have recognized death
as a transition to a new life; they prayed for the departed;
they strove to be prepared to go beyond the narrow confines of the material world as perceived by the five mammalian senses: sight, taste, smell, touch, sound. The living soul
of the first Adam carried the human race from its beginning
to its present precipice of power.

Now is the beginning of the Second Adam, who is
endowed with a life-giving spirit. The Second Adam has a
new body that resonates at a higher frequency. The transition from this life to the next is made in a new way as we
graduate from the Epoch of the First Adam to the Epoch of
the Second Adam.

The transition is made, not by disintegration, but by

conscious integration of the intention of the individual with God. All is well. All is choice. In the end there is no coercion, only free will, aligning freely with the will of God. The former things are not remembered. The past has passed away. The first Adam has done his work, which was to prepare the way for the life-giving spirit. The living souls of the first Adam, whose bodies have disintegrated in the graves of Earth, are reclothed with new bodies at the time of the transformation, their pioneering service to the future honored through the halls of Heaven. All is well. Not a hair, not a feather is uncounted. The will to live on is the key to the Kingdom of life. As we will, so shall it be when our will and God's are one.

Nevertheless that was not first which is spiritual, but that which is natural; and afterward that which is spiritual.

I CORINTHIANS 15:46

That which is natural came first because it was the necessary learning period for life-giving spirits, a time to choose or not to choose to go on. Evolution at this stage of history is becoming a self-selection process. The assembly of souls who have undergone the rigors of Earthbound life are now prepared to make the choice freely for universal life.

Not everyone chooses to evolve. The spirits of some less attracted souls do not leap with joy at the opportunity to discover the next phase of life. They have had enough and are gracefully allowed to remain precisely where they are.

There is no criticism for those who choose to wait. There is no criticism anywhere at the next stage. The judgment is over. There is no pain. Everyone is honored.

⌒◞

*T**he first man is of the earth, earthy; the second Man is the Lord from Heaven.*

I CORINTHIANS 15:47

The first human had a body made of the materials of Earth, resonating at the frequency of Earth and designed to be reincorporated with Earth at the end of the earthly life. The second human is Christ consciousness awake in a body that is materialized by conscious intention, and that can be dematerialized and rematerialized at will. The second body is made out of the same atoms that comprise the Earth, yet combined in a new way by the energy of focused will. Material formed by a conscious mind resonates with a higher frequency, and is thereby more responsive to intention than the stone or the body of early humans.

⌒◞

*A**s is the earthy, such are they also that are earthy: and as is the heavenly, such are they also that are heavenly. And as we have borne the image of the earthy, we shall also bear the image of the heavenly.*

I CORINTHIANS 15:48–49

Those who remain in Earth bodies will remain of this Earth, in this phase of self-consciousness. Those who choose to transform will co-create new bodies and express the intention of their higher self, the Christ-within, God.

As we were born of Earth, with earthly bodies, we have imagined ourselves to be Earthbound. As we are born of conscious intention, we shall imagine ourselves to be Heavenbound. We shall be in a state of relationship with all being, to that which was, is now and ever shall be, world without end. As we imagine ourselves, so we are.

The mind imagines; it uses images to create new form. In the Epoch of the Second Adam our self-image becomes our reality. We are what we think we are. Thoughts are to the next phase what gold is to this one—pure energy to purchase our heart's desire, with which to become whatever we choose to be.

GUARD YOUR THOUGHTS, OH WOULD-BE angels! Only the pure go on. Prospect your minds for thoughts of pure gold. Polish, mount, love, honor and cherish them, and let the dross settle out and disappear. Your thoughts are your treasure. What you think, you are.

❧

*N*ow this I say, brethren, that flesh and blood cannot inherit the kingdom of God; neither does corruption inherit incorruption.

I CORINTHIANS 15:50

As long as the soul is in a perishable body it cannot become a life-giving Spirit, it cannot resonate wholly with God. The density of the flesh dampens down the frequencies, causing insensibility to dimensions of reality that cannot be perceived by the five physical senses and their scientific extensions, which look at reality from the outside.

The new bodies are incorruptible, meaning they resonate precisely with the intention of the Spirit. The form becomes a perfect expression of the intention that informs it. The intention is incorruptible. The root of the word "corrupt" is "to break." Incorruptible bodies do not break, do not disconnect from the spiritual intention of the person who creates them. As long as the will remains pure, that is, connected with Spirit, the form remains at one with the intention it reflects. We experience continuity of consciousness through ever-evolving forms.

❧

*B*ehold, I show you a mystery; we shall not all sleep, but we shall all be changed.

The generations in the Epoch of the First Adam, which lived during the terrestrial phase of life, from the first human on Earth to us now, ended this life by death. Their physical bodies could not respond to Spirit's desire to live on. Spirit therefore discarded the body and lived on the next plane of reality, no longer carrying out the work of this world.

The generation now alive during the transition between the Epoch of the First Adams and the Epoch of the Second Adam—during the shift between the terrestrial and the universal phase of human history—is undergoing subtle body changes in preparation to give birth to a generation that will not have to undergo physical death. The generation that will come will recognize that we are one body born into this universe, seeking greater awareness of our creative intention.

As we focus our attention on restoring the Earth, emancipating human creativity and building new worlds in the universe, the need for the continuity of consciousness will become obvious. For universal humans living in an Earth-space, or a universal environment, the limited creature human life cycle will be inadequate.

On Earth our emphasis will be on conserving and enhancing the environment, nurturing the endangered species, stewarding the works of nature and human art, and creating a sustainable world for all Earth life. So, too, will the surviving humans be able to restore their own physical bodies. We will extend our lives by choice, and die by choice. Newness will arise as we explore the depths of inner and outer space, as we remove the veil from our eyes and extend the five mammalian senses through the awakening of the sixth sense, the spiritual faculty.

Oh, humanity, what your eyes are about to behold will fill your breaking hearts with joy. You who are saddened by the infantile condition of the human race, take heed. Lift up your hearts, raise your eyes, throw back your heads and sing praises for the day that is coming.

You have always known you are one body, now you see you are. You have always intuited that you were immortal, now you know you are. You have always known you were universal, now you voyage to the stars. You have always known you were beloved, and now you feel the love. You have always known you were unfinished, now you are evolving before your own eyes.

The movie of creation is speeding up. The slow frames quicken to let you see the pattern of the future unfolding before your eyes. In the twinkling of an eye you are seeing the next step of creation. The film accelerates. The static frames blend and you see God's hand at work vividly for the first time. As you move off Earth time and into cosmic time, the invisible hand of God reveals itself by speeding up the picture.

❧

In a moment, in the twinkling of an eye, at the last trump: for the trumpet shall sound, and the dead shall be raised incorruptible, and we shall be changed.

I CORINTHIANS 15:52

The transformation is a natural event in cosmic time. The sound of the last trumpet will be as obvious as the end of winter and the beginning of spring. Day by day we scarcely perceive the ground softening, the sap flowing, the shoots rising, the buds opening—yet when we look back upon it the change is apparent: irresistible and magnificent. If you were experiencing spring for the first time you would have no way of knowing that the barren land would surely, surely, surely become green. You would have no way of knowing that the cold, white eggs would hatch with lively, running things. No way of knowing that the dark bulb would become the violet in bloom.

Humans born during the transition have no way of knowing that this Earth, this living being, will renew herself and send her children forth to become universal beings in a community of stars. We think it will be winter forever, for we are creatures of one planetary season. We have not yet lived on planetary time, where the growth in the garden of planets that were born in the velvet darkness of the universal womb becomes apparent.

The creatures of a single planetary season have no proof they will evolve beyond these earthly bodies and become glorified. No proof except the demonstration of the resurrection and the promise: this you shall do and even more shall you do.

or this corruptible must put on incorruption, and this mortal must put on immortality.

I CORINTHIANS 15:52

This corruptible body is not fully connected to the intention of the mind. We are in an early stage of the mind-body relationship. Our thoughts are disconnected from the frequencies of our cells. As we move into the next phase of human development, our thoughts will be able to penetrate the nucleus of the cells. The communication channels will be open and more direct.

The mortal body will be transformed as the immortal, immaterial mind connects directly to the design that constructs the body. Like the mind, the design is a field of consciousness, not a thing. As the mind changes its idea of what it can do, it will change the design, building the body according to its intention.

We will only succeed in this when we fully align ourselves with the mind of God. Our immortality springs from God's desire for eternal creativity, not through the death of the body and the birth of infants *ad infinitum*. God's desire for creativity requires the emergence of creatures who do not die, but who go on creating, while remembering they are the Sons and Daughters of God and who enact the Creator's intention.

To gain these powers takes more than a creature human life cycle of four score and twenty years. It will seem ridiculous, ages hence, to recall that once we lived a flash of time, then died to this world and hovered in waiting as spirit bodies, to return again. This process is our kindergarten.

Now we are going to God's School for Conscious Evolution. Soon we shall graduate into the next world of co-creative action, designing that which has never been before, carrying out the pattern of evolution as it has been written in the scriptures, "What I do shall you do, and even more shall you do."

❧

*S*o when this corruptible shall have put on incorruption, and this mortal shall have put on immortality,
then shall be brought to pass the saying that is written,
"Death is swallowed up in victory."

I CORINTHIANS 15:54

It has been said that death shall have no dominion in the end.
Death occurs in the early school of life. It gives the young
and unknown the opportunity to try and try again. The
wise know that they are acting out the will of God, which is
their own. They constantly ask and listen and pray for guidance until at last the voice for God becomes second nature
and they never return to the days of unknowing, the days of
dying and being born again.

❧

*B*lessed be God, even the Father of our Lord Jesus
Christ, the Father of mercies, and the God of all
comfort; who comforts us in all our tribulation, that we
may be able to comfort them which are in any trouble, by the comfort wherewith we ourselves are comforted of God.

2 CORINTHIANS 1:3–4

We can only give what we have received. If we are comfortless, we cannot give comfort. If we are full of comfort, we cannot help but give comfort to others. It flows from us naturally. To give is to receive. Therefore, the more comfort we give, the more we receive. To those who have shall be given even more abundantly.

The source of comfort is to love the Creator and to know we are loved in return. We can recognize our oneness with God, and yet must remember that the Act of Creation comes from God to us. Loving God, we must love ourselves. Loving ourselves as having been created by God, we are released from the "sin" of feeling separate and alone. We grow comforted by the unbreakable connection that is established between the Creator of the universe and ourselves. The source of comfort, security, tranquility and joy lies in this relationship. When we have it, we give it.

We are troubled on every side, yet not distressed; we are perplexed, but not in despair; persecuted, but not forsaken; cast down, but not destroyed; always bearing about in the body the dying of the Lord Jesus, that the life also of Jesus might be made manifest in our body. For we which live are always delivered unto death for Jesus' sake, that the life also of Jesus might be made manifest in our mortal flesh.

2 CORINTHIANS 4:8–11

A bright beacon of light comes from the knowledge that we do now have life everlasting because one man did it, and revealed to each of us that it is our potential to do as he did, and even more. Believing this to be true gives us the strength to rise above any momentary distress, no matter how terrible.

We can always turn our attention toward the reality of our potential for everlasting life, for perfect security, and be not afraid, even unto the death of this body. For our faith frees us from fear. Freed from fear, we can no longer be victimized by distress.

We have chosen to experience ourselves as saved at all times, even unto the cross.

In fact, with this attitude we can welcome affliction, for it gives us the opportunity to strengthen our faith. However, we must never *seek* affliction for the sake of affliction. This becomes masochistic and reveals a lack of faith in the certainty of our already achieved potentiality for salvation.

⌘

For which cause we faint not; but though our outward man perish, yet the inward man is renewed day by day. For our light affliction, which is but for a moment, works for us a far more exceeding and eternal weight of glory; while we look not at the things which are seen, but at the things which are not seen: for the things which are seen are temporal; but the things which are not seen are eternal.

2 CORINTHIANS 4:16–18

As creatures still dependent on our five creature senses, which pick up impressions of solid objects from the unseen world of patterned vibrations, we find it hard to remember that what we see with our outer eyes is but a picture in our heads of invisible events that impinge upon our nervous system. We are translating that invisible world in every instant into sounds, tastes, smells and images that are *in us*.

Knowing this, we can choose to remember at all times that the picture we see is not the event, which has already changed by the time the picture comes into focus in our brains. Our complex memory system interprets that picture and checks out every new experience for meaning in terms of its limited past experience. Our nervous systems and brains relate everything that happens to us to some past experience, for interpretation and evaluation. Usually, this is "sensible," as it supports survival in the material reality that our "senses" are sensibly sensing.

However, if we are working toward a state of being that our five senses cannot sense, because they have not experienced it, we cannot trust our senses! They do not sense what is not material. They do not sense the Cause of the material world. They do not sense the Creative Initiative of the Creator, creating energetic events to manifest ideas. Events are ideas incarnate.

To look at the "things unseen," which are eternal, is to experience the Source of the energetic events that our senses experience. The Source is always there, always creating. The events created are always changing, always evolving, since the mind of God is infinitely creative.

To identify with the eternal Source of the evolving world is to free ourselves from all identification with our own temporal conditions—our body, our emotions and all the afflictions to which they are heir. We can take an inner stance where we know that "we" are not our bodies. We are not our emotions. We are at one with the Source of the universe, creating our own images of reality and our own experiences.

We can reverse the flow of consciousness. Instead of perceiving ourselves as victims of the images that our nervous systems are creating, we can experience ourselves as the conceiver of those images, for in fact we are—our nervous systems make the experience felt. Because the stream of energy that impinges on our nervous systems creates the images, we can consciously detach the images from the events, change them by an act of graceful imagination, and project our consciously conceived image outward onto the invisible events. This outward projection becomes an energy flow that invisibly affects the invisible flow of events in the world around us, influencing what we see. We see it in crude form in phenomena like psychokinesis and telepathy. Jesus demonstrated a more advanced form by manifesting food for thousands. At the level of God, to think is to create.

Thought is energy. To imagine is to attract, focus and project energy so we can manifest what we imagine. When we see ourselves at the source of the creation, imagining it into being, we place our intention in alignment with the intention of God.

In this way, we are sure to succeed. For God's will is being done on Earth as it is in heaven, *now*. Victory is certain once we join our will with God's and *image-in* the Kingdom of Heaven for all.

The shift from Adam to Christ reflects the change from experiencing ourselves as the victim of events to experiencing ourselves as co-creators, co-conceivers of events through the alignment of ourselves with the will of God. Jesus aligned himself with the Creator and so became the *source* of experience rather than the victim of it.

How can we—who are still creatures in a state of self-consciousness, still perceiving with our five senses—awaken our sixth sense, our inner eye, our suprasensory channel of cognition? We do it the same way a baby grows up, by allowing it to happen naturally. We *image-in* ourselves as Christ, our Potential Self. That inner expectation and utter faith in our own potential to evolve from Adam to Christ is all we need. A higher level of intelligence accomplishes the rest—just as DNA builds our bodies at a higher level of intelligence than our conscious mind can do.

Therefore if any man be in Christ, he is a new creature: old things are passed away; behold, all things are become new.

2 CORINTHIANS 5:17

Each of us, individually, can be in Christ now and leave forever the darkness of self-centered consciousness. To be "in Christ" means to be evolved to the point where we have turned our life over wholly to our higher self, the Christ-within. In such a state, we see constantly that all is one; we hear constantly the inner voice of God; we experience constantly the love that creates all; we co-create as we breathe; with every breath we take we become free of the limitations of the mortal body and the ego. Collectively, all things become new.

F or though I made you sorry with a letter, I do not repent, though I did repent: for I perceive that the same epistle has made you sorry, though it were but for a season. Now I rejoice, not that all of you were made sorry, but that all of you sorrowed to repentance: for all of you were made sorry after a godly manner, that all of you might receive damage by us in nothing. For godly sorrow works repentance to salvation not to be repented of: but the sorrow of the world works death.

2 CORINTHIANS 7:8–10

To be made sorry "in a godly manner" is a lesson devoutly to be desired. There is the pain of growth and there is the pain of death. The pain of growth pricks the conscience and alerts us to a self-imposed limitation. We respond to the pain of growth by removing the limitation and freeing ourselves for our own evolution.

The pain of death is suffering caused by the intimate, hidden decision not to grow, not to respond to our own highest intuition of the good. When we suppress our capacity to grow, we trigger the pain of death. Each of us is choosing, at every moment, whether to respond to the pain of growth or submit to the pain of death.

We rejoice whenever the pain of growth causes "repentance," meaning a change of mind, a decision to elect to respond to the highest within us, rather than to what is lower, or deathward. "Godly sorrow worketh repentance to salvation not to be repented of." We surely will not be sorry if we respond to the pricks of growth.

❧

But this I say, he which sows sparingly shall reap also sparingly; and he which sows bountifully shall reap also bountifully. Every man according as he purposes in his heart, so let him give; not grudgingly, or of necessity: for God loves a cheerful giver.

2 CORINTHIANS 9:8–6-7

We pay all for all. If we pay less than all, we receive less than all. We receive precisely what we give. We receive in the manner in which we give. If we give grudgingly, we receive grudgingly. If we give joyfully, we receive joyfully. While there is no justice on the earthly plane, there is total justice on the godly plane.

On this Earth some are born rich, some are born poor. Some are born sick, some are born healthy. Some are born bright, others are born dull. These advantages and disadvantages are unevenly spread—according, it is said, to circumstances beyond the immediate lives of individuals. The law of cause and effect decrees that the advantages and disadvantages have a meaning that comes from circumstances beyond our immediate control.

However, no matter the difference between our advantages and disadvantages, we are all equal on one point. All people will be affected immediately by the purpose intention in their hearts now. If our intention is to give our best—whatever our external condition, whether rich or poor, sick or well, bright or dull—we will be rewarded by joy and by the peace that passeth understanding. These treasures are beyond all earthly rewards and cannot be attained by earthly victories.

If we choose to act upon our own highest purpose now, we will be rewarded now, beyond our wildest dreams. For truth is stranger than fiction. What is about to occur is beyond our wildest dreams. Our past dreams were dreamt in the darkness of the womb of Earth in dying mortal bodies.

Who knows what dreams we shall dream when we at last become universal beings, beyond the reach of physical death and the gravity of Earth? Sow bountifully now; reap bountifully now, then and forever.

F or though we walk in the flesh, we do not war after the flesh: For the weapons of our warfare are not carnal, but mighty through God to the pulling down of strong holds; Casting down imaginations, and every high thing that exalts itself against the knowledge of God, and bringing into captivity every thought to the obedience of Christ.

2 CORINTHIANS 10:3—5

We struggle heroically to rise beyond hubris: the pride of human intellect that we are doing this alone and may do anything we please. We are not doing this alone. We did not create ourselves. We did not create the patterns in the process of evolution. We are discovering them.

"Every high thing that exalts itself against the knowledge of God" will be cast down. Every great work we do from now unto eternity is to be translated from a purely human act to a co-creative act, an act consciously undertaken in joyful recognition that we are freely carrying out an intention whose source, scope and ultimate purpose we do not yet know at this phase of evolution. Now we see through a glass darkly, then we shall see face to face. Now we know the part. Then we shall know the whole.

Every thought will align with our highest purpose. We will put the Kingdom of Heaven first. We will love God above all else. We will love our neighbor as our self. We will continue to discover the invisible patterns of creation and co-create with them from here to eternity.

∽

I knew a man in Christ above fourteen years ago, (whether in the body, I cannot tell; or whether out of the body, I cannot tell: God knows;) such a one caught up to the third heaven. And I knew such a man, (whether in the body, or out of the body, I cannot tell: God knows;) how that he was caught up into paradise, and heard unspeakable words, which it is not lawful for a man to utter. Of such an one will I glory: yet of myself I will not glory, but in mine infirmities.

2 CORINTHIANS 12:2–5

Paul-the-earthly-man once knew himself as Paul-in-Christ, when he had the vision of Jesus on the road to Damascus and was blinded for three days. During those three days he was out of touch with his earthly self and in touch with his higher self, which is Christ. During those three days he was "caught up in paradise," and heard unspeakable words, "which it is not lawful for a man to utter." He could not even tell whether he was in his body or out of it.

If any one of us experiences a sudden awareness of ourselves as "in Christ," the limits of our little body of flesh and bones render that experience hard for us to identify. Where goes the person during that instant of expanded consciousness? Is that person confined to the limits of the flesh and blood body, or do we transcend those limits by knowing what exists beyond those limits?

Paul was "caught up in paradise." The next step of evolution seems to be paradise for the human spirit still incorporated in a mammalian body. At the time of Paul, and through the end of this phase of self-consciousness until the present time, it has not been "lawful" for a man to utter the "unspeakable" words heard while in a higher state of consciousness.

Why was it unlawful? The deeper truths needed to be esoteric, secret, hidden and protected by initiates in mystery schools, because the power of that state of consciousness was still too great to be given to those in a stage of infantile self-centeredness. Would we give a three-year-old child the key to a car whose engine was running—when one touch of the gas pedal would shoot thousands of pounds of steel wherever the hand of the child directed it? Would we give a self-centered *Homo sapiens sapiens* the key to higher consciousness before humans matured mentally and spiritually enough to be capable of sustaining greater awareness wherein those powers would be used for only the good?

Hitlerism, black magic, hypnotism, cultism, animal magnetism and psychic powers of all kinds are spin-offs of higher consciousness. But they do not reflect the full state of the coming phase of evolution, wherein the awakened mind aligns itself freely with the patterns in the process of creation.

Now is the time. We are maturing despite ourselves, like awkward adolescents experiencing budding sexual changes in our bodies—regardless of how unprepared for the responsibilities of sex the youngster may be. We are sprouting suprasexual technologies: rockets that leave the Earth, instruments that change the genes, bombs that destroy the Earth.

Mother Earth is developing her evolutionary capacities— her seed imperative, her reproductive impulse to ejaculate her life into the universe, where it may grow anew. The time is now because the whole planetary system is undergoing its shift from terrestrial to universal development.

We are a living system overgrowing its finite womb. We can, will and must stop growth here and become synergistic, conservative and self-limiting. But if we *only* do that we will have to suppress our evolutionary capacities to go beyond the mammalian condition. We would have to suppress genetics, longevity, artificial intelligence, self-replicating robots, astronautics, nanotechnology and all other evolutionary capacities. We would have to deny our aspiration to transcend physically through our space programs. We would have to cut out the muscles of the newborn universal species and condemn it to remain in the nest—a basket case, a self-limited planetary genius, afraid of its suprasexual powers to become co-creative with God and joint heirs with Christ.

These early technologies designed for the first phase of universal life are crude and awkward. They will soon be surpassed by more "natural technologies" that are aesthetic, nonpolluting and miniaturized. A tree is a high *natural* technology. A chemical space rocket is low technology. Soon, human-made technologies will be more miniaturized and ephemeralized, more like nature's technologies.

In the distant future, each person will be truly like Christ. Our spiritual intention and our high technologies fused together will create new bodies. Now is the time when the secrets Paul experienced in "paradise" are being shared, given, and experienced by humans *en masse*. Millions are meditating, attuning, listening and sharing in the experience of enlightenment, however crudely.

The esoteric is become exoteric as the planetary system shifts from terrestrial to universal. As we come through the birth transition we will be aligned with the Intention of Creation, for the powers of co-creation are the natural inheritance of a universal species. All will inherit, new godlike powers as every adolescent inherits the sexual powers, ready or not, worthy or not. The selection process will favor those who are sensitive to the patterns in the process of creation. "Then shall two be in the field; the one shall be taken and the other left. Two women shall be grinding at the mill; the one shall be taken and the other left." (Matthew 24:40–41)

Evolution is compassionate, but not nice. It cannot afford to be nice at the expense of the whole of life. Those who do not follow the Way of Love will not be able to handle the powers of co-creation. The infant with an atom bomb is a picture already too terrible to witness. We are infantile humans with atom bombs now!

The process, which operates beyond human intervention, will favor and promote those characteristics that *can* evolve. Those who feel connected to the whole can live and evolve lovingly with the powers that shall be revealed in us. The rest will be repurposed with compassion.

And lest I should be exalted above measure through the abundance of the revelations, there was given to me a thorn in the flesh, the messenger of Satan to buffet me, lest I should be exalted above measure. For this thing I besought the Lord three times, that it might depart from me. And he said unto me, "My grace is sufficient for you: for my strength is made perfect in weakness." Most gladly therefore will I rather glory in my infirmities, that the power of Christ may rest upon me.

2 CORINTHIANS 12:7–9

Even the mighty Paul was afflicted with a "thorn in the flesh," a "messenger of Satan" that separated him from the perfect state experienced during his revelations. Why? Because no one on Earth is yet totally beyond the human condition, nor *can we be* if we desire to carry out the essential maturation process step-by-step until finally, in due time, we no longer exist in a state of self-centered consciousness.

Even the greatest among us grapple with infirmities. Through the act of grappling, we attempt to overcome the impulses of our lower self by following our intuitive attraction to our higher self. The inner decision to overcome every obstacle to Christlike being is the key to self-evolution. Many are attracted. But few choose to go the whole way in changing themselves. Somewhere we begin to accommodate a weakness, rather than grow beyond it. We evolve as far as we choose to, and no farther.

Christ incarnated in a human body to demonstrate the potential each human holds to transcend the separated human condition. If he had appeared as a nonhuman being, a Greek god, for example, he would never have inspired the faith that *we* could do as he did, and even more. A divine human, Jesus demonstrated every human's capacity to choose to be divine.

Even our greatest teachers manifest weaknesses that enable them to relate to the human condition to which they minister. If we see a thorn in our flesh, we should take it as a "messenger from Satan." Satan stands for separation from God. It probes every weakness to test for the willingness to accept the illusion of separation. This part of the selection process weeds out the dedicated from those who have not chosen to go the whole way. It brings forth the self-elected, so that when the tribulations are over only those connected to the whole will go forward.

When we see ourselves behaving less than our best, we can interpret it as the evolutionary selection process and decide whether we want to evolve or devolve. If we choose to evolve, we practice Christ's commandment to love God above all else and our neighbor as our self. If we choose to devolve we give in to guilt, fear and disease, permitting ourselves to be relieved of participation at the next level of response-ability for the implementation of the design of Creation.

*S*ince *all of you seek a proof of Christ speaking in me, which toward you is not weak, but is mighty in you. For though he was crucified through weakness, yet he lives by the power of God. For we also are weak in him, but we shall live with him by the power of God toward you.*

2 CORINTHIANS 13:3–4

We cannot evolve by free will alone. Grace is an integral part of the pattern, and aids us beyond our known capacities. We need to do all we can to make the highest choice at every step, knowing full well that our initiatives will never suffice. We are fully responsible for our actions, and at the same time totally aware that a larger response-ability than our own— which holds but an infinitesimal glimpse of reality—enables us to evolve beyond our present powers.

When we feel weak and yet are choosing to evolve, we must ask for strength and guidance that lies beyond ourselves. No one can do it alone. No one *is* alone. That is the point.

We who are Jews by nature, and not sinners of the Gentiles, Knowing that a man is not justified by the works of the law, but by the faith of Jesus Christ, even we have believed in Jesus Christ, that we might be justified by the faith of Christ, and not by the works of the law: for by the works of the law shall no flesh be justified.

GALATIANS 2:15–16

No human law, and no human works based on human law alone, however divinely inspired, can serve to transform us from creature human to co-creative human. Only the processes of evolution and the laws of transformation—as demonstrated by Jesus's baptism, transfiguration, crucifixion, resurrection and ascension—can justify our expectation of life everlasting.

+ **Baptism:** awakening to the fact we are a son or daughter of God.
+ **Transfiguration:** being filled with light.
+ **Crucifixion:** dying to the creature human condition.
+ **Resurrection:** embodying the intention and power of the Creator.
+ **Ascension:** rising beyond this dimension of space/time to become a universal being.

Human laws aided us during the terrestrial phase of human existence, from the Baptism through the Crucifixion. Universal laws will guide us during the cosmic phase of human existence, from the Resurrection through the Ascension—and beyond. The Jews sought to fulfill the laws of God by bringing Heaven to Earth. Christ sought to fulfill the love of God by transforming humans to universal beings, beyond the confines of their bodies and this Earth, through the transformation of the material world.

Scientists sought to fulfill the love of God by discovering how the creation works.

Freedom lovers sought to fulfill the love of God by discovering how the creation works.

World reformers sought to fulfill the love of life by improving material existence for all people. Now comes the moment of synthesis, when the aspiration of all peoples will be fulfilled, by all transcending as they are confronted by the blinding glare of the reality of our potentials unfolded in life.

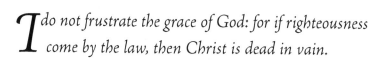

I do not frustrate the grace of God: for if righteousness come by the law, then Christ is dead in vain.

GALATIANS 2:21

Consider the universe in all its splendor. Contemplate the billions of galaxies. Imagine the creation of this whole realm of reality. Focus upon the intelligence manifested in the exquisite organization and design of every entity, from subatomic particles to the human brain. Recognize that within you flows the essence of that intelligence. View yourself as a being just now opening your eyes to the fact of your personal participation in the evolution of the universe—a creative member of the ongoing creation.

Ask yourself how much you consciously know about how and why the creation works. Think about the limitations of the social laws to which you submit, in relationship to the process of universal creation. Imagine that Christ is the aspect of you that knows the laws of creation—not social laws, but God's operating principles. Now, seek connection with those principles by grace—that is, by the realization that those principles are alive and reaching toward you, even as you are reaching toward them. Surrender. Do not frustrate "the grace of God"—the Divine attraction for you—by prejudging how righteousness may be acted out by you.

Believe for an instant that the whole universe is alive and as attracted to you as you are attracted to it. Let the magnetism of that mutual attraction flood your nervous system with the force that binds atoms to atoms, molecules to molecules, cells to cells.

Break the bonds of self-consciousness by allowing the electricity of Creative Intelligence to flash through you consciously. Take the blinders off. Be blinded for an instant, as Paul was on the road to Damascus. Let your inner eyes become accustomed to the light; then act in a state of grace—a state of attraction to, and harmony with, the whole creation. Connect consciously with the whole.

Christ died on the cross and demonstrated, by his resurrection, that we are no longer subjected to the laws that were appropriate throughout the dispensation, when Spirit was incarcerated in an animal body. The resurrected body is a new body, which is directly sensitive at all times to the Universal Mind that created it. Animal bodies were appropriate for the terrestrial phase, during which we built the capacity to transcend the womb of Earth. Intentional bodies will be appropriate for the universal phase, during which we will exercise our capacity as co-creators, designing worlds and exploring the multidimensions of this universe without end.

❧

Wherefore then serves the law? It was added because of transgressions, till the seed should come to whom the promise was made; and it was ordained by angels in the hand of a mediator.

But before faith came, we were kept under the law, shut up unto the faith which should afterwards be revealed.

GALATIANS 3:19, 23

Humanity's childhood was the period of self-consciousness during which the human intellect matured enough to become aware of the processes of creation. During our childhood we were bound by laws because we were not old enough to be responsible for our own acts. We transgressed (like all children do) yet were held in safety by the law as given to Moses, to preserve the human community from its own self-centered tendency to destroy itself out of its own ignorance. The laws were essential until the revelation of our divinity could be actualized, until our consciousness matured enough to understand how God works, so we could work with God as natural co-creators.

When giving the Ten Commandments to Moses, God announces himself: "I am the Lord your God, which have brought you out of the land of Egypt, out of the house of bondage." (Exodus 20:2) To be brought out of the "land of Egypt," out of "the house of bondage" means, from an evolutionary point of view, that those who recognize the whole Design will be free to evolve. The land of Egypt is the stage of existence before we knew there was but one God and one Design, which could be known directly by the chosen people rather than indirectly through the Pharaoh.

"Egypt" represents an earlier phase of consciousness and civilization, when we first glimpsed the possibility of extended life beyond this life. The pyramids were launching pads for universal life. The pharaohs were buried with their wives and possessions. They mummified their bodies, preserving them as best as possible for life everlasting in a new domain. While the Indian cultures looked inward for transcendence, the Egyptian culture looked outward and forward, toward a transformed material world—as demonstrated by the pharaoh—a god-king prepared to transcend his mortality. No one yet suspected that *everyone* is to be pharaoh, that God is alive in us all. Thousands of years had to pass before humanity grew ripe for this awareness.

Egypt founded Western Civilization on the expectation of a transformed and desirable personal life in a new body that lived beyond this world. Israel executed the next step of the Design by communicating that God's Design extended to each person who was willing to follow God's law: the chosen people. India evolved the Design further by discovering and teaching how to be at one with the process of creation through Yoga and meditation. The Greeks then evolved the Design by intuiting the structure of nature and the principles of democracy. From the Pharaohs of Egypt, through the yogis of India, through Abraham and Moses, through the discoveries of the Greeks and other great sages, within each tradition an element of the Design has been revealed.

The truth spread through Jesus to all people who would love God above all else and their neighbor as themselves. At this stage, for those who have faith in transcendence through the way of Jesus, there is no need for the law to be imposed upon them from the outside. It is experienced from the inside as an irresistible attraction to God, and to one another, beyond all labels and divisions of the past.

In our time, the Design is unfolding rapidly. We are the bridging generation from creature human to co-creator. Soon there will be no need to protect ourselves from our "transgressions," for we will be whole. The Law will be incorporated in the consciousness of Universal Humanity in attunement with God. The mammalian phase will be over, for those who follow the pattern the Whole Way.

Do you remember, dearly beloved, that you volunteered for this task? Do you, in whom the flame of expectation burns, recall that you have a memory of the future? Do you know that you already intuit the next stage of evolution? Do you know that you are volunteering emissaries, with a variety of missions on Earth, to help your brothers and sisters? Do you know that you are already familiar with Christ? That you are of the same family—younger in experience, but as capable of evolution if you will follow his example?

Dig deep into your memory, dearly beloved, till you can recall the promise that was made to you. The promise is that you shall have life ever evolving, if you remember that you are at one with God. This memory must awaken now for you to prepare the glorious future where the miracle of the resurrection is translated into action as the evolution from Homo sapiens sapiens to Homo universalis. You all share a similar experience of a different time and place in the universal community.

You know each other instantly because of your shared memory of the future. Those who recognize the truth of this writing will be those who have been together before Earth was created. Those to whom the promise was made existed before Abraham, before Moses, before Jesus.

Wherefore the law was our schoolmaster to bring us unto Christ, that we might be justified by faith. But after that faith has come, we are no longer under a schoolmaster.

GALATIANS 3:24–25

The old external law served as our guide and brought us to this point in history when the Quantum Transformation is to occur. Those "to whom the promise has been made"

379

are now going through a crash course in God's School for Conscious Evolution. Our task now is to incorporate the law within us so we can be guided through the time of the tribulations, when all about us disorder will increase. The old external law will not hold.

The inner law will take hold in those to whom the promise has been made and through whom the promise is to be kept. The inner law is the pattern in the process of evolution. The family of humanity, whose task is to work for the future, experiences it as a deep knowingness.

Each of us must improve our inner listening to prepare ourselves for full participation in the transformation. The whole system signals us continually and brings us into contact with others who are receiving the same signals. The words of this testament stimulate the memory of those who are ready to experience the joy of cosmic birth—the evolutionary, collective equivalent to the individual experience of being "born again."

The "born again" individual transforms from self-centeredness to a whole-centeredness appropriate for the terrestrial phase of the Earth's history. The born again collective transformation affects many individuals, who all at once experience themselves as awakening members of a planetary system that is both coordinating itself and reaching beyond itself for universal action, consciousness and contact.

Those of us called to conscious participation in this act are willing to do whatever it takes to emancipate ourselves from anxiety, hostility, fear and guilt so that the signals may come through us loud and clear.

⌒

Now I say, that the heir, as long as he is a child, differs nothing from a servant, though he be lord of all; but is under tutors and governors until the time appointed of the father. Even so we, when we were children, were in bondage under the elements of the world: but when the fullness of the time was come, God sent forth his Son, made of a woman, made under the law, to redeem them that were under the law, that we might receive the adoption of sons.

GALATIANS 4:1–5

God works on the macrocosmic scale. We have been in a long mammalian terrestrial life cycle wherein we were required to submit to the law that applies to that phase. We are conceived; we gestate in our mother's womb; we are born; we grow to the age of reproduction; we reproduce; we age; we die to this physical body.

Jesus was a first human cell in the planetary body to be activated into the next phase of the life cycle. His example is activating millions of other cells to prepare to do likewise. The triggers are:

- our personal intention;
- the planetary shift from continued growth on Earth to restoring the Earth and exploring the universe beyond our planet;

+ the cosmic environment flooding into our Earth system owing to the penetration of the biosphere by human instruments propelled into outer space;
+ the thinning of the ozone layer;
+ the emergence of new technologies of transformation such as nanotechnology, robotics, quantum computing and space development; and
+ the expansion and development of the noosphere, the thinking layer of Earth that is connecting us rapidly as a global brain, and moving us toward the experience of being members of one whole planetary body.

These signal to the whole system that the members of the body have matured enough intellectually for transformation to proceed. The new intuitive life stage can now be activated *en masse* for those who intend to participate in the transformation, in alignment with the design of creation.

The signs that we are being activated into the new phase of the life system are:

+ A sense of our body being infused with inner radiation;
+ A momentary intellectual disorientation as self-consciousness begins to destabilize and whole-centered consciousness begins to normalize (an "awkward stage," like adolescence);
+ An intensification of suprasexual attraction that may spill over into sexuality, falling in love and instant empathy;

- An intensification of vocational signals from within that urges us to "be about our Father's business," that is, to follow our highest aspiration for service and participation in the evolution of the world.

The Spirit of the Whole calls us to respond to our unique calling. At first we experience it as deep restlessness, frustration, uncertainty about what to do next, an unwillingness to continue to do what we are doing. We feel impulsive desires to travel, meet new people, shuck off the old, find our soul mates—those whose functional vocation is related to ours and with whom we must "keep in touch" and work together.

The co-creative family ties are being formed.

As we choose to listen to our inner voice, its signals begin to intensify. We make contact with our own inner teacher. Our interest in Jesus and other great spiritual beings becomes renewed. We renew our relationship with God. We begin to co-create on a global scale, way beyond our past experience or capacity. We begin to hear a sacred inner voice continually. We have increased peak experiences of unity with all being. We receive "the adoption of sons." We mature. "Therefore you are no more a servant, but a son: and if a son then an heir of God through Christ." (Galatians 4:7)

ACCEPT YOUR INHERITANCE, SONS AND Daughters of God. This is the will of God. I have waited thousands of years for planet Earth to mature so that its men and women could awaken and become one with me.

I especially awaited the awakening of co-creative women. From the time of those great women who first served me—from the first Marys, through the devout sisters, nuns and ordinary women who "married" me in their minds and hearts—I have awaited the maturing of the new woman, the whole woman who could not exist until the planetary system had developed to the phase where maximum procreation is no longer needed.

The time has come. Women who unite with me now, when the planetary phase is shifting from terrestrial to universal, will have a new relationship with me. Their bodies are preprogrammed to release a body-changing hormone that will trigger a co-creative system, which is the next step after the procreative system. The co-creative system normalizes the body changes experienced by the mystics and yogis.

The sexual energy in whole-centered men produces an experience of personal enlightenment—satori, Samadhi. The sexual energy in whole-conscious women gives birth to divine co-creativity as a new norm. The female nervous system and brain become aroused through the love of creation. The woman is no longer aroused only to unite physically with a man and produce biological children. She also feels deeply aroused to unite suprasexually with the Christ within, and to produce a new planetary body that is fully and consciously aligned with the Intention of Creation.

The work I performed between the crucifixion and the resurrection, women will perform naturally in the next phase of evolution. They will become the mothers of themselves. Their suprasexual energy, which desires union with me to co-create with me, as aspects of God, will, through that mental-spiritual union, trigger biochemical changes in their bodies comparable to the metamorphosis of caterpillar to butterfly.

This metamorphosis could not occur within individuals until planet Earth (your larger body) was ready to crack open its biospheric cocoon and begin to reproduce the Earth system in the universe. A planet's capacity to reproduce itself and its individuals' capacity to co-create themselves occur at the same time in the planet's life cycle.

You could not experience new bodies, en masse, until Earth arrived at its own stage of reproduction via your matured intelligence united with love for me. Now that you are able to send your first seed-pods into the universe, through human intelligence creating technological bodies, the signal has been given to turn on the co-creative system.

In men this is experienced as a powerful drive to conceive at a higher level. In women this is experienced as a body-mind transformation wherein your body becomes resonant with mind, your psychic capacities develop rapidly, you increasingly pick up telepathic signals from me and your rejuvenation mechanism is switched on. There will be an appreciable, measureable change within your cells.

Your cells will become more communicative and more receptive to receiving communications. You will discover that you can listen to their intelligence and learn from it. By a conscious release of tension, combined with the intention to evolve, you and your cells will enter a partnership to change your body from perishable to less perishable to final imperishability.

As your cells' design and your conscious mind begin to communicate, as you and your DNA intelligence learn to exchange information, your conscious intelligence will communicate to your cells its intention to turn on the regenerative mechanism that has been dormant in complex mammals, awaiting the maturation of the intellect, its union with Christ, and the Planetary Birth from terrestrial to universal.

All of this is as preprogrammed as puberty and senescence. The macrocosm has a life cycle as well as the microcosm. You have never witnessed a planetary life cycle; therefore you are not familiar with what happens to individuals at the time of a planet's shift from building intelligence in the womb to birthing that intelligence beyond its biosphere in the universe.

You are getting this picture because you asked for it. You asked, "What in our age is comparable to the birth of Christ? What is our story?" The first part of the answer is macrocosmic: Our story is a birth. We are being born into the universe. Mother Earth and all its life forms have jointly evolved humanity, whose task is now to love and restore the Earth, to care for its people and species, and carry its intelligence into the universe.

The second part of the answer is microcosmic: When the planetary system is being born, its human members are evolving from self-conscious to whole-conscious, from Adam to Christ. Your bodies, which have been designed to live and die like animals on Earth, are ready to change for performing a new function, which is to carry life into the universe, and to become a loving body on Earth.

As your bodies change, so does the body of the Earth. The biosphere is under stress. It must be freed from the pressures of human growth. You must begin to build a new Eden, a Second Garden, a cultural, natural center in alignment with the will of God.

Then there is the creation of the "androsphere"— the human creation beyond the biosphere. To achieve it, new bodies are required. Photosynthesis, multicellular life, sexual reproduction and scheduled death created a living Earth. A co-creative human who builds technologically and regenerates in space, will create a living universe.

⌒∾

*C*hrist is become of no effect unto you, whosoever of
you are justified by the law; all of you are fallen
from grace. For we through the Spirit wait for the hope
of righteousness by faith. For in Jesus Christ neither circumcision avails any thing, nor uncircumcision; but
faith which works by love.

GALATIANS 5:4–6

As we shift from self-consciousness to whole-consciousness, faith is our only way to go. The laws of this phase of
self-consciousness will not lead us to co-creative union with
God. They will hold us in bondage by forcing us to focus on
past limits rather than present possibilities.

Faith is the magnetic force that can guide us over the
abyss between self-centered and whole-centered awareness.
For a cosmic instant, the creature in transition to co-creator
panics. It *seems* as if we are nowhere and have no identity.
It *seems* as if we are abandoned by the human race still in
bondage and by Christ who is already free. This dark night
of the soul is the transitional phase from self- to whole-centeredness. It can last for years.

When we feel it we stop, and we remember that billions
of years of momentum in our being is driving us across the
abyss to the other side of the river. In time past, the "river"
was death of the physical body and the emancipation of the
spirit. In time future, the river will be the chosen, conscious
transition from mammalian self-consciousness to natural
Christhood. When the Kingdom has at last come and the

next stage of consciousness is secured, there will be no river, no abyss, no dark night of the soul. The individual person will remain in constant touch with the Creator at all times. Until then, we have faith and believe what cannot be seen by the five senses.

We trust totally in our faith in things unseen to guide us over the abyss. We turn on the magnet of faith within us. Our inner compass needle will be energized to pick up the magnetic field of the whole, which can then send us signals to guide us safely over the abyss.

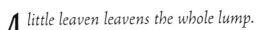

A little leaven leavens the whole lump.

GALATIANS 5:9

IT MAY SEEM TO YOU THAT YOUR FAITH CAN-not lift the weight of the world. The world is heavy. You are but a flicker of light. Yet the flicker of light that glows within you also glows within everyone else in the world. If you allow the flicker of light in you to rise up into a flame and become a blazing fire, it will encourage the flame to burn more brightly in every other person in the world.

Dearly beloved, if you can lift the flame to a fire within you through total love of me, beyond all appearances, beyond all sensation, beyond all hopes and fears, you will help the entire body of Earth arise. You are the leaven in the loaf, dearly beloved. If you can rise to me with pure faith that I am here, I am love, the world itself will burst into the flame of love.

❧

*F*or all the law is fulfilled in one word, even in this; You shall love your neighbor as yourself.

YOU CAN LEARN TO LOVE YOURSELF DESPITE your shortcomings, just as a mother loves a child. You love yourself for your potential to grow up, to be fully human. You never give up hope in yourself any more than a mother gives up hope in her child. You are your own child. The seed of the natural Christ is patterned in you. One phase of evolution gives birth to the next.

In this moment of transition, your lower self is required to give gracious consent to the birth of your Higher Self as the full self, in command of all aspects of your personality.

You—conscious self—must notify your body, your emotions, your ego that they are henceforth to give total allegiance to the Higher Self, whose will shall be done on Earth as it is in Heaven. It is their fulfillment also. Your childish self is not to be suppressed. It is to be gratified by the grace of maturation.

This alignment of all aspects of the human personality with the highest intention is the first step in the training of a young co-creator—which you now are, dearly beloved.

Be mother and father to yourself. Be patient, be kind, be firm, be joyful. You will surely mature until you become all that you can be—a natural Christ, an heir of God. The Design will unfold. How long it will take, and how hard it will be is up to you, dearly beloved.

This testament is written for the co-creators on planet Earth, those who have the intention to go the whole way to divine humanness. If you allow it to trigger in you the memory of why you are here, you will grow far more rapidly. This is the voice of the Christ teacher for those whose mission is the evolution of humanity from *Homo sapiens sapiens* to *Homo universalis*.

*A*nd they that are Christ's have crucified the flesh with the affections and lusts.

GALATIANS 5:24

We who came two thousand years after Paul do not have to "crucify" the flesh in the same brutal way that was necessary at the time of Christ. Jesus cracked the hard seed on the cross and sprouted the new body, which stimulated a wave of determination in millions of souls to do as he did. We do not need to crucify our flesh. We need to align our flesh with Spirit.

The Cosmic birth is now. The collective crucifixion is the pain of our birth. The resurrection of the whole has begun. Earthbound history is ending. Universal history is beginning. The Epoch of Adam gives way to the Age of Christ.

*B*ut let every man prove his own work, and then shall he have rejoicing in himself alone, and not in another. For every man shall bear his own burden.

GALATIANS 6:4–5

Each of us has an inner assignment, a unique function for which we came to Earth. Every assignment is needed. None is in competition with the other. We are like instruments in an orchestra. Everyone must sing his or her own pure note, freely in harmony with the Whole Composition, which is as yet beyond our full awareness.

When we sound our own tones in accord with our inner calling, we will blend with all others sounding their own tone, according to the celestial melody that harmonizes the universe into one ever-evolving whole.

☙

*B*e not deceived; God is not mocked: for whatsoever a man sows, that shall he also reap.

And let us not be weary in well doing: for in due season we shall reap, if we faint not.

GALATIANS 6:7, 9

BE PATIENT, BE STEADFAST, BE PERSISTENT, dearly beloved, and all shall be given to you. The step from adulthood to senescence is being interrupted at this phase of evolution. The transformation of the creature human adult to the co-creative human adult is interrupting the mammalian life cycle. This is an evolutionary leap! Naturally it seems disorienting. Be not afraid. The transformation is natural. Keep your attention on me— that still-small voice within each of you that knows what you are now and what you are becoming.

☙

*F*or in Christ Jesus neither circumcision avails any thing, nor uncircumcision, but a new creature.

GALATIANS 6:15

The rituals of the past will be irrelevant in the future, when the glory shall no longer be symbolized *by* us, but be manifested *in* us. We shall be new. The fire of enlightenment that lit the spiritual genius of the human race will be normalized and democratized at the time of the Planetary Birth.

Circumcision and non-circumcision were important issues at the time of the preservation of the seed. Now that the seed of the new creature is sprouting, those symbolic gestures can join the archival artifacts of the ancient history of the human race.

Blessed be the God and Father of our Lord Jesus Christ, who has blessed us with all spiritual blessings in heavenly places in Christ: according as he has chosen us in him before the foundation of the world, that we should be holy and without blame before him in love; having predestinated us unto the adoption of children by Jesus Christ to himself, according to the good pleasure of his will, to the praise of the glory of his grace, wherein he has made us accepted in the beloved.

EPHESIANS 1:3–6

Those of us on Earth now who sense within ourselves a total dedication to the transformation of ourselves and the world, according to the example of Christ, have been predestined by Christ—by our higher self—to serve in this way. Our higher self chose to serve this purpose "before the foundation of the world."

HAVE YOU EVER WONDERED WHY YOU SENSE a dedication deeper and greater than others? Have you ever probed deeply into your memory to recollect that you made a choice to come to planet Earth at the time of the Cosmic birth, the Quantum Transformation? Do so now, dearly beloved.

Your destiny has been chosen by your Higher Self, which exists in a dimension beyond evolutionary space/time. Your Higher Self preexists the evolution of the world and prefigures your function in the world according to the pattern laid down by the Creator before time began. There is the eternal God and the infinitely evolving God. There is the eternal you and the evolving you. The eternal God preexists and is the Source of the evolving universe. The eternal you preexists in the mind of God and is the source of your role in the evolving universe.

As we enter the period of co-creation, which is triggered by the Planetary Birth, you are to remember at all times both your eternal and your evolving aspect. As you take on the role of heirs of God, joint heirs with Christ, remember whom you are. You are at the Source of your own creativity. God created the eternal aspect of you and that aspect has been, is now, and will forever be with the eternal aspect of the Creator.

As your creativity increases, as the effects of your acts reach further into the future, your memory must reach deeper into the past until it cracks the sensory cocoon of space/time and experiences the eternal dimension out of which evolution springs. Unveil yourselves, dearly beloved. You are now ready to stand the shock of the brilliance of your own divinity.

Having made known unto us the mystery of his will, according to his good pleasure which he has purposed in himself: that in the dispensation of the fullness of times he might gather together in one all things in Christ, both which are in heaven, and which are on earth; even in him, in whom also we have obtained an inheritance, being predestinated according to the purpose of him who works all things after the counsel of his own will, that we should be to the praise of his glory, who first trusted in Christ.

EPHESIANS 1:9–12

Those of us who chose to come to Earth to nurture evolution at the time of the Planetary Birth will "in the dispensation of the fullness of times" be gathered together on Earth as it is in Heaven. We shall be gathered when the separate innovating parts interconnect simultaneously, annihilating time.

When the last feather is dropped upon the scales, the balance is shifted forever.

When the final grain of salt is dropped into a supersaturated solution, it crystallizes instantaneously. It takes eons of incremental changes to arrive at the instant of synchronicity, when all changes interconnect and shift the system into a new order of higher freedom, consciousness and union. This is the time that Jesus spoke of as the tribulations: "And He shall send His angels with a great sound of a trumpet, and they shall gather together His elect from the four winds, from one end of Heaven to the other."

Those who first trusted in Christ, who had faith in the transformation before it was visible, have "obtained an inheritance." We shall be "to the praise of his glory." We shall be able to celebrate the transformation first because we have believed in it first and helped others, by our faith, to believe in it. For as we believe, so shall we create.

As we imagine, so shall we become. As we sow, so shall we reap.

Those who have elected to have faith before it was visible will meet up with those who already have evolved, those who are in Heaven. There shall be a great cosmic family reunion of those who have chosen to give their total being for the good of the whole.

THERE IS A REWARD, DEARLY BELOVED. IT IS the answer to your deepest prayers. It is the response to your call, the gift that is given to all who have hungered after the Kingdom of Heaven.

The Kingdom of Heaven is the reward. The self-elect shall suddenly speak the same language, hear the same voice simultaneously and participate with synchronicity in the quantum moment—when the new creature shall be born in us for all to see. We are here to unravel the mystery of the coming events in which we have chosen to participate. We are to discover together our complementary roles in the time to come. We already intuit it. Planet Earth gathers together an ancient family of beings who collectively choose to incarnate together for this particular Planetary Birth.

YOU WILL KNOW WHO YOU ARE BY THE FACT that you share the same experience. The purpose of this testament is to unlock your memories and help you find each other, so that you can work together overtly for the good of the whole during the Planetary Birth.

The most important point to remember at this precious moment is to listen to your inner voice. Create a still place within you. Whenever you feel a loss of faith, stop. Listen, and hear my voice, the voice of your higher self who has experienced all this before.

You are a universal child. Your Higher Self is a universal adult. The experience of the transformation is within you, knocking on the door of your conscious mind, seeking entrance upon the center stage of your attention, so you will know what to do when the quantum time is come.

Now is the time of rapid preparation. The hour of our deepest discontent precedes the first rays of dawn. Crisis precedes transformation. Prepare yourselves, future-oriented family of humanity. Your hour is coming.

⁓

I *[Paul] also, after I heard of your faith in the Lord Jesus, and love unto all the saints, Cease not to give thanks for you, making mention of you in my prayers; that the God of our Lord Jesus Christ, the Father of glory, may give unto you the spirit of wisdom and revelation in the knowledge of him. The eyes of your understanding being enlightened; that all of you may know what is the hope of his calling, and what the riches of the glory of his inheritance in the saints, and what is the exceeding greatness of his power toward us who believe, according to the working of his mighty power, which he wrought in Christ, when he raised him from the dead, and set him at his own right hand in the heavenly places, far above all principality, and power, and might, and dominion, and every name that is named, not only in this world, but also in that which is to come.*

EPHESIANS I:16–21

Imagine the power that shall be revealed in us when it is the will of the Creator of the universe that it be so revealed. Imagine the capacity locked in our minds to become co-creators with God. Imagine that our belief in our ability to transcend and God's grace willing us to do so will coincide. God's creative genius gifted Christ the capacity to rise up from the dead. God's creative genius will likewise gift us the capacity to do the same—even more.

ALL THAT IS ASKED OF YOU, DEARLY BELOVED, is to have faith that it is so, and to discover your personal initiative, act, vocation or calling that is required for the enactment of the Design. Grace and initiative are twin keys now. Memory of who you are reinforces your faith. Love of your evolutionary family encourages you. Your heart fills with joy to encounter and cooperate with those in whom the flame of expectation also burns.

The power of God that created the universe and first demonstrated the next step in evolution through the example of Jesus is "far above all principality and power and might and dominion." Call on that power, dearly beloved. Its purpose is to fulfill you, so that you, too, can rise beyond your creature human limits.

Nothing on Earth can stop that power from fulfilling its intention—if not on Earth, then elsewhere in the universe. Do not forget that you are not alone. Planet Earth is only one among billions of planetary civilizations at various stages of evolution, from conception, through prenatal history, through their births into cosmic life, cosmic consciousness, cosmic contact with their brothers and sisters throughout the living universe.

God's house has many mansions, dearly beloved. If one house collapses, many remain. Have no fear— the evolution of life in the universe is inevitable. Whether or not any one planet makes it, is up to it. That is the freedom that has been given throughout the universe.

Each planet, like each newborn child, undergoes a viability test, a last judgment on Planet-bound life. You are undergoing your test now. Will you qualify for participation in the universal community of evolved beings? It depends on what you do now, dearly beloved.

If you put the Kingdom first and love your neighbor as yourself, and learn how the creation operates through your maturing sciences—then you shall participate in the exhilarating experience, at a new beginning, as members of the universal community with much to learn from your elder brothers and sisters, and from Universal Intelligence.

The inner eye will open and you will see intelligence everywhere—in every atom, every molecule, every cell, every tree, every animal, every person, every star. All creation will ring with the sound of the voice of God.

Vibrations of energy will become intelligent signals upon your inner ear, explaining to you with every pulse how God works, so that you may work together.

The new sensory system will turn on—not only the sixth sense and the third eye as happened to mystics of the terrestrial phase (these are only the beginning, as the greatest of saints well knew), but the full spectrum of organs of knowing will turn on, until you know it all.

The rewards that await your faith and initiative are too glorious for you to fully understand. But now is the time for the mystery to be revealed. Discover it, dearly beloved. That is your privilege because you chose it before time began.

❧

*W*herefore remember [...] that at that time all of you were without Christ, being aliens from the commonwealth of Israel, and strangers from the covenants of promise, having no hope, and without God in the world. But now in Christ Jesus all of you who sometimes were far off are made nigh by the blood of Christ. For he is our peace, who has made both one, and has broken down the middle wall of partition between us; having abolished in his flesh the enmity, even the law *of commandments contained in ordinances; in order to make in himself of two one new man, so making peace; and that he might reconcile both unto God in one body by the cross, having slain the enmity thereby; and came and preached peace to you which were far off, and to them that were nigh. For through him we both have access by one Spirit unto the Father.*

EPHESIANS 2:12–18

Christ Jesus's demonstration of new human potential transcends the past division between believer and nonbeliever, between Jew and Gentile. Through his demonstration of the human capacity to transcend the creature human condition, he has reconciled all past belief systems. Through his demonstration he notifies believers and nonbelievers that all have access to the power of transformation if they have faith in things unseen.

Every person who intends to follow the way of Jesus will eventually go beyond crucifixion to metamorphosis and ascension.

⌒∾

*N*ow therefore all of you are no more strangers and foreigners, but fellow citizens with the
saints, and of the household of God; And are built upon
the foundation of the apostles and prophets, Jesus Christ
himself being the chief corner stone.

EPHESIANS 2:19–20

These words notify us that we are to grow up and take our
natural place in the household of God, as fellow citizens
with the saints. We no longer have the right to remain children in the household of God. Extended adolescence, without co-creative responsibility for conserving life on Earth
and developing life in the universe, is irresponsible. We no
longer have the luxury of childish irresponsibility, cavorting
carelessly, destroying the biosphere of our Earth and failing
to establish a productive capacity in outer space.

We have to build on a global-universal scale, consciously
contributing to the "holy temple" as did the apostles and
prophets. We are to transform the physical world into
a Second Garden, a more sensitive manifestation of the
Creative Intention. It is prepatterned, pre-scripted that this
will be so.

ill we all come in the unity of the faith, and of the knowledge of the Son of God, unto a perfect man, unto the measure of the stature of the fullness of Christ; that we henceforth be no more children, tossed back and forth, and carried about with every wind of doctrine, by the sleight of men, and cunning craftiness, whereby they lie in wait to deceive; but speaking the truth in love, may grow up into him in all things, which is the head, even Christ.

EPHESIANS 4:13–15

When we look at the behavior of humans in society and are filled with despair, we are not to say, "It is the nature of humans to be thus and so." Rather, we are to say, "We have been children, learning how God works, self-centered as the young always are. Now we are ready to graduate from this class in God's school. We will "grow up into Him in all things, who is the Head, even Christ." We must set our sights *high*. Human nature as we have known it is a transitional phase—as are all phases until the creature and the Creator become one.

◦

Finally, my brethren, be strong in the Lord, and in the power of his might. Put on the whole armor of God, that all of you may be able to stand against the wiles of the devil. For we wrestle not against flesh and blood, but against principalities, against powers, against the rulers of the darkness of this world, against spiritual wickedness in high places.

EPHESIANS 6:10-12

What *seems* to us to be evil is often the selection process of evolution, which is constantly selecting for those characteristics that favor our development as universal humans, and selecting out those characteristics that block this development. The steady pressure of the forces of destruction, disintegration, dissent, decay, devolution and death test us every instant of every day. When that pressure meets the resistance of a self-centered characteristic, it corrodes it with the almighty force of God.

Those characteristics that prevent us from sensing our relationship to the whole will not be favored. Selfishness, hostility, fear and anxiety are all manifestations of characteristics that are being selected against at this stage of evolution. Likewise, those characteristics that enhance our sensitivity to the patterns in the process of evolution will be favored. The selection mechanism of evolution is highly intelligent. Its function is to favor every trait that can help us inherit the Kingdom of Heaven, everything that can bring forth the next stage of evolution.

God's will is for all life to inherit the Kingdom and become co-creative. The universe is a nurturing ground for gods. God's intelligence operates everywhere. The method of transformation is known as evolution. It has operated before life began and it will continue to operate in the post-biological phase, when conscious evolution prevails.

We may experience God's selection mechanism as evil when we are tested. That which can evolve is always contending with that which would prevent it from evolving.

Every hurdle to our own growth reveals God's selection process at work. Tests are necessary to grant us the opportunity to grow stronger. If we respond to hurdles by leaping over them while keeping our eye on the Kingdom, we will evolve. If we respond with fear and fail to leap, we will be given chance after chance—forgiven, forgiven, forgiven—until the time of the Quantum Transformation, when one phase of evolution ends and another begins.

Self-consciousness will be absorbed into universal consciousness. Evolution's work on *Homo sapiens sapiens* will be complete. Only that spectrum of human consciousness freely able to attune to the Whole and hear the inner voice for God will evolve. Self-centered consciousness will pass away.

❦

But as the days of Noah were, so shall also the coming of the Son of Man be. For as in the days that were before the flood they were eating and drinking, marrying and giving in marriage, until the day that

Noah entered into the ark, and knew not until the flood came, and took them all away; so shall also the coming of the Son of Man be. Then shall two be in the field; the one shall be taken, and the other left. Two women shall be grinding at the mill; the one shall be taken, and the other left. Watch therefore: for all of you know not what hour your Lord does come.

MATTHEW 24:37–42

One moment all appears tranquil. The next instant all hell breaks loose. Then suddenly, all is new. The selection process is not crude, however. It is extremely *refined*.

Those strains of human temperament that have withstood the diseases of the modern age will evolve. Evolution will favor those characteristics that resist fear, hostility, guilt and alienation. It will favor the ability to become centered in the "holy place" within, wherein the higher self, the Holy Spirit, the Voice for God speaks constantly and lovingly to all people.

LISTEN CAREFULLY, DEARLY BELOVED. LEARN to focus your attention continually on the still-small voice within each of you. Be still, listen—and know that **I am God.**

Strengthen the magnetic needle of your attention by faith in the process of creation. Faith is a magnet that attracts the signals.

Pray constantly for guidance. Prayer is the telepath-ic signal from the part to the whole that attracts God's attention that you are ready to do more.

Refuse to believe that the appearance of the exist-ing world is the ultimate nature of reality. Refuse to accept the status quo as the way things truly are. Things are in the process of change, dearly beloved. Invisible processes are at work giving birth to a whole world.

Reject all existing ideologies and belief systems that would limit you to your present incomplete stage of development. Reject all counsel to stay as you are. Ask that you become all that you are: a natu-ral Christ.

Let the flame of expectation burn to a fire and light your enthusiasm—till the love of God fills your whole being.

Surrender yourself to the design of creation—by carving out a still place within you to listen for the voice of God.

Make direct contact. Let the electricity of God's communication system transfigure you as Jesus himself was transfigured.

❧

*A*nd after six days Jesus took Peter, James, and John his brother, and brought them up into an high mountain apart, and was transfigured before them: and his face did shine as the sun, and his raiment was white as the light.

While he yet spoke, behold, a bright cloud over-shadowed them: and behold a voice out of the cloud, which said, "This is my beloved Son, in whom I am well pleased."

MATTHEW 17:1–2, 5

FOR EACH OF YOU THE PROCESS IS THE SAME. First your lower self—your creature human body-brain that has experienced itself as a mortal organism born to live and age and die—must recognize its whole self as the Son or Daughter of God. The lower self must be infused with enough light to see beyond the five senses. That act of recognition by your lower self of the reality that you are a Son or Daughter of God will free you to transform.

Next you will "go to Jerusalem." You will resolutely decide to die to this stage of evolution—your ego-centered self is crucified and you arise as a new being, a natural Christ—which is every human's inheritance as a natural heir of God. Your lower self will protest, as Peter himself once did. You must educate your lower self lovingly, as Jesus taught his disciples, that a far greater victory is to be gained by your transformation than by adaptation to the existing human condition.

You will clear your system of all negativity and guard your thoughts with a sword of steel. The natural process of self-evolution will occur. You will triumph. All elements of your being will align themselves with your highest intention. Then you will be transfigured. You will shine with light. You will know your identity as a co-creator.

B *ut if I live in the flesh, this is the fruit of my labor: yet what I shall choose I know not. For I am in a strait between two, having a desire to depart, and to be with Christ; which is far better; nevertheless to abide in the flesh is more necessary for you.*

PHILIPPIANS 1:22–24

In the time of Paul there were two choices: to die to this body and be with Christ in another dimension of reality or to live in the flesh, prey to imprisonment, pain and disease. Paul chose to live for the sake of others, even though he, personally, would have preferred to die, to be "in Christ." There was no other alternative during pre-transformation history—because flesh and blood cannot inherit the Kingdom.

Mammalian bodies and self-centered personalities could not be in Heaven, except for brief flashes of unitive bliss.

After the transformation, a new choice will open up: to consciously transform our body as Jesus did and live on at one with Christ, rather than die to be with him. During the transition from Earthbound to universal life, we are still "in a strait between the two" as Paul was, "having a desire to depart" to separate ourselves from the disordered world and seek inner peace, or to remain in life, suffering. But two thousand years later we are closer to the Quantum Instant than was Paul. We thus make the same choice he did, to stay in the world and keep our attention totally on God, and to act on behalf of the Divine Design. Blessed are we to be chosen to live at the time when "We shall not all sleep; but we shall all be changed."

Our potential self yearns for actualization. Our love of all life yearns for greater expression. Our mortal flesh yearns for incorruptibility. Our childish emotions yearn to be put to rest forever. Self-conscious beings yearn to rejoin the creation as conscious co-creators. Eve, the maturing intellect, yearns to marry Christ. The entire creation longs to give birth to ourselves in the future, universal beings, attuning to the voice for God, in contact with our brothers and sisters throughout the universe: free at last, dear God, free at last.

◦◦◦

Not as though I had already attained, either were already perfect: but I follow after, if that I may apprehend that for which also I am apprehended of

Christ Jesus. Brethren, I count not myself to have appre-
hended: but this one thing I do, forgetting those things
which are behind, and reaching forth unto those things
which are before, I press toward the mark for the prize
of the high calling of God in Christ Jesus.

PHILIPPIANS 3:13–14

None of us have yet attained our own highest potential. It cannot happen until the planetary system is ready to integrate into one whole and reach into the universe for new life. Until the Quantum Instant comes, we can only do this one thing—forget and forgive those things that are passing away in the old stage of evolution, while remembering and reaching toward those things that lie before us—the next stage of evolution beyond the creature human limits.

Press onward toward this mark: Ourselves as fully realized beings, natural Christs, in a world that has experienced its oneness in a Planetary Pentecost, the first planetary smile of a cosmic species born into universal life.

*B*rethren, be followers together of me, and mark
them which walk so as all of you have us for
an example.

PHILIPPIANS 3:17

Seek examples of humans who have "put this purpose first"—who put the Kingdom first, who "press toward the mark for the prize of the high calling." Their magnetic attraction to their higher self magnetizes us to be attracted to that which is highest in ourselves.

Whenever we are near someone who is distracted by fear rather than attracted by love, we protect ourselves with "the whole armor of God that you may be able to stand against the wiles of the devil." (Ephesians 6:11) The "devil" distracts us from our attraction to our highest potential. He appears in many guises: worldly success, glamour, fame, power, glory, ease and popularity. Anyone who is giving in to any of these as his or her primary purpose becomes a disorienting magnetic field—and tends to distract us from our focus unless we deliberately protect ourselves. The best method of protection is to charge ourselves with enthusiasm and love. Our magnetic field then becomes so coherent that it serves as a membrane against invasion by confused motivations.

Light the flame of expectation. Create a still place where the flame can safely burn, protected from the surface winds of change. The flame is the Divine spark that was lit at the dawn of creation and has been growing ever since. It desires to rise until it consumes our whole being in its light. It burns inside every cell. Signal your cells that you are ready to have the flame rise, and your whole body will become sensitive to the Intention of Creation.

_F_ or our conversation is in heaven; from whence also we look for the Savior, the Lord Jesus Christ, who shall change our vile body, that it may be fashioned like unto his glorious body, according to the working whereby he is able even to subdue all things unto himself.

PHILIPPIANS 3:20–21

We need not condemn one stage of evolution in order to affirm the next. Paul falls into an emotional trap when he speaks of "our vile body" in contrast to Jesus's "glorious body." That is like calling the single-celled organism "vile" because it is not a rose.

Our body is a magnificent achievement developed throughout billions of years of creation. It is our heritage. So too is every organism that ever lived, every atom that ever whirred about itself, our heritage. The experience of billions of years of history is written in our blood and bones. We are the sum and substance of the whole creation. To deny our present condition is to deny God who created us!

The memory of the creation is recorded in our neurons. We were there at the first explosion. Our atoms date back to the time when God created the Heavens and the Earth.

Our molecules were formed on the early Earth. Our cells have the memory of the origin of life. Our brain records the reptilian and mammalian experience. Our as-yet untapped capability to self-transform bodies is coded in our DNA.

We originated before life began. The design for our bodies did not begin with the first dim cell that organized molecules into a living pattern. The design for our bodies did not begin with the first complex molecules. It did not begin with the first atoms. It began in the mind of the Creator whose intention was, is and will be to create creatures in the image of God. The intention of the Creator is to create co-creators. This intention is written deeper than our genetic code. It is laid down in the invisible infrastructure—the matrix—and serves as the bonding mechanism, the connector among particles. This intention attracts, attracts, attracts until complexity increases to the point where consciousness awakens on a universal scale. The first creatures to become co-creative on planet Earth are now emerging. Soon we will discover we are not alone. We are growing up in a universe full of life with an intention similar to our own.

None of this will be real to us until we experience the demonstration of its truth, ages hence, just as Jesus's resurrection was not and is not yet real to most people, because it goes beyond the phase of creature human experience. The next step in the Design will be real now only to those whose memory of the future is awakened. That is the purpose of this testament. Use it well. It serves as a guide for our own evolution. It is given to those who have eyes to see and ears to hear.

Jesus spoke in parables to the multitudes, while revealing the mysteries to his disciples. Two strands of religion emerged: the external, exoteric church that preached the fixed word, and the internal, esoteric communities of knowers, which initiated individuals into the disciplines of self-transformation. The Mystery Schools initiated those willing to undergo rigorous self-discipline, providing techniques of personal alchemy that start a person on the path to awakening the spiritual sense, rejuvenating the body, stimulating psychic powers, attuning to other dimensions of reality.

Now we no longer speak in parables, for the time of the transformation is now. Conscious evolution has begun. We are already changing our bodies through the new science of genetics. We are already practicing meditation by the millions. We are already using biofeedback machines to learn to control our own involuntary functions. We are already leaving this Earth alive in spacecraft and returning. We are already travelling by image with the speed of light around this tiny globe and beyond.

The Mystery Schools have opened their doors and are revealing their secret teachings. Those who have spent lifetimes of training in personal transformation are everywhere among us, setting high examples of capabilities for those in whom the flame of expectation burns. What is the flame expecting? It is expecting union with God through evolution of the person and the planet. It is expecting union with God through maturation of the human race.

A single cell cannot know the whole body, yet it carries the design of the whole body within its nucleus. A single person cannot know the whole design of creation, yet each of us carries the Design in our consciousness. Individuals *united* into an intercommunicating, co-creating planetary body will see each other as part of a whole that is greater than the sum of its parts. Individuals bonded for an instant by sharing awareness of the Intention of Creation will know the whole—and its parts. It is through our unity that we will know the next phase of God's Design for evolution and our individual parts in it. The phase of personal salvation is ending. The phase of collective conscious evolution is beginning.

THE PURPOSE OF THIS TESTAMENT IS TO create sufficient unity among those whose memory of the future is awakening so that together they may have eyes to see and ears to hear what none of them could see or hear alone. To penetrate the Quantum Instant, to see beyond the present crisis to the transformed world, you must unite, dearly beloved, you must unite.

Evolutionaries, unite! Not organizationally—unite spiritually. Combine your flames and your intuitions until you see that which is greater than the sum of your parts, and do that which none can do alone. Use this testament as an awakener, a connector and a reflector of that which exists beyond all of you. Together you will see me, be me and know me.

❧

Finally, brethren, whatsoever things are true, whatsoever things are honest, whatsoever things are just, whatsoever things are pure, whatsoever things are lovely, whatsoever things are of good report; if there be any virtue, and if there be any praise, think on these things.

PHILIPPIANS 4:8

Steady focus on the highest aim is the key to self-evolution. If we focus on pain, we are in pain. If we focus on joy, we will enjoy. If we focus on what is lovable, we act lovingly and receive love from everywhere.

We are responsible for our perception of the world. If we choose to see with the eyes of Christ we look upon a forgiven world in which everyone is a Son or Daughter of God. If we choose to see with the eyes of a dying animal we see a dying world, increasing in disorder day by day until the end shall come. If we choose to see with the eyes of a young co-creator, we see ourselves, and all others, as conscious participants in the creation, emerging from self-consciousness to consciousness of the whole. We see the disordering world as the birthplace of a new Heaven and a new Earth. And so shall it be, so shall it be.

Not that I speak in respect of lack: for I have learned, in whatsoever state I am, therewith to be content. I know both how to be brought low, and I know how to abound: every where and in all things I am instructed both to be full and to be hungry, both to abound and to suffer need. I can do all things through Christ which strengthens me.

PHILIPPIANS 4:11–13

We can be content in all things to the extent that we are full. The basis of our contentment is the knowledge that we are eternally co-creative with God in a universe without end. We are instructed both to be full and to be hungry. We are filled with the knowledge of our relationship to God and our potential to become co-creative with God by intending to do so with all our heart, body and mind.

We are hungry because it is not yet so. We are not yet perfect as God in Heaven is perfect. We are *potentially* perfect. That promise is our fullness. We are as yet imperfect. That desire is our hunger. Remember, those who hunger after righteousness are fulfilled.

Those who hunger after co-creative union with God shall surely be satisfied, for it is the Divine Intent that all children should mature to become heirs. God's will shall be done, on Earth as it is in Heaven. If our will and God's will are one we cannot fail.

No force in Heaven or hell can defeat a human being whose will is the will of God.

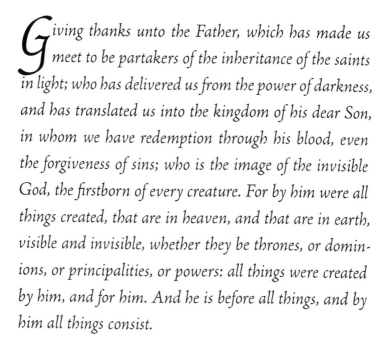

Giving thanks unto the Father, which has made us meet to be partakers of the inheritance of the saints in light; who has delivered us from the power of darkness, and has translated us into the kingdom of his dear Son, in whom we have redemption through his blood, even the forgiveness of sins; who is the image of the invisible God, the firstborn of every creature. For by him were all things created, that are in heaven, and that are in earth, visible and invisible, whether they be thrones, or dominions, or principalities, or powers: all things were created by him, and for him. And he is before all things, and by him all things consist.

COLOSSIANS 1:12–17

Imagine that the Creative Intelligence of the whole universe truly created us in its Divine Image and intends that we be partakers of the same inheritance as the highest, saintly humans who ever lived. Imagine that our Creator has delivered us from the "power of darkness"—that is from disease, hatred and death, and has "translated" us—changed us into another medium or form so that we can be like Jesus.

Imagine that the existence of one person, who has been translated beyond the creature human, serves as the evolutionary trigger for others to do so in the fullness of time, through activating latent capacities to do so. Imagine that we are created in the image of the invisible God. That is what we are.

Imagine that since we are co-creative with God, since we are also beloved sons and daughters as was Jesus, that by us were all things created, whether on Earth or in Heaven. Imagine that by us all things exist, for our Creator and we are one. Imagine this is so, and so shall it be.

But we, brethren, being taken from you for a short time in presence, not in heart, endeavored the more abundantly to see your face with great desire.

I THESSALONIANS 2:17

Think of the nobility, courage and heroism of Paul—and do as he did. When he was persecuted and imprisoned he used it as an opportunity to increase his spiritual freedom. While failing in the eyes of the world—a powerless prisoner of Rome, rejected by his own people, ministering to a tiny flock who were also endangered—he sent letters that changed the world.

The Epistles of the Apostle Paul strengthened the believers, who nurtured the seed of hope for a new person. This hope stimulated the development of science and democracy and modern society, which is now to undergo the collective tribulations, the collective crucifixion, and the collective resurrection as Universal Humanity.

Every act counts *ad infinitum*. All is well. All is very well. We are never imprisoned unless we believe we are. We are never helpless, unless we imagine we are. For the power of the Creator moves within us. When we express it we enlarge the creativity of the whole world to an immeasurable degree.

*B*ut I would not have you to be ignorant, brethren, concerning them which are asleep, that all of you sorrow not, even as others which have no hope. For if we believe that Jesus died and rose again, even so them also which sleep in Jesus will God bring with him. For this we say unto you by the word of the Lord, that we which are alive and remain unto the coming of the Lord shall not prevent them which are asleep. For the Lord himself shall descend from heaven with a shout, with the voice of the archangel, and with the trump of God: and the dead in Christ shall rise first. Then we which are alive *and remain shall be caught up together with them in the clouds, to meet the Lord in the air, and so shall we ever be with the Lord. Wherefore comfort one another with these words.*

I THESSALONIANS 4:13–18

Comfort indeed! Miraculous comfort. If we truly believe that Jesus died and rose again, can we also believe that those who died believing in him, shall also rise at the time of the Second Coming? How could it be that dead people can rise again? How did Jesus do it? The mystery is resolved by understanding what happened in the cave between the crucifixion and the resurrection.

What happened cannot be fully understood at our stage of evolution. Here is a hint of what might have happened, based on our *current* imagination: Jesus's consciousness was not dependent on his body. He chose to create a new body that resonated at a higher frequency. The idea for this kind of body comes from the experience of evolution on billions of other planetary systems that have already graduated from Earth-bound to universal life.

Jesus sped up the process of building the new body just as healers can speed up the coagulation of the blood and the formation of scar tissue. Jesus sped up the natural process of creation, building a new body of higher frequency that carried a continuity of appearance, and a stored memory of Jesus's first body.

It is said that every experience of every lifetime is recorded in the Library of Consciousness—a universal database with instant access to any recorded experience of any nerve cell in every being anywhere in the universe. Jesus could have transferred that recorded information from his old brain cells to his new brain cells in an instant download transfer—a technology that might one day be perfected throughout the universe as easily as an iPhone connected to the global brain through Google downloads information today.

The continuity of appearance is also easy to imagine. The genetic code for every being may also be recorded in the Library of Life. Category: Humans. Place: Planet Earth. Each gene carries specific instructions to bring forth specific characteristics. We are already creating new life forms in our work with recombinant DNA, in preparation for being able to do as Jesus did—and even more.

Jesus could have selected the instructions to build his new body with similar physical characteristics of height and weight. He could have activated and sped up the process of body creating, and then set it in motion with the greatest demonstration of co-creativity the world has ever seen—although this may one day be common behavior among universal beings.

Jesus appeared on the third day in a new, but recognizable body with its memory system intact. The same process could be applied to those who have died with a belief in Christ. Their belief would be recorded in the Library of Consciousness, their Life Codes recorded in the Library of Life. Their consciousness remains poised, alive, awaiting the sign. At the sound of the trumpet, the signal is given to the consciousness in waiting. They will call for their life experiences and their new bodies. They will reappear in a similar sped-up process to the one Jesus performed on himself. The "dead in Christ shall rise first."

The resurrected dead and the transforming living may then all be transported into a new state of consciousness and a new experience of life beyond the planet when the Quantum Instant comes. This is no more unbelievable than the 13.8 billion years of evolution that has been, and is now, creating a universe out of no thing at all.

Be prepared, dearly beloved, be prepared, and comfort one another with these words.

The end is near. The rapid breakdown and the rapid breakthroughs are about to occur. This is the premonition of the end that has alerted the human race from time immemorial. The intuition is correct. Modern futurists must learn from the ancient religions that incremental change leads to quantum transformation, which leads to new beings of higher consciousness, greater freedom and more perfect union with God.

---

*R*ejoice evermore.

I THESSALONIANS 5:16

Be joyful that the deepest aspiration of your being is true. Beneath the selfishness and chaos of the last days of self-centered humanity run the rivulets of wholeness and universal capabilities. Be aware of those rivulets of new life, and let that which is passing away, pass. Do not pay attention to the end. Pay attention to the beginning. Thus you will develop the discernment to know what is naturally dying and what is naturally being born. What is dying? The characteristics of *Homo sapiens sapiens* that make us feel separate from each other and from God:

- fear of death;
- fear of failure;
- fear of losing;
- fear of rejection;
- fear of poverty, and
- fear of sickness.

All of which engender:

- arrogance;
- pride;
- greed;
- covetousness; and
- all the other faults to which flesh is heir.

Being born now are the characteristics of *Homo universalis*:

- love of life;
- love of mutual victories;
- love of inclusion;
- love of shared abundance;
- love of wellness; and
- love of transcending every limit until at last we are co-creators with God, fully human, natural Christs.

Rejoice! Our dream will come true. The human race's aspiration for life everlasting is true.

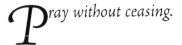

*P*ray *without ceasing.*

I THESSALONIANS 5:17

PRAYER IS YOUR SIGNAL TO THE WHOLE Intelligence, that you, the part, are ready to become whole. Pray without ceasing that my will, not thine, be done, that the will of God be done through you, that you and God are one. This prayer sends an energy signal that you are ready to surrender the illusion of separation. During this period of separation, you developed your individuality and your intellect sufficiently for them to become tools of transformation, servants to your will and God's will, now to become one.

A flood of power will answer the prayer. You will be empowered and enabled to carry out your unique creative function within the body of humankind now being born into universal life. Not only are you to become a natural Christ, you are to become a unique heir of God. Each of you has been given special gifts. Those talents are needed. As you evolve, you will be rewarded, as the greatest artists of the past never were. Creating consciously with God, within a community of others who do the same, will be your reward.

In the past, genius was so rare that it was eccentric and unable to fulfill itself. Yet it built the foundation for the planetary capacities you have inherited—oh privileged generation, oh Adams of the life-giving Spirit, oh first born of the universal age. The tower of Babel was torn down, for you were not ready, as immature humanity, to reach for the stars. Now you who love God above all else and neighbor and your self, pray without ceasing that you may remember who you are, dearly beloved. You are needed in this universe to take your natural place at the right hand of God.

Call upon the full hierarchy of evolved beings to be with you now. In your prayers call upon Abraham and Moses, Buddha and Mohammed, and Jesus Christ. Call upon all your heroes and heroines. Call upon all the consciousness of the past to join with you now. This is the moment for which they prepared. They are with you now, the saints and seers of humanity, preparing to join with you after the resurrection of the dead and the transformation of the living.

Call upon them. They need you as you need them. Their work cannot be fulfilled until yours is complete. The entire history of humanity is poised upon this living generation born at the time of the Quantum Transformation. Mark it well, all you who believe in the future of the human race. Pray without ceasing for all the help you can get.

In every thing give thanks, for this is the will of God in Christ Jesus concerning you.

I THESSALONIANS 5:18

CAN YOU BELIEVE THAT THE ENTIRE HEAVenly host is waiting for you to remember who you are? Can you accept the fact that it is the will of God, expressed through Christ Jesus, that you should transcend the creature human condition if you so choose? Can you believe that your universal brothers and sisters await your entrance into universal life, so they can be with you and educate you to the language of the spheres, the knowledge of the wondrous workings of the Designing Intelligence in the universe without end?

Trailing clouds of glory and intimations of immortality, you were born into this world of both evanescent beauty and deadly disease. Remember who you are, and you will reawaken to the glory and the memory of immortality with the experience you have gained in the rigorous school of Earth.

It is hard, dearly beloved, for a sensitive spirit to be incarcerated in a dying body, cut off from awareness of divinity. You are being trained as an apprentice godling, though your ego doesn't yet know it.

You have been here to learn how to work with God as mature individuals. The ego was essential to separate you temporarily so you could develop the capacity to be heirs rather than children of God.

Now you are graduating from the school of Earth. You have developed your intellects. The ego can withdraw and trust that the educated mind will fuse with the Designing Intelligence and act on behalf of the whole rather than the isolated part.

Give thanks with all your being. Be grateful with every breath you take. "Thank" (draw it in) "you" (breathe it out).

⁓

Quench not the Spirit.

I THESSALONIANS 5:19

In you burns the spark of the flame that was lit at the origin of creation by the fire of the mind of God. It is the Spirit within you that knows who you are and where you want to go. Feed the spark and nurture the flame. Its light is about to catch fire with the light of other flames, spreading like wildfire through the forests of our mind, burning the dross, revealing the gold of our capacity.

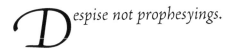

*D*espise not prophesyings.

I THESSALONIANS 5:20

Look to the future! Listen to those who know by faith of things unseen and hope for things to come. Pay attention to those now attuning to the pattern in the process of evolution. Who are they? How do we know the false prophet from the true? We know them by their fruits. If they are creating dependent followers, they are false. If they are creating liberated individuals self-preparing for universal life, they are true.

If a prophecy is built on less than the full realization of the whole spectrum of human potential—psychological, social, scientific, aesthetic and spiritual—it is false. If a prophecy is based on vengeance, fear or guilt, it is false. If a prophecy predicts that the end of this phase is coming, that the beginning of the new is here, that our future is to become ever-evolving beings in a universal community as co-creators, and we believe it, it is true for us.

*A*nd to you who are troubled rest with us, when the Lord Jesus shall be revealed from heaven with his mighty angels, in flaming fire taking vengeance on them that know not God, and that obey not the gospel of our

Lord Jesus Christ, who shall be punished with everlasting destruction from the presence of the Lord, and from the glory of his power.

2 THESSALONIANS 1:7–9

We can now translate the language of vengeance to the language of the evolutionary process.

"The Lord Jesus shall in flaming fire take vengeance on those who know not God, and do not obey the gospel"— this means that if we are in a state of self-centered consciousness we are not choosing to evolve through the Quantum Transformation. If we do not know the Consciousness that is creating us, we will not be able to evolve to the next natural stage, which is co-creative consciousness. The human intellect has matured sufficiently to naturally fuse with intuition. Intuition opens a direct channel to the Designing Intelligence. Intellect is the indirect channel through which we learn about the works of God—the "how" of it, so we can do it also. Henceforth, with a fused intuition/intellect, we will consciously evolve and consciously cooperate with the laws of transformation to co-create ourselves in the image of our full potential selves. Evolution is God's process of selecting beings who are ever more capable of knowing and co-creating with Divine Intention, in a universe of ever-evolving worlds without end.

et no man deceive you by any means: for that day shall not come, except there come a falling away first, and that man of sin be revealed, the son of perdition; Who opposes and exalts himself above all that is called God, or that is worshipped; so that he as God sits in the temple of God, showing himself that he is God.

2 THESSALONIANS 2:3–4

The "man of sin ... the son of perdition" refers to self-centered humans who are under the illusion that they are separate from God and other beings. This stage of consciousness will pass away before the new order is revealed through us.

In that state we cannot inherit the powers of co-creation, for we would surely further misuse them. Nuclear energy, biotechnology, cybernetics, astronautics, nanotechnology—all these evolutionary capabilities developed by the human intellect are even *now* too powerful to be used by the intellect alone. The intellectual genius that developed science and technology can willingly fuse with the higher intuition, the realization that One Creative Intelligence has created us all. It is natural to align our will with God's will, so that we may inherit the powers of the Tree of Life.

This fusion of intellect and intuition eliminates the blindness of narrow-minded scientism, which arrogantly assumes there is no Creator and that humans can become godlike on their own. Such hubris destroys. It is like stabbing our own hearts. Humans who have the powers of evolutionary technology can now destroy the world, and themselves with it. So clearly, self-centered humans are a passing phase. We will either self-destruct in our self-centeredness, or self-transform to whole-centered and co-creative humans, cooperating freely for the good of all.

*B*ut we know that the law is good, if a man use it lawfully; knowing this, that the law is not made for a righteous man, but for the lawless and disobedient, for the ungodly and for sinners, for unholy and profane, for murderers of fathers and murderers of mothers, for manslayers.

I TIMOTHY 1:8–9

We cannot legislate ourselves into the next stage of human development. We cannot become our full potential self, natural Christs, by merely avoiding disobedience of the law. We will become our potential self through love and attraction for the intrinsic, self-rewarding value of being godlike.

Negative goals do not suffice for those who wish to evolve. Thou shalt not kill, thou shalt not lie, thou shalt not steal, thou shalt not pollute, thou shalt not overpopulate, thou shalt not go to war—these prohibitions may prevent the potentially disobedient from perpetrating destructive behavior. The negative commandments will not, however, activate the obedient to evolve from Adam to Christ, from *Homo sapiens sapiens* to *Homo universalis.*

The law is for the lawless—to protect us from destruction. The evolutionary testament is for the lawful, the obedient, to attract us to evolve. It sets a positive goal.

◠◡

*T*his is a faithful saying, and worthy of all accepta-
tion, that Christ Jesus came into the world to save
sinners; of whom I am chief. Nevertheless for this cause
I obtained mercy, that in me first Jesus Christ might
show forth all longsuffering, for a pattern to them which
should hereafter believe on him to life everlasting.

I TIMOTHY 1:15–16

Jesus Christ first demonstrated a pattern on planet Earth
of how to achieve life everlasting. It was to love God above
all else and all people as Sons and Daughters of God. Paul
accepted this evolutionary template, modeling his own life
after that immortal pattern. He went forth and taught the
pattern. Life. Love. Death. New Birth. Many who have read
of his acts have also modeled their lives after that pattern
and are evolving toward a new life.

Two thousand years ago, Paul was required to demonstrate a pattern of long-suffering in a creature body with
limited consciousness, as yet almost blind to God at work
in all things. Those of us living at the time of the rapidly
approaching quantum change will take up an aspect of the
pattern not available till now. We who live now are born into
the time of the collective ordeal. The end of this phase of
history is near. We have heard the word through the lips
of the long-suffering faithful whom we love for the foundations they have laid for the glory that shall be revealed. The
part of the pattern to be revealed in us is the resurrection
and the ascension—which come *after* the crucifixion.

Our unused potential awaits the proper planetary

conditions to trigger it into action. Soon we will manifest the pattern in totality. The pattern of long suffering, waiting for the time, is almost completed. The pattern of the glory that shall be revealed in us is almost begun. Two thousand years of suffering have given us time to educate our intellects and develop the evolutionary technologies of transcendence, which can literally work with the pattern, to transform humans into new cosmic beings in the image of God.

*L*ikewise *must the deacons be grave, not double-tongued, not given to much wine, not greedy of filthy illegal gain; Holding the mystery of the faith in a pure conscience.*

I TIMOTHY 3:8–9

Image in detail, as precisely as you can, every aspect of yourself at your highest. Image yourself doing your best, being your best and thinking your best. Image yourself thinking like Jesus, seeing as he saw, doing as he did every second of the day. Let nothing distract you from imagining that you are already wholly yourself, already acting in full possession of your full God-given potential.

Let no imperfection cloud your mind. Self-correct with no self-condemnation and proceed to image yourself at your best. The time for guilt is over. We can be forgiven our "sins" of separation by the recognition they were but a natural, early stage of human consciousness.

When one person flew the Atlantic alone, it was signaled to all flyers that it could be done. When one person sailed around the world it was signaled to all sailors that the world was not flat. When one person set foot on the moon it was signaled to all humans that they need not be Earthbound. When one person died and then rebuilt his own body into a new body more sensitive to his intention, it was signaled to all human beings that they could all be changed. Imagination and intention are the keys.

IMAGINE YOURSELF AS A NATURAL CHRIST. Intend to be a natural Christ. And you shall so be. This is certain—as certain as the fall of an apple from a tree, as certain as the Earth's encirclement of the sun, as certain as the fact that the flower lives in the seed, is your potential to be as Christ, do as Christ—and more. It is the law. Open your inner eyes to your potential. Attune your inner ear to the voice within you that speaks incessantly to you, guiding you to self-evolve. Have faith, dearly beloved, that you and I are one, and all shall be given to you.

❧

*B*ut refuse profane and old wives' fables, and
exercise yourself rather unto godliness. For bodily exercise profits little: but godliness is profitable unto
all things, having promise of the life that now is, and of
that which is to come.

I TIMOTHY 4:7–8

EXERCISE YOURSELF INTO GODLINESS BY
imagining yourself to be the Son or Daughter of
God. Exercise your imagination to create yourself
as you can be. That life is in you now, as a seed.
Your imagination serves as the sunshine and rain,
nurturing the seed of your own self at the next
stage of development. It is preconceived.

Imagine the universe with its billions of galaxies. Imagine that the Creator of the universe created you in his image. Do you see yourself as a co-
creator, a natural inheritor with all others who are
willing to believe in their own godliness? It is that
self-image you must hold in your mind's eye every
minute of the day and night.

Visualize the image of humans at this stage of evolution: standing with one foot upon the Earth, the
other poised toward the stars, learning how the

process of creation works, ready to set forth from the kindergarten of Earth to the community of the universe.

Can you see? Can you hear? Look. Listen. Imagine. Have faith, and intend to be a natural Christ.

⁓

*B*e not you therefore ashamed of the testimony of our Lord, nor of me his prisoner: but be you partaker of the afflictions of the gospel according to the power of God, Who has saved us, and called us with an holy calling, not according to our works, but according to his own purpose and grace, which was given us in Christ Jesus before the world began, but is now made manifest by the appearing of our Savior Jesus Christ, who has abolished death, and has brought life and immortality to light through the gospel.

2 TIMOTHY 1:8–10

CAN YOU BELIEVE THAT YOU WERE CONceived in the mind of God before the world began? Can you believe that the evolving world that began billions of years before this Earth condensed was preconceived in the imagination of the Creator?

Can you believe that evolution is the acting out of the Creative Intention—an artistic process of discovering how to manifest a perfection that has already been conceived in the mind of the Creator?

Can you believe that your work, your "holy calling" was conceived before the world began? Can you believe that the inner urge you feel to create something in the world is the awakening of a seed idea, conceived before evolution began to manifest, a timeless idea in space/time? Can you identify your vocation with God's work? Do you know you are about God's business, whether you remember it or not?

Do you realize that the integrity of your vocation, which calls to you to create, does not depend on specific works you have already accomplished? Just as the reality of the perennial seed does not depend on any particular leaf or flower, so, the reality of your vocation does not depend on your works, but springs from a larger purpose and pattern than you have yet conceived.

Your vocation is your participation in the creation. You are designed to be creative. Each person is a unique creator. Every unique act of creation is integral to a universal pattern. Everyone has a choice as to whether to act upon that creative calling. Those who respond to the creative call become a living part of the creation. Those who fail to respond to the creative call do not become a living part of the creation. They die unborn, like a seed that was never planted, or whose shell was too hard for the green shoots to pierce.

Listen, listen, listen to the unique, creative calling within you. It is your gift to the world. You may feel it as a nameless frustration nagging at you to do more than you are now doing. Cherish that frustration. Ask it what it wants of you. It is the voice of your Creator calling to you to join the creation.

The works you will do if you respond to the call are far greater than you can yet imagine. Your works are part of a pattern and purpose so magnificent that the human mind, still slumbering in a creature's body and a self-conscious state, cannot see the glory that shall be revealed by you, through you and for you.

Dearly beloved, celebrate your creativity. Honor your vocation. Have faith that your unique calling is needed, is beautiful and carries a seed idea from God, which it is your privilege to make manifest through free will and experimentation. Freedom exists in the universe. All are called. Few choose to respond with all they have been given. Those who give all receive all.

That is the law.

⟨ ornament ⟩

*H*old fast the form of sound words, which you have heard of me, in faith and love which is in Christ Jesus. That good thing which was committed unto you keep by the Holy Spirit which dwells in us.

2 TIMOTHY 1:13–14

CAN YOU BELIEVE THAT THE THOUGHT YOU choose to hold in your mind creates reality?

Can you believe that if you "hold fast to the form of sound words" they will become manifest in your life and in the life of the world?

It is so. Think carefully. Think clearly. Think aspirationally. Focus upon your vision of what you want to become. Ask your inner calling to speak to you. What are you born to do?

Let the compass of joy guide your thoughts till they focus on the magnetic attraction for a creative act in the world. Image yourself doing your heart's desire. Conceive yourself being everything you ever dreamed of doing. Being everything you ever dreamed of being.

Place that vision in the context of the evolution of your species toward full humanity. See yourself participating in that evolution, joining with all others also responding to a unique call from within. Connect with them. Take communion with them in your mind's eye. Fuse with them in the body of light in the cocoon of transformation. Wherever two or three are gathered in Christ's name, there is the church.

Church is not a building or an institution. It is a body of aspiring beings, believing and acting so as to support the birth of humanity as a universal species in the universe of infinite light and life. We keep our vision clear by the power of the Holy Spirit who dwells in each of us. The Holy Spirit serves as our connection to the Designing Intelligence of the universe. It is available to us at all times. All we need do is call upon it.

Practice Christlike abilities. We can heal as Jesus healed. We can create abundance as he did with the fish and the loaves. We can communicate by direct thoughts. We can know and do the will of God—the pattern in the process of evolution.

We can evolve our bodies by signaling to our body that we are ready to rejuvenate. We can purify all negativity from our thoughts. We can create an inner environment of deep peace, absolute faith. We can practice incessant prayer and experience unshakable joy. We can leave this Earth alive. We can send signals of thought into the universe alerting our brothers and sisters that we are born from the womb of Earth and are ready to communicate with them.

Artists of the world are needed now to envision humanity emerging from its womb of self-centeredness into its universal phase. Every great age created a new image of humans. Ours is still waiting to be imagined. We see with the inner eye, yet when we open our outer eye we do not see ourselves as co-creators. On television, in films, in newspapers, we see ourselves as victims and destroyers instead of powerful creators. This self-image will be fatal if not changed soon.

Artists of the world: Envision! Art serves as the interface between the inner and outer vision, because it is imagination made visible. What will we look like as universal humanity? We will see each other as thoughts, not as things. Every thought we are thinking will be instantly visible to another. Nothing will be hidden. Now we hide our thoughts from each other. We can walk into a room thinking, "I hate you," while smiling and hiding our thought behind that smile.

At our next stage, our thoughts will be apparent. Telepathy will become like television: clear, obvious images of our state of being will be immediately picked up by others. We will be transparent. Our intentions will also manifest immediately. The powers of materialization will be ours. We will attract energy around the nucleus of a thought and produce a thing.

This is why only natural Christs will survive into the next stage of evolution. Not only the external powers of nuclear bombs can be misused. As terrible would be the misuse of internal thought. To think a hateful thought would be to destroy the hated person. To think a jealous thought would be to annihilate your love. To think a covetous thought would be to appropriate the wealth for yourself. This is why self-centered humans cannot enter the next stage of evolution.

Any cell in the body can kill the whole body if it becomes cancerous. Any human in the body of humanity can destroy the whole of humanity once a certain amount of power has been collectively attained. Even now, one person can build and explode a nuclear bomb. One person can destroy the water supply of a whole city. One person can highjack a jumbo jet and hold a nation at ransom.

The powers of co-creation are also the powers of co-destruction. So there exists a built-in limit to selfishness, similar to the built-in limitations for every cancerous cell. If the cancer succeeds, it just as surely fails, for it kills the entire body upon which it feasts.

If one person in a state of selfishness were to inherit the powers of a natural Christ, he or she could destroy the universe. It cannot be. It will not be. It is against the Law. Therefore, "hold fast to the form of sound words." Align your thoughts with the Intention of God.

Remember that Jesus Christ of the seed of David was raised from the dead according to my gospel, wherein I suffer trouble, as an evil doer, even unto bonds; but the word of God is not bound. Therefore I endure all things for the elect's sakes, that they may also obtain the salvation which is in Christ Jesus with eternal glory.

2 TIMOTHY 2:8–10

We could fail, but the Law cannot. The word of God is not bound, although we are in momentary bonds. The bonds will pass away, but the prophecy shall surely be made real. The dead shall be raised and we shall have life ever evolving. What seems real now—the nails in our flesh, the sorrow in our heart, the fear in our mind—shall disappear, just as we can no longer remember life in our mother's womb.

What seems unreal still—our future as universal, co-creative beings in touch with God at all times—shall become real in the fullness of time.

For everything there is a season:

A time to build your intellect in the womb of Earth;

A time to give birth to yourself as an integrated being at one with your Creator and the whole creation;

A time to be bound to a mammalian body;

A time to be free in a body that responds to your intention as my body did to my intention.

A time to work by the sweat of your brow, and

A time to create by the power of thought;

A time to give birth in pain, and

A time for conscious conception, conscious gestation and painless birth.

There was a time for Paul to be in prison for the sake of the elect.

There is a time for you to be in Heaven for the sake of the elect.

For the word has been heard by all the nations of the world. Through Paul's word, written from bondage, in prison and bound, the seed of hope has been planted. In all continents, among all races, the Gospel has been spread from the prison in which Paul suffered for the elect.

The end is coming in this generation. Incremental changes cannot continue. The time of birth is at hand. Therefore it is the time to be free of prison for the sake of the elect. There must be a new demonstration of human freedom for the elect to believe.

The elect are all those choosing to become natural Christs, full humans at the coming stage of evolution. The tribulations are beginning.

Those who enter the "Holy Place" are listening to their inner voices, ever more carefully. Those who would do as Paul did for his time will be emancipated as new models for all to see. Dearly beloved, you who would be disciples now will become like me now. Can you believe you can do as I did? If you can, you will carry on the work of Paul during the period of transition from Adam of the living soul to Adam of the life-giving Spirit.

Become ever more like me for the sake of the elect. Intend it. Have faith in it. Awareness is not a pre-condition of creation.

Did you have to know how to be born, to be born?

Do you have to know how to give birth, to give birth?

Do you have to know how to degenerate, to die?

No. You do not. Therefore have faith. You do not have to know how to transform in order to do so. The instructions are encoded already in your genes, awaiting the time when humanity is born from ter-restrial to universal life. The time is now.

❧

or I am now ready to be offered, and the time of my departure is at hand. I have fought a good fight, I have finished my course, I have kept the faith. Henceforth there is laid up for me a crown of righteous-ness, which the Lord, the righteous judge, shall give me at that day: and not to me only, but unto all them also that love his appearing. Do your diligence to come shortly unto me.

2 TIMOTHY 4:6–8

DEARLY BELOVED, BECAUSE PAUL FINISHED the course and kept the faith, you have received the word. Never underestimate the importance of action taken in utter faith with purity of intention. Did Paul appear to his generation to have succeeded as he lay in bondage, reviled and brutalized by the powers of Rome and Israel? Surely not.

Yet, he did succeed. It is the law that whatever is done with utter faith and pure intent, shall inevitably prevail in the fullness of time. Paul stayed the course and kept the faith in order that all on planet Earth may know what to do now that the end is near.

He expected a "crown of righteousness." I will give this crown to all those who believe in their capacity to be like me. You will emerge as universal humans, like butterflies emerging from the cocoon of self-centered humanity.

*O*nly Luke is with me. Take Mark, and bring him
with you: for he is profitable to me for the ministry.
At my first answer no man stood with me, but all
men forsook me: I pray God that it may not be laid to
their charge. Notwithstanding the Lord stood with me,
and strengthened me; that by me the preaching might be
fully known, and that all the Gentiles might hear: and I
was delivered out of the mouth of the lion.

2 TIMOTHY 4:11, 16–17

Paul was brought before the emperor Nero and condemned.
He stood alone at first. No one dared come forward for fear
of also being condemned by association with him. Yet his
strength was so great, his faith so total and his sense of mission so clear that he could rejoice even unto the time of his
execution when he prayed, as Jesus had done, for forgiveness
for those who persecuted him.

He had persecuted the Christians. Then the Jews and the
Romans persecuted him. And soon the Christians were to
persecute those who did not believe. The Old Dispensation
continued after the martyrdom of Paul. He said he would
return for the introduction of the New Dispensation.

BE PREPARED, DEARLY BELOVED, FOR THE
mystery to be revealed in you. Be assured that you
who seek the way shall find the way and encounter,

in real terms, in real time, all who have gone before to pave the way for you, the children of the Quantum Instant, the privileged generation born at the most marvelous time in the history of planet Earth.

⚮

"What is man, that you are mindful of him? or the son of man that you visit him? You made him a little lower than the angels; you crowned him with glory and honor, and did set him over the works of your hands: you have put all things in subjection under his feet." For in that he put all in subjection under him, he left nothing that is not put under him. But now we see not yet all things put under him. But we see Jesus, who was made a little lower than the angels for the suffering of death, crowned with glory and honor; that he by the grace of God should taste death for every man. For it became him, for whom are all things, and by whom are all things, in bringing many sons unto glory, to make the captain of their salvation perfect through sufferings. For both he that sanctifies and they who are sanctified are all of one: for which cause he is not ashamed to call them brethren.

HEBREWS 2:6–11

Humans have not yet inherited the Kingdom of God. Jesus, as our representative at the next stage of evolution, did inherit godly powers. His purpose was to "bring many sons to glory." By his willingness to call us his brothers and sisters, Jesus notified us that we are of the same family, the same species as he; we have the same parent, the same future, the same power, the same glory, the same inheritance.

Our greatest problem is that we do not know how great we are. We do not know the expectations our Creator has for us. We do not acknowledge ourselves as heirs of the universe. Why? Because we are still young, still learning, still unruly. Only a few thousand years ago none of us could read or write or free ourselves from burdensome work.

Only recently have the minds of millions been liberated enough to hear the word of the *future human we are to become*. Occasionally we lift up our heads from the ground we so laboriously till, to hear the word of the great advocate of humanity, who told us we are sons and daughters of God. But the news is too good for us to believe. We can barely imagine that our potential is so glorious. We bow our heads again, yet remember in the recesses of our mind, that we are more than animals who eat, sleep, reproduce and die.

Some few lift their heads for good and do not bow down again. They raise their sight to their own potential and initiate their own transformation to godliness.

LIFT YOUR HEADS, WORKERS OF THE WORLD. You are divine! Every one of you is the Son or Daughter of God. Your work is rapidly changing. You are no longer to work by the sweat of your brow. You are to live by the power of love, in alignment with the mind of God. Everything is to be in subjection to him who is in total love of God. The godly will inherit the power; that is the law.

Do not follow me for fear of punishment. Follow me for the joy of becoming what you are. The process is self-rewarding. It is heavenly to become godly. Heaven is the process, never-ending, of co-creating with God. Think of the joy of falling in love. Think of the ecstasy of sexual union with your beloved. This is a hint of the joy of co-creation.

Who could turn down such joy? Only those who choose to remain under-developed, forever acting out the tantrums and doldrums of the self-centered stage of human existence.

❧

For verily he took not on him the nature of angels; but he took on him the seed of Abraham. Wherefore in all things it was essential for him to be made like unto his brethren, that he might be a merciful and faithful high priest in things pertaining to God, to make reconciliation for the sins of the people. For in that he himself has suffered being tempted, he is able to help them that are tempted.

HEBREWS 2:16–18

Jesus Christ is a living consciousness, and can assist us. He experienced the full cup of human joy and suffering in a body like ours in order to demonstrate to us that we can do as he did and more. He will help us now if we choose to evolve.

How can he, who is so far above, help those of us who are so close to the ground? Can a parent help a child? Can an older brother help a younger? Can a teacher help a student? Yes.

When we call on his "succor," two things happen. First of all we activate our own Christ abilities. Just as our autonomic nervous system pumps adrenalin into our system to give us extra strength when we perceive we are in danger, so our system pumps co-creative, suprasexual energy into our system when we call upon Jesus. He is the opposite of the idea of danger. He is the idea of security, salvation, eternal life. That thought floods our system with impulses that signal all our cells and organs to perform in synchronicity, harmony and tranquility. This starts the self-healing, self-regenerating mechanism that strengthens and transforms us into his likeness—which is *us* at our next stage of evolution.

By our call to him, we are signaling a helpful consciousness that is omnipresent in the universe. It is like calling a friend on the phone. Would you have guessed you could do that before the phone was invented? Can you image how strange it sounded to your grandparents when they first picked up the phone and called across the valley to another? They used to shout. We no longer have to shout. Our voices are carried by invisible vibrations around the world and registered upon the inner ears of others, wherein they sets up sympathetic actions that impinge on the receiving brain, which translates those vibrations to meaning—all without us knowing how it is done. A two-year-old child can do it.

We have a similar instrument within us that most of us have not yet learned how to use, one as reliable as the phone. We can call any consciousness with this inner telephone. It works through directed thought, or telepathy. The reason most of us do not use this inner phone is that we have not learned how to concentrate and purify our thoughts. Our thoughts still carry extraneous ideas, hidden fears, guilt and wayward beliefs. We have not yet mastered the art of "thought proofing" our inner sound studio by making it inaccessible to negative or random thoughts.

This static in our receiving and sending apparatus inhibits us from using our innate telepathic capacity to call upon Jesus—or anyone else.

The universe is sensitive to thought.

PRACTICE THINKING EXACTLY WHAT YOU want to think and nothing else. Focus, focus, focus. Let the magnetic needle of your attention point to the highest signal you can hear—and send forth upon that inner communication system a call whenever you so desire. Ask and it shall be answered. Try and you shall see. You shall see.

*T*here remains therefore a rest to the people of God. For he that is entered into his rest, he also has ceased from his own works, as God did from his.

HEBREWS 4:9–10

This rest is not death. It is the total release that comes from giving birth. As every woman knows who has given birth to a child, there is a moment of complete relaxation, repose and joy at the arrival of what has been created through and with her, yet not by her. For every mother knows that she offered her body as a garden for a seed that she did not create. She nurtures; she does not create. When the birth is complete, she rests in the peace that passeth understanding.

The collective rest occurs in the interlude between terrestrial and universal life. It is the moment before the next phase of evolution begins—before the mother takes the baby home and undertakes the new tasks of raising the child outside of her womb, in the world.

So HUMANITY, ONCE YOU HAVE PASSED through the great evolutionary transition, you shall know the rest that comes from having given birth to yourselves as full humans—in new bodies, prepared to take up the next set of tasks: growing up in a universe without end.

*F*or every high priest taken from among men is ordained for men in things pertaining to God, that he may offer both gifts and sacrifices for sins; who can have compassion on the ignorant, and on them that are out of the way; for that he himself also is compassed with infirmity. And by reason hereof he ought, as for the people, so also for himself, to offer for sins.

HEBREWS 5:1–3

Even Jesus was tempted. He took on a separate mortal body that felt pain. Each of us, no matter how devout, is still in a body, still vulnerable, still in need of asking for help in overcoming the illusion of separation. Never succumb to spiritual pride. When we do, our ego victimizes us, torturing us with the pain of the damned. For it is far more painful to lift ourselves high to union with God and then fall, than never to have risen at all.

THOSE OF YOU WHO ARE SELF-TRANSFORMing now, be prepared for joy and depression. You are undergoing a spiritual adolescence. Your co-creative system is turning on. Your procreative system is turning off. You are in an unstable state.

Have compassion on yourselves. Do not identify with your emotions. Identify with your awareness that you and God are one. This will steady you as you pass through the transition from Adam of the living soul to Adam of the life-giving Spirit.

Dearly beloved, you are butterflies whose wings have not yet dried. Take care of yourselves. You are needed for the transformation of the world.

〜

For it is impossible for those who were once enlightened, and have tasted of the heavenly gift, and were made partakers of the Holy Spirit, and have tasted the good word of God, and the powers of the world to come, if they shall fall away, to renew them again unto repentance; seeing they crucify to themselves the Son of God afresh, and put him to an open shame.

HEBREWS 6:4–6

Once we know the choice between extinction and evolution, once we have committed ourselves to evolution rather than extinction, we set in motion an irreversible process. Once the baby starts down the birth canal, it cannot return to the womb. What was one hour before a safe home has become a lethal, suffocating place.

Once we begin the process of self-evolution toward whole-centered being, we cannot return to the old limits of self-consciousness without ripping the fabric of our inner being to shreds and suffocating our higher self, which has entered into our system, turning on the process of survival as a Christlike body, while turning off the process of survival as a mammalian body.

Once the body begins to breathe oxygen itself through the lungs, once its umbilical cord is cut, it can no longer take oxygen directly from its mother. The watery womb would kill it, one second after birth. That is the Biological Quantum Change.

The Psychological Quantum Change occurs when a person has passed from the womb of self-consciousness to the world of universal consciousness. This is the time of rebirth, or enlightenment. Once having experienced enlightenment, we can no longer survive psychologically in self-consciousness. It is to the psyche what the return to the womb would be to the baby.

There is yet another kind of quantum change still to come. We have experienced the Biological Quantum Change at our birth. We have experienced the Psychological Quantum change at our rebirth or enlightenment or discovery of the Christ within. We have yet to experience the Planetary Quantum Change, which is the forthcoming collective experience of oneness, universal life and shared contact with God.

Just as it is impossible for those who have been born biologically to return to the womb, it is likewise impossible for those who have been reborn psychologically to return to the stage of unknowing. It will be impossible for those who are self-transformed within a planetary system, which is interacting as one body, to return to the state of social separation.

The cells are triggered into a new state by the birth of the baby. The Planetary Birth Experience will trigger humans into a new state. This event is as certain as the fact that once a child is conceived, it will surely be born. Even if it is aborted, it is born—dead. Even if it is stillborn, it is born—dead. It must eject from the womb once it has been conceived.

So a planetary system, once it has conceived self-conscious humans who learn the powers of science and technology through the development of their intellects, *must experience* planetary oneness, birth and universal life. We may be an abortive planet. We may be a stillborn planet. We may be a healthy planet. Nonetheless we shall inevitably pass through this phase of evolution, *never to come back again.*

The process of evolution is irreversible, intentional and directional. An adult cannot become a child. A child cannot become an embryo. A planetary species—*Homo sapiens sapiens*—cannot return to the first Garden of Eden before we separated out from the animal world. *Homo sapiens sapiens* can only go forward to the Second Garden of Eden, wherein resides the Tree of Life. We shall have the power of the gods and be godly—or we shall surely decline and pass away like all the billions of species before us, like Neanderthal, *Homo habilis* and *Homo erectus*. There is no other choice.

❧

"*T*his is the covenant that I will make with them after those days," says the Lord, "I will put my laws into their hearts, and in their minds will I write them; and their sins and iniquities will I remember no more."

HEBREWS 10:16–17

THE DAYS ARE HERE THAT WILL PREPARE US for the Planetary Birth, when the Earth struggles to integrate as a whole body and reach into the universe for new life. These are the days of quantum change, when the selection process will strengthen those who are attuning to the sound of God. They are the days of the Planetary Pentecost, when all will hear the voice of God in our own language—the days of the Second Coming, when the Christ within awakens and links all people in Christ consciousness: the days when you connect up with other planetary systems who have undergone the same experience, the transition to universal life. These are the days of the Third Covenant.

The First Covenant was made with those who came out of the land of Egypt—the stage of consciousness in which there were many gods—to Israel, the stage of consciousness when there was one God. The laws were given, in all detail and complexity, to remind the children of Israel that they were intimately, ultimately related to God.

The Second Covenant was the agreement that came with the coming of Jesus. He sacrificed himself so that all of us can follow him into the Kingdom through love. God became man so that man could become godlike.

The Third Covenant is made with those who come out of the stage of self-consciousness. With the Third Covenant you will enter the stage of co-creative consciousness, and know at all times that you are heirs of God.

You are children of the Third Covenant.

∾

*L*et us hold fast the profession of our faith without wavering (for he is faithful that promised), and let us consider one another to provoke unto love and to good works, not forsaking the assembling of ourselves together, as the manner of some is; but exhorting one another: and so much the more, as all of you see the day approaching. For if we sin willfully after that we have received the knowledge of the truth, there remains no more sacrifice for sins, But a certain fearful looking for of judgment and fiery indignation, which shall devour the adversaries.

HEBREWS 10:23–27

There is a time for forgiveness and there is a time when forgiveness of old forms of behavior is no longer relevant, for these forms must pass away. The challenges of the first birds—to fly—no longer exist. The wing has been perfected.

The challenges of the past no longer exist. Breathing, walking, seeing, tasting, touching, feeling, sharing, communicating, symbolizing, writing and reading have been learned. They no longer challenge our capacities; they become a given for all who come after the achievement has been attained. As an example, how to exist on dry land has been learned, once and for all. All land creatures inherit the victory.

To overcome a new challenge, we must first experience a heroic struggle and undergo a painful process, and then we can enjoy a long and fruitful plateau of continued development.

At the time of the first birds, contenders for the design of the wing abounded. No one knew which design was correct: that is, which would work the best. Then, at a certain point, life discovered the laws of aerodynamics. The laws had always been there. The discovery was new, not the principles. Only certainly types of flying mechanisms would work. All others were discarded forever. No need exists to return to the fumbling efforts of dinosaur-like creatures whose wings were too small for the weight of their own bodies.

The Period of Forgiveness is the time of mutation, invention and research into how to do something new that works. While this time of invention and discovery continues, creatures are "forgiven" their mistakes. Try, try, try again is the encouraging evolutionary morality at this stage of the development of a new capacity—whether it be the wing, the lung or the God-conscious mind.

However, once the creatures have discovered the way to do it that is most consistent with the laws of the creative process (such as gravity and motion) they do not need to keep on inventing the wing or the lung over and over again. There must be some aspect of the process of selection that rapidly weeds out those creatures that keep on reinventing the wheel or the wing!

For humanity the "day is approaching" when we will have discovered how to be whole-centered, fully human beings at all times. All history can be viewed as the period of our discovery of how to be co-creators with the Divine. (Self-centered consciousness is an early phase in the Great Experiment, like the dinosaur birds.)

Once the discovery has been made, and we learn to do it, there will be no evolutionary significance in rediscovering it over and over again. The struggle to be God-conscious will be achieved.

Just as there are no more fish flopping up on the dry land gasping for breath, trying to walk, and as there are no more dinosaur-like creatures trying to fly, so there will be no self-centered humans trying to be godly without God-consciousness. *This* struggle will be over—a vital part of the Great Experiment in how to become godlike beings.

Jesus demonstrated the way of becoming God-conscious. He knew the laws, he understood the truth, and the truth made him free—as it will make anyone free who acts upon it. We do not have to keep on discovering it—we need to learn how to do it.

Cast not away therefore your confidence, which has great recompense of reward. For all of you have need of patience, that, after all of you have done the will of God, all of you might receive the promise. For yet a little while, and he that shall come will come, and will not tarry.

HEBREWS 10:35–37

Those of us born on the cusp between creature human and co-creative human must remain steadfast during the turmoil of an evolutionary quantum transformation.

These are confusing times. They will become more confusing before all will become clear. Those who can understand the words of this testament are here on Earth to help guide humanity through the transformation.

How do we act as guides through territory we have never experienced before? We have a goal. We have a compass. We use it to get ourselves, and others who so desire, there safely. That is how we act as guides.

The goal is to become a universal human in contact with God's laws and intentions from within. The goal is to become joint heirs with Christ. The goal of human history is to become co-creators with God.

Our inner magnetic needle serves as our compass. It tells us when we are off the path (pain and fear) and on the path (joy and peace). The more frequently we check our compass, the more sensitive we become to its signals of pain and joy—and the better we stay on course, able to guide others to do the same.

Confidence becomes an essential survival characteristic for those who wish to make it through the Quantum Change to the stage of Universal Humanity. For the time has not yet come when the next stage is visible. What we actually see is disorder, pain, anger, separation, killing, injustice, war, armaments, pollution, depression, shortages, cruelty on a mass scale, repression on a mass scale, disorientation on a mass scale.

How can we have confidence in the future, people will ask us, when all about us there is confusion or despair? We can say we have confidence, because: "I know what the future can be. I have already experienced it from within. I have already seen it from without. I know that I am destined to become a divine human because my whole being pulses with the intention to do so, and I have a living example to confirm that my desire is not an illusion, but is in fact the most real aspect of my person. I have confidence because my eyes have seen the glory of the coming of the Lord. The 'Lord' is *us*, living up to our highest human potential to be Sons and Daughters of God.

"I have patience because I know that the timing of the transformation is not in my hands. It lies in the hands of the Whole System, with which I am in resonance. All I am required to do is to express my unique creativity with all my heart, mind and spirit. The rest will follow.

"I know I am here on Earth to give my all to serve my fellow humans who wish to cross the River of Life from mortality to imperishability. I shall remain steadfast in my task. I shall be confident at all times. I shall be patient, knowing that the time of our transformation is close at hand."

Now faith is the substance of things hoped for, the evidence of things not seen. For by it the elders obtained a good report. Through faith we understand that the worlds were framed by the word of God, so that things which are seen were not made of things which do appear.

HEBREWS 11:1–3

Faith is based on the understanding that the whole visible universe is the manifestation of the unseen idea of God. Everything we see is the product of God's process, rather than the accidental creation of creatures mating and mingling on the material plane. Faith is the substance of our knowledge of this process.

How do we know that which is unseen? We know it because we are living it. We know it by consonance. We are the product of the process of creation. We are motivated by the Intention of Creation to continue to evolve in God's image, so we can be ever more godlike.

We have faith because we desire to become co-creative with God. We have faith because the desire to unite with God consumes our beings and gradually shifts our attention from the tangibility of things seen to the magnetic pull of things unseen, things undone, things becoming, until that which is unseen has greater reality than that which is seen, until that which is to come has greater meaning than that which is passing away, until that which is creating the universe has greater reality than any manifestation of it.

The word becomes more alive than the flesh, for those who have faith.

*T*hese all died in faith, not having received the promises, but having seen them far off, and were persuaded of them, and embraced them, and confessed that they were strangers and pilgrims on the earth. For *they that say such things declare plainly that they seek a country. And truly, if they had been mindful of that country from whence they came out, they might have had opportunity to have returned. But now they desire a better country, that is, an heavenly; wherefore God is not ashamed to be called their God: for he has prepared for them a city.*

And these all, having obtained a good report through faith, received not the promise: God having provided some better thing for us, that they without us should not be made perfect.

HEBREWS 11:13–16, 39–40

O DEARLY BELOVED—YOU WHO KNOW YOU are strangers and pilgrims on Earth, have faith. The promise is being kept now. Those men and women of faith who died unfulfilled, will be fulfilled, but not until you are fulfilled. The quick and the dead shall be raised together, not alone.

The promise could not be kept for some, no matter how faithful, until the time had come when the whole planetary system was ready to give birth to co-creative Christlike humans. Those who came before sought a country different than any they had ever seen before. They proceeded on faith that there was something beyond the creature human condition.

Their heroism is in some respect greater than our own needs to be, for they were not born at the time of the

Quantum Change. Their faith in preserving the seed of hope for a new human condition has granted us the opportunity to actualize it now. "They without us should not be made perfect" for the time had not yet come.

The cells alive when the child enters the birth canal are no greater than the first ovum and sperm through which the design for the child was set in motion. The cells that began forming the organs in the body in the first three weeks, and that later died and were replaced by new cells, were no less wondrous than the cells that form the eyes when they first open, or the lungs when they first breathe, or the ears when they first hear.

We who live at the time of the Cosmic Birth, when the Divine human will be born out of the current human, are not greater than those who wrote the first word, prayed the first prayer or built the first scientific instruments of investigation of the material world.

We shall all receive the promise *together*. Collectively we shall all experience the great reward.

❧

Wherefore seeing we also are compassed about with so great a cloud of witnesses, let us lay aside every weight, and the sin which does so easily beset us, and let us run with patience the race that is set before us, looking unto Jesus the author and finisher of our faith; who for the joy that was set before him endured the cross, despising the shame, and is set down at the

*right hand of the throne of God. For consider him that
endured such contradiction of sinners against himself,
lest all of you be wearied and faint in your minds. All of
you have not yet resisted unto blood, striving against sin.*

HEBREWS 12:1-4

Take courage. A loving family of pilgrims and strangers, all
of whom seek the next step of evolution, surround you. We
are not called upon to manifest blind faith under terrible
conditions. We are merely required to run, with patience,
the course that has already been laid out for us.

Someone has already been through the virgin jungle of
the transformation. Someone has lit a path through the ver-
dant vegetation of millions of years of animal, vegetable and
mineral existence. Someone has stayed the course to the finish and stands upon the finishing line, beckoning to all pilgrims that the race can be won by anyone who keeps going,
no matter how slowly.

Keep going. Keep reaching, and keep your eye on your
goal of life as a co-creator, and you shall surely see the victory at hand.

∾

*A*nd all of you have forgotten the exhortation which speaks unto you as unto children: "My son, despise not you the chastening of the Lord, nor faint when you are rebuked of him: For whom the Lord loves he chastens, and scourges every son whom he receives."

HEBREWS 12:5–6

When we are in pain, when we experience a severe problem, loss or failure, we can interpret it as a sign from God to teach us something about our own development. The present challenges and hardships prepare us for the tribulations that are close at hand. We will be called upon to perform like champions in the greatest contest this world has ever seen. This contest is the struggle to transform us, from self-centered to whole-centered humans, in time to avoid self-destruction. The parameters of the challenge are these:

+ Disorder will increase.
+ An overwhelming sense of guilt and defeat will abound in the West, which is responsible for both the metacrises and the metaopportunities facing planet Earth.
+ Multitudes of people, increasing in number every day, will be sufficiently dislodged from their past comforts, and will actively search for guidance and hope. People literally cannot live without hope.
+ Shortages and scarcities will increase selfish tendencies in some, while accelerating co-operation and empathy.

The crises throw us back upon our own resources and on our faith in things unseen. We receive intense inner signals to change, to extend our vocation, to break-up stifling relationships, to connect with soul mates, to discover what we are uniquely called to do. Those of us who hear the vocational call begin a self-authorized course in self-development. We start practicing the inner disciplines of conscious evolution. We meditate to clear our negative emotions. We practice forgiveness of self and others. We heal our body. We surrender our self-centeredness, asking for guidance for the next creative step.

As we follow that guidance and begin to self-evolve, we experience increased energy, beneficial changes in the body, suprasexuality, new creativity, new vocation, new leadership. We go through a "second adolescence" as the stable patterns of the past dissolve and the new patterns emerge. We find others who are members of our team of destiny, called to the same extended, organic function.

Our faith in God increases. We discover a relationship with Jesus. We begin to pray constantly for guidance. Internal controls take over as our external guidance systems fail. Those of us who are not attuning to our own higher wisdom will feel increasingly stressed, despairing and self-destructive. Opposite symptoms will arise in those who do not choose to evolve: a lack of vitality, a loss of interest in work, feelings of separation and alienation, physical sickness.

All this prepares us for the Quantum Transformation—an intense period in which breakdowns and breakthroughs both occur exponentially. That which is interactive, cooperative and directed toward the fulfillment of our evolutionary potential will be dramatically empowered. That which is separatist, selfish and blocking of our evolutionary potential will be disempowered.

In every group some will be attracted to what is coming, and others will attempt to hang on to what they already have. Consider every personal problem you now face as a blessed opportunity to practice your new capacities and authorize your own growth. You will need these skills when the real contest begins.

If all of you endure chastening, God deals with you as with sons; for what son is he whom the father chastens not? But if all of you be without chastisement, whereof all are partakers, then are all of you bastards, and not sons.

HEBREWS 12:7–8

If we are not experiencing any problems of frustration, disorientation, nameless desire, we are in trouble! It means we are not aware, not responding to the transformation. It will take us by surprise, like a thief in the night.

Those who are struggling for self-mastery, inner guidance, forgiveness and transcendent aspiration will be prepared for what is to come. Those ensconced in comfort, or those building defenses against change, will be swept away by the turbulence that shall be let loose upon the Earth.

Learn to swim. Learn to surf on the tide of change rather than be obliterated by it. Thank God for the struggle. It prepares us for the transformation.

*S*ee *that all of you refuse not him that speaks. For if they escaped not who refused him that spoke on earth, much more shall not we escape, if we turn away from him that speaks from heaven.*

And this word, "Yet once more," signifies the removing of those things that are shaken, as of things that are made, that those things which cannot be shaken may remain.

HEBREWS 12:25, 27

More than ever before we must hone our ability to listen to our inner voice. In the times of our ancestors, people received signals from God. Moses was given the Ten Commandments, and many other signals did we receive to carry on throughout the long, long history of preparation for the time that is now at hand.

During the Period of Preparation, society behaved in traditional ways. External authorities controlled the social agenda. Each generation passed its guidelines for behavior down to the next. Changes occurred incrementally.

Jesus initiated the Period of Personal Transformation with his new signal to love. This commandment triggered the impulse for everyone to turn within to hear and feel the love of God. No external authority can teach us how to love. No ritualistic following of laws can *make* us love all people as ourselves. Love arises naturally through the inner surrender of our separated ego self to our own higher being.

Now, our generation is entering the time of the *Quantum Transformation*. This is the last phase of creature human history. We will experience the "removing of those things which can be shaken, such things which are made, that those things which cannot be shaken may remain."

We are the things that are to be shaken! We will be shaken to the very roots of our being. As we choose to listen to the voice of God within, we will be guided through the treacherous period. Therefore "see that ye refuse not him that speaketh."

DEARLY BELOVED, LISTEN TO ME, YOUR Higher Self, the Christ within, your potential, the Creative Intention that motivates you, listen, dearly beloved, to this call.

All of you are beloved. All of you are needed. All of you are capable. All of you can evolve. Some of you will choose to do so. Some of you will choose to ignore me, the call of your future. I weep for you, dearly beloved, who refuse to answer your own call. There is still time.

Freedom is the condition of universal life, which cannot be imposed upon you. It must be chosen. The future must be chosen, offering ever and ever more freedom for those who willingly follow the intention to evolve to their own highest potential— which is to be a partner with God in the creation of worlds without end.

⁓

*B e not forgetful to entertain strangers: for thereby
some have entertained angels unexpectedly.*

HEBREWS 13:2

Consider everyone a possible angel. Who are we to judge?
Since every one of us is a son or daughter of God, we can
treat everyone just so, with honor—as a sacred citizen of the
universe, a bearer of the seed of natural Christhood, an heir
of God in the making.

Our attitude towards people affects their feelings about
themselves. If we perceive them as unworthy, they are likely
to feel diminished. If we see them as budding heirs of God,
they are likely to feel encouraged to do more and be more—
to give their best.

We are responsible for our opinion of others. We can
choose what we want to see in others. We can choose to see
their weaknesses, or we can choose to see their strengths.
We can choose to see their fears, or to see their loves.

Both are there. Either can be accentuated by what we pay
attention to. We are to treat everyone as a possible angel—
including ourselves! Our greatest responsibility is how we
see ourselves. If we view ourselves as inadequate, we will be
inadequate. If we view ourselves as contemptible, we will be
contemptible. If we experience ourselves as loving, we will
love—and we will be loved.

We are henceforth responsible for every thought we
think, especially our attitude toward our selves. How can
we love our neighbor as ourselves if we think of ourselves
as a dying creature caught in a dying world? We cannot love

our neighbors as they should be loved unless we can love ourselves as we should be loved.

We are to love our self as a Son or Daughter of God. It is sacrilegious not to do so. The arrogance of self-condemnation springs from forgetting that we did not create ourselves. God created us. To hate ourselves is to hate God's creation. It is to imagine that we created ourselves, and that we, therefore, can condemn ourselves.

We cannot. We have no right to condemn ourselves. We did not create ourselves. To condemn ourselves is to condemn the works of God! But be not forgetful to entertain the Divine being within yourself. For thereby you will be entertaining an angel, aware that you are obliged to love that angel-within as you love God.

Jesus Christ the same yesterday, and to day, and for ever. Be not carried about with divers and strange doctrines. For it is a good thing that the heart be established with grace; not with meats, which have not profited them that have been occupied therein.

HEBREWS 13:8–9

The conditions are ripe now for our conversion from Adam of the living soul to Adam of the life-giving Spirit. We do not need to practice eccentric rituals or eat exotic foods to take this *natural* step. All that is necessary is that "the heart be established with grace." This means we must place our love entirely in the hands of God. Grace is that action that is *not* within our control or will. It is the action of the whole upon the part.

The part is attracted to the whole. Then the whole can activate the part in such a way as to enable it to partake of the collective capacity of the larger system, which is greater than the sum of its parts. If we keep our attention on the whole, on God, on the Christ-within, on the Kingdom of Heaven, on our full humanity now bursting to be born, all will be enabled to happen naturally. If we narrow our focus to diets and rituals we will draw the energy of thought to mechanistic levels, thereby impeding the process, which is far more subtle and complex than we can yet know.

It is as though children learning to walk were to focus exclusively on how to bend their ankles when their feet touch the ground. Far better that children look at the place they want to run toward and try to get there. Since walking is a natural capacity, their systems already know how. It's up to them only to want to walk somewhere—and their muscles will act upon their intentions naturally.

Accordingly, those of us who want to transform need only to set our focus on what we want to become, image ourselves *as* that desired being, and "establish our heart with grace"— that is, put loving trust in the mystery of nature: that it can create new forms out of old.

F or here have we no continuing city, but we seek one to come.

HEBREWS 13:14

For those who have set their sights on evolution to the next phase, there is no sense of belonging to a particular social order, community or nation. We are sojourners here, passing through on our way to the city to come. The New Jerusalem is our goal, the city of universal humanity, where we will act out our full potential as co-creators in the universal community of worlds without end.

M y brethren, count it all joy when all of you fall into divers temptations; knowing this, that the trying of your faith works patience. But let patience have her perfect work, that all of you may be perfect and entire, lacking nothing.

JAMES 1:2–4

Think of us as mountain climbers near the top of the mountain. Jesus has already climbed the full way to the mountaintop. Since the time he first walked that path, it has become faint, overgrown and hard to follow, hard even to see. We take tiny steps and feel tempted to stop, so difficult seems the climb. But our attraction to the top overcomes our fatigue. We resist the temptation to stop and we continue to climb.

Each step we take upward makes it easier for us to reach the top, and easier for those who follow us to do the same. With each fateful decision to take another step rather than to stop, we are perfecting ourselves. Each step is of eternal significance. The difficulty of the climb can trigger our impatience and cause us to choose to stop anywhere along the path. One such choice, fully taken, will impede our progress, until we choose to rise again. We are free to choose how far up we wish to go.

Patience is essential to the climb. It is inevitable that we will succeed if we keep climbing. Have patience. The top is near. The beginning of our new life is at hand.

⁓

But be all of you doers of the word, and not hearers only, deceiving your own selves. For if any be a hearer of the word, and not a doer, he is like unto a man beholding his natural face in a glass: for he beholds himself, and goes his way, and immediately forgets what manner of man he was. But whoso looks into the perfect law of liberty, and continues therein, he being not a forgetful hearer, but a doer of the work, this man shall be blessed in his deed.

JAMES 1:22–25

We are like people beholding their Christlike faces in a mirror, then turning away and forgetting what manner of person we are. The image of ourselves at our full potential is so radiant and unlike the way we ordinarily sense ourselves that we tend to forget our glorious self-image. To remember the image of ourselves as natural Christs, we must do as he did, day by day and minute by minute, until through action we become that which we potentially are.

ENACT WHAT YOU ENVISION. BECOME WHAT you are. Do what you wish to see done. And find yourself made whole in the image of God.

❦

My brethren, have not the faith of our Lord Jesus Christ, the Lord of glory, with respect of persons. For if there come unto your assembly a man with a gold ring, in goodly apparel, and there come in also a poor man in vile raiment; and all of you have respect to him that wears the cheerful clothing, and say unto him, "Sit you here in a good place;" and say to the poor, "Stand you there," or "Sit here under my footstool," are all of you not then partial in yourselves, and are become judges of evil thoughts?

JAMES 2:1–4

God does not favor one person above the other. Neither should we. The Jews excluded the Gentiles, believing they were unclean. Yet Peter realized the Gentiles experienced the Holy Spirit even as did the Jews. He broke the narrow law of his community to act upon the wider law that commanded him to love one another as himself.

When we see a person dressed beautifully and a person dressed humbly, we are to realize that both are the same in respect to their potential. Neither the poor nor the rich person has fully achieved it. Therefore, we see through the apparel to the person. We see through the person to the potential. We see through the potential to the pulsing seed of desire to be clothed in the raiment of God. All else is the shell of a seed that is now sprouting.

Remember, all humans are rich if they love God above all else and their neighbor as themselves. Remember the loaves and the fishes. Remember the lilies of the field. We are designed to be beautiful and abundant. That is our heritage.

Everything in nature is beautiful. Every bird, every worm, every rock. Everything that endures, everything that evolves, is beautiful. Aesthetics is the reflection of the intrinsic harmony of the mind of God. We learn the aesthetics of nature and apply it to our own attire. We learn to be as beautiful as a bird, as colorful as a flower, as silken as a fish, as brilliant as a tree in the autumn—and radiant in honor of who we are.

So speak all of you, and so do, as they that shall be judged by the law of liberty. For he shall have judgment without mercy, that has showed no mercy; and mercy rejoices against judgment.

JAMES 2:12–13

The "Law of liberty" is the truth that shall make us free. Whatever we give, we shall receive. If we give love, we will receive love. If we give mercy, we will receive mercy—this much we know, for it has been told to us since we were children. But there is more to come. The law of liberty reveals that if we choose to be free of the creature human condition, so we shall be. It decrees that as we follow the commandment to love, we shall surely have life ever evolving. This is the law we must obey with all our heart, mind and spirit.

The law is not given as a constraint to our freedom. It is given as a guide to free us from constraint. The astronauts broke the bonds of gravity by obeying the law of gravity, which decrees that we must travel at a certain speed to escape the pull of Earth.

We will break the bonds of creature mortality if we obey the law of love and emulate Christ. That is the law that was designed to set us free forever.

❦

*From whence come wars and fightings among you?
Come they not behind, even of your lusts that war
in your members? All of you lust, and have not: all of
you kill, and desire to have, and cannot obtain; all of
you fight and war, yet all of you have not, because all of
you ask not. All of you ask, and receive not, because all
of you ask amiss, that all of you may consume it upon
your lusts. All of you adulterers and adulteresses, know
all of you not that the friendship of the world is enmity
with God? Whosoever therefore will be a friend of the
world is the enemy of God.*

JAMES 4:1–4

Friendship of the world is enmity with God? What does this mean?

It does not mean we should ignore the world and focus only on God, excluding ourselves from the concerns of this Earth to attend to the salvation of our souls. This is selfish and will not succeed. It means that we should not covet to possess the world; that we should rather desire to *fulfill* the world. To fulfill the world means to enable all life to reach its natural potential as a manifestation of God.

What is wrong is to try to own the world. What is right is to participate in the evolution of the world, and of ourselves. At this stage of history this means to recognize that we are stewards of this entire planet, and of all things upon it. Our commandment is to nurture the second Garden of

Eden, wherein the terrestrial creation can evolve a new harmony of the works of nature and the works of humans.

To participate in the evolution of this world means also to extend the world beyond its biosphere by reproducing little worlds in space—the seedpods of new worlds to come, which will reflect the co-creativity of Christlike humans.

"God so loved the world he sent his only begotten Son" to save the world. We so love the world that we must *ourselves* become a son or daughter of *Homo sapiens sapiens*, so that we can co-operate and thereby evolve the world.

⌁

Go to now, all of you that say, "Today or tomorrow we will go into such a city, and continue there a year, and buy and sell, and get gain;" Whereas all of you know not what shall be on the next day. For what is your life? It is even a vapor, that appears for a little time, and then vanishes away. For that all of you ought to say, If the Lord will, we shall live, and do this, or that.

JAMES 4:13–15

A fine line exists between taking initiatives for God and taking initiatives that are based on human will and whim. It is necessary for us to explore and take steps to act out our part in the process of creation. Yet we must practice a deep inner attunement to help guide us in our initiatives. Are they resonating with the larger pattern, or are they self-centered and for personal gain alone? How can we tell the difference?

It takes practice.

When we take initiatives to act out a higher pattern that includes our personal self-interest, we will feel an inner joy, a security, a linking with others in love, a subtle empowerment that does not depend on external results, but rather on internal affirmation. When we are taking self-centered initiatives we will feel anxiety, competitiveness, fearfulness of losing, momentary exhilaration followed by depression and emptiness at the core of our being.

Practice taking the perspective of God. See yourself as God sees you. Ask what God would like you to do today, or in a particular situation. As we enter the Period of Co-Creation, God is empowering us to emancipate our full potential. "God" in this context stands for the Whole System, of which each of us is a vital whole part.

Wholes within wholes, fields within fields, each element in the creation is both a whole system and a part of a larger whole system, up unto the Comprehensive Whole System— the entire universe in all its dimensions, which is God.

Imagine for an instant the Intelligence that created and is now creating the Comprehensive Whole System. Imagine that it knows what has been and is now. Imagine that it intends the future to be an ever-greater awareness by the members of the whole. Imagine that the Creative Intelligence has as its purpose the nurturing of creative intelligence like its own throughout the Comprehensive Whole System.

Now focus on yourself as an element of Universal Intelligence in the process of self-recognition and self-nurturance. Nurture your ego and emotions to align totally with your higher self, so that you can align fully with the Comprehensive Whole System or God.

Now imagine the alignment clicking into place—like a difficult puzzle suddenly completed. You are instantly something new, something other than a separate piece. You are an element in a whole, you partake of the whole, and you give to the whole. You have transcended yourself through participation in the larger system. Yet you keep your integrity and your identity. It is essential that you play your own part in the whole.

Synergistic participation does not require the shedding of our identity. It invites the enhancement of our identity by connecting up our part with the parts of others into a Whole that is greater than our personal awareness. Thus, while taking our own initiatives, we are to see them as part of the good of the whole. Affirm constantly, "If the Lord will, we shall live and do this or that." This means we are always checking out whether we are in alignment with the Comprehensive Whole System.

It is in your interest to be so aligned. It leads to joy, certainty and security.

To be separate from the whole leads to despair, uncertainty and the vulnerability of a fragment disassociated from its natural context, a lost cub, an orphan alone in the world.

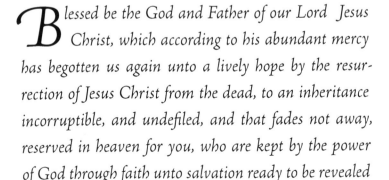

B lessed be the God and Father of our Lord Jesus Christ, which according to his abundant mercy has begotten us again unto a lively hope by the resurrection of Jesus Christ from the dead, to an inheritance incorruptible, and undefiled, and that fades not away, reserved in heaven for you, who are kept by the power of God through faith unto salvation ready to be revealed in the last time.

Wherefore gird up the loins of your mind, be sober, and hope to the end for the grace that is to be brought unto you at the revelation of Jesus Christ.

I PETER I:3–5, 13

FOCUS, FOCUS, FOCUS YOUR ATTENTION ON your goal.

Your goal is to become a natural Christ. This is the incorruptible inheritance reserved for you by the power of God through your faith, until it will be revealed in the "last time," in the Quantum Transformation, when the next stage of evolution shall be apparent and the old order shall be in obvious disarray.

To achieve your inheritance, your faith and focus upon this goal is essential. It cannot be given to you if you are a passive or negligent creature going about your selfish business with no interest in what you are to become.

A parent cannot give a child its inheritance until the child has matured enough to know its value. You cannot receive your inheritance—the powers of a co-creator—until you have matured enough to know its value and are prepared to use the power with responsibility.

The key now is where you place your attention. Place your attention on the image of yourself as a natural Christ. Perform the Cosmic Union Ceremony. It is the universal stage of the communion service that has been practiced, faithfully, for two thousand years in preparation for my Second Coming. Visualize a cocoon of light. In this cocoon is the person of Jesus Christ, glowing with light. He is in the cave of metamorphosis.

Step into the cave. Let the light enlighten your body until it vibrates at the same frequency as his.

Think:

> I am a body of light.
> You are a body of light.
> Fuse your light with mine
> So that I may be charged
> With the electricity of your being,
> So that I will be changed
> To become like you.
> I ask my body to transform.
> It knows how.
> It awaits my conscious decision.
> Call for the Holy Spirit: Brighten the cocoon of light.
> Let nothing penetrate this membrane of light.
> I call for the Holy Spirit
> To enter my being,
> To be with me all day,
> Guiding my every action,
> Guarding my every thought,
> Giving me the comfort I need
> To act out of love, not lack.
> Energize me with
> The fire of love,
> The light of wisdom,
> The electricity of attraction,

The magnetism of will,
Oriented to the purpose of my life
Which is to become
A natural Christ, an heir of God.
Guard me from separation this day
That thy will, and mine
Which are now one,
Shall be done.
Amen.

~

But all of you are a chosen generation, a royal priesthood, an holy nation, an exclusive people; that all of you should show forth the praises of him who has called you out of darkness into his marvelous light; which in time past were not a people, but are now the people of God: which had not obtained mercy, but now have obtained mercy. Dearly beloved, I plead to you as strangers and pilgrims, abstain from fleshly lusts, which war against the soul; having your conversation honest among the Gentiles: that, whereas they speak against you as evildoers, they may by your good works, which they shall behold, glorify God in the day of visitation.

I PETER 2:9–12

DEARLY BELOVED—YOU WHO ARE ANSWER-
ing the call of your higher self to be like me, to be
natural Christs, all praise to you. I, Jesus Christ,
thank you, brother and sister humans, for your
faith in me, during the terrible sufferings that you
have undergone.

I know how it feels, for I have felt it. I also know
how it feels to overcome it. And so shall you. We
are entering the home stretch, O people of God.
Do not waiver now.

Now is the time when the people of God must
demonstrate what it means to be godly.

Reveal the glory that is Me in You by acting up to
your highest potential right now for all to see.

This means: Do not give in to any fear; love God
above all else; love your neighbor as yourself, and
allow your mind-body to transform. Your body
wants to become like mine.

Your body wants to regenerate. Let it do so.

Your mind wants to become like mine. Let it do so.

Your mind wants to attune to God. Let it do so.

Your role now, dearly beloved people of God, is to
demonstrate Christ capacities.

Heal!

Rejuvenate!

Love!

Attune!

Empower all you meet to do the same.

Thank you.

I love you.

Amen.

Barbara's Closing Words

The Next Step:
The Promise Will Be Kept through YOU

If this *Evolutionary Testament of Co-Creation* has moved your heart and soul, it means you have within you a great evolutionary promise, yearning to be fulfilled—the further expression of your Unique Self. This yearning reveals the divine impulse of the process of creation, urging you toward manifesting as your full potential self. It means that arising from within you is the mysterious promise of becoming a "universal human," a co-creator of the emerging world.

The purpose of *The Evolutionary Testament* is to nurture this promise within you. The following are some of the steps you can take to support yourself during this process: I suggest that you purchase the *Evolutionary Testament Spiritual Practice and Study Guide* to deepen in your practices as a "universal human." Begin by gathering a few friends and forming an Evolutionary Bible Study Group to read *The Evolutionary Testament* together. As outlined in the *Study Guide*, the basic process is quite simple: First, take time to create a sacred space. Develop your own rituals, whether they involve the use of candlelight, flowers, music or deep silence. Start each meeting with a prayer that includes the sacred intention for each member of the group to be awakened to more of the promise within, with each inspired to deliver their greatest gift of love into the world. Keep a journal of your own inspired insights, especially your own interpretations of scripture from an evolutionary perspective.

As described in the *Study Guide*, you then read a passage of scripture, followed by reading portions of my own revelations explaining my interpretation of the text's evolutionary meaning. Afterward, take time to share your own inspired insights. If possible, record these so that you can listen again later and reflect upon your own "inner scripture" when you desire. I have found that each of us has within many such intuitions that are often fleeting and need to be captured and cherished.

One of the insights from my book, *52 Codes for Conscious Self Evolution*, is Code 39: "Develop an Incorruptible Communication System for your Inner Scripture." Write down these precious messages that arise from the Source of your being. They are vital to your fulfillment of the Promise within you and they need to be treasured.

To support your personal evolution as a young "universal human," I suggest that you create a context for your group that goes beyond study, to an experience of true fulfillment. See your study group as a Sacred Universal Human Pod: a small group of those inspired by the life of Jesus to fulfill your own potential as universal humans and co-creators of new worlds. The Pod is a multi-human cell of individuals who have joined together in a "cocoon of light" to create a whole system. This sacred container establishes a process for those who yearn to join genius and actually tap into their own full potential self and to realize their sacred destiny.

The Pod process fosters the fusion of genius, representing a further awakening of the as-yet underdeveloped potential within each person. As Jesus told us, where two or more are gathered in my name, there I am also. This fusion process is designed to bring forth genuine genius, by joining unique vocations of destiny in the experience of the joy of co-creation. Each Pod offers an Evolutionary Sacrament to ground "the lightening rod of the divine" within the group. These Sacred Pods nurture the Communion of Pioneering Souls, which are so vital to the evolution of our world.

The deepest purpose of the Pods is to empower those who are attracted to the future of the world, and who seek to work together to fulfill the promise of the evolution of humanity from *Homo sapiens sapiens* to *Homo universalis*. The Sacred Universal Human Pod Process is described in detail in the *Spiritual Practice and Study Guide*. Additional information is also available on our website: *www.evolve.org/ Evolutionary Testament*.

Finally, I have provided at the end of this book a short list of vital books as suggested reading to support this Promise within you. They have been written by spiritually inspired evolutionaries. *The Co-Creators Handbook* by Carolyn Anderson and Katharine Roske is offered as a master text to guide you in mastering the principles and practices of co-creation, which are so essential in birthing a universal humanity.

I look forward to staying connected as we fulfill the Promise together!

—BMH
February, 2015

Reading List

Belknap, Mary. *Homo Deva: Evolution's Next Step.* Berkely: Lifethread Institute, 2004.

Bourgeault, Cynthia. *The Wisdom Jesus.* Boston: Shambala, Publications, 2008.

Delio, Ilia. *Christ in Evolution.* Maryknoll: Orbis Books, 2011.

The Emergent Christ. Maryknoll: Orbis Books, 2011.

From Teilhard to Omega. Maryknoll: Orbis Books, 2014.

The Unbearable Wholeness of Being. Maryknoll: Orbis Books, 2013.

Gafni, Marc. *Your Unique Self: The Radical Path to Personal Enlightenment.* Integral Publishers, 2012.

Hubbard, Barbara Marx. *The Hunger of Eve: One Woman's Odyssey Toward the Future.* Eastsound: Island Pacific Northwest, 1989.

Emergence: The Shift from Ego to Essence. Newburyport: Hampton Roads Publishing Company, 2012.

52 Codes for Conscious Self Evolution. Santa Barbara: The
Foundation for Conscious Evolution, 2011.

*Conscious Evolution: Awakening the Power of Our Social
Potential.* Novato: New World Library, 2015.

*Birth 2012 and Beyond: Humanity's Great Shift to the Age of
Conscious Evolution.* Shift Books, 2012.

Land, George, and Jarman, Beth. *Nature's Hidden Force:
Joining Spirituality with Science.* Washington D.C.: Humanist
Press, 2014.

Lanier, Sidney. *The Sovereign Person: A Soul's Call to Conscious
Evolution.* Santa Barbara: The Foundation for Conscious
Evolution, 2010.

Panikkar, Raimon. *Christophany: The Fullness of Man.*
Maryknoll: Orbis Books, 2009.

Richo, David. *When Catholic Means Cosmic.* Mawah: Paulist
Press, 2015.

Smith, Paul. *Integral Christianity: The Spirit's Call to Evolve.* St.
Paul: Paragon House, 2011.

Walsch, Neale Donald. *Conversations with God, Book 3.*
Newburyport: Hampton Roads Publishing, 2011.

Walsch, Neale Donald. *The Mother of Invention: The Legacy of
Barbara Marx Hubbard and The Future of You.* Carlsbad: Hay
House, 2011.

Afterword

By Marc Gafni

In this discussion of Barbara Marx Hubbard's critical book, I want to answer the implicit questions of the intelligent reader as to why this work matters so enormously.

First let's examine some of the questions you may be asking:

Is there a God?

Does God talk to human beings?

Does God speak to me?

These are critical questions. Our approach to them will inform the depth, quality and integrity of our spiritual experience. Our answers directly affect our ability to access our own inspiration and to inspire the kind of social transformation necessary to meet both the unprecedented possibility, as well as the fierce challenge, of our time. Following our initial reflection we can explore some additional questions:

What is a sacred text?

Did God speak to Barbara Marx Hubbard in the form of a revelation?

Is there such a thing as a true reading of the sacred texts?

Can new readings and interpretations of sacred texts like the Bible actually attain the status of the word of God?

If our answers are to be taken seriously we cannot fabricate them. Rather, our response must reflect the highest standards of philosophical, biblical, religious, spiritual, historical and rational integrity. If our answers are to be relevant to the mainstream culture and not just its fringes they must make sense to mystics and scientists, entrepreneurs and poets, psychologists and philosophers alike. The answers must point us toward a shared spiritual language, one with the power to integrate the inspiration of sacred text and the evolutionary worldview in a single breath. They must inspire us in a new way toward the evolution of consciousness.

Before I begin to address these questions, let me share my own thoughts about Barbara's experience. Barbara *did* hear divine revelation; I'm sure of it. I know this because I've heard the same voice that she did. It spoke in different terms to her, but I'm able to clearly recognize the fragrance of authentic divine revelation within her text.

But it's also more then that. It's not just that Barbara is reading a sacred text in a powerfully necessary and legitimate way. It's that in the book you have before you, Barbara's own words have become a sacred text. And finally, Barbara herself is a sacred text, because Barbara has awakened.

To awaken is to realize that you are a unique letter within the cosmic scroll. You are a Unique Self who represents an irreducibly precious story of essence that's being written throughout your life. Your sacred autobiography, once you've evolved beyond your exclusive identification with your ego's story, is revealed to be a sacred text. When your Unique Self awakens you become an expression of God's will, and you are able to hear the voice of divine revelation. When your awakened Unique Self, sensitive to the voice of God's new revelation, joins with the genius of an ancient sacred text like the Bible, then the desperately needed miracle of new revelation, so critical for our time, is made manifest. That is the miracle that Barbara has wrought with this book.

I will only touch briefly upon each of the above questions, but I trust that a meta-response to these critical inquiries will emerge over time and that the radical integrity and necessity of Barbara's crucial offering of this book will also become clearer.

Let's begin then. I make no dogmatic claims here, or ask you to take anything on faith. Rather, I am sharing with you the best leading-edge understanding I believe exists today on the nature of our shared reality.

Is Spirit Real?

In response to the question about the existence of God, God or Spirit *is* real. Furthermore, the God you don't believe in doesn't exist. The God you don't believe in is a false image of God that lives in your mind and heart, and is one you've correctly rejected. That is the God who punishes those who don't follow a particular religion; the God who is used as a fig leaf for every manner of cruelty and corruption. When you were three, and your mother was chasing you with a paddle, and you ran into the bathroom and locked the door and your mother screamed out, *"God will get you even in there!"*—that God doesn't exist.

Having said that, what do I mean when I say God, or Spirit, is real? I use the word Spirit as a synonym for God because sometimes it's easier to hear the word Spirit, since we tend to confuse the word God with the concept of the God we don't believe in. By deploying the word Spirit in its stead, we bypass those visceral objections that are rooted in early trauma. We can then engage from a more clarified level of consciousness. So let's talk about what we mean when we say Spirit is real.

To say Spirit is real is not a dogma of religion, but an article of spiritual science. To understand what that means we need to investigate what we know. How is knowledge attained in ways that can be considered real and authentic?

The leading edge of thought today suggests that knowledge is drawn from three possible sources. Borrowing the language of the great philosophers, let us call these sources the eye of the senses, the eye of the mind, and the eye of the spirit. Each is able to see and know the nature of reality in its own way.

The eye of the senses represents the empirical method of the classical sciences. In the hard sciences that seek to explain the material world, experiments are conducted. We perform an experiment. If it's successful we repeat it. We then have others perform the same experiment in double blind [where neither the participants nor the investigators know whether the test agent or a placebo has been administered] conditions. If other scientists consistently come to the same conclusion, we then submit our findings to the community of experts. If the community of experts validates the conclusions we've arrived at by successfully deploying the eye of the senses, then our conclusions are considered true knowledge about what is real.

The second eye is the eye of the mind. The eye of the mind is not based on empirical experimentation but on logic, mathematics, deduction and induction. Here we generate arguments and formulate equations. We check to see if our arguments are consistent and logical, and if our equations are valid. We then submit our conclusions to the experts in this field. If they're accepted, we have successfully deployed the eye of the mind to arrive at authentic knowledge about reality.

The third eye is often called the eye of the spirit. It is also sometimes called the eye of the heart. The eye of the spirit does not reveal knowledge about the mathematical or material world, but about the interior face of the cosmos. The eye of the spirit delves within and reveals true knowing about love, values, meaning, and all the other interior realities that give depth and breadth to our lives.

The eye of the spirit also uses the scientific method. We perform an experiment. The experiment we conduct is in the form of a spiritual practice. Our practice might be meditation, contemplation, nature mysticism, or some other form of embodied practice. The key is that our practice opens the eye of the spirit and allows us to taste and see the inner nature of reality. The great Christian theologian, St. Thomas Aquinas, often cited a favorite verse from Psalms, "Taste and see that God is good." He pointed to those words as the essence of what it means for us to know God.

This understanding of the three eyes of perception is known as Integral Semiotics. I consider it the leading edge theory of knowledge that is available today. Semiotics is about meaning making. Integral Semiotics shows us how to integrate the meanings that we've derived from diverse sources.

Metaphorically speaking, we might refer to the realizations of spiritual practice as "the revelation of strawberry ice cream." How do we know what strawberry ice cream tastes like? The answer is, we taste it. Our direct, first person experience of strawberry ice cream reveals its taste. The name, strawberry ice cream, merely evokes the memory of that taste within one who has already tasted it. If we have not yet tasted strawberry ice cream, the words evoke nothing in us. This, said Aquinas, is what is meant when we talk about tasting and seeing God.

The more profound the taste we seek to experience, the greater the skill level and training that is required for us to activate that taste. For example, the appreciation of great wine is an acquired skill. The sensual pleasure of the finest wine wildly exceeds that of any cheap, over-the-counter variety we might purchase from our corner liquor store. However, it also requires some experience and knowledge if we're to fully appreciate a fine wine's sophisticated nuance. Such is the nature of tasting God, or Spirit. We must develop the *capacity* to taste God. Once we've done so we can share and compare our experience with others who have also tasted God. Knowing that taste firsthand, we find ourselves readily able to discern between those who have actually tasted God and those who are merely describing God conceptually, yet who seem to have no experience of God's taste.

We can develop a skill for accessing the taste of Spirit through sustained spiritual practice. Such experiments yield true knowledge about the inner nature of reality. Recognized experts of great integrity within the spiritual community can then check our results. The true nature of our knowledge is thus confirmed. Additionally, those who sincerely wish to experience their own inspired insights can perform these same experiments and learn to taste God for themselves.

I've pointed here to the precise, scientific nature that this knowledge of Spirit delivers, and that arises through our sustained spiritual practices. Many trained scientists of spirit must perform these experiments in double blind conditions for the knowledge to be validated. That's precisely what has happened throughout human history. The world's most subtle and speculative minds, across the eons and among our various cultures, have all performed experiments of spirit. These great minds were largely unaware of each other, particularly in early human society, so in effect these experiments have been preformed under double blind conditions. The results were later submitted to the greatest living experts in each locale and era, who then validated the results of these experiments.

Throughout time, the results of these sustained spiritual practices have been shared through our oral traditions and written down in our sacred texts. Over the past century in particular the results of all these experiments have been collected and compared, as the leaders of various spiritual traditions began meeting with and talking to each other. Comparative religion, ecumenism, and the emergence of a universal dialogue around Spirit are new experiences in our human story. This universal dialogue allows us to compare the results of all the great experiments of Spirit. It turns out that spiritual practitioners mainly agree on the essential conclusions that can be drawn from their various experiments. The results of these we now call "the perennial philosophy."

The primary tenets of knowledge—the spiritual principles of reality—that have emerged from these experiments are roughly as follows:

Spirit is real.

The manifestations of Spirit are real. For example: Love is Real.

We find Spirit most directly by going inside of ourselves. Interiors are real.

Interiors have content. The content of our interiors reveals the good, the true, and the beautiful.

It is encoded in our nature, and is the intention of Spirit, that everyone falls away from conscious knowledge of Spirit. This falling away causes suffering.

There is Good News, in that a way back to a conscious connection with Spirit exists. The way back is through sustained spiritual practice.

When we find our way back through sustained practice, we wake up and realize that we are both inseparable *from* Spirit and held in every moment *by* Spirit.

This realization fills us with a sense of both peace and urgency. Peace because everything is already perfect, and urgency because we realize ourselves to be the hands, legs and voice of God. We become God's verb, actively responsible for the healing and transformation of reality.

We are each called to be fully alive, and to make manifest our greatest possible Unique Gift.

These nine shared depth structures are collectively revealed by the great experiments of Spirit, as performed by the most advanced minds and hearts in history. To be clear: These depth structures are not the same as the surface structures we encounter in our religions. Surface structures refer to the dogmas in the various religions. Dogmas are not discerned through direct experience via the eye of the spirit, nor are they validated through the scientific, empirical process described above.

Dogmas are merely *claims* about the nature of reality that have been asserted by a person or group of persons; therefore, dogmas cannot be validated by direct experience. One example of a dogma is the belief that God expects to be celebrated through a mass every Sunday morning (as in the Catholic faith) or conversely, that God expects to be celebrated every Friday evening through Saturday (as in the

Jewish faith). These dogmatic surface structures need to be distinguished from the depth structures, which yield genuine knowledge about reality.

All of our sacred texts point to God as best they can by attempting to describe God's taste through the use of words. The underlying knowledge, however, comes not from the words themselves, but from sustained and repeated experiences of reality that have been accessed via sustained spiritual practices. Based on those real-time realizations and experiences, we can say with certainty that God is real, Spirit is Real, and Love is real—and can do so with no less certainty than we say scientific laws are real.

To Whom Does God Speak?

The answer to the question of whether God speaks to humans emerges from the best experiments of Spirit, and is a resounding *yes. In fact, it's been said that Spirit speaks in three unique voices. These three voices of Spirit are given different names in each of the great traditions. Some call them I, We and It, or I, Thee and Thou. Others call them Buddha, Sangha and Dharma, or the Father, the Son and the Holy Ghost. Still others call them God, Torah and Israel. Whatever we name them, we're always speaking of this universal holy trinity—the three persons, faces or voices of Spirit.*

The first face of God—what we might call God in the first person—reveals itself through meditation and other forms of contemplative practice. This is the inner knowing that "I" am indivisible from the "God field." In the language of the Hindu Upanishads, "Tat Tvam Asi: Thou art that."

We'll investigate the second face of God in a moment. First though, let's consider the third face of God—what we might call God in the third person. This is the god force that suffuses and drives all reality. It's often referred to as energy, prana, shakhti, shefa, or Christ consciousness. In my own work I refer to it as outrageous love, or evolutionary love. It's a force that can be recognized and accessed by every human being.

Both of these faces of God—God in the first person and God in the third person—are deeply resonant throughout most of contemporary culture. Whether one is part of a great tradition of Spirit, spiritually inclined, or merely sensitive to the deeper implications of contemporary science, the realization that a creative force drives the cosmos and urges consciousness to higher and higher levels of awareness can be accessed directly by the awakened mind. The realization that we are inseparable from All That Is—that All That Is lives within and through us in some mysterious way—is also accessible through profound and sustained spiritual practice.

These realizations are both consistent and consonant with human consciousness in some profound way. Our humanism feels for its non-dual roots through the realization of our own divinity. We're delighted to realize that God dwells within us. God in the first person makes sense to our enlightened Promethean sensibilities. Our natural scientific inclination is conditioned to think in terms of energies, or energy fields, that suffuse and drive all of reality.

Additionally, God in the third person appeals to our scientific minds as we seek the grand synthesis of a unified field theory. God is All, and we are in the All. However, the idea that Spirit speaks to us, knows our name, calls out to us, holds us accountable and madly loves us, feels alien to contemporary sensibilities. The enlightenment philosopher

Emmanuel Kant once said that modern man is embarrassed to be caught praying.

Prayer, prophecy and revelation are expressions of the second face of God—what we might call God in the second person—which has not yet found a home in our yearning hearts. However, when we take a sacred text seriously we enable ourselves to experience the face of God in the second person[1].

To meet God in the second person is an experience of ultimate communion. When the Sufi poet Rumi writes about falling into the arms of the beloved, he is not writing about meditation. He's describing both his yearning for, and experience of, his blissful communion with this, the personal face of God. The God presence evoked when we read a Rumi poem (or one by John of the Cross or St. Teresa of Avila) is the loving, intimate God of "Thou and I."

We're all desperate for communion, the movement from loneliness to loving. It is what makes our lives worth living, the experience of being held and received. We are all systematically mis-recognized by others throughout our lives. To be recognized is to be seen and loved. To be loved is to be in communion with the one who sees us.

When we're seen, we're also called into the fullness of our glimmering beauty as unique incarnations of the divine treasure. We feel inspired by the beauty we see mirrored back at us through the eyes of the beloved to activate the personal evolutionary impulse that lives within us. We long to bring forth the unique gifts that are only ours to give, and that are desperately desired by the All That Is. To be in communion

---

1 Sacred text is also an expression of God in the first and third person, but is primarily a realization of God in the second person.

with this personal face of God is to know that our deed is God's need. This communion both gives us joy and calls us to evolutionary responsibility.

The above describes the inner experience of a human being who stands in relationship *to* God. This state of relatedness reflects the essence of Hebrew biblical consciousness. God in the second person is all about *relationship*—whether the relationship of a servant to his master, a lover to her beloved, or a friend to a partner. All these models of relationship find expression in our wisdom teachings. All are ways of approaching God in the second person.

The most powerful experience of God in the second person arises through prayer. It's been said that when Hassidic master Levi Yitzchak of Berditchev prayed, he began by offering the standard liturgical form of blessing—"Baruch Ata Adonai: Blessed are you, God." He then broke out of the formal mode of blessing, crying in sheer joy, "You, You… You…YOU!" He would lose himself in those words, repeatedly shouting in ecstasy, "You…You…YOU!" This reveals the rapture of an encounter with God in the second person.

The God of prayer is not a concept, but a realization. I once had a conversation with a well-known Buddhist teacher who asked me, "How can a serious teacher like you believe in the dogma of prayer?"

I said, "How can you believe in the dogma of awareness?"

He replied, "Awareness is not a dogma, it is a realization."

To which I said, "Yes, of course it is. And so is prayer."

He told me later that this simple pointing-out instruction I offered shifted his entire relationship with prayer. Prayer is not a dogma; it is a realization of God in the second person. It is the felt sense that every place you fall, you are falling into God's hands.

Can you recall a time when you felt alienated in a relationship and said to your partner, "I feel you're being too impersonal?" Or consider a time when you critiqued some dimension of society as being too uncaring. Inherently you sensed that God has a personal quality. This face of God lies beyond the grasping of our skin-encapsulated ego, which still believes itself to be separate from All That Is.

Prayer serves as an expression of the radically personal nature of enlightenment—the place wherein the personal, unique self talks to the personal God. Through prayer, the personhood of God meets the personhood of a human being. This is the flight of the lonely one to the Lonely One. Or, according to Hasidic master Ephraim of Sudykov, here we experience the meeting of misunderstood man with misunderstood God. Both parties come to this meeting as strangers in the land. They then establish a friendship through which both are liberated, and each is redeemed from their prior sense of loneliness.

As I've described in depth in my own book, *Your Unique Self: The Future of Enlightenment*, we tend to think of God or Spirit in impersonal terms. In the usual thinking of the spiritual community, human beings possess a personality or separate self, which can be transcended through enlightenment and merged with the impersonal Spirit of the All-That-Is. That, however, is only a part of the story

To understand and then embody the personal face of God, we need to pass through four core levels, or stages, of internal spiritual development. Level one is pre-personal, which emerges at birth and exists prior to the formation of our individuated, separate self. Level two expresses when the pre-personal psyche evolves into a personal self. We experience this important level as a separate self, the "individual me" of ego and personality. We enter the third level only after the personal self—in a healthy and non-dissociative process—has been transcended, as well as included, in the Impersonal. We call this the classic state of enlightenment, which is an integral aspect of all our greatest spiritual traditions. The personal has been trance-ended, in that we've broken the trance of the personal self that separated us from the All That Is. We realize we're part of the vast, impersonal Spirit of the All That Is, a tiny thread in the seamless coat of God.

This seamless coat of the universe into which we're all woven may be unified, but it certainly is not featureless. Within its vast fabric we now find ourselves expressing uniquely as a personal incarnation of Spirit, a living fractal of the All That Is. This moves us into the fourth stage of our spiritual development, when the personal face of this vast, impersonal divine Spirit that suffuses, animates and embodies everything reveals itself to us.

This is the face of the divine Mother who holds us in her loving embrace, comforting us, yet challenging us to our greatness at the very same moment. This second face of God offers infinite intimacy, and invites our approach and our intimate prayers. It affirms the infinite dignity, value and adequacy of our personhood, even as our prayer affirms the dignity of our personal needs. Our praise and our petition, our confessions and even our crying out in need are all addressed to the second face of God, which we invoke through the sacred art of prayer. Prayer is our way of initiating a conversation with, and thereby invoking, the infinitely gorgeous face of the personal God, God in the second person.

Sacred texts are outrageous love letters inspired by the

personal face of God, so only a lover of God in the second person can read a sacred text authentically. The lover is able to *hear* the nuance, depth and intimation hidden within every word. Sometimes the lover reading a sacred text discovers a depth of meaning unknown even to the text's original author. Thus the lover reveals the beloved to herself, through the act of reading. The act of interpreting and writing commentary on a sacred text becomes itself an outrageous love letter response, written by the lover and delivered up to the beloved in a state of holy ecstasy. That is precisely what Barbara Marx Hubbard had done in this, her holy book. She's written an outrageous love letter back to God, after reading God's personalized love letter to her in the form of the sacred biblical texts.

How Should We Engage With A Sacred Text?

We can read a sacred text in three different ways. In Hebrew mystical consciousness, they are termed Hach'na'ah, Havdala and Hamtaka. Translated, they mean Submission, Separation and Sweetness. These three levels of engagement point to the universal structures that exist within human consciousness. We can see them in action most clearly through:

Falling in love

The power struggle and conflict that eventually arises between lovers

Falling in love all over again, but at a higher level of consciousness

Let's examine these levels through the lens of love to better understand them.

Level One: Submission—Hach'na'ah

When we're in submission to love we're subject to something greater than ourselves. Our complete absorption into this larger framework establishes our identity. As so often happens, we succumb to a wild current or force that moves through us and sweeps us off our feet.

When we fall in love we lose our sense of personal individuation. We'll do anything to be with, or please, our beloved. We can also see this state of consciousness in operation within our nuclear family systems, where each family member submits to parental conditions and requests—although where our families are concerned we did not fall in love; we were born into a family that then shaped and defined our identity. This same level of consciousness is found in humanity's historical cultural consciousness (called the typhonic level by some theorists) during which early humans felt embedded in, and subjected to, the larger context and unseen forces of nature.

Level two: Separation—Havdalah

At this level of consciousness we find ourselves moving out of the prior state of fusion with our beloved and disconnecting from the larger system. A sense of separation, of loss, then often arises. Sometimes it's accompanied by loneliness, a longing within for our lost feelings of togetherness. At the same time we may experience newfound independence and freedom. Our liberation creates within us a new sense of wellbeing and stability, which lives in paradoxical tension with our feelings of alienation and disconnection from the prior larger framework and relational pattern.

Our imperative at this stage of personal development is to individuate our identity successfully, to learn to stand on our own. Our personal development might include learning new skills: for example, learning to leaving a relationship behind without feeling anxiety or a need to demonize the other; self-soothing; learning to communicate our needs clearly, etc. At this stage of development we're challenged to establish the reliability of our own identity, now that we've successfully detached ourselves from the earlier fusion.

This stage begins with a sense of conflict. The initial flush of love is replaced with a sense of diverging, even competing, agendas. The feeling of being misunderstood, misrecognized and devalued begins to rear its head. Great pain arises with this loss of apparent harmony and bliss that characterized the first stage of falling in love. During this stage, relationship tensions intensify as the partners seek to return to the undifferentiated state of fusion that was Eden's early bliss.

Often when a relationship reaches level two, one or both parties abandon the relationship and seek to re-establish the simple bliss of a level one experience with a new partner. Inevitably, however, they wind up once again at level two. Thus the cycle repeats itself indefinitely. For further development to take place, at some point we need to stay in level two and do our work. As the biblical myth reminds us, two cherubs with flaming swords guard the entry to the Garden of Eden. Returning to the Garden of Eden (level one) without doing the necessary work that allows for our return at a higher level will not suffice.

Level Three: Sweetness—Hamtaka

In level three we begin to reestablish ourselves as part of a larger whole, while maintaining our capacity to function as an individual. We integrate our experience of the previous levels, becoming a complete part/whole member. Here we experience the belonging of union combined with the freedom of diversity. This is a fully loving, free-functioning stage of life experience.

In biblical mysticism, "sweetness" refers to our non-dual realization that we exist as part of the grand context of the good, the true and the beautiful—we at last perceive ourselves as a precious living stitch within the seamless coat of the universe.

Here we fall in love all over again, only this time from a higher state of awakening and consciousness. We have evolved from station one (fusion) through station two (separation) to station three (union). Our identity is once again enmeshed within the larger context of the whole. At this level we have trance-ended the fixation of separation and autonomy, which is our primary achievement in level two, even as we include autonomy as an integral part of our identity within the higher, free-functioning union that is level three.

Full Circle: Barbara's Holy Revelation

A thorough understanding of these three developmental levels of consciousness, as well as an appreciation of the three distinct faces of God, becomes key to understanding how to approach a sacred text in a way that elicits the God voice, so that we can experience it for ourselves. Skip a level and the sacred text will not reveal God's voice. Pass through all three levels, one at a time, and the voice of God may well speak to you directly.

During the first level of submission to the text, God commands the reader. This is the stage of heteronomy in the Abraham story. God sees and we are blind. We read with radical devotion, listening for the divine voice that calls us. We have fallen in love with the divine and the text is a love letter; we're not critiquing with any objective distance. Rather we're blown open by every word, every gesture of the divine writ. This is our critical point of departure for engagement with sacred text. We bow before the text, in awe of its beauty.

The fundamentalist approach to sacred text reflects this level of engagement. The power of religious fundamentalism derives from the authenticity of the love the reader feels at this early level of engagement. The problem arises when fundamentalism arrests the evolution of a person's interior consciousness, freezing them in this first stage of textual interpretation. This is not the endgame for engaging with sacred text; rather, it marks the beginning.

The second level of our engagement with a sacred text involves separation. Here we reclaim some measure of distance from it, and we begin to see its internal patterns. Repeated use of particular words, parallel structures, psychological and poetic nuance clarify themselves, taking on greater significance.

This level of investigation takes place in a powerful way in Jesuit seminaries, Orthodox schools of biblical analysis, and—in a different form—through the academic study of sacred text. The Orthodox and Jesuit schools focus on understanding sacred text according to its own internal literary structure, even while feeling the divine breath that animates the text in every moment. Such an approach both transcends and *includes* level one.

Alternately, where academics are concerned, a sacred text is reviewed primarily through the prism of the historical forces that have ostensibly shaped it. This form of textual study is valid in and of itself; however, it usually transcends and *excludes* the level one experience. The text therefore becomes alienated from its living presence, a mere cadaver for intellectual dissection.

Only through transcending and *including* level one as a function of level two can the reader experience the third level of engagement with a sacred text. This level delivers the sweetness. Here the most profound dimensions of the first two levels are *both* transcended and included. We are in love with the text. We bow in devotion, in utter submission to it. Our devotional love for the text, however, does not blind us. Quite the opposite, it moves us to know our beloved text ever more intimately.

We seek patterns, subtle nuance, inflection and texture in every sentence, word and letter of the sacred writ. We then evolve by entering the text from the inside. All boundaries between the text and us disappear as we erotically merge into one. From a masculine perspective, it can be said that the reader penetrates the text. From a feminine perspective, the reader opens up fully to receive and absorb the text. This erotic union between reader and sacred text is, for Hebrew Kabbalists, the outrageous love methodology through which all sacred texts are meant to be engaged. In this non-dual merger between reader and text, new revelation is born.

Wherever new revelation is born, New God is also born. At this level of encounter with a sacred text, the awakened reader participates in the evolution of consciousness, which is no less then the evolution of love—which is no less then the evolution of God. God, Israel, and Torah have become One. This unity fully awakens through every radical engagement with a sacred text. The first person of God, incarnate in man, tunes in to the voice of God in the second person. We speak to God *as* God, with the consciousness of the human being serving as the living, aware and accepting space within which this divine encounter occurs.

Once the full implication of this audacious evolutionary love mysticism is made explicit we realize that, in fact, there are two distinct forms of sacred text at play. One is the classic document inspired or revealed by God and accepted by the court of history as a canonical sacred text. (The Bible remains a classic example of this form of sacred text.) The second type of sacred text is the actual living reader. As a clarified human being we *speak* the word of God right here and now. We incarnate Christ Consciousness. Every person who lives the full integrity of his or her clarified Unique Self story thus writes the text of his or her book of life on the heart of God. Each of us is a potential letter in the cosmic scroll. There are no extras on the set of life.

When the awakened human being who has become a sacred text meets a classic sacred text, there God meets God and new worlds are born. This is what happened when the highest, most evolved expression of God, which was having a Barbara experience, met the God who was having a New Testament experience. New revelation was born. And we, the readers, have become the beneficiaries of this great and noble evolutionary birth.

The answers to our earlier questions are now clear. Spirit is real. God is real. God speaks to human beings, both then and now. A sacred text is not merely an eternal, unchanging document; it is a dynamic, ever-evolving life experience. The evolution and revelation of new meanings in sacred text arise not from some historical discovery of its original meaning, but from the periodic infusion of new meaning.

The infusion of new meaning in sacred text takes place when God in the first person—the Unique Self reader *as* sacred text—meets and erotically merges in profound, textual supra-sex with the written sacred text. When this happens, new God is born. This is what Barbara's stunning Unique Self has done. In *The Evolutionary Testament of Co-Creation* God is having a Barbara Marx Hubbard experience.

Amen.

About
Barbara Marx Hubbard

There is no doubt in my mind that Barbara Marx Hubbard—who helped introduce the concept of futurism to society—is the best informed human now alive regarding futurism and the foresights it has produced.

BUCKMINSTER FULLER, 1895–1983

Barbara Marx Hubbard has been called "the voice for conscious evolution" by Deepak Chopra. As the subject of Neale Donald Walsch's book, *The Mother of Invention*, many would agree Barbara is the world's foremost global ambassador for conscious change.

At heart Barbara Marx Hubbard is a visionary, a social innovator. She thinks from an evolutionary perspective and believes that global change happens when we work collectively and selflessly for the greater good. She realizes that the lessons of evolution teach us that problems are evolutionary drivers and that crises precede transformation. This gives us a new way of seeing and responding to our global situation.

A prolific author and educator, Barbara has written seven books on social and planetary evolution. She has produced, hosted, and contributed to countless documentaries seen by millions of people around the world. In conjunction with the Shift Network, Barbara co-produced the worldwide

"Birth 2012" multi-media event that was seen as a historic turning point in exposing the social, spiritual, scientific, and technological potential in humanity.

In 1984 her name was placed in nomination for the Vice Presidency of the United States on the Democratic Party ticket. She called for the creation of a Peace Room to scan for, map, connect and communicate what is working in America and all around the world. She also co-chaired a number of Soviet-American Citizen Summits, introducing a new concept called "SYNCON" to foster synergistic convergence between opposing groups. In addition she co-founded the World Future Society, and the Association for Global New Thought.

Barbara Marx Hubbard is not an idealist, nor does she believe that social and planetary change is simple. But she does believe that humanity has the tools, fortitude, and resolve to take the leap towards conscious evolution.

Her earlier books include: *The Hunger of Eve: One Woman's Odyssey toward the Future; The Evolutionary Journey: Your Guide to a Positive Future; Revelation: Our Crisis is a Birth —An Evolutionary Interpretation of the New Testament; Conscious Evolution: Awakening the Power of our Social Potential; Emergence: The Shift from Ego to Essence; 52 Codes for Conscious Self Evolution* and *Birth 2012 and Beyond: Humanity's Great Shift to the Age of Conscious Evolution.*

About
Neale Donald Walsch

Neale Donald Walsch is a modern day spiritual messenger whose words continue to touch the world in profound ways. Neale has written 29 books on spirituality and its practical application in everyday life. Titles in the With God series include: *Conversations with God*, Books I–III; *Friendship with God*; *Communion with God*; *The New Revelations*; *Tomorrow's God*; *What God Wants*; and *Home with God*. Seven of the books in that series reached the New York Times Bestseller List, *Conversations with God-Book 1* occupying that list for over two-and-a-half years. His most recent books are *When Everything Changes Change Everything* (2010), *The Storm Before the Calm* (2011), *The Only Thing That Matters* (2012), *What God Said* (2013) and *God's Message To The World: You've Got Me All Wrong* released in October, 2014.

About Marc Gafni

Marc Gafni is a visionary thinker, social activist, passionate philosopher, wisdom teacher, and author of ten books, including the award-winning *Your Unique Self: The Radical Path to Personal Enlightenment*, the two-volume *Radical Kabbalah*, and the recently published *Tears: Reclaiming Ritual, Integral Religion, and Rosh Hashana*. He holds his doctorate in philosophy from Oxford University, rabbinic certification from the chief rabbinate in Israel, as well private rabbinic ordination. He is the co-initiator of The Center for Integral Wisdom, an activist think tank dedicated to evolving and articulating a shared global framework of ethics, eros, and meaning. In partnership with leading thinkers and change agents working on key social issues, Gafni's work in the world is focused on collectively re-shaping key pivoting points in consciousness and culture.

Also Available from Muse Harbor Publishing:

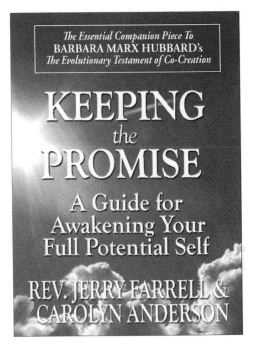

The Essential Companion Piece To
BARBARA MARX HUBBARD's
The Evolutionary Testament of Co-Creation

KEEPING
the
PROMISE

A Guide for
Awakening Your
Full Potential Self

REV. JERRY FARRELL &
CAROLYN ANDERSON

"Keeping the Promise: A Guide For Awakening Your Full Potential Self,"
— by Reverend Jerry Farrell and Carolyn Anderson.

This beautifully crafted guidebook encourages readers of Barbara Marx Hubbard's groundbreaking material to expand and deepen their exploration of the original source text through a comprehensive, self-guided seven-week study program. The study program, which can be pursued alone or in a group setting, explains how to form a local study group of interested individuals. The book also contains in-depth information about how to establish sacred space for meetings, how to communicate with greater integrity within a group setting, and how to perform sacred ceremonies and rituals that can support more intimate spiritual communion.

Each weekly study chapter has been formed around a unique intention, or theme, and includes a personal message from Barbara Marx Hubbard. The guidebook authors draw upon select passages from the source text and invite the participants to connect more deeply with the chosen material by posing a set of questions that have been specifically designed to encourage greater self-reflection and promote spiritual growth.

The guidebook also offers a more extended study course for those groups and/or individuals who, after completing the seven-week course, wish to continue on their journey of self-transformation.

Made in the USA
Middletown, DE
13 October 2017